Blockchain Technology Applications in Businesses and Organizations

Pietro De Giovanni
Luiss University, Italy

A volume in the Advances in Data
Mining and Database Management
(ADMDM) Book Series

Published in the United States of America by
   IGI Global
   Business Science Reference (an imprint of IGI Global)
   701 E. Chocolate Avenue
   Hershey PA, USA 17033
   Tel: 717-533-8845
   Fax: 717-533-8661
   E-mail: cust@igi-global.com
   Web site: http://www.igi-global.com

Library of Congress Cataloging-in-Publication Data

Names: De Giovanni, Pietro, editor.
Title: Blockchain technology applications in businesses and organizations / Pietro De Giovanni, editor.
Description: Hershey, PA : Business Science Reference, [2022] | Includes bibliographical references and index. | Summary: "This book investigates the true advantages that blockchain entails for firms by creating transparent and digital transactions, resolving conflicts and exceptions, and providing incentive-based mechanisms and smart contracts"-- Provided by publisher.
Identifiers: LCCN 2021026041 (print) | LCCN 2021026042 (ebook) | ISBN 9781799880141 (hardcover) | ISBN 9781799880158 (paperback) | ISBN 9781799880165 (ebook)
Subjects: LCSH: Electronic commerce. | Blockchains (Databases) | Business enterprises--Technological innovations.
Classification: LCC HF5548.32 .B58 2022 (print) | LCC HF5548.32 (ebook) | DDC 381/.142--dc23
LC record available at https://lccn.loc.gov/2021026041
LC ebook record available at https://lccn.loc.gov/2021026042

This book is published in the IGI Global book series Advances in Data Mining and Database Management (ADMDM) (ISSN: 2327-1981; eISSN: 2327-199X)

British Cataloguing in Publication Data
A Cataloguing in Publication record for this book is available from the British Library.

All work contributed to this book is new, previously-unpublished material.
The views expressed in this book are those of the authors, but not necessarily of the publisher.

For electronic access to this publication, please contact: eresources@igi-global.com.

Advances in Data Mining and Database Management (ADMDM) Book Series

ISSN:2327-1981
EISSN:2327-199X

Editor-in-Chief: David Taniar, Monash University, Australia

MISSION

With the large amounts of information available to organizations in today's digital world, there is a need for continual research surrounding emerging methods and tools for collecting, analyzing, and storing data.

The **Advances in Data Mining & Database Management (ADMDM)** series aims to bring together research in information retrieval, data analysis, data warehousing, and related areas in order to become an ideal resource for those working and studying in these fields. IT professionals, software engineers, academicians and upper-level students will find titles within the ADMDM book series particularly useful for staying up-to-date on emerging research, theories, and applications in the fields of data mining and database management.

COVERAGE

- Database Testing
- Data Warehousing
- Database Security
- Educational Data Mining
- Data Quality
- Association Rule Learning
- Predictive Analysis
- Data Analysis
- Web Mining
- Decision Support Systems

IGI Global is currently accepting manuscripts for publication within this series. To submit a proposal for a volume in this series, please contact our Acquisition Editors at Acquisitions@igi-global.com or visit: http://www.igi-global.com/publish/.

Titles in this Series

For a list of additional titles in this series, please visit:
http://www.igi-global.com/book-series/advances-data-mining-database-management/37146

For an entire list of titles in this series, please visit:
http://www.igi-global.com/book-series/advances-data-mining-database-management/37146

701 East Chocolate Avenue, Hershey, PA 17033, USA
Tel: 717-533-8845 x100 • Fax: 717-533-8661
E-Mail: cust@igi-global.com • www.igi-global.com

Table of Contents

Detailed Table of Contents

This chapter analyses the blockchain implemented by Genuino in the collectibles industry. Since collectibles are subject to high risk of counterfeiting and fake replications, blockchain technology can help substantially to ensure transparency, originality, ownership, and data security and protection. Two methods to use blockchain in the industry seem to be the most widespread today: creating digital native collectibles on blockchain and transposing physical objects into the blockchain by creating digital twins. By using blockchain, new consumer clusters emerge, highlighting the need to modernize both the traditional economies and the current business models.

The agri-food sector is the highest application of blockchain technology to track and trace components and raw material along the supply chain. Blockchain presents many potential advantages; however, small and medium enterprises often lack the means and knowledge to exploit this technology fully. This chapter presents a case study of blockchain application, namely Trusty, a platform for the notarization of fully traceable information on blockchain in the agri-food sector. Thanks to its limited up-front implementation costs and its modularity, it seems particularly suitable for use by SMEs. The authors' goal is to identify some useful issues for practitioners and inspiration for future research for academics. The most relevant topics that will be placed are (1) needs and expectations of SMEs in the agri-food sector towards the blockchain, (2) difficulties of introducing blockchain into SMEs, (3) the agnostic approach to blockchain, (4) the different value of notarized information for B2B and B2C companies, and (5) limits of some blockchains compared to others.

Chapter 3

This chapter identifies the existing challenges in the winery industry and proposes to analyze their resolution by the adoption of blockchain technology. Blockchain allows the traceability of the whole process linked to wine production, from the cultivation of the grapes to the distribution of the bottles. Blockchain allows winery firms to unlock the potential value existing in some processes, especially when they create a competitive advantage. The chapter investigates these concepts within the case of Cantina Volpone, which has been the first case in Italy to adopt blockchain technology in the winery industry. This chapter studies the implementation path for blockchain technology in the winery industry and highlights the operational and financial challenges emerging from its adoption.

Blockchain is proven to support businesses in traceability, data reliability, and data retrieval in all the steps of the supply chain, but still has limited use in the food sector. Through the EU-Horizon 2020-backed example of an Italian regional milk value chain, the chapter describes a real case toward the implementation of such technology in the food sector for the benefit of multiple stakeholders. The case sheds light on the gathering of information concerning the milk production through a network of advanced internet of things sensors, the output of which is employed both for data-driven decision-making and for information certification through blockchain. This trustable and certified information could be shared and employed by other stakeholders to get informed about the status of the production process and, in turn, to potentially deliver an enlarged set of details about the product, progressively up to the end consumers, with implications of technology adoption for food tech-firms and on related impacts on a circular economy.

In the era of tech-driven globalization, supply chains are becoming increasingly complex, with an increasing number of stakeholders spread across continents. A complex supply chain requires complex management systems. Supply chain management digitalization and information technology have advanced simultaneously in time, but a more technological and connected society calls for more information, uncovering the limits of supply chain management tools available today, which, while providing efficiency, automation, and organizational capabilities, are quite scarce in providing transparency. Consumer awareness on sensible issues such as climate change, human rights, or counterfeiting is increasing.

Biopharmaceutical companies and health authorities continuously exchange information to provide safe and effective therapeutics. The interactions between the two require transparency and extensive documentation exchange concerning the processes which extend from the development through the manufacturing phase. The current processes rely on paper documentation, notebooks, and point-to-point electronic data interchange (EDI) for the storage of data. Thereby, generating challenges of data integrity within the internal siloed structures and the traceability of the medicinal products in the pursuit to avoid counterfeiting. With Industry 4.0 and blockchain, the authors envisioned a reinvented workflow that helps to 1) manage data integrity with decentralized trust and 2) improve the track and trace capabilities. Hence, biopharmaceutical companies can manage data in a more trustable manner while maintaining security and privacy, further enabling the external ecosystem with track and trace to ensure complete transparency until the therapeutics reach patients.

Chapter 7

Conrad Kraft, University of Nicosia, Cyprus
Mariana Carmona, University of Nicosia, Cyprus

Grant management is a vital process that enables organisations to successfully deliver programmes that address social, economic, environmental, and other challenges. Globally, grant transfers represent significant sums, and their management is fraught with deficiencies that undermine the impact of the donated funds. Among the most urgent challenges in grant management are to improve transparency and reduce high administration costs. Digital transformation has done much to enhance efficiency, transparency, and accountability in grant administration; however, numerous shortcomings still exist. Blockchain, smart contracts, and tokenisation can be combined to achieve greater levels of efficiency and control in grant management than is currently possible. Through the study of fundamental blockchain concepts, the authors propose a grant-management solution that tokenises every expenditure item and uses smart contracts to automate payments, reporting, and budgetary compliance.

Chapter 8

Audet Victoire Malonga Bibila, Luiss University, Italy
Pietro De Giovanni, Luiss University, Italy

The study aims at investigating the potential use of blockchain technology in procurement processes. To better understand how the procurement process works, the case study of Eni is analyzed. Eni seeks to decarburize all its products by 2050, and its fight towards the energy transition is committed to working with suppliers ready to support it in this vision. After understanding the procurement process within Eni and identifying the potential uses of blockchain within these processes, the chapter proves that blockchain could be a powerful tool for the procurement process, especially for supplier qualification.

Chapter 9

Bernardo Nicoletti, Temple University, Italy
Andrea Appolloni, University of Rome Tor Vergata, Italy

Blockchain technology is one of the most vital and exciting technologies available today. It can transform the business world and the organizations' functions. It offers several possibilities to flourish existing businesses, grow entirely new ones, and severely disrupt traditional organizations. This chapter aims to study the applications of blockchain in procurement, to improve at the same time effectiveness and sustainability, and to define its critical success factors. The chapter presents a model and then describes its application in a real business case. It highlights the critical challenges in this blockchain implementation and the potentials of blockchain in managing sustainable procurement in support of utilities. This blockchain application is for smart metering. The blockchain solution contributes to the three bottom lines: economic, social, and sustainable. It can help support sustainable procurement, reduce errors, improve organizational functions and procedures, and prevent fraud. The chapter includes some challenges and their possible remediations.

Chapter 10

The aim of this work is to investigate emerging research trends and propose an evidence-based roadmap for encouraging further research into the management of blockchain technology. A bibliometric analysis is proposed, with a focus on intellectual property (IP) issues, in the field of blockchain technology. Then, the study highlights the main benefits that blockchain provides as well as the main difficulties, barriers, and challenges that emerge from the literature. The present study provides a reference for scientific communities to understand the current state of blockchain technology, thereby contributing to future research in the area. Moreover, it offers industrial implications and recommendations for entrepreneurs, managers, and practitioners.

As a decentralised digital ledger, blockchain has become a buzzword in the recent years, due to its advantageous characteristics. The application of blockchain has been associated with different implications, ranging from trust generator to increased efficiency. Recently, blockchain application has gained momentum by being implemented by different governments and public bodies, as a solution for tackling different issues, with the intent of providing more efficient public policies. Different blockchain-based systems and platforms have been increasingly introduced as a more secure and orderly alternative of delivering various public functions and services. Given the expansion of use cases in different countries and the scattered information in this regard, this chapter develops a taxonomy of blockchain outcomes in the public domain by identifying the emerging patterns and subcategories. The proposed taxonomy can support decision makers and researchers to better identify the various blockchain applications, alongside their benefits, implications, and possible associated risks.

Preface

Nowadays, the curiosity and interest around blockchain are definitely being followed with skepticism and uncertainty due to the immaturity of this technology and its historical connections with the world of financial transactions and trades. However, the properties and main features of blockchain can bring considerable improvements to businesses and organizations, even when used in non-financial applications. How can firms benefit from blockchain technology? How should firms modify their business models to accommodate blockchain technology? How will supply chain relationships and networks transform when blockchain activates smart contracts? These questions challenge firms and businesses as well as governments, international bodies, and policy makers. Consequently, society at large requires knowledge on blockchain to assess its real potential and evaluate both its business opportunities and social implications.

One of the first steps to undertake when evaluating blockchain is to modify the data management systems to accommodate the new technology. During recent decades, firms have experienced important changes in data management due to specific mega trends, including corporate social responsibility (CSR), modern solutions like Industry 4.0 technologies, or disruptive events like the Covid-19 pandemic. In each of these instances, firms have adjusted their business models and data management systems to remain competitive and successful. As with e-commerce before and Industry 4.0 technologies afterwards, blockchain requires significant advancements in the digital transformation process. In more recent years, the adoption of digital solutions has been both fashionable and appealing due to their potential benefits and the role they play in the digital world (Ivanov et al., 2019; Frank et al., 2019). However, firms and supply chains require a more comprehensive analysis and evaluation of the digital transformation process. Many investments in Industry 4.0 have been pursued to exploit financial and fiscal opportunities rather than to successfully use potential new technology. Therefore, a deep analysis of the blockchain is needed to better understand such rapid and increasing trend and to recognize whether digitalization through blockchain can supply real business advantages and concrete market opportunities along with social and environmental benefits (De Giovanni, 2020). In fact, it seems clear that firms need three things to understand how blockchain can benefit them: a comprehensive analysis of the strategic behavioral changes required to properly select and use blockchain technology, an accurate estimation of their economic outcomes, and a careful assessment of the implications for the whole supply chain network (Ivanov et al., 2019; Saberi et al., 2019).

Within the context of operations and supply chain management, blockchain technology allows firms to perform transparency, verify the originality of raw materials and goods, and ensure traceability and business risk mitigation. These targets can be achieved by collecting real information about the business model in a digital environment, recording them in an immutable dataset, and then making the whole batch of information available to all stakeholders, including consumers. In general, a blockchain consists of a set of digital applications enabling firms to track, trace, and verify how goods move along the supply chain, from the manufacturers to the retailers through to the distribution centers and logistics facilities (Cole et al., 2019). Such shared information on a blockchain platform allows supply chain members to be updated, integrated, and involved in any transaction (Pournader et al., 2020); therefore, blockchain seeks to better monitor both the firms' and the suppliers' actions and activate the smart contracts accordingly (De Giovanni, 2019).

Today, businesses are geographically extended and dispersed, making the boundaries of their affairs and competition difficult to identify (Saberi et al., 2019). In addition to the intricate network of relationships that firms can establish worldwide, issues like inefficient transactions and supplier performance, frauds and fake deals, unethical practices and routines, use of environmentally harmful processes and supplies, cultural barriers and language differences, international regulations and legislative constraints, and lack of trust and commitment of some suppliers call for additional information visibility, transparency, and verifiability to better manage and control the supply chain network, remove all potential business risks, and mitigate the inefficient transactions characterizing the supply chain linkages (Dolgui et al., 2019). Blockchain technology enables trustless networking, because the parties can make transactions even though they do not trust each other; therefore, their applications can considerably increase the chances for firms to create an efficient and effective supply chain network (De Giovanni, 2021).

In fact, the implementation of blockchain applications requires that all supply chain members take into account the complex regulatory, tax, auditability, risk, and compliance implications linked to any global transaction platform (Cole et al., 2019). Restrictive legislations, reputational pressures, corruptions, fake news and products, human rights and gender violations, unknown working conditions, and security are only some of the social factors that cannot be handled by using traditional data management systems. Today's firms and supply chains struggle to demonstrate their performance in these dimensions, which are quite complicated and require intricate verification and communication systems. Instead, blockchain can substantially help to achieve these outcomes and leverage the firms' businesses and sustainable actions (De Giovanni, 2021).

Within this framework, this book seeks to contribute the state of knowledge on how firms are currently reengineering their business models to accommodate blockchain technology. It sheds light on the business motivations for adopting blockchain, the types of improvements the blockchain can guarantee, and the modifications occurring in supply chain relationships and offers a comprehensive assessment of both the strengths and the weaknesses of blockchain in business, including the economic implications. Finally, the book offers thoughts for reflection about the possible adoption of blockchain in businesses and organizations through a lens on operational changes, contractual agreements and relationships, and emerging economic trade-offs.

TARGET AUDIENCE

This book is a collection of case studies and business applications relative to the experiences of blockchain adoption and implementation. Therefore, professionals, executives, and business leaders will be able to acknowledge the blockchain's potential and gain unique inspirations on whether to embrace this technology within their business models.

Researchers and Ph.D. students will find in this book a way to challenge traditional economic models and negotiation processes. For example, how do pricing strategies change when implementing blockchain? What are the goodwill and brand implications? How does blockchain interface and complement the transaction cost theory? How does the digital world around blockchain work parallel to the physical world? How do supply chain partners and members modify coordination mechanisms and agreements by shifting from traditional to smart contracts? This book will provide evidence and directions on how the business world changes through blockchain and leaves opportunities to develop quantitative and theoretical research starting from the book's outcomes.

This book can be also used by graduate and undergraduate students in programs like operations management, supply chain, international business, and negotiations. Students will gain an understanding of how the digitalization induced by blockchain technology changes firms' strategies at both the corporate and functional levels and highlights the new competences that managers, strategists, and entrepreneurs should acquire in modern economic systems and businesses.

BLOCKCHAIN WITH ORACLES, TOKENS, AND SMART CONTRACTS

Since this book seeks to provide a set of case studies that have implemented the blockchain, I hereby present a quick overview of the technical and technological aspects of blockchain, including oracles, tokens, and smart contracts. These ingredients are common parts of all the chapters of this book and, therefore, this section allows readers to quickly get acquainted with how blockchain functions, interacts with oracles, generates tokens, and activates smart contracts.

Developed in 2008 by Satoshi Nakamoto, blockchain is a distributed dataset system that records transactional data after verifying them through a consensus reached within a network of relationships. The data recorded in the blockchain are organized in blocks, and all parties can recognize and access to transactions through hashes (or cryptographic fingerprints) that are impossible to tamper with. Therefore, the network of links corresponds to peer-to-peer transactions, which can be either based on financial transactions or based on information to be continuously monitored and traced.

When a member of the network initiates a transaction, all details are transmitted to the full network, checked by all other users, and recorded if a consensus is reached among all these parties. By doing so, the blockchain develops and maintains a distributed ledger, that is, a dataset of replicated nodes where information is stored in an immutable way. One important element of blockchain is the absence of a given entity that controls the transactions. In fact, the blockchain solves all issues when the parties of a transaction have different interests through smart contracts, protocols, and negotiation clauses. When a transaction is validated, it is grouped in a block of other transactions where a cryptographic algorithm protects the information; the cryptographic algorithm includes private keys to sign any transaction, hash functions to link blocks among themselves, and the consensus mechanisms to guarantee the transaction's irreversibility. If a party tries to change any information recorded in the blockchain, the modification can occur only if all parties of the network simultaneously agree on that change. Therefore, the blockchain mitigates fraudulent behavior in a transaction, either based on financial assets or based on operational practices and performance.

In the past, firms have used enterprise resource planning (ERP) systems for managing data; nowadays, the blockchain technology can represent an important new information system that can resolve issues and exceptions, for example, the parties' reconciliation. These are, in fact, managed through digital cryptocurrencies and tokens to facilitate the transactions and then mitigate time-consuming and expensive bank transfers and oversee conversions and interactions among the network parties. The blockchain allows firms to share data within the network to create a trustable set of transactions that are regulated by protocols, rules, and standards negotiated and set by all network parties. Therefore, the blockchain collects and records all data by private networks, intelligent sensors, mobile apps, and all possible traditional data sharing and collection systems to make the transactions and the quality of the data secured and trustable. By doing so, blockchain can create verifiable digital chains through tokens and then unlock business opportunities in production, inventory, procurement, quality control, financial assets, and promotion. In fact, blockchain provides real-time data to the network from the origins of resources to sales, level of stocks, delivery, and after sales services. This is an important feature of blockchain technology in supply chain management, since end-to-end transactions and their transparency allow small- and medium-sized firms to unlock the value linked to features and business peculiarities that are real sources of competitive advantages and that are not identifiable through traditional ERPs. For large firms, it allows them to properly manage their networks of firms dispersed worldwide.

Because the blockchain can potentially change the way businesses are carried out and how supply chains are managed, the multiple unanswered questions around the technology can result in diffused skepticism throughout firms and organizations when they turn to blockchain implementation and adoption. One clear evidence for this is that blockchain can lead companies to reach a high level of integration without being legally vertically integrated. Therefore, the blockchain allows companies to mimic the vertical integration by executing contracts according to the parties' performance and behavior. This is the main smart contract duty, that is, executing the contract according to the parties' real performance. In supply chain management, De Giovanni et al. (2016) and De Giovanni (2018) mathematically created a contract that is called an incentive mechanism, according to which the supply chain members are penalized economically every time one deviates from the optimal strategies defined by the vertical integrated solution. While this remains a theoretical exercise, the blockchain offers the chance to make this framework executable through smart contracts. For example, in a traditional transaction, a seller and a buyer agree to finalize a certain delivery in 5 days. In a traditional framework, the transaction of money from the buyer to the seller occurs before the buyer receives the goods from the seller and, then, when the buyer places the order. Afterwards, when the delivery is finalized and the buyer receives the goods, the presence of any operational issue like quality, delays, or nonconformities induces the buyer to initiate a complaint process that should lead to the parties' reconciliation. In contrast, when using blockchain, the buyer does not pay the seller when they place the order; rather, a certain amount of digital assets from the buyer's wallet are frozen when the seller sends the goods. Then, the amount is unlocked when the delivery is finalized and after the buyer has checked the quality of the goods received, reviewed possible delays, or identified any defects occurring in the packaging. According to the real performance of the seller, the buyer will then decide to pay the seller by unlocking the amount from its wallet.

Indeed, this is a very important revolution for supply chain management and for negotiation processes in general. All these features must be controllable by using oracles, such that the buyer's information is verified and checked, registered in the blockchain, and used to activate the smart contract by also considering the possible emerging issues or underperforming situations, such as a clause in the smart contract that penalizes the seller if there is a delay. In such a case, the smart contract would not unlock the full amount from the buyer's wallet, but rather a reduced amount is automatically computed according to the clause. Through these mechanisms, all parties have incentives to stick with the contract terms and behave as if they were vertically integrated.

Indeed, the most precious work is done by the oracles. To execute a smart contract, the blockchain needs access to external data through the oracles present within the eco-system and that connect the physical world with the digital world, and then allow one to verify and authenticate the smart contract clauses as well as to pursue its execution. The oracles can be classified as follows:

- Software oracles, which gather data and information from online sources (e.g., Google maps, the Financial Times) and feed them into smart contracts.
- Hardware oracles, which provide data from physical devices dispersed over a certain territory and that generally serve other purposes. For example, the sensors and video devices used to pay the highway tolls can gather information to be injected in the smart contract and lead to its execution.
- Human oracles, which refer to a network of people being physically present within the eco-system who can verify some information if they are connected to the blockchain system. The individuals send information to the blockchain through their devices and, when a consensus is reached among them, the blockchain activates the smart contracts.
- Inbound oracles, which are offline sources of information that go from the eco-system to the blockchain and that are recorded somewhere. For example, data recorded on the quality of water for a certain river in the past 20 years is used to estimate the quality of fishing from that river when writing a contract. The smart contract can activate the payment when the real quality corresponds to the estimated quality.
- Outbound oracles, which are offline sources of information going from the blockchain to the eco-system. For example, the records on the quality of today's fishing show that fishing was of low quality; hence, smart contracts containing information about quality for tomorrow's fishing should set the expected level of quality according to that information.

Clearly, these oracles are able and willing to collaborate with the blockchain's owner if they are to receive a proper reward, which takes the form of tokens. Tokenisation is the process of creating digital assets and currencies according to the contribution provided in verifying the blockchain protocol. These digital assets can take the form of fungible and non-fungible tokens. The former are "coins" of the same value that are interchangeable and divisible. The latter are unique assets corresponding to something special with a value that is not interchangeable or divisible. For example, the token linked to a song file is not interchangeable or divisible because the properties of that song are unique.

BOOK ORGANIZATION

This book is organized into 11 chapters. Each chapter analyses how blockchain can be implemented in a specific business context and framework using tokens, smart contracts, and oracles when needed. A brief description of each chapter follows below.

Chapter 1 introduces the case in a collectible industry. Collectibles are, in fact, subject to a high risk of counterfeiting and fake replicas. Blockchain helps to guarantee the originality and the transparency of the products. This chapter is organized around the case of Genuino, which uses blockchain to extract the value behind collectible objects, connect them to digital platforms, and manage the data value through non-fungible tokens. The use of physical oracles along with Internet of Things (IoT) helps to capture and record the right information and make the application of blockchain technology in the collectible industry successful.

Chapter 2 is an application on the Agri-food sector, which informs on how customers are increasingly paying attention to healthy, high quality, and environmentally friendly products. The case develops around the case of Pastificio Mancini, which applies the blockchain developed by Trusty. Thanks to the transparency offered and guaranteed by blockchain technology, the company is able to communicate the real product's quality to customers, gain trust about their offers, and acquire more customers over time.

Chapter 3 develops a case in the winery industry where Cantina Placido-Volpone uses blockchain to ensure wine traceability, which results in trust, consumer protection, and anti-counterfeiting options. Customers can connect to the blockchain using a QR code, through which a web page ensures access to various information regarding the wine, such as the geographical context, the cultivation procedure, and the wine production steps. The use of blockchain allowed the company to carry out an internationalization strategy, increase their financial performance, and better forecast the future demand for their products.

Chapter 4 analyzes the application of blockchain in the food industry, focusing on milk production and distribution. The chapter develops around a milk supply chain comprising several companies that implemented a blockchain project to guarantee the traceability of milk, from the production through sales. Metrics related to cows, such as health state, certifications, medicines, and antibiotics, are progressively tracked through an immutable set of information stored in a dedicated blockchain system. Customers and other actors can use the blockchain technology to read the information and verify the product's authenticity and safety prior deciding whether to purchase the milk.

Chapter 5 introduces a case in the saffron industry in which Arte Zafferano implemented the blockchain within different functions and activities, including purchasing, production, inventory management, selling strategy, and customer relationship management. Within each of these functions, the company uses blockchains to unlock various business potentials, although it also has encountered several barriers linked to either the implementation cost, the supply chain, or the public domain. A comprehensive analysis of both operational and economic performance highlights both the strengths and the weaknesses of blockchain.

Chapter 6 introduces the application of blockchain within the biopharma industry, with a focus on quality control systems. In the biopharma industry, blockchain technology can be used not only for ensuring the distribution and the proper sale of both medical and health care products but also to align their production systems with regulatory guidelines. The blockchain helps to ensure data integrity, transparency, and trust within multiple external stakeholders and coordinates the internal procedures of the ecosystem, including with the patients. The chapter introduces a proof of concept to see the benefits that blockchain provides comparatively to traditional quality control systems.

Chapter 7 investigates blockchain technology in the service industry, with a particular emphasis on grant management. Instead of only focusing on tracking and reporting issues, using blockchains allows firms in the grant industry to avoid issues like misappropriation and over-expenditure of funds. This chapter also proposes a smart contract concept that unifies the interests and values of the stakeholders in a grant project, including donors, fiscal authorities, grantees, and beneficiaries.

Chapter 8 describes how blockchain can be used in the energy sector, specifically, in the procurement process of Ente Nazionale Idrocarburi (ENI). This chapter shows how blockchain helps in defining the smart contracts and obtaining several benefits, like saving time compared to traditional qualification systems, decreasing the supplier risks, mitigating the need for compliance, matching the smart contract with the legal issues, and providing real incentives to customers and suppliers through smart contracts. At the same time, new challenges emerged in the procurement function due to the application of blockchain technology, such as the need for specialized operators, the energy consumption rates, transaction date and time, and the culture for using the blockchain properly. Finally, the chapter shows how blockchain can be helpful in the supplier's qualification process.

Chapter 9 elaborates on the application of blockchain in the food industry, specifically for quality assurance targets in procurement, with a focus on the wine industry. This chapter shows that blockchain solutions can better manage procurement in terms of quality of product and service along with their sustainability goals, highlighting that blockchain can be a disruptive innovation for sustainable procurement although it provides several benefits in terms of security, cost effectiveness, and number of intermediations.

The last two chapters make a collection of case studies and analyze the blockchain applications. Chapter 10 groups the cases into four clusters. After carrying out a bibliometric analysis on papers dealing with blockchain technology implementation and adoption, the identified intervention areas are: blockchain as a social driver, blockchain technology as a strategic lever, blockchain as new emerging business models, and blockchain technology as a solution for ensuring security and traceability. The chapter ends by identifying new directions and challenges that blockchain implies for firms and policymakers. Chapter 11 searches the taxonomy dimensions of blockchain by analyzing legal cases, benefits, risks, challenges, and public value. The cases are then clustered according to the blockchain usages, which can be linked to digital records, supply chain management, identity management, bills and payments, welfare, e-voting, and legal enforcements. These two final chapters offer a rich overview of the current applications and leave reflections for future studies in the area and possible business developments.

IMPACT ON THE FIELD AND CONTRIBUTIONS

This book proposes a set of case studies and business applications to shed light on the motivations that push firms to implement blockchain. A comprehensive analysis of the technology's strengths and weaknesses for each case allow one to appreciate its real potential and to better evaluate its possible future adoption. All business cases developed in this work highlight the need to undertake two directions. On the one hand, light implementation processes are possible when blockchain technology should be embedded within a specific function, thus requiring procedures and routines to be rewritten. On the other hand, the implementation of blockchain requires deep modifications in the business models, the relationships with suppliers and consumers, and adjustments to data management systems. The cases reported throughout this book show that the blockchain can play different roles within the business model. These roles can be either operative, where they aim at increasing the goods' traceability, security, and originality, or strategic, where they seek to reshape the corporate strategy, modify the supply chain networks through smart contracts, and ensure the integration of all business parties spread all over the world. Beyond traditional (operational and economic) targets, blockchain turns out to be a great technology to demonstrate firms' social impact and contribution to the environment by recording information regarding both pillars. In general terms, the blockchain finds promising and fruitful applications when a firm has a competitive advantage that cannot be acknowledged by using traditional data management systems.

One additional important dimension that emerges from this book is that blockchain technology should be supported by other digital technology to pursue its objectives and exploit its full potential. In fact, the blockchain records data and information in a digital space, data and information that are received—most likely—by other digital technologies like IoT. Furthermore, the cases that are reported in this book do not all rely on oracles to make the blockchain work. Instead, oracles allow firms to connect the physical world with the digital world and, consequently, monitor and manage the physical world through the blockchain and the related smart contracts. Future developments and applications should evaluate the possible exploitation of oracles to unlock the blockchain's potential. Finally, this book seeks to highlight the real advantages of blockchain technology and how it can be used in practice. The readers will then decide whether it is time to either surf this new technological wave or stay away from it and take the risk of being disrupted.

Pietro De Giovanni
Luiss University, Italy

REFERENCES

Cole, R., Stevenson, M., & Aitken, J. (2019). Blockchain technology: Implications for operations and supply chain management. *Supply Chain Management*, *24*(4), 469–483. doi:10.1108/SCM-09-2018-0309

De Giovanni, P. (2018). A joint maximization incentive in closed-loop supply chains with competing retailers: The case of spent-battery recycling. *European Journal of Operational Research*, *268*(1), 128–147. doi:10.1016/j.ejor.2018.01.003

De Giovanni, P. (2019). Digital supply chain through dynamic inventory and smart contracts. *Mathematics*, *7*(12), 1235. doi:10.3390/math7121235

De Giovanni, P. (2020). Blockchain and smart contracts in supply chain management: A game theoretic model. *International Journal of Production Economics*, *228*, 107855. doi:10.1016/j.ijpe.2020.107855

De Giovanni, P. (2021). Smart Contracts and Blockchain for Supply Chain Quality Management. In *Dynamic Quality Models and Games in Digital Supply Chains* (pp. 91–110). Springer. doi:10.1007/978-3-030-66537-1_5

De Giovanni, P., Reddy, P. V., & Zaccour, G. (2016). Incentive strategies for an optimal recovery program in a closed-loop supply chain. *European Journal of Operational Research*, *249*(2), 605–617. doi:10.1016/j.ejor.2015.09.021

Dolgui, A., Ivanov, D., Potryasaev, S., Sokolov, B., Ivanova, M., & Werner, F. (2020). Blockchain-oriented dynamic modelling of smart contract design and execution in the supply chain. *International Journal of Production Research*, *58*(7), 2184–2199. doi:10.1080/00207543.2019.1627439

Frank, A. G., Dalenogare, L. S., & Ayala, N. F. (2019). Industry 4.0 technologies: Implementation patterns in manufacturing companies. *International Journal of Production Economics*, *210*, 15–26. doi:10.1016/j.ijpe.2019.01.004

Ivanov, D., Dolgui, A., & Sokolov, B. (2019). The impact of digital technology and Industry 4.0 on the ripple effect and supply chain risk analytics. *International Journal of Production Research*, *57*(3), 829–846. doi:10.1080/00207543.2018.1488086

Pournader, M., Shi, Y., Seuring, S., & Koh, S. L. (2020). Blockchain applications in supply chains, transport and logistics: A systematic review of the literature. *International Journal of Production Research*, *58*(7), 2063–2081. doi:10.1080/00207543.2019.1650976

Saberi, S., Kouhizadeh, M., Sarkis, J., & Shen, L. (2019). Blockchain technology and its relationships to sustainable supply chain management. *International Journal of Production Research*, *57*(7), 2117–2135. doi:10.1080/00207543.2018.1533261

Acknowledgment

The success of this book is due to commitments of several parties. I would thank all the authors who have contributed to this book for their time and their dedication. Furthermore, I would thank all the reviewers, who always offer their free and sincere contribution to the developments of both the scientific community and the society at large. I would also thank all companies and stakeholders who have interacted with us during the whole journey. A big thank goes to my wife, Maria, and to my kids, Maria Greta and Riccardo, who always support me with care and love and push me to be on top. Finally, a sincere thank goes to my parents, Domenico and Angelina, who always believed and trusted me – even without using any blockchain technology– especially when I was a young scholar. I dedicate to them this book along with the whole journey of my career.

Chapter 1

How Genuino Applies Blockchain Technology in the Collectibles Industry

Daniel Ruzza
Luiss University, Italy

Gabriele Bernasconi
Genuino, Italy

Pietro De Giovanni
https://orcid.org/0000-0002-1247-4807
Luiss University, Italy

ABSTRACT

This chapter analyses the blockchain implemented by Genuino in the collectibles industry. Since collectibles are subject to high risk of counterfeiting and fake replications, blockchain technology can help substantially to ensure transparency, originality, ownership, and data security and protection. Two methods to use blockchain in the industry seem to be the most widespread today: creating digital native collectibles on blockchain and transposing physical objects into the blockchain by creating digital twins. By using blockchain, new consumer clusters emerge, highlighting the need to modernize both the traditional economies and the current business models.

DOI: 10.4018/978-1-7998-8014-1.ch001

INTRODUCTION

The collectibles market has experienced an important modification with the e-commerce revolution, which moved the collectibles trade from shops to online platforms such as eBay (Heitner, 2016; Seideman, 2018). However, this shift implied a considerable increase of fakes. Among the technologies available to mitigate such risks, the blockchain technology is now emerging as a possible solution to these business issues. Among the full set of options and features, the blockchain enables firms to create non-fungible tokens, which turn out to be secure and unchangeable and whose uniqueness, originality, and ownership are guaranteed through the blockchain (Tapscott and Tapscott, 2016). Research has already documented the adoption of blockchain to mitigate the risks of counterfeiting items (Debayouty et al., 2021), which makes blockchain the ideal technology to solve this issue also for collectibles. In particular, two methods seem to be the most widespread today, whose application in the collectible and memorabilia industry is definitely feasible: 1) creating digital native collectibles on blockchain and 2) transposing physical objects into the blockchain by creating digital twins.

The option of creating digital native collectibles on blockchain has upfront advantages in the collectible and memorabilia industry. In fact, the blockchain protects related tokens, which are impossible to destroy, counterfeit, or replicate. Hence, users can engage in ownership and trade them easily (Rensing, 2021). Recently, Dapper Labs created and sold CriptoKitties, (https://www.dapperlabs.com), which are fully digital and unique carton cats. Only two months after their launch in 2018, Dapper Labs managed to generate a turnover close to $20 million (Zorloni, 2018). Given the great success with the CriptoKitties, Dapper Labs then turned to sports collectibles by creating the NBA Top Shots in collaboration with the NBA (Browne, 2021). NBA Top Shots invented a new category of collectibles: the key moments of NBA games. Through this type of collectible, consumers can buy videos of key moments of a certain match and become exclusive owners (Guzman, 2021). The business model linked to NBA Top Shots created a turnover of $50 million in the first 30 days (Guzman, 2021). After purchase, moments can be traded between fans. For example, a key moment in a match with LeBron James has been sold for $208,000 (Browne, 2021). Alternative approaches consist of digital collectible cards, which have the same functionalities of the physical ones. Anyways, there are several applications suitable for these options. Dapper Lab created tokens for Mixed Martial Arts MMA (Roberts, 2020), Sorare (https://sorare.com), and Fantastec Swap (https://www.swap-fantastec.com). Player Tokens Inc., turned to baseball (https://playertokens.co), while Animoca Brands (https://www.animocabrands.com) entered the world of Moto GP and Formula 1 (Schmidt, 2020). Finally, some companies embrace more sports simultaneously, such as Ex Sport (https://www.ex-sports.io).

A different, more complex approach to tokenization consists of bringing physical sports collectibles into the digital world through blockchain technology. The physical object "transposition" involves creating a digital twin in the blockchain. Fantastec Swap (https://www.fantastec.io/#home) uses a hybrid approach by both creating full digital collectibles and turning some physical objects into digital ones. A typical example of such applications are autographs. The Fantastec Swap's partners are some top international soccer clubs such as Real Madrid, Borussia Dortmund, and Arsenal. These partnerships provide an example of the economic value of following the business model. A similar approach has been taken by Collectable.com (https://collectable.com), who searches for high-value sports collectables, verifies their authenticity, and makes sure that they are conserved in the best possible way. The physical collectibles are then held by Collectable.com, which creates a Digital Twin on the blockchain. Collectable.com customers can then purchase the digital twin entirely or in fractions thereof and hold them in their portfolio. In the Collectable. com marketplace, consumers can trade with collectables and create a secondary market that works similarly to the stock market.

Along with the aforementioned wave, new approaches to digitalization are emerging in the collectibles industry. Among those, Genuino has certainly taken a different and original approach to manage collectibles (https://genuino.world/page.html). The Genuino's final goal is to combat counterfeiting in the sports collectibles market while allowing enthusiasts to hold physical and digital objects and exchange freely. Genuino's idea is to digitalize collectibles by applying t-shirt patches that collect information on sport events. Examples of information are the athlete's name, whether he played a game, the performance, the amount of time he played, and its roles. The patch receives information and signals from physical oracles, located throughout the playing field and integrated within all sport facilities. The collected information is then recorded to the blockchain, becoming then trustable, traceable, valuable, and original. Considering the different approach adopted by Genuino, we will go through the full case to highlight how the blockchain is used, the possible advantages linked, as well as the emerging threats.

The chapter is organized as follows. Section 2 provides an overview of the collectibles industry to highlight its importance, while Section 3 describes the idea behind Genuino's solution. Section 4 introduces the certification process, while Section 5 explains the integration of blockchain with other technologies. Section 6 discusses the case, and Section 7 analyzes emerging threats and opportunities. Finally, Section 8 briefly concludes and identifies the future research directions to be undertaken.

AN OVERVIEW OF THE COLLECTIBLES INDUSTRY

The collectibles market is a growing industry worth around $370 billion a year (Heitner, 2016; Ito, 2020). People buy collectibles for several motivations: pure passion, affirmation of a social status, social consensus, philanthropy, and speculative investment (Bleve et al., 2018). Collectables are often assimilated into real luxury goods that reflect the owners' passion and lifestyle (Hechler-Fayd'herbe and Picinati di Torcello, 2020). According to a survey conducted by the Credit Suisse, more than 70% of customers are collectors and buy collectibles most likely to cultivate their passions. Furthermore, collectibles have recently gained great popularity as a form of investment, which can diversify one's portfolio (Bleve et al., 2018; Kiesnoski, 2019). This finding is especially true for ultra-high-net-worth individuals, as collectibles count between 5% and 10% (with peaks of 15%) of the total amount invested (Hechler-Fayd'herbe and Picinati di Torcello, 2020). These percentages are in line with other consulting and professional advice and reports (Kiesnoski, 2019). Although investments on collectives are currently increasing in the range $250 and $5000 (Hechler-Fayd'herbe and Picinati di Torcello, 2020), Deloitte highlights that the attention for collectibles depends on its low correlation with traditional assets (Bleve et al., 2018), which is a proxy of a diversified portfolio.

Figure 1.

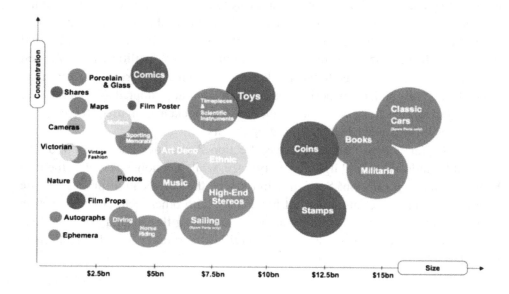

Figure 1 (Ito, 2020) shows the most common categories of collectibles classified by size and concertation. The latter consists of the number of items included in each category and their impact on the within-category sales. The colors identify clusters of goods. The size of the bubbles indicates the category's global trade volume. Accordingly, art, classic cars, wine, coins, stamps, and sports memorabilia are the most prominent collectibles. In this chapter, we focus on the sports memorabilia market, since it offers numerous opportunities to apply the blockchain technology given its size and growth (Seideman, 2018). In fact, millennials and members of Generation Z, who have the financial means to enjoy collections, are often willing to collect this type of objects (Weil, 2019). Sports memorabilia represents a fundamental segment of the collectibles market, involving 67 million people a year (Heitner, 2016) and about $10 billion globally, with approximately half from the United States (Seideman, 2018). Jerseys used by sports superstars can often be valued at hundreds of thousands of dollars (Weil, 2019). In June 2019, Babe Ruth's New York Yankees jersey from 1928-1930 has been sold at auction for $5.64 million, making it the most expensive sports memorabilia item ever sold (Weil, 2019). The most popular items are those that belonged to the 6-time NBA champion and superstar Michael Jordan (Heitner, 2016), whose popularity is constantly growing thanks through the recent ESPN docuseries, "The Last Dance" (Red, 2020). The jersey wore by Jordan during the farewell match with the Chicago Bulls was auctioned for $173,000 (Heitner, 2016).

The high risk of fraud and counterfeiting is one of the most recurrent problems within the sports memorabilia market (Red, 2020). In the past, William Mastro, also called "The King of Memorabilia" and owner of Mastro Auction (Crosby, 2015), was accused and later sentenced to 20 months in jail for defrauding his clients; he tampered with sports memorabilia and sold fake items for more than 7 years (Crosby, 2015). However, Mastro's case is not isolated. The "Bullpen" investigation conducted by the FBI starting in the 1990s reveals that about 50% of sports memorabilia sold in the United States are counterfeit, while certain items present a counterfeit rate of up to 90% (The Federal Bureau of Investigation, 2005). These estimates make the sports memorabilia market very risky and uncertain, as confirmed by the United States Postal Inspection Service (2019).

The most important threats persisting in the sports memorabilia market relate to the difficulty to verify an object's originality, the peculiar skills requested and the high experience needed to verify the originality, and the exchange system regulating the objects' transactions (Weil, 2019; Thomas, 2020; Red, 2020). To date, collective objects are exchanged between fans and collectors either through independent auctions or generalist websites such as eBay (Seideman, 2018). According to Pownall (2017), private sales mobilize 70% of the total value of sports memorabilia market, whose transactions are most likely finalized online, without any face-to-face meeting, through payments that are not guaranteed, and with uncertain shipment to the buyer's location. Therefore, the buyer is unable to verify the originality of a collectible object before receiving it physically. Hence, buyers have insufficient operational tools against possible scams, while they can look at the price as a proxy that signals the items' originality. In fact, a price outside the market price – either above or below – could warn buyers of possible scams (Weil, 2019; Thomas, 2020). Alternatively, buyers can collect information about the sellers, verifying features like their presence in the market or their reliability in past transactions (Weil, 2019). Items can also be either certified and authenticated by professional organizations like the Professional Sports Authenticator JSA and Beckett or purchased from these sources (Red, 2020). However, several issues remain, like the cost and timing for the authentication procedure as well as the risk of false certificates and certifiers' mistakes (Thomas, 2020).

THE GENUINO CASE STUDY

Genuino is an innovative startup within the ICT sector, funded in the USA in 2018 and established in Italy on February 1, 2019. Genuino is a decentralized protocol to certify, authenticate, and trade digital collectibles backed by certified physical assets, which integrates blockchain, IoT, and Artificial Intelligence technologies into a proprietary web app and mobile app (Genuino, 2020). By combining all of these technologies, Genuino connects both the digital and physical worlds. The company's motto is: "Collect Digital. Own Physical". The idea for this application comes from the awareness that we live in an era of post truth, in which it is difficult to blindly trust regarding product genuineness based only on the sellers' communication and advertising. Genuino knows that the new primary consumers' needs are to verify a product first hand and to gain understanding and gather evidence on a product. Companies should adapt to this need and inspire the trust of consumers, creating transparency relative to a product and along the whole supply chain. The certification protocol that Genuino has created meets these needs; the system collects data within the production processes while minimizing the risk of manipulation and increasing the product's authenticity. Genuino's mission is to enhance quality and guarantee the traceability, sustainability, and anti-counterfeiting of the product, thereby safeguarding the final consumer, the product manufacturer, and all stakeholders. Although Genuino knows the potential of its blockchain approach, today, it tests and applies its solution to the food sector by exploiting a partnership with Daruma sushi, as well as in the sports collectibles thanks to the partnership with ACF Fiorentina. The latter represents the main sector of Genuino's business today and in the near future. Genuino seeks to create a solution against counterfeiting and to empower brands. These dual targets will allow them to tell their stories and engage their fans through NFTs connected to physical certified assets. To this end, Genuino's solution must achieve three primary objectives: guarantee the authenticity of a jersey and distinguish between "Match Worn" or "Match Prepared", trace the constituent elements of the shirt, and trace the creation and transfer of ownership events.

Genuino was created in 2018 based on the ideas of Gabriele Bernasconi and Eleonora Mulas, two Italians abroad with the desire to bring a little Italianism out of their country of origin. To do this, they first turned their attention to the food sector, for which Italy is recognized all over the world, trying to certify the quality of products with the blockchain. However, they quickly realized that this was probably not the best sector, especially because of the scale-up issues linked to the blockchain technology (De Giovanni, 2020). In contrast, people within the sports sector are much more willing to adopt new technologies, and that has allowed for greater and faster mass adoption. In February 2019, Genuino was founded as a company in Italy and, after acquiring further skills and capital, Genuino developed the first prototype of blockchain technology with ACF Fiorentina. The prototype has been tested in the last two rounds of the Serie A 2019/2020 championship: Fiorentina-Roma and Fiorentina-Inter. Meanwhile, Genuino was selected to participate in the CES in Las Vegas, one of the largest events in this sector in the world. The project with ACF Fiorentina soon evolved and moved from just the certification of the jerseys to the creation of a marketplace with a series of digital collectibles to engage with their fans. The product will be launched in July 2021 for the start of the new sporting season and will include both physical and digital collectibles.

GENUINO'S CERTIFICATION PROCESS

Through the certification process, Genuino seeks to guarantee the authenticity of jerseys worn by players during official matches. In fact, especially when objects have high economic value, a high counterfeiting rate exists (De Giovanni, 2019). This is a demanding challenge, since the protocol developed must guarantee the certification of the object on the blockchain with the use of all required technologies and without interfering with the usual activities of staff and athletes before, during, and after the match. Although Genuino's prototype has been created for football games, it can be easily applied to other sports. Each football jersey is created from a virgin anonymous jersey plus a set of patches that can be applied via a thermal press. The jerseys prepared for an event become two types: *match worn* or *match prepared*. Match-worn jerseys are the jerseys worn and that actually entered the field during the game phase. Two shirts enter the field (one during the first half and one for the second half). One is left to the football team for sale, and the other remains available to the player who wore it. Match-prepared jerseys are prepared and/or worn jerseys that have not actively participated in the match. Match-prepared jerseys can be used at a later event if they have not been stressed. For each match played, the following are prepared: two shirts for each player, two shirts per goalkeeper in three possible colors, and about ten neutral jerseys to customize during the moment in case of need.

To ensure the achievement of the certification objectives, each jersey must be uniquely identified both in the physical and digital settings. For this reason, a smart patch containing identification passive tags are added to each shirt. A Non-Fungible Token (NFT) will also be created on the blockchain for each jersey. The smart patch is the connection between the physical object to the digital one. A gate records the passage of the jersey once the player enters and exits from the pitch. All recorded data is directly registered on the blockchain without third-party intermediation. Once this background process has been completed, it will be possible to sell the shirts and tokens that represent them digitally. The jerseys can be purchased and exchanged through the Genuino Marketplace.

How can buyers verify the originality of a jersey? The verification of the authenticity of the jersey can be performed using the Genuino app, upon framing the patch. The transfer of jersey ownership takes place in two steps, a physical transfer and a digital one. Once the buyer has transferred the agreed-upon fee, the seller transfers the jersey as a physical object and the digital NFT token representing the certificate of shirt ownership to the buyer. The NFT token transfer takes place like a normal wallet transaction as the NFT token is transferred from one wallet to another, once the jersey authenticity is validated by the buyers through the Genuino app.

BLOCKCHAIN AND OTHER TECHNOLOGIES

Within the certification protocol described above, blockchain and non-blockchain technologies are applied. Given the positioning of Genuino's "Collect Physical. Own Digital" mission, blockchain technology alone is not enough to guarantee an object's originality. Other technologies are needed to connect the physical object with the virtual token created on the blockchain (De Giovanni, 2021). In fact, the transition from physical to virtual is one of the most delicate phases in the certification process on the blockchain, since it is the easiest step to counterfeit. In this section, we will determine the fundamental technologies used by Genuino in this phase. In particular, we will see how the blockchain, NFTs, and patches work altogether.

One of the fundamental choices that Genuino made was the selection of the blockchain to use when registering the NFTs linked to the physical object and based on which the transactions take place. Initially, Genuino's choice was Ethereum, which is particularly effective and suitable for operations of this type. Ethereum is one of the most important public blockchains and guarantees the solidity and reliability of the recorded information. Furthermore, Ethereum creates NFTs called ERC 721, which lend themselves to this type of use. However, due to the increase in the cost of gas, Genuino had to revise its choice. Gas refers to the amount of money required by miners to perform operations such as transactions and smart contracts on Ethereum (Kay, 2021). The amount of gas required is not the same for each operation but depends on the speed with which you want the operation to be completed, the complexity of the operation, and the number of pending transactions in the network (Kay, 2021). With the outbreak of Decentralized Finance in the summer of 2020, the number of complex transactions in Ethereum increased considerably, leading to network congestion (Haig, 2021). This has resulted in average transaction fees exceeding $20 per transaction (Foxley, 2021). In a traceability protocol like that of Genuino, in which it is important to write every relevant event on the blockchain, the cost to write the information on the blockchain would have been prohibitive. So, Genuino had to review the choice and rely on L2 EVM. The two main advantages of using L2 for the application of Genuino are that it allows one to perform transactions with a very low commission in gas (e.g., up to 500 transactions can be made for few cent of a dollar), and it allows one to create a block and, therefore, to record the information very quickly. Furthermore, as an Ethereum side chain, it "bridges" with Ethereum and accommodates any request to transfer the tokens to Ethereum.

NFTs are created on the L2 blockchain. "Non-fungible tokens are unique, digital items with blockchain-managed ownership" (Finzer, 2020). Non-fungible goods are all objects that are not interchangeable, in contrast to fungible goods, such as money, which are perfectly interchangeable. It makes no difference whether a person has one 10€ banknote or another, because the banknotes have exactly the same value. Thanks to the blockchain, it is possible to assign the ownership of these objects to subjects who can hold them in their wallets and manage them as they like. NFTs can move across different ecosystems and across different Blockchains (Finzer, 2020). Another interesting feature of NFTs is that they can be traded and sold, and the high speed with which this can take place gives them high liquidity (Wintermeyer, 2021). Examples of NFTs include collectibles, game items, digital art, event tickets, domain names, and even ownership records for physical assets (Finzer, 2020).

NFTs are tools used by Genuino to represent physical shirts in the virtual world, functioning as real certificates of ownership of the jersey. The connection between the physical shirt and the digital NFT takes place through a smart patch applied to the shirts and the stadium gate. Patches are applied to the game jerseys. Using the patches, the virgin jersey can be customized with the sponsors, the players' names, and information about the competition during which the jersey was used. In the world of football, the patches applied to the jerseys are produced by a single supplier and made of different materials. There are two main patch packages: front patches, which represent sponsors and other ancillary info, and back patches, which indicate the player's name and jersey number. To recognize the t-shirts on the Genuino's blockchain, an additional small patch is applied to each t-shirt (Figure 2) without disturbing the operations or the activities linked to the game preparation, including the game jerseys. The patches are applied once to the blank jerseys, and their preparation process varies only marginally, considering the different types of patches. This new smart patch was developed by Genuino in partnership with DekoGrapics, one of the world leaders in the sector. The challenges that characterized the research and development phase were mainly due to the sensor durability embedded in the patch. In fact, the sensors are subjected to stresses when applied to the t-shirt as well as during the washing phase.

Figure 2. Example of Genuino's patch

CASE DISCUSSION

Genuino's solution creates benefits for both firms and consumers (Table 1). On the one hand, firms mitigate the counterfeiting issues by attaching a digital ownership certificate to their physical objects. This allows them to improve the brand value by protecting imitations and increasing transparency. On the other hand, consumers can quickly and effectively verify and validate the product by having proof of originality and ownership in just a few seconds. Using Genuino, consumers can see the jersey's chain of ownership by tracing the object life and the full batch of information connected to it. Furthermore, consumers can access an efficient and secure platform to sell and exchange the jersey in future transactions. In this sense, it is worth mentioning that Genuino opens the sports collectibles market to three types of people: collectors, fans, and crypto enthusiasts. The first category includes the classic collectors of collectibles and memorabilia. These people collect objects independent of the blockchain; however, they can easily and safely exchange objects through Genuino. Furthermore, the fans and supporters teams are generally discouraged from purchasing sports collectibles due to their low purchasing skills. Genuino supports them by simplifying the purchasing process and involving them in the new market platform.

Finally, crypto enthusiasts are more familiar with the blockchain world than with sports sector. This category is well informed on the crypto world dynamics, and are mainly interested in investment and speculative opportunities. crypto enthusiasts know the success of CryptoPunk and CryptoKitties, whose digital collectible NFTs value increased exponentially in a few months. Therefore, they can invest in sports collectibles and their respective NFTs hoping to follow the same path.

The Genuino solution raises some concerns when connecting physical and digital worlds and the related processes, which can take place both on and off the chain. Although the data is recorded on the blockchain, thus making it unchangeable and guaranteed, the insertion phase offers opportunities for falsification. Therefore, the data entry process is the weakest and most complex task in most applications. Genuino has invested massively to limit these issues, especially when the process takes place off chain or outside the blockchain. Genuino's motto is "Collect Digital. Own Physical." Therefore, unlike the full digital collectibles, it is impossible to manage all tasks on chain. Off-chain steps are required for physical objects, specifically jerseys. To ensure their correct identification and prevent illegal actions like the use of stolen tags or cloning of serial numbers, the NFT token is generated when the owner establishes the association between the patch and the product. From this point, the falsification opportunities are extremely limited, since all data is recorded by the sensors (physical oracles) and without any human intervention. When the jersey worn by the player enters or leaves the field, the sensors capture this information and record it on the blockchain. Overall, Genuino achieves the target of limiting falsifications during the phases of data collection and record on the blockchain using IoT sensors.

EMERGING TREATS AND OPPORTUNITIES THROUGH BLOCKCHAIN

Despite the numerous advantages that Genuino brings to customers using the blockchain, this solution is highly challenging. Among the challenges faced, we previously mentioned the development of identification tags to be embedded into the jersey, subject to many stresses like pressure, temperature, and body fluids. In addition to this issue, we identified three further challenges: the patch sensors can be either damaged or broken, legal issues can arise, and the possible pricing bubble linked to NFTs (Table 1). The smart patch and its sensors are the link between the virtual NFT and the jersey. The sensors associate a jersey with the NFT on the blockchain. There is a rare possibility that the sensors are broken. In fact, collectors are used to conserve and prevent match-worn jerseys from being worn or washed and, therefore, preserve the whole market value. To avoid this risk, Genuino carried out various stress tests on the patches to ensure their resistance through the use of several machine washes. The patches have shown good resistance in combinations of various situation. However, for any poorly performing patch, Genuino has developed a procedure for a prompt replacement that involves checking the actual sensor breakage from the back end. The damaged jersey is then sent to Genuino, the damaged patch is replaced, and a new NFT is created and associated with the new patch. To preserve all of the information recorded in the NFT connected to the broken patch, Genuino transfers the entire batch of information to the new NFT, preserving the whole history of the shirt, and ensuring total transparency to the customer. Another challenge that Genuino faces concerns the legal aspects linked to anti money laundering (AML) with the related issue of Knowing Your Customer (KYC) as well as the privacy issues. The KYC falls under the AML legislation, including the KYC law that provides obligations for the charged parties. Usually, the subjects charged are qualified subjects such as lawyers, notaries, accountants, banks, and financial institutions. These institutes are used to identify (either manually or automatically) the clients who contact them for any service by crossing data linked to difference sources. While this legislation only applied to the charged parties till the cryptocurrencies have been introduced in the business world to manage transactions and mimic the behavior of traditional currencies. Tokens linked to blockchain (such as NFTs) can be added to cryptocurrencies, considering that the NFT is not a currency in itself. However, it can be linked to a shirt, a painting, a video, etc. Selling the NFT does not signify selling a currency; instead, it implies selling an object, thus signaling that the NFT has value and is very often used in a speculative way similar to cryptocurrencies.

This paradigm has created confusion among Italian and European regulators, who consider all crypto-assets as a sector with high potential risk of money laundering.

Therefore, they have created a new category of subjects charged with carrying out crypto activities. The Italian legislative Decree 231/2007 and the fifth European AML directive of 2019 identify new subjects charged. Legislative Decree 231/2007, Article 1 letter FF identifies the following as charged subjects: *"Service providers relating to the use of virtual currency: any natural or legal person who provides third parties, on a professional basis, even online, with functional services use, exchange, storage of virtual currency and their conversion [...] as well as issuing, offering, transfer and clearing services and any other service functional to the acquisition, negotiation or intermediation in the exchange of the same currencies; ff-bis) digital wallet service providers [...]. "* Genuino falls into these categories, both for receiving and guarding digital currency and converting them into further digital value representations such as Genuino's NFTs. Therefore, Genuino must perform these tasks to avoid legal problems.

The procedure that Genuino put in place includes customer identification with first name, surname, date of birth, identity card, and photo. Then, it must keep this data secure and report to the authorities any suspicious transactions that exceed certain amounts and/or that can be considered anomalous by law. Much software has been developed that pursues these targets along with data collection and reporting. Genuino acquires the data and fulfills these obligations only for customers who purchase NFTs and carry out transactions to prevent the money loundering.

The second legal issue emerging through Genuino's blockchain is the potential compromise of privacy. In Europe, the General Data Protection Regulation (GDPR) 679/2016 became fully applicable in all European countries in 2018. Since 2018, all European countries are obliged to comply with the GDPR regulation, which also applies to companies with registered offices outside the European Union any time European Union citizens are involved. When Genuino acquires users' personal data, it must comply with this regulation. Genuino possesses sensitive data related to consumers, knows how many NFTs a person has, and knows that each person could have an NFT worth millions of euros. Therefore, Genuino could have information impacting individuals' freedom and rights. Genuino pays particular attention to privacy, not only surrounding the possible legal burdens, but also because it will play a key competitive role in the future. In fact, customers are increasingly careful of how their data is processed by firms, especially in the crypto world.

The measures adopted by Genuino to mitigate the privacy issues must be analyzed on both technical and formal levels. From a technical point of view, Genuino adopts all available technologies such as server partitioning, encryption, and backups. From a formal point of view, it identifies an extremely restricted list of employees and managers who have the credentials to access the data.

The last weakness of Genuino's solution lies in the possible bubble of NFTs. Indeed, while NFTs supporters believe that NFTs are the future of collectibles and the digital economy, a growing number of people believe that NFTs could create a bubble that eventually will burst (Wintermeyer, 2021). NFTs linked to collectibles or arts experience a constant increasing value and are traded at important speculative prices. One example is the NFT of a digital art by Beeple, one of the greatest digital artists, sold in March 2021 for nearly $70 million (Reyburn, 2021). As a result, the vast majority of buyers buy NFTs to speculate on and earn from a future sale (Turley, 2021). It is extremely difficult to assess the evolution of the NFT market, since there are countless factors that influence it, such as the interest of speculative investors, gas prices (in particular on Ethereum), and the possible emergence of dedicated blockchains focused on NFT (Wintermeyer, 2021). Therefore, Genuino must operate within this changing and highly unstable context. The main risk for Genuino's users could be the drastic reduction in their value when increasing the NFTs available. Then, no one would buy NTFs, which will become illiquid. For this reason, Genuino is now working on a solution based on decentralized finance systems to ensure that its NFTs maintain a certain liquidity in any situation.

Table 1. Treats and opportunities of blockchain applied in the collectible industry

Opportunities	Treats
Mitigate the counterfeiting issues	Data entry process into the blockchain could be an opportunity for falsification
Improve the brand value	Patch sensors can be damaged or broken
Quickly and effectively verify and validate the product	Legal issues: anti money laundering (AML) and Know Your Customer (KYC)
Marketplace	Legal issues: Privacy
Opens the sports collectibles market to three types of people: collectors, fans, and crypto enthusiasts	Possible pricing bubble linked to NFTs and possible token liquidity issue

On the positive side, Genuino uses blockchain technology to develop its idea and business strategy. It will launch its product on the market in July 2021 with the kickoff of the Serie A 2021/2022 season in partnership with some Serie A teams including ACF Fiorentina. Genuino is also working on further developments of its product in addition to the certification process. The most important of those is the marketplace for the exchange of NFT tokens and physical t-shirts and for the sale of full digital collectibles. Consistent with Genuino's motto of "Collect Digital, Own Physical", the marketplace includes three main phases with the aim of tradability and fan engagement. The first phase is called "Collect Digital". In this phase, it is possible to collect digital objects that consumers can obtain by participating in drops or by purchasing virtual packages of collectibles. The second phase is called "Own

Physical". In this phase, collectors must complete challenges and missions when collecting digital NFTs. Upon completion of these missions, they will receive the physical object as a reward. These first two phases are aimed primarily at collectors and fans, while the third phase is aimed at all three categories of Genuino customers. The third stage is called "Unleash Defi". This phase, combining the Genuino token with a decentralized finance system, allows the creation of value through farming and staking. Moreover, these dynamics ensure the NFT liquidity in case no one wants to buy the item.

CONCLUSION

This chapter analyzed the case of Genuino, which applied the blockchain technology to the sport collectibles to extract the value behind the industry objects and connect these physical objects with a digital platform through the blockchain. The presence of blockchain in the Genuino's business activates three consumers' categories, specifically collectors, fans, and crypto enthusiasts. Each has different motivations for accessing the blockchain solution, which is fully managed through NFTs linked to physical objects.

The blockchain uses physical oracles, most likely IoT linked to patches to collect information during sports events and to register everything in the blockchain to increase the collectibles' values. This method of recording information offers advantages in terms of mitigating counterfeiting issues; providing proof of the collectibles' originality; provide incorruptible details regarding the event, the player, and the collectibles; and ensure that the items registered on the blockchain platform can be exchanged within the Genuino's platform in a secure and authorized environment.

Although the business model is quite promising, Genuino still has some challenges to face. From the operational side, the patches' conformance and durability can create some issues throughout the entire process. Since several types of agreements exist in traditional partnerships (Preeker and De Giovanni, 2018), Genuino could bring the partnership with DekoGrapics to a higher level, integrating the contractual agreements within the blockchain as well. Furthermore, legal issues must still be understood and governed. Being a completely new business model and a different environment, the exchanges and the rules being part of the entire set of transactions must be rethought and reengineered dynamically. In this sense, Genuino must still solve the issue of money laundering, since the NFTs are not cryptocurrencies to be exchanged in the stock market, but they carry out economic value as they were cryptocurrencies. This kind of situation can create resistances from consumers who are not familiar with such types of applications as well as from regulators and legislation that need integration in comparison to traditional transactions. Finally,

Genuino needs to set a plan of investments and strategic actions to guarantee the stakeholder's privacy at large. In fact, stakeholders should provide and exchange confidential information, which can be subject to cyber warfare and cyber espionage over time. The challenge is to guarantee confidentiality through ad hoc and updated protection systems.

The experience of Genuino's blockchain will facilitate research in future directions. First, the existence of new consumer clusters inspires research on strategic consumers who adjust their purchasing behavior according to the market conditions and opportunities. Within the Genuino framework, the NFT value and market perception can modify the purchasing attitudes of collectors, fans, and crypto enthusiasts. Second, future research should analyze how the formation of the collectibles' price changes according to the teams' performance and, consequently, the convenience of adopting blockchain technologies. Third, Genuino can evaluate the possibility to acquire knowledge regarding making the patches, with the objective of mitigating any operational issues emerging from suppliers. Finally, the current blockchain technology created by Genuino links most likely to physical oracles located all over the playing field. Additional oracles as well as other digital technologies can be generally adopted to increase the object originality and value (De Giovanni and Cariola, 2020). For example, human oracles could be linked to the fans' tickets. Important moments in a match are then collected by the IoT system, and the information is exchanged with the human oracles. The fans receive tokens for any verified information, which is then transferred and recorded to the blockchain when the human oracle consensus is reached. Other types of oracles to be adopted are software oracles as well as inbound and outbound oracles.

REFERENCES

Bleve, D., Costa, M., Ghilardi, R., Lanzillo, E., Picinati di Torcello, A., Ripa, P., & Tagliaferri, B. (2018). Il Mercato Dell'arte e Dei Beni Da Collezione Report 2018. Italia.

Browne, R. (2021). *Crypto collectibles are selling for thousands — and celebrities like Mark Cuban are cashing in*. CNBC.

Crosby, R. (2015). King of Memorabilia sentenced to 20 months in prison for fraud. *Chicago Tribune*, pp. 1–7.

De Giovanni, P. (2019). Digital supply chain through dynamic inventory and smart contracts. *Mathematics*, 7(12), 1235. doi:10.3390/math7121235

De Giovanni, P. (2020). Blockchain and smart contracts in supply chain management: A game theoretic model. *International Journal of Production Economics*, *228*, 107855. doi:10.1016/j.ijpe.2020.107855

De Giovanni, P. (2021). *Dynamic Quality Models and Games in Digital Supply Chains: How Digital Transformation Impacts Supply Chain Quality Management*. Springer Nature.

De Giovanni, P., & Cariola, A. (2020). Process innovation through industry 4.0 technologies, lean practices and green supply chains. *Research in Transportation Economics*, 100869. doi:10.1016/j.retrec.2020.100869

Finzer, D. (2020). *The Non-Fungible Token Bible: Everything You Need to Know about NFTs*. Available at: https://opensea.io/blog/guides/non-fungible-tokens/#:~:text=Non-fungibletokens(NFTs),ownership records for physical assets.

Foxley, W. (2021). *Ethereum Transaction Fees Hit Record Highs as Ether, DeFi Coins Soar*. Yahoo Finance.

Genuino. (2020). *About us*. Available at: https://genuino.world/page.html

Guzman, Z. (2021). *This blockchain startup selling collectible NBA highlights just had $50 million in sales in 30 days. Yahoo!* Finance.

Haig, S. (2021). *Ethereum posts new highs as DeFi gas fees go through the roof.* Cointelegraph.

Hechler-Fayd'herbe, N., & Picinati di Torcello, A. (2020). Collectibles: An Integral Part of Wealth. Academic Press.

Heitner, D. (2016). Playing Ball In The Multi-Billion Dollar Sports Collectible Market. *Forbes*, 2–7.

Ito, R. (2020). The future of collectibles is digital. *Tech Crunch*. Available at: https://techcrunch.com/2020/03/25/the-future-of-collectibles-is-digital/

Kay, G. (2021). *Selling crypto art can come with huge hidden fees, leading some people to lose hundreds of dollars*. Business Insider.

Kiesnoski, K. (2019). *Are collectibles for collecting or investing? Advisors weigh in*. Available at: https://www.cnbc.com/2019/06/21/are-collectibles-for-collecting-or-investing-advisors-weigh-in.html

Pownall, R. (2017). *TEFAF Art Market Report 2017, The European Fine Art Foundation (Tefaf)*. Helvoirt. Available at: www.ideebv.com

Preeker, T., & De Giovanni, P. (2018). Coordinating innovation projects with high tech suppliers through contracts. *Research Policy*, *47*(6), 1161–1172. doi:10.1016/j.respol.2018.04.003

Red, C. (2020). Sports Memorabilia Is Booming, But Industry Has Its Share Of Past Scandal. *Forbes*, 1–6.

Rensing, L. (2021). *The future of sports is embracing digitisation*. SportsPro.

Reyburn, S. (2021). Art's NFT Question: Next Frontier in Trading, or a New Form of Tulip? *The New York Times*, pp. 3–7.

Roberts, J. J. (2020). *UFC and Dapper Labs offer crypto collectibles of MMA fighters*. Fortune.

Schmidt, S. L. (2020). *21st Century Sports: How Technologies Will Change Sports in the Digital Age*. Springer Nature. doi:10.1007/978-3-030-50801-2

Seideman, D. (2018). Tech Entrepreneur Determines First Estimate Of U.S. Sports Memorabilia Market: $5.4 Billion. *Forbes*, 5–10.

Tapscott, D., & Tapscott, A. (2016). *Blockchain Revolution: How the Technology Behind Bitcoin Is Changing Money, Business, and the World*. Penguin Random House LLC.

The Federal Bureau of Investigation. (2005). *Operation Bullpen*. Available at: https://archives.fbi.gov/archives/news/stories/2005/july/operation-bullpen-overview

Thomas, M. (2020). *Sports Memorabilia Market Estimated at $5.4 Billion, but Beware of the Fakes*. Sports Casting.

Turley, C. (2021). *If you haven't followed NFTs, here's why you should start*. Tech Crunch.

United States Postal Inspection Service. (2019). *Fake Sports Memorabilia*. United States Postal Inspection Service.

Weil, D. (2019). The Market for Sports Memorabilia Continues to Score Big. *The Wall Street Journal*, pp. 1–2.

Wintermeyer, L. (2021). Non-Fungible-Token Market Booms As Big Names Join Crypto's Newest Craze. *Forbes*, 1–7.

Zorloni, L. (2018). Cryptokitties, il Tamagotchi con i gattin che si paga in criptovaluta. *Wired*, *11*, 1–7.

Chapter 2
Blockchain Application to the SMEs in the Food Industry:
Trusty Case Study

Daniel Ruzza
Luiss University, Italy

Lorenza Morandini
Luiss Business School, Italy

Alessandro Chelli
Apio S.r.l., Italy

ABSTRACT

The agri-food sector is the highest application of blockchain technology to track and trace components and raw material along the supply chain. Blockchain presents many potential advantages; however, small and medium enterprises often lack the means and knowledge to exploit this technology fully. This chapter presents a case study of blockchain application, namely Trusty, a platform for the notarization of fully traceable information on blockchain in the agri-food sector. Thanks to its limited up-front implementation costs and its modularity, it seems particularly suitable for use by SMEs. The authors' goal is to identify some useful issues for practitioners and inspiration for future research for academics. The most relevant topics that will be placed are (1) needs and expectations of SMEs in the agri-food sector towards the blockchain, (2) difficulties of introducing blockchain into SMEs, (3) the agnostic approach to blockchain, (4) the different value of notarized information for B2B and B2C companies, and (5) limits of some blockchains compared to others.

DOI: 10.4018/978-1-7998-8014-1.ch002

INTRODUCTION

The agri-food sector, valued at around $8 trillion per year, faces significant changes due to the shift in people's consumption habits towards healthier and environmentally friendly products. Consequently, companies are dramatically changing their value proposition and product offering to suit these expectations better. In this context, blockchain technology allows companies not only to create a relationship of trust with consumers but also to create a platform to communicate with them directly (De Giovanni, 2020). Traditionally, the investments and the efforts to drive such a change are significant and often barely affordable by SMEs, which may remain for the most part excluded: they often lack the resources or skills to implement such technologies. This is the niche that Trusty has entered, and this chapter analyzes the Trusty case study. Trusty is a Software as a Service platform blockchain-based. It aims to improve customer engagement, improve information disclosure, build a positive brand reputation, reduce waste, and optimize the supply chain. Trusty, created by Apio, aims to promote the application and deployment of blockchain in the Agri-food industry, starting from the smaller players (e.g. SMEs). Thanks to a Freemium business model (consisting of three packages: Free, Basic, and Premium), Trusty allows SMEs to adopt blockchains with a modular approach, limiting initial investments and overcoming many of the limits of more demanding solutions as IBM Food Trust. With Trusty, the initial implementation costs can be pretty limited at the beginning because investments can be scaled up easily overtime when the blockchain starts bringing tangible results. The onboarding process on Trusty involves typically four steps: analysis, data entry, implementation, and roll-out. In this chapter, to present a practical application of Trusty, the authors deal with the case of Trusty applied to Pastificio Mancini. Pastificio Mancini is an Italian company that produces high-quality pasta, taking care of the value chain from the cultivation of raw materials to the final product. Pastificio Mancini has chosen to use Trusty to communicate to its customers the quality and the value of its production, developed with full respect to the environment. Pastificio Mancini was one of the first companies to apply the Trusty Premium package. With this package, various automations were developed, such as the automatic insertion of data on the blockchain and the automated printing of QR-Codes on pasta packages. Some exciting issues emerge from the case, such as (i) specific needs of SMEs, (ii) the agnostic approach to the blockchain used by Trusty, (iii) different information needs of B2B customers compared to B2C customers. There are also some challenges or weaknesses of this application. The authors identify at least three: (i) limits of some blockchains such as Bitcoin compared to other blockchains, (ii) difficulties in the introduction of blockchain in SMEs, (iii) particularities of the Pastificio Mancini case that make it an "easy" case. Through the presentation of this case, the authors intend to present a successful case of blockchain application to an often-neglected category of companies that is useful both for practitioners and for giving interesting research ideas to academics.

INDUSTRY, SECTORAL DATA, PROBLEMS, AND OPPORTUNITIES

Agri-food is one of the most important sectors from an economic, social, and environmental perspective. The food industry is worth about $8 trillion a year and accounts for 10% of total consumer spending by employing 40% of the world's workforce (Esther Rodriguez, 2018). It is an industry that presents numerous challenges and opportunities throughout the value chain (Goedde et al., 2015). Among the most relevant trends, we can identify the growth of the world population that will lead the caloric needs to grow by 70% by 2050 (Eliaz and Jagt, 2020a), food waste that amounts to 1.6 trillion tons per year (Hegnsholt et al., 2018), climate change and environmental sustainability (Riedmatten et al., 2013), the polarization of the sector towards larger or smaller organizations (Goedde et al., 2015). To face these challenges, it becomes essential for the companies to adapt the entire value chain. The value chain in the agri-food sector includes the network of parties involved in the production, processing, and sale of food from the farm to the consumer's table (Riedmatten et al., 2013). It includes producers, processors, distributors, final consumers, and governments (Santhanam et al., 2018). Each actor is responsible for its part of the value chain (De Giovanni, 2021). However, given the high level of interdependence between the parties, only through the collaboration of all the stakeholders in the chain is it possible to face the challenges that characterize it (Riedmatten et al., 2013).

Consumer's attention to these issues is increasing, and they are changing their consumption habits to favour the approach they believe the most. This phenomenon is because of the growing level of education, urbanization, health consciousness, and the availability of new technologies to consumers (Pinder et al., 2017). Among the main concerns for consumers, on the one hand, we find the attention to health, food quality, and food safety (Figure 1) (Rogers and Pieters, 2020), on the other hand, the desire for responsible and sustainable food consumption (Dongoski and Ramsey, 2020). Starting from the first point, today, more than ever, consumers are food and health-conscious and want to know how and where their food is grown (Dongoski and Ramsey, 2020). As a result, the demand for healthy, organic, and GMO-free food is constantly increasing (Eliaz and Jagt, 2020b). As a result, the global-health-and-wellness beverage and packaged food market represents a growth rate of over 3% per year and expects to reach $851 billion by 2022 (Santhanam et al., 2018). Shifting the focus to environmental sustainability, an Accenture survey shows that more than 55% of consumers are willing to pay more for environmentally friendly products (Pinder et al., 2017). While if we consider millennials alone, 73% are willing to spend more on sustainable products (Eliaz and Jagt, 2020b).

Furthermore, products marked as sustainable grow 5.6 times faster than products that are not (Eliaz and Jagt, 2020a). Therefore, healthy and environmentally sustainable food is increasingly seen as a premium product. As a result, companies need to demonstrate to their customers that their products meet specific standards. This has caused the growth of special tools and labels to communicate the product's characteristics to the consumer (Santhanam et al., 2018). The special labels that are growing the most are "Organic" and "non-GMO" (Deines and Linhardt, 2020).

Figure 1. Consumer main concerns
Source: Rogers and Pieters, 2020

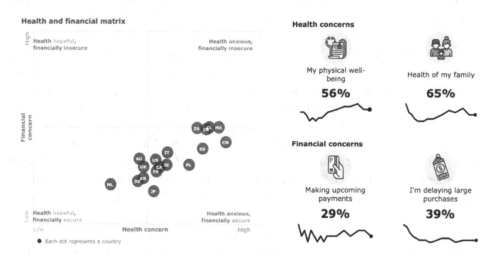

The new habits of consumers and their willingness to pay more for products with the characteristics just seen have led to an increase in fraud involving counterfeit food products (De Giovanni, 2019). The 2019 European Union report shows how the number of European Union intervention requests for fraud involving food has doubled from 2016 to 2019 (Publication office of the European Union, 2020). In particular, 47% of the requests concern cases of mislabeling, 20% Replacement / Dilution / Addition / Removal in product, 16% Unapproved treatment and / or process, 15% Absent / Falsified / manipulated documentation (Figure 2) (Publication office of the European Union, 2020). Therefore, consumers are often not getting what they are paying for (Kruh, 2019). Among the most counterfeit products there are fats and oils, fish and related products, meat and related products (Figure 3) (Publication office of the European Union, 2020). In addition to the economic damage to the sector, estimated by KPMG at more than $ 100 Billion (Kruh, 2019), the danger to consumers' health is concrete. On average, over 300 food recalls are reported in the U.S. each year, which translates into over 75 million foodborne illnesses, 325,000 hospitalizations, and 5,000 deaths (Riedmatten et al., 2013). If we look at the origin of counterfeit products, Spain and Italy are among the first in terms of the number of cases (Publication office of the European Union, 2020). Therefore, traceability and transparency become fundamental for companies to convey to the consumer the efforts made to face these challenges and to meet their needs (Eliaz and Jagt, 2020b). It also becomes crucial for the consumer to understand which value chain companies have aligned with their new habits and demands (Pinder et al., 2017). Technology is a fundamental tool to limit or solve these problems.

Figure 2. Most common frauds
Source: Publication office of the European Union, 2020

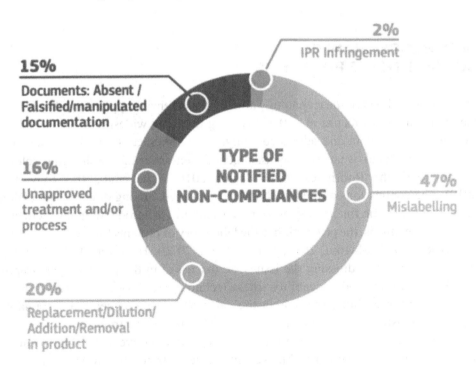

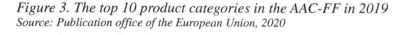

Figure 3. The top 10 product categories in the AAC-FF in 2019
Source: Publication office of the European Union, 2020

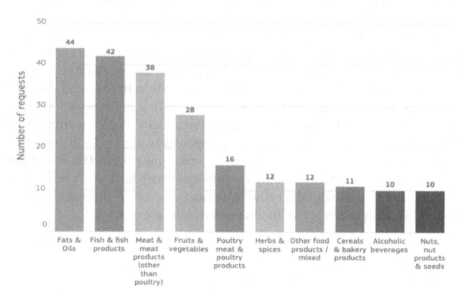

HOW BLOCKCHAIN COULD HELP SOLVING THESE PROBLEMS

In the agri-food sector, the technology already has extensive application throughout the value chain (Walker et al., 2020). Among the most widespread technologies, we can find: big-data and advanced analytics, robotics, aerial imagery, sensors, sophisticated local weather forecasts, genetic engineering, biohacking, cloud technology (Esther Rodriguez, 2018; Magnin, 2016; Pinder et al., 2017; Sylvester, 2019). The applications of these technologies have led, among others: to precision agriculture, specific financial systems for agriculture, the production of genetically modified organisms, the production in the laboratory of proteins for food use (Esther Rodriguez, 2018; Magnin, 2016; Walker et al., 2020). However, the technology most interested in addressing the issues we discussed in the previous paragraphs is technologies for food traceability. These technologies make it possible to create visibility and traceability throughout the value chain, guaranteeing a sustainable supply, increasing income for farmers, a reduction in food fraud, a reduction in waste (Bakker et al., 2020). The most promising and effective technology for food traceability is blockchain. The blockchain increases transparency by creating an immutable record of the life of products from the farm to the consumer (Sylvester, 2019). There are different approaches in applying the blockchain depending on the type of blockchain chosen, the tracking technology, the method of entering data into the blockchain, the way of managing and storing data, the practice of communicating data to consumers (Köhler and Pizzol, 2020). If we look at the type of blockchain used, the primary choice is between public, private, or hybrid blockchains. Some examples of the use of public blockchains in the industry are Provenance, OpenSC. TE-Food uses a hybrid approach, while FairChain and IBM Food Trust use private blockchain (Köhler and Pizzol, 2020).

To track the products along the value chain, different technologies are applied to support the blockchain, such as RFID tags, QR codes, NFC tags (Ge et al., 2017). For example, BeefLedger has combined different technologies in addition to blockchains such as Internet of Things (IoT), analytics, smart contracts, and digital tokens to trace the origin, simplifying payments and limiting the risk of fraud in the quality and sustainability of the livestock farming in Australia (Leong et al., 2018). The insertion of data in the blockchain represents one of the most critical steps of the tracing process since it is the easiest to tamper. Therefore, different strategies are applied in this phase, such as GPS sensors, IoT sensors, or so-called oracles (Sylvester, 2019). Oracles are trusted intermediaries that connect the real world to the blockchain to acquire information (Sylvester, 2019). Once collected, the data must be managed and stored.

In some cases, there is the insertion of data directly on the blockchain, in others, they use external databases, and they record on the blockchain only the hash (Leong et al., 2018). Finally, the data can be communicated to consumers in different ways. In most cases, a QR code or an NFC sensor is used (Köhler and Pizzol, 2020). In the next paragraph, we will see the approach used by Apio and its solution for the application of blockchain to the food supply chain called Trusty. Then, we will see what strategies are adopted and the reasons that led to these choices.

APIO HISTORY AND MILESTONE

Apio is a Venture Builder, a company dedicated to systematically producing new Software as a Service Platform and scale it through Industrial Partnerships. Apio was founded in 2014 by four young professionals from the Marche Polytechnic University, and it is composed of IT engineers, software developers, and business developers. It helps large companies create new products and services through Digital Transformation. The core business of Apio is connectivity, transmission, and data analysis technologies. Apio stands out to mix specific skills such as cloud computing, web development, system integration, embedded development, and hardware design. Apio starting in 2017, develops Blockchain solutions for large corporates, mainly in the energy sector. In 2017 Apio and Acea, Indra, Cisco, and

Enea delivered the first Italian project in the energy market with Blockchain and Internet of Things technologies. They develop an innovative solution for energy data timestamping. Apio, Acea, and Indra patented the project's workflow, and today, Apio and Acea are developing the approach within a European Project. At the end of 2018, thanks to the know-how acquired in this Blockchain project, Apio became the first Trusted Partner of IBM Food Trust worldwide.

Apio understands how to integrate IBM's solution with Track & Trace Software. The expertise required to integrate Track & Trace Softwares with IBM Food Trust includes developing microservices that send GS1 EPCIS Events to the IBM Blockchain. Electronic Product Code Information Services (EPICS) is a world standard developed by GS1 that allows creating and sharing data on visibility events within the same company and between different companies. Thanks to EPCIS, it is possible to identify origin/production location based on the Global Location Number (GLN). The codes can trace the plant or farm where production occurs, identify the products, the packaging, and pallets through the Global Trade Item Number (GTIN). In August 2020, Var Group, one of the leading Italian System Integrators, made a capital increase in Apio to facilitate the scale-up of innovative solutions through access to financial capital and a multi-certified companies' ecosystem. Var Group is a strategic partner for Apio because it is part of the SeSa Group, a reference operator in Italy in technological and digital innovation, supporting the partners and client companies in their evolution path.

TRUSTY: WHAT IS IT AND HOW IT WORKS

Given the importance of the blockchain-related business for Apio and the specific skills required for its development, Apio has developed a business line dedicated to Trusty. Trusty is a Software as a Service platform to improve customer engagement, positively impact brand equity, reduce waste, and optimize the supply chain. One of the peculiarities of Trusty is that it was explicitly developed to be easily implemented by small and medium enterprises SME, a category until initially mostly excluded from the adoption of the blockchain. Trusty can be used by any player alongside the supply chain to authenticate information such as purchase order, dispatch advice, receiving advice quantities, and products related to it. In particular, the platform helps the food producers improve customer's experience through a full disclosure about the provenance and ingredients of products, journeying through the entire supply chain with a simple scan of a QR code. Trusty uses Blockchain technology to verify and secure all the information about a product. The traceability events shared with the customers are retrieved from IBM Food Trust or other Blockchain platforms following an agnostic approach to blockchain. Unlike most other traceability platforms, Trusty enables food producers to upload descriptions, pictures, and videos of company facilities and products. The information is shared with the final consumer thanks to a QR-Code that can be printed in the product's packaging or other places to which it is easy for the consumer to have access. The consumer only has to scan the QR code with his smartphone, and he will have access to the web page with all the information of that specific product. He can look at the company description and information, the product description and features such as its allergens, the product and company certifications, the traceability events on the blockchain. The level of detail of the information available depends on which package of services the manufacturing company has decided to use.

Trusty is based on a Freemium business model. The customer can choose between three different packages for functionality and costs: free, basic, and premium (Table 1). The free version provides basic features, and it is the best option for SMEs that want to approach blockchain technology. With the free version, it is possible to generate unlimited information on lots and QR-Codes, notarize information on the Bitcoin blockchain, and have basic statistics on user interactions and QR-Codes. For example, how often has someone scanned the QR Code, from which place it was scanned, and the average age of those who search or buy products. Of course, the free version also has limitations. In the free version, the company should put the information on the blockchain manually, and it has limited access to statistics about customer activities within the web page that contains the information on their products. In addition to free services, the Basic package allows you to enter data on Trusty in an automated way and export the data recorded on the blockchain on platforms external to Trusty, such as e-commerce or a company website. The price for the Basic package is €250 per month. The €250 includes 1000 lots to be registered. If a company needs to register more lots, it can purchase them separately. The integration between the company's IT systems and Trusty for automated data entry can be done independently by the customer's staff or by Apio for an additional price, generally between €3000 and €10000. The Premium package includes all the customized projects requested by companies with specific needs and carried out by Apio through the development team. In the Premium package, it is possible to include almost any type of customization such as the complete customization of web pages, the integration of Trusty with IoT or Industry 4.0 sensors for the automated recording of data on the blockchain, the use of other blockchains different from Bitcoin such as Ethereum o IBM Food Trust.

Moreover, Trusty can collect relevant information on customers based on their interaction with the product web page. Customer companies can use this data to improve customer engagement and create new marketing campaigns based on a transparent and secure supply chain. The Premium service cost depends on the customer's requests and starts from € 3000 up to several thousand euros.

Table 1. Trusty's packages costs and features

	Free	Basic	Premium
Features	• Generate unlimited information on lots and QR-Codes; • Notarize information on the Bitcoin blockchain; • Basic statistics on interactions between users and QR-Codes.	All the Free package features plus: • Automation on the data entry process on Trusty; • Exporting the data recorded on the blockchain on platforms external to Trusty, such as e-commerce or a company website	All the features of the other packages plus: • Custom template creation; • Integration with Internet of Things and/or Industry 4.0 systems; • Use of company domains; • Integration with other Blockchains;
Costs	Free	€250/month €3000-10000 for API integration	€3000-40000+

There are four onboarding phases for accessing Trusty: analysis, data entry, implementation, and roll-out. The level of detail and the effort of Apio and the client required for each phase depend on the package that will be chosen. In this section, we will look at the case of a complete Premium package. A series of aspects are investigated in the analysis phase. First of all, it is necessary to understand the company's expectations regarding the project it wants to develop with Trusty. Typically there are three main objectives: increasing transparency towards consumers, increasing the operational efficiency of the supply chain, accessing new sales channels. Then, they need to define the products for which you want to start the traceability project. They could be all the products or just some to make a first test of the solution. For each product, the phases we intend to trace on the blockchain and which supporting data we need are identified. Based on this, it is then necessary to identify where the products are grown or processed and any third-party suppliers. The last steps of the analysis phase foresee the definition with the customer of the data entry interfaces on Trusty and the interfaces to visualise the data by the consumer. The analysis phase allows you to produce a project document that evaluates all activities. For each activity, timescales and a budget will be defined for their implementation. In the data entry and implementation phase, the agreed project will be developed, and the client company's staff will be trained in the use of the platform. Finally, in the Roll-out phase, the access credentials will be shared with the company and all the actors identified during the analysis phase.

The timescale required to complete all phases and have Trusty operational vary according to the project's complexity and may range from a minimum of 2 up to a maximum of 6 months. Once Trusty is operational, assistance and maintenance are simple and do not require any particular or complex task. As we have seen in the previous paragraphs, direct costs for the client company depend on the package they choose. In any case, approaching the expenses from the company's point of view and including all opportunity costs, we must also include the expenses related to the person who must be freed from their current jobs. In the initial phase, one or two people are typically trained to use the platform. This starts from the analysis phase, which is done in synergy with 1 or 2 people from the client company. Collaboration at this stage also increases the level of satisfaction once the platform is implemented. This is followed by the training of the company's staff. During the training, the company's employees are trained on the platform, on the public page, on storytelling, certified info, and the technologies used. Indicatively, one day a week for a month is required for the people that the client company decides to dedicate to the project with Trusty. Furthermore, we can see how the Free package is offered for free with a low or zero initial cost. However, it has a high price for a company in terms of employees dedicated almost daily to manually entering data within the platform. On the contrary, the more elaborate packages integrate much automation that decreases the running costs of Trusty. The higher the price paid for the solution, the higher the level of automation, the lower the opportunity cost due to dedicated internal staff required to make Trusty running.

TRUSTY APPLICATION EXAMPLE: PASTIFICIO MANCINI

In this section, we analyze the Pastificio Mancini case, an example of Trusty application to an SME. Pastificio Mancini (https://www.pastamancini.com) is based in the central region of Marche, Italy. It was founded in 2010 by Massimo Mancini, and today it counts 35 employees with an annual turnover of around € 3,5 Million. The primary market for its products is Italy, however, about 30% of the products are exported, mainly to the United States, the United Kingdom, China, and Russia. The pasta produced by Pastificio Mancini has a quality and price above the average. Therefore, customers of Pasta Mancini are mainly chefs and premium consumers. The formers look for excellent quality raw materials to raise the standard of their services. This type of customer is focused on the product, its origin, and characteristics to be told as a unique story of values "from farm to fork". Over the years, Pastificio Mancini has developed a series of best practices to satisfy the quality demands of this high-level clientele. High quality is achieved through in-house management of the entire production chain, from the cultivation of raw materials to the delivery of the product to the final consumer. Pastificio Mancini deals directly with selecting the seed to be planted, the management of the fields in which wheat crops are alternated with other crops to regenerate the soil, the harvesting of the cereal and storage. The whole agricultural process is carried out in compliance with Good Agricultural

Practice (BPA), which contains all the rules applied to have the raw material of the highest quality and healthiness while respecting the environment. Pastificio Mancini then deals with the transformation of the raw material into pasta. This process also follows strict rules for grinding wheat, bronze drawing, pasta drying up to the packaging that must respect the environment. Given all the efforts made to achieve these standards of quality and respect for the environment, Pastificio Mancini needs to have a tool to communicate these efforts to its customers. Indeed, traceability and secure information can play a strategic role to influence and confirm customers' choices. The most suitable tool to reach this goal was identified in the blockchain and the solution developed by Apio.

Apio and Pastificio Mancini work together to create a digital identity for the pasta made by the company. With Trusty, Pasta Mancini is one of the first food companies that open a direct communication channel with its customers. From January 2021, through a QR code printed on the label of the pasta's packaging, the company open up a virtual window in the whole company's supply chain (Figure 4). QR codes connect the costumers with the product's identity, distinguishing it from other brands and information written on the blockchain. By scanning the QR code placed on the bottom of the new packages, the customers have access to a web page where they can know instantly and without intermediaries all the information about that specific pack of pasta. Moreover, the manufacturer can customise the webspace with documents, including descriptions and certificates, photos, videos, creative content, and all the information that the consumer needs to immerse himself in the brand's story. Trusty creates a digital space that breaks down the barriers between producers and consumers, establishing an authentic and transparent relationship of trust.

Figure 4. Pastificio Mancini's packages and the web page

From an operational point of view, the project developed for Pasta Mancini is a Trusty Premium package. Pasta Mancini transforms the raw materials from wheat to pasta, and therefore it wants to share information, photos, and documents about every batch of pasta. In addition, Pastificio Mancini aims to track wheat fields, automate data entry and automate QR codes printing on products through blockchain and the internet of things. To achieve the Pasta Mancini Goals, Apio implemented the following stages: analysis of the company's data model; creation of the company in the platform (and associated users); data entry for facilities; data-entry for products; micro-services for data entry automation; public page customization (Table 2). The first step is the analysis of the company's data model. In this phase, Apio carries out research of the company and all its products. During the product analysis, for each product, the information that Pastificio Mancini wants to share with the consumer is identified through an analysis of the elements of value that the company is interested in communicating. The parts of the supply-chain chosen are the same for all 103 products of Pastificio Mancini and are four: threshing, milling, drawing, and packaging. For each of these four phases, the company's data model is analyzed. The company's data model is the methodology applied by the company to collect the data of these four elements of value. It is interesting to see that for all Pastificio Mancini products, the same four elements of value were identified. Consequently, all products are described in the same way. This has considerably simplified the work required compared to projects where the part of the supply chain are different for each product.

Table 2. The Trusty's onboarding phases applied to Pastificio Mancini

Trusty's onboarding phases	Pastificio Mancini case
Analysis	Analysis of the company's data model
Data entry and implementation	Creation of the company in the platform (and associated users)
	Data-entry for facilities
	Data-entry for products
	Micro-services for data entry automation
	Public page customization
Roll-out	Credential share

The second phase is the creation of the company and associated users in the platform. It is a process that is carried out the first time that a company joins the Trusty platform. Apio creates the client company's account on Trusty and, at the same time, the profiles of the users who can modify the company's information. Once the company is into the platform, the profile of the company, the facilities, and the individual products are created. For the company, Apio declares on Trusty, the company description, the website, the geographical information, and other information that the client company wants to communicate. For the facilities, the name, traceability codes, and location. While for the products, the process is longer. Apio created for all the 103 products sold by Pastificio Mancini, a photo of the product, a background photo, a description of the product, and other additional information such as the cooking times. After creating the single product sheets, Apio creates the four parts of the supply chain for each product.

The next phase is the development of microservices for automated data entry. Until now, none of the information entered on Trusty uses blockchain technology. It was only the construction of a structure to create the company profile on Trusty. From this stage, we begin to develop and build the tools for entering traceability information. Trusty provides several possibilities for inserting traceability information on the blockchain, ranging from manual entry by the company to the automatic transmission of data on the blockchain through IoT sensors. In the case of Pastificio Mancini, an intermediate solution was applied. It provides the automatic insertion of data on the blockchain from the company's information system. Apio created a software automation system that integrates Trusty with the Pastificio Mancini existing Manufacturing Execution System (MES) to make it possible. This Software performs an automatic daily analysis of the information that Pastificio Mancini has in its MES and records the new ones on the blockchain. This procedure takes place every evening and relieves Pastificio Mancini from the burden of manually entering information, thereby also limiting the possibility of error. A further step, carried out in Pastificio Mancini, consists of the printing automation of the QR code in the product packaging by making Trusty communicate with the printing machine through an API. In fact, in this case, the QR codes printed in the packs of pasta are all different and specific to the product inside each pack. To make this possible, it is necessary to create particular QR codes and communicate them to the printer, who must print the correct QR code. This solution increases the informative potential of the Trusty service. The last phase is the customization of the public page. This step consists of customizing the web page that the customers have access through the QR code. It must be in line with the graphic style and Design desired by Pastificio Mancini. Therefore, the corporate colours, the template, and the images are customized to be consistent with the style and communication strategy of Pastificio Mancini.

Another interesting aspect to analyze in the Pastificio Mancini case is the blockchain used to record the information. Trusty follows an agnostic approach. Therefore, with Trusty, it is possible to record information on many blockchains according to the customer's needs and requests. In the case of Pastificio Mancini, the Bitcoin public blockchain was chosen. Even before the invention of blockchain, companies' traceability information was declared, so the fact of communicating traceability information is not new. The novelty lies in using an external platform that guarantees the notarization of the information and its immutability once registered. They chose Bitcoin for mainly two: efficiency reasons due to the Open Timestamp protocol; it is public, reliable, and completely independent.

Starting from the first point, the notarization on Bitcoin takes place with a standard procedure using an open-source protocol called Open Timestamp. Open Timestamp provides a standard format for time stamping on Bitcoin. Time stamping demonstrates in an unchangeable way that certain data existed before a specific date. Open Timestamp is a widely developed and tested protocol with a lot of documentation available, commonly accepted, and reliable. Furthermore, one of the main advantages of this protocol is the limited transaction costs required to record information on the blockchain. Recording information on the blockchain is not free, but transaction costs vary based on various factors. Open Timestamp allows you to take advantage of the network to reduce these costs. The protocol aggregates a packet of information and inserts it into the blockchain every two hours by performing a single transaction. This allows you to divide the registration costs among all the subjects who have entered the information in the package. From a practical point of view, Trusty creates a PDF file with the MES of Pastificio Mancini information that must be entered on the blockchain. The file is then placed in a package with other information that, through Open Timestamp, are recorded on Bitcoin. The Open Timestamp output is an OTS file with all the information of the Merkle Tree.

The second point is that Bitcoin is the first blockchain platform created, so it is very widespread, increasing its solidity. Furthermore, it is a public blockchain. Therefore, it is the ideal choice to protect the consumer of the products registered in it. It is entirely independent of the producers who cannot modify the information once it has been entered on the Bitcoin blockchain. With a solution of this type, once the data has been entered on the blockchain, he would have only two possibilities if a producer wants to "cheat" the consumer. To declare to have lost the PDF and OTS files that the blockchain generates once the data has been recorded or record the information multiple times with multiple PDF files. In the first case, the role played by Trusty limits this possibility because Trusty keeps all the files related to the notarization on blockchain always organized and present. In the second case, the final consumer can always see all the recorded files and the dates on which they were recorded. By comparing these documents, he can understand any changes that would lead to a lack of consumer trust in the manufacturer if the manufacturing company did not adequately justify them.

STRENGTHS AND OPPORTUNITIES

Trusty and the application case at Pastificio Mancini highlight some interesting aspects about the blockchain application that need to be discussed. These aspects are: the needs of the SMEs that intend to use blockchain; the agnostic approach to the blockchain; the differences in strategic requirements between B2B customers and B2C. Trusty is designed mainly for small and medium enterprises, which, due to their size, do not have the economic and technological resources of the large enterprises. In the attempt to promote IBM Food Trust among SMEs, Apio realized that they need blockchain mainly for marketing purposes to communicate the excellence of their brands and products. If, on the one hand, there are companies like Walmart or Maersk that have been using the blockchain developed by IBM to track their supply chains for years, on the other, there are a significant number of SMEs that have different needs and problems. However, IBM Food Trust is one of the largest networks that connects participants across the food supply chain through a Distributed Ledger Technology. IBM Food Trust offers to the company that joins the network benefits such as: supply chain efficiencies, brand trust, food safety, and so on. The IBM Food Trust solution was, therefore, mainly aimed at making the supply chain more efficient. This is a long and complex process that requires the collaboration of all actors in the supply chain and a considerable amount of time to get up and running effectively (Roettgers, 2020). Otherwise, those kinds of benefits are crucial for large organizations with an international and anonymous supply chain composed of thousands of suppliers; on the other side, SMEs are most interested in creating a Direct-to-Consumer Channel to improve the Brand Positioning and Brand Awareness. Moreover, the onboarding process on IBM Food Trust requires several identifiers (GS1 Identifiers, GLN Identifiers, and GTIN Identifiers) that usually are not quickly available in a small and medium enterprise. The most crucial feature of IBM Food Trust is linked to Track and Trace. IBM Food Trust gives every supplier the possibility to access information about food products. The main challenge of this kind of approach is that there is no guarantee that workers at all the businesses in a company's supply chain will insert data, and there are not incentives for suppliers to log everything in blockchain correctly (Roettgers, 2020). While large companies like Walmart can force their suppliers and companies to take part in blockchain and traceability systems taking advantage of their role as the group leader or leading distributors, this is not possible for SMEs. Apio has decided to develop Trusty to place itself in this market niche left uncovered by the best-known solutions to meet the needs of SMEs. For this reason, Trusty provides a series of packages that can be modulated according to the needs and financial resources of the company. From this perspective, the plan offered for free by Trusty plays a fundamental role in favouring the mass adoption of blockchain technology. Moreover, thanks to the agnostic approach, Trusty can modulate the costs, and the level of service offered, offering the choice between blockchains with less economic and management costs or others more expensive but also with a better service.

Adopting a blockchain agnostic approach means that the platform, in this case, Trusty, can support many blockchains without preferring any in particular (Nasdaq, 2017). Trusty's current implementation can notaries traceability events with: Bitcoin, IBM Food Trust, and Ethereum (included Ethereum side chains such as XDai and VSC). Using one blockchain rather than another in a project depends mainly on the needs of the client company and its economic resources. We have already seen that Bitcoin, thanks to the Open Timestamp protocol, allows containing costs and, at the same time to record information in one of the most solid and reliable blockchains. However, it does not allow you to register the identity. Identity consists of the association of data on the blockchain with the public key of the actor who reported it. In Bitcoin, with Open Timestamp, it is not the client company that records the information directly but the Open Timestamp protocol to which Trusty provides the data. This could represent limitations for some companies wishing to register also the identity. Thanks to the agnostic approach for companies with this need, Trusty can provide its Ethereum-based solution where it is possible to write identity. Similarly, for larger companies that need to improve long and complex supply chains, Trusty can suggest IBM Food Trust. While on the one hand, the agnostic approach represents a solution to best satisfy the client company's requests; on the other, it represents insurance for the future of Trusty itself. Using an agnostic approach is consistent with the development phase of the technology because a standard has not yet been identified, and consequently, there is no certainty about the future (Abuhantash et al., 2019). If this standard is determined, Trusty must be ready to include that blockchain and that technology in its system. Otherwise, it risks being out of the market. From this perspective, adopting an agnostic approach is an insurance towards a context characterized by sudden changes and the future not yet defined (Abuhantash et al., 2019).

Another interesting issue that the Pastificio Mancini case raises concerns the different strategic reasons that determine the use of Trusty by companies that have the consumer as their final customer (B2C), and companies that sell their products to other companies (B2B). The communication strategy, relevant information, and strategic objectives of these two categories are different. Companies that sell their products directly to the final consumer in a B2C perspective choose Trusty to pursue "customer relationship management" strategies mainly. This strategy consists of increasing the business and customers by ensuring their satisfaction with the company and its products (Strauss and Frost, 2014). A common practice in this strategy is to create contact points with the client and give them all the necessary information at every possible opportunity (Strauss and Frost, 2014). Thanks to Trusty, a new point of contact is created between the customer and the manufacturing company, and the information is communicated more securely and directly. On the contrary, in the case of Pastificio Mancini, most of its customers are B2B customers. They are part of the HORECA sector, including hotels, restaurants, trattorias, pizzerias, bars, catering, etc. Pastificio Mancini sells a small amount of its products to the final consumer. In this case, Trusty helps Pastificio Mancini to pursue an ingredient branding strategy (Gassmann et al., 2013). This strategy is accomplished when a product is purchased as a part or ingredient of another product. The ingredient product is advertised as a significant component of the final product that elevates its characteristics and performance (Gassmann et al., 2013). The product ingredient increases the perceived quality of the final product within which it is inserted in the eyes of the final consumer. Perhaps the most famous example of this strategy is Intel Inside. The Intel Inside label placed on Intel-based PCs is a strategy to communicate to the consumer the quality of a PC's processor, ensuring him of the performance and durability characteristics of the computer as a whole. Similarly, in our example, Mancini Pasta becomes a fundamental ingredient of the Chef's dishes capable of raising its quality and ensuring its origin. Therefore, on the one hand, the Chef can ask the end customer for a premium price due to the high quality of the raw material used in his dishes, on the other hand, Pastificio Mancini makes his products known. Furthermore, for the Chef, traceability through Trusty becomes a form of guarantee that allows him to demonstrate the origin of the products he uses to his customers. In the case of problems related to flawed or poor-quality products, the Chef can easily trace the packages to be eliminated, always guaranteeing the customer a high-level service.

THREATS AND WEAKNESSES

The application of Trusty to the Pastificio Mancini case has clear advantages, however, some weaknesses need to be discussed. In this section, we identify three weaknesses: the limits of Bitcoin and Open Timestamp; the difficulties in introducing blockchain in SMEs; the fully integrated value chain compared with a more disaggregated value chain. The use of Bitcoin and Open Timestamps has some advantages in terms of ease of use and limited costs. However, it also has disadvantages. The most obvious of these is the possibility of proving the Timestamp but not the actor's identity who records the information. Identity consists of the association of data with the public key of the actor who registered it. Through identity, it is possible to demonstrate that specific information has been written by a specific public key attributable to a company. Using Open Timestamp, the data is aggregated into packets and recorded on Bitcoin by the Open Timestamp protocol. With this solution on the blockchain, it can be seen that the Open Timestamp protocol enters the information and that Trusty generated the PDF with the data. Therefore, it does not appear on the blockchain that the information was written on the blockchain by Pastificio Mancini. This is a solvable problem. Thanks to the agnostic approach adopted by Trusty, it is possible to use other blockchains that allow identity registration, such as Ethereum. However, the costs of solutions that enable identity registration are significantly higher due to the transaction costs required to register every transaction on the blockchain. Furthermore, to date, there is not commonly recognized open-source protocol such as Open Timestamp on Ethereum. Consequently, they would have to develop a protocol internally with the associated costs. For the needs of Pastificio Mancini, it was not necessary to resort to solutions of this type. Another aspect of weakness linked to the Pastificio Mancini case is in the data entry phase. In the case of Pastificio Mancini, the data are taken by Trusty from the company's MES. This could leave some space for possible scams. Trusty or Pastificio Mancini itself could tamper with the data before it is recorded on the blockchain. The solution presented in this case involves a certain measure of consumer trust in Trusty and Pastificio Mancini. This does not precisely meet the trustless relationship expectations that the blockchain promises to achieve. Again, in this case, the problem is easily solvable because Trusty allows more advanced solutions. Data are recorded directly on the blockchain by IoT sensors placed on the plants, limiting as much as possible any form of intermediation and eliminating any possibility of a cheat. What we have seen with Pastificio Mancini is a simple approach that allows containing costs. This is the approach chosen by most of the SMEs who turn to Trusty to approach blockchain technology, intending to adopt more advanced solutions if they see a tangible advantage. Therefore, if, on the one hand, the approach used in the Pastificio Mancini case has limitations, on the other hand, it is essential to bring SMEs closer to blockchain technology. SMEs often do not know blockchain and are not willing to invest tens of thousands of euros without first understanding the advantages. The Trusty approach allows SMEs to gradually increase blockchain adoption in terms of the solution complexity and required investment. Without a flexible and modular approach, Trusty's customers would be forced to make a considerable investment upfront to adopt blockchain. Most SMEs may be deterred by this investment and may choose not to use blockchain. The Trusty team evaluated the gradual approach to the blockchain as the best solution in this phase of development of the technology.

Although the modularity of the service offered by Trusty facilitates home boarding, this is not enough to solve the adoption of this technology by SMEs. One of the most relevant challenges faced by Trusty is due to the characteristics of the Italian SMEs, which make the onboarding process complex and expensive in most cases. While large companies have developed information systems and relevant internal skills to which it is possible to connect Trusty, in most of the SMEs, this has not happened. So, right now, the biggest weakness of the solution is related to scalability. The level of digitization of Italian SMEs is so low that the onboarding activity must often be accompanied by professional resources that identify virtuous paths for companies. Trusty must engage not only in the traceability service through blockchain but very often it must provide for a minimum digitization path to make it possible to use Trusty itself. This limit slows down the adoption process and does not fit well with Software as a service business model based on rapid customer acquisition and conversion. The solution's novelty, the lack of knowledge of the blockchain of agri-food companies, and the legislative vacuum on the subject also slow down investments in this area. Finally, we cannot refrain from recognizing that the case of Pastificio Mancini is particular and relatively simple. Pastificio Mancini has a vertically integrated supply chain and directly controls every step of the supply chain. Therefore, it is easy for Pastificio Mancini to carry out traceability of its supply chain since it is not necessary for the blockchain to be adopted by other actors in the supply chain to be effective. On the contrary, in the case of very disintegrated supply chains with a plurality of actors, perhaps in international contexts, the adoption is more complex. If, on the one hand, the benefits of blockchain in situations of this type are greater, on the other hand, all the actors in the supply chain must adopt the blockchain. If one actor in the supply chain decides not to use it, the chain falls, and the solution becomes useless for all the other actors.

CONCLUSION

In this chapter, the authors analyzed the Trusty case study. A case of application of the blockchain to SMEs in the Agrifood sector is undergoing substantial changes due to more aware and informed consumers. Consumers are increasingly paying attention to healthy, high-quality and environmentally friendly products. While it is growing the need for businesses to have a simple and affordable tool to effectively and securely make visible their efforts in a mutable and sustainable market environment, Trusty represents a possible solution, that leverages blockchain, to give SMEs these tools. The analysis of Trusty and the case of application of Trusty to Pastificio Mancini allowed us to discuss some interesting issues that we have summarized in Table 3. The first topic is the blockchain application to SMEs. A considerable part of SMEs shows different needs compared to large companies (that use blockchain mainly to lower cost and wastes along their supply chain). SMEs seem more interested in communicating the quality of their products directly and reliably to their customers. This represents an opportunity for Trusty and a strength of the solution developed by Trusty. At the same time, the application of Blockchain to SMEs encounters considerable challenges given the limited budget of these companies and their often low level of digitalization. The second overarching issue concerns the type of blockchain used for notarization and traceability solutions such as Trusty. The agnostic approach used by Trusty is an excellent solution does not commit to a specific blockchain from the beginning, neither Trusty nor Pastificio Mancini. This represents an opportunity and an advantage both in strategic and economic terms. In fact, if in the future a standard blockchain for operations of this type will emerge, Trusty would be ready to adopt it. From a cost point of view, some blockchains allow information to be notarized at lower costs, therefore they are ideal for certain SMEs that do not have particularly complex needs. However, Blockchains with limited expenses such as Open Timestamp also have significant limitations, such as the inability to register the identity. Finally, some specific issues emerged in the case of Trusty's application to Pastificio Mancini. Pastificio Mancini sells almost all of its products in the HORECA channel. Consequently, these products are purchased by highly competent people who include them as an ingredient in their dishes. As a result, their information needs are different from customers who buy pasta at the supermarket. Furthermore, the Pastificio Mancini case has a fully integrated value chain, from raw materials to the finished product, in these conditions, applying the blockchain for traceability reasons are easier than in companies that have a very disaggregated value chain.

Table 3. Summary of the main topics of the chapter

MAIN TOPICS	STRENGTHS AND OPPORTUNITIES	TREATS AND WEAKNESSES
Blockchain and SMEs	The needs of the SMEs that intend to use blockchain.	The difficulties in the introduction of blockchain to SMEs.
The type of blockchain	The agnostic approach to the blockchain.	The limits of Bitcoin and Open Timestamp.
The peculiarities of the case considered	The differences in strategic needs between B2B clientele compared to B2C.	Fully integrated value chain and more disaggregated value chain.

REFERENCES

Abuhantash, A., Grabski, J., Kobeissi, H., White, M., & Sykes, O. (2019). Establishing Blockchain Policy. Academic Press.

Bakker, P., Holdorf, D. B., & Cairns, A. (2020). *CEO Guide to Food System Transformation*. Available at: https://www.wbcsd.org/Programs/Food-and-Nature/Food-Land-Use/Resources/CEO-Guide-to-Food-System-Transformation

De Giovanni, P. (2019). Digital supply chain through dynamic inventory and smart contracts. *Mathematics*, *7*(12), 1235. doi:10.3390/math7121235

De Giovanni, P. (2020). Blockchain and smart contracts in supply chain management: A game theoretic model. *International Journal of Production Economics*, *228*, 107855. doi:10.1016/j.ijpe.2020.107855

De Giovanni, P. (2021). *Dynamic Quality Models and Games in Digital Supply Chains: How Digital Transformation Impacts Supply Chain Quality Management*. Springer Nature.

de Riedmatten, A., Barr, P., Ringquist, J., & Eng, V. (2013). *The Food Value Chain A Challenge for the next Century Contents*. Deloitte.

Deines, G., & Linhardt, K. (2020). *Nourishing the Food Industry with Profitable Growth*. Available at: https://www.accenture.com/us-en/_acnmedia/pdf-70/accenture-future-of-food-new-realities-for-the-industry.pdf

Dongoski, R., & Ramsey, N. (2020). *Vertical Integration in Food and Agribusiness*. Available at: https://www.google.com/url?sa=t&rct=j&q=&esrc=s&source=web&cd=&ved=2ahUKEwjJjorF66rwAhXdwQIHHUbXAbsQFjAKegQIIhAD&url=https%3A%2F%2Fassets.ey.com%2Fcontent%2Fdam%2Fey-sites%2Fey-com%2Fen_us%2Ftopics%2Fconsumer-products%2Fey-vertical-integration-in-food-and-agribusiness.pdf%3Fdownload&usg=AOvVaw3hMrD8qsc3B94tWYYjm3Vc

Eliaz, S., & Jagt, R. (2020a). *The global food system transformation The time to change is now*. Deloitte. Available at: https://www2.deloitte.com/global/en/pages/consumer-business/articles/global-food-system-transformation.html

Eliaz, S., & Jagt, R. (2020b). *Future of Food : Responsible Production Connecting yield increase and sustainability*. Deloitte. Available at: https://www2.deloitte.com/global/en/pages/consumer-business/articles/gx-future-of-food-responsible-production.html

Gassmann, O., Frankenberger, K., & Csik, M. (2013). *The Business Model Navigator: 55 Models That Will Revolutionise Your Business*. FT Publishing.

Ge, L., Brewster, C., Spek, J., Smeenk, A., & Top, J. (2017). *Blockchain for Agriculture and Food*. Wageningen Economic Research. Available at: www.wur.eu/economic-research

Goedde, L., Horil, M., & Sanghvi, S. (2015). *Pursuing the Global Opportunity in Food and Agribusiness*. Available at: https://www.mckinsey.com/insights/Food_Agriculture/Pursuing_the_global_opportunity_in_food_and_agribusiness?cid=other-eml-alt-mip-mck-oth-1507

Hegnsholt, B. E., Unnikrishnan, S., Pollmann-larsen, M., Askelsdottir, B., & Gerard, M. (2018). *Tackling the 1.6-billion-ton food loss and waste crisis*. BCG Henderson Institute. Available at: https://www.bcg.com/it-it/publications/2018/tackling-1.6-billion-ton-food-loss-and-waste-crisis

Köhler, S., & Pizzol, M. (2020). Technology assessment of blockchain-based technologies in the food supply chain. *Journal of Cleaner Production*, *269*, 122193. Advance online publication. doi:10.1016/j.jclepro.2020.122193

Kruh W. (2019). *Consumer Currents*. Available at: https://www.google.com/url?sa=t&rct=j&q=&esrc=s&source=web&cd=&cad=rja&uact=8&ved=2ahUKEwjc2b7q66rwAhWD7KQKHZhwCrcQFjABegQIAhAD&url=https%3A%2F%2Fassets.kpmg%2Fcontent%2Fdam%2Fkpmg%2Fxx%2Fpdf%2F2019%2F05%2Fconsumer-currents-issues-driving-consumer-organizations.pdf&usg=AOvVaw0MQAkem-_mCZ1OQVwkSKMA

Leong, C., Viskin, T., & Stewart, R. (2018). *Tracing the Supply Chain: How Blockchain Can Enable Traceability in the Food Industry*. Available at: https://www.bcg.com/publications/2020/benefits-of-automation-in-the-agriculture-industry

Magnin, C. (2016). *How Big Data Will Revolutionize the Global Food Chain*. Available at: https://www.mckinsey.com/business-functions/mckinsey-digital/our-insights/how-big-data-will-revolutionize-the-global-food-chain

Nasdaq. (2017). *Cryptocurrency Agnosticism and a Vision for Privacy*. Nasdaq. Available at: https://www.nasdaq.com/articles/cryptocurrency-agnosticism-and-vision-privacy-2017-09-08

Pinder, S., Walsh, P., Orndorff, M., Milton, E., & Trescott, J. (2017). *The Future of Food: New Realities for the Industry*. Accenture.

Publication office of the European Union. (2020). *Annual Report 2019 - The EU Food Fraud Network and the Administrative Assistance & Cooperation System*. . doi:10.2875/326318

Rodriguez. (2018). Agrifood: The $8 Trillion Industry That's Worth Your Salt. *Tech Crunch*. Available at: https://techcrunch.com/2018/11/01/agrifood-the-8trn-industry-thats-worth-your-salt/

Roettgers, J. (2020). Who is buying into IBM's blockchain dreams? *Protocol*. Available at: https://www.protocol.com/ibm-blockchain-supply-produce-coffee

Rogers, S., & Pieters, L. (2020). Small positive signs in the consumers' dual-front crisis The road to recovery may be opening, but. *Deloitte Insight*. Available at: https://www2.deloitte.com/us/en/insights/industry/retail-distribution/consumer-behavior-trends-state-of-the-consumer-tracker/covid-19-recovery.html

Santhanam, N., Varanasi, S., Surana, K., Jacobson, Z., & Zegeye, A. (2018). *Food Processing & Handling Ripe for Disruption?* McKinsey & Company.

Strauss, J., & Frost, R. (2014). *E-Marketing* (S. Wall, Ed.). Pearson.

Sylvester, G. (2019). E-Agriculture in Action: Blockchain for Agriculture Opportunities and Challanges. Academic Press.

Walker, D., Van Wyck, J., Nannes, H., & Pérez, D. (2020). *The Future of Food Is Automated*. Boston Consulting Group. Available at: https://www.bcg.com/publications/2020/benefits-of-automation-in-the-agriculture-industry

Chapter 3
Blockchain Adoption in the Winery Industry:
The Case of Cantina Placido–Volpone

Matteo Pio Prencipe
Luiss University, Italy

Behzad Maleki Vishkaei
Luiss University, Italy

Pietro De Giovanni
iD https://orcid.org/0000-0002-1247-4807
Luiss University, Italy

ABSTRACT

This chapter identifies the existing challenges in the winery industry and proposes to analyze their resolution by the adoption of blockchain technology. Blockchain allows the traceability of the whole process linked to wine production, from the cultivation of the grapes to the distribution of the bottles. Blockchain allows winery firms to unlock the potential value existing in some processes, especially when they create a competitive advantage. The chapter investigates these concepts within the case of Cantina Volpone, which has been the first case in Italy to adopt blockchain technology in the winery industry. This chapter studies the implementation path for blockchain technology in the winery industry and highlights the operational and financial challenges emerging from its adoption.

DOI: 10.4018/978-1-7998-8014-1.ch003

INTRODUCTION

The agri-food sector in Italy can no longer ignore new innovations such as blockchain-based traceability. In Italy, in the wine sector, companies are able to transmit the main values of their product (territory, method, and professionalism) to the end customers with great difficulty. These values are the main guarantors of the quality and authenticity of the products. There are companies abroad that cannot guarantee the quality of Italian products and tend to deceive consumers with the "Italian sounding". The annual losses due to the phenomenon of counterfeiting in the wine sector are estimated at about 2 billion euros per year, a loss that can adversely affect the economy of this country.

Consumers are increasingly careful about the origin of the products, raw materials used, and the quality of the methods used to cultivate the food destined to reach their tables. Based on a survey, 71% of consumers are willing to pay a higher price if the information related to quality, transparency, and provenance is provided, 60% of consumers check the label for sustainability, 74% of consumers are influenced by transparency and traceability and 89% would like to know the criteria for a certification of origin (E&Y Report, 2019).

The current practice of traceability in the agriculture supply chain largely suffers from data fragmentation and centralized controls which proves vulnerable to both data modification and management. In the event of contamination, identifying the source and isolating the product swiftly from the supply chain requires close coordination among multiple stakeholders in the agricultural supply chain (Storoy et al., 2013). These technologies cannot guarantee with certainty to consumers that the information presented is true and has not been altered. Specifically, in the food sector, it is harder to know where the products came from and where they are as they make their way into a vast network of physical or digital distribution channels involving multiple actors. The solution to address the food safety and quality concerns is to improve traceability, transparency, security, durability, and integrity (Feng et al., 2019; Tsang et al., 2018; Helo and Hao, 2019; Banerjee et al., 2018; Li et al., 2017). Blockchain has been widely accepted as a solution to the underlying trust and security issues in information transparency and prevention of tampering with (Ølnes et al., 2017). The contribution that Blockchain could make is very large in traceability; in fact, Blockchain is an innovative application of distributed data storage, peer-to-peer transmission, consensus mechanism, encryption algorithm, and other information technologies.

Blockchain-based traceability is a technology that is presented as a solution that enables the tracking and tracing of finished goods and materials, providing users with a high level of trust that the data they view is correct and has not been altered by an unauthorized party. Blockchain-based traceability allows the creation of a form of identification and enhancement of products offered in the form of virtual KM-zero. The solution gives the possibility to increase a digital certified information relationship between the producer (wherever he is) and the final consumer (wherever he is).

In the wine sector, the bottle of wine is presented with an intelligent label that allows identifying the producer through the digital signature. Moreover, information about the entire cultivation process, the methodologies used for the production and transformation of the wine are provided by the producer and other operators in the supply chain. Consumers can obtain this information by scanning the QR Code on the label of the bottle. The Blockchain allows fixing an indelible and secure photograph of all those steps, creating and strengthening the relationship of trust between the producer and the final consumer.

Although blockchain-based traceability is seen as a breakthrough in the agri-food sector, in literature there are not yet many studies. In fact, a real definition for this technology does not exist. There are few studies that show how the blockchain can be useful to traceability systems or what benefits it can bring to companies. This chapter addresses these significant research gaps through the research questions which are mentioned in figure 1.

Figure 1. Research questions of this chapter

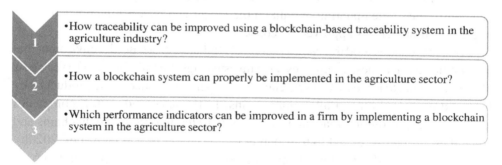

Therefore, this chapter identifies a definition for blockchain-based traceability, reviews the main benefits, limits, and challenges, analyzes the blockchain implementation in the traceability systems, and estimates the possible performance improvements. Moreover, to clarify the benefits and the performance related to the implementation of this solution, a business case is provided. The business case is related to "Cantina Placido-Volpone", which is the first firm in the world to implement the blockchain in traceability systems.

LITERATURE REVIEW

Blockchain is defined as a digital, decentralized, and distributed register, in which each transaction is recorded and added in chronological order, with the aim of creating permanent and non-alterable evidence and traces. In different words, blockchain can be defined as a new type of data system that records and stores data allowing multiple stakeholders to share in a confidential manner, and to access the same data and information in the future (Horst Treiblmaier, 2018). The first block in the chain is called "genesis block" because it has no "relatives" (previous blocks), while each block that is added to the chain refers and connects to the previous one, called "parent block", through a hash value. Given the continuous addition of blocks, the size of this chain is bound to grow over time because each new set of information corresponds to a block. This chain, however, has an immutable nature and when its content is once written, it is no longer modifiable or eliminable, unless the entire structure which is guaranteed by the use of cryptographic primitives, can be invalidated. In summary, the Blockchain can be defined as an ordered, incremental, solid, digital chain of cryptographically linked blocks (De Giovanni, 2020a).

The blockchain can be of two types, public or private. In the private ones, the actors can operate independently, but only one or more pre-selected actors perform the function of validators in the network, in the public ones, each member of the network can contribute to the updating of data on the ledger and have all the unchangeable copies of all operations approved by consent.

In recent years, as food traceability is closely linked to cross-border environmental and public health issues, companies have invested significantly in order to seek new alternative tools to increase transparency, consumer confidence in the products they buy, and accountability in all supply chains. In the agri-food sector, companies are looking for a solution that can be easily integrated into their supply chains and solve their problems related to transparency and reliability (De Giovanni, 2020b). In order to fully understand blockchain-based traceability, it is important to give a brief explanation of what traceability and blockchain really are.

Blockchain and Traceability

When it comes to the meaning of the word traceability, in order to not get confused, it is necessary to refer to some definitions included in main national and international norms. Table 1 describes some of these definitions.

Schwägele (2005) defines "tracing" as the integration of the focal firm and its customers, and "tracking" as the integration of the focal firm and its suppliers. Jansen-Vullers et al. (2003) use both an up and downstream approach to integration to define the two concepts in relation to traceability. The difference between "track-

and-trace" and traceability is that traceability includes the ability to point out the position of an item in real-time (Duhaylongsod and De Giovanni, 2019; Preeker and De Giovanni, 2019).

Table 1. Traceability definitions based on national and international standards

Reference	Definition
UNI EN ISO 9000	The ability to trace the history, application, or location of an entity
UNI 10939	The ability to reconstruct history and follow the use of a product through documented identifications related to material flows and supply chain operators
Regulation (EC) 178/2002 of the European Parliament	The ability to trace and follow a food, feed, food-producing animal or substance intended to be, or expected to be incorporated into a food or feed, through all stages of production, processing, and distribution

Traceability can be categorized into two types, internal and external traceability (Zhang and Batt, 2014). Internal traceability refers to the processes that individual firms use which link the identities of the products that enter the firm's operations and the products that leave its operations. Individual firms will also generate and store additional data reflecting changes that occur during the processing and transformational processes, which is added to product identification. External traceability refers to the ability of firms in a value chain to communicate information about products from some or all stages of transformation to some or all parties in the value chain. Firms generally assign a unique product identifier and adopt some method for its communication (Zhang and Batt, 2014).

In recent years, a number of companies, researchers, and key players along the supply chain have examined the applicability of blockchain technology in the traceability sector (Roberto Casado-Vara, 2018). The blockchain, thanks to its intrinsic characteristics and structure, offers the possibility to face one of the most difficult challenges of agri-food companies, the total and reliable registration of information and data related to the food. Indeed, instead of storing data in an opaque network system, with the blockchain, all the information of the food products can be stored in a shared and transparent system for all the members along the supply chain (Tian,2017).

Blockchain-Based Traceability in the Agri-Food Sector

Due to human error and criminal behavior, actual traceability systems are deeply imperfect. Traceability systems have repeatedly betrayed consumers, companies, and European and international institutions in various ways in recent years, and there has been a need to implement more transparent and sustainable solutions in this sector. Databases are highly vulnerable to inaccuracies and hacking systems, as well as intentional defects caused by corruption and fraudulent behavior.

Currently, many technologies such as RFID[1] have been used in the food industry to solve frequent food safety incidents (Aung, M.M.; Chang, 2014). For example, RFID technology can be used for data acquisition of raw material procurement, production processing, warehousing management, logistics, and transportation (Zhang, 2019). However, traditional models using RFID technology have problems such as low efficiency. As an instance, the centralized storage of data increases the possibility of information loss and tampering. The tools and techniques used for the product's traceability, before the implementation of blockchain, was characterized by a centralized organization that can be a vulnerable target for bribery. Another potential risk of the centralized system is that it becomes a single point of failure (Tian, 2017).

Blockchain-based traceability facilitates the establishment of a data structure that can be used by smart contracts to automate assertions, certifications, and market operations (De Giovanni, 2019b). There are three elements to explain why the food supply chain can benefit from the blockchain concept which is described in figure 2.

The transparency and the accuracy, guaranteed by blockchain, allow the customers and operators to trace every single product along the supply chain in a few seconds.

Blockchain-based traceability could solve several problems that the original traceability was not able to overcome. The most important issue of traceability is related to the coordination of transaction activities. Blockchain technology uses distributed digital databases where the blocks are linked together in a linear way and cannot be tampered with. The second issue is the difficulty of connecting physical flows to information flows. Blockchain technology can be easily linked to sensors, IoT platforms, and readable electronic tags such as RFID and barcode.

Blockchain-based traceability provides targeted and accurate information regarding a specific product to the customers and it enables the customers to reach crucial information related to food safety and quality (De Giovanni, 2020c). Thus, customers with food's traceability feel more confident and they will be willing to pay a higher price for those products, which guarantee information on high quality and desired origin (De Giovanni and Zaccour, 2019). Consequently, companies that can provide such effective traceability systems for their products not only increase safety precautions in operations but also enhance customers' confidence and trust through the assurance of quality and safety (Shanahan et al., 2009, Mai et al., 2010).

Figure 2. The main benefits of blockchain for the food supply chain

Transparency

- Blockchain enables the exchange of information with ease, generates a twin of information, and controls quality throughout the chain. Participants in this process by sharing information, evidence, and evaluations of each other's food declarations, allow these goals to be achieved.
- The journey of food along the supply chain is captured in a blockchain object called a "food bundle". When the "food bundle" reaches the last step of the supply chain, it is completed with all the information shared by the operators involved throughout the life of the food. In this way, the information can be a very effective tool in indicating the attributes of the food, quality, taste, and land of origin (Juan F. Galvez, 2018).

Efficiency

- A blockchain is a piece of infrastructure that enables new transactions between players not knowing or trusting each other yet.
- Smart contracts are instructions that interface with the blockchain protocol in order to automatically evaluate and possibly post transactions in the blockchain (M.Raskin,2017).
- All the participants can evaluate the assertions made, and notify their account holders when matches in quality, timing, quantity, etc., are found.
- Buyers and sellers are matched by a shared but trusted need for data, which can then be combined and used by either party. In this way, traceability does not have to wait for large company consortiums to use standards, and/or semi-mandatory or concentrated business practices to access the information (Juan F. Galvez, 2018).

Security and Safety

- Blockchain has the ability to generate and manage the creation of unique cryptographic tokens. The purpose of creating the tokens is to represent the value in escrow between two participants (e.g., future production to be farmed in a particular field lot). In fact, tokens do not need to take the form of value exchange for financial settlements of invoices and contracts. Rather, they represent a license to publish information that becomes uniquely valued in proportion to the needs of others in the blockchain (Juan F. Galvez, 2018).

Proper blockchain-based traceability systems also have the potential to help a supplier or an operator with responsibility for a product safety problem by providing well-documented traceable data to prove that they comply with regulatory requirements and do not present risks (Meuwissen et al., 2003; Sahin et al., 2007; Fritz and Schiefer, 2009). In that condition, liability claims and lawsuits will be avoided and the company's image will not be affected (Mai et al., 2010; De Giovanni and Ramani, 2017). Blockchain-based Traceability can support product claims and in general, it provides product information that everyone can rely on and it is a perfect strategy for the brand's protection, complementing both quality and goodwill (Buratto et al., 2019).

As shown by an experiment conducted by Walmart, one of the most important benefits of adopting this technology is the speed of tracing every single product's information. Based on a survey, Walmart wanted to trace the origin of mangoes in one of its shops. Using traditional linear methods to trace a package from the orchards in Ecuador to the Los Angeles supermarket took six days, 18 hours, and 26 minutes. The time taken to complete and submit all the information using the blockchain was only 2.2 seconds. In case of food contamination, six days is an eternity! The blockchain also allows specific batches to be identified at any time without food waste. Contaminated or counterfeit products can be traced quickly, while safe goods would remain on shelves instead of ending up in landfills (Kamath,2018).

Therefore, blockchain-based traceability is a solution that enables the tracking and tracing of finished goods and materials, providing users with a high level of trust that the data they view and store on the chain is correct and has not been altered by an unauthorized party (Deloitte,2018).

Several studies have been carried out on the blockchain as a solution to the problems of traceability and, although in some projects excellent results have been recorded (IBM Food Trust, Walmart, E&Y blockchain Hub), the blockchain remains a "new" technology with a high level of risk (De Giovanni, 2019a). Even if Blockchain technology looks like an important innovation for food traceability, there are some limits that have to be analyzed. The Global Food Traceability Centre has identified six different challenges that it is important to overcome in order to use blockchain-based traceability successfully. The first challenge is related to consumers' preferences, which change over time, and their confidence, which tends to be increasingly fragile. The Centre also identified the disorder created by national regulators, who are often at odds with each other on the issue of traceability. The third challenge concerns the possible difficulty in data analysis because there are not unifying requirements. The fourth challenge, on the other hand, is to explain the complex difference between the various food sectors. Later the Centre pointed out that neither traceability nor blockchain could not prevent human errors in the recording of information. Finally, the last challenge is represented by the weak technical systems that do not allow fast and effective response times. Overcoming these challenges will not be easy and will depend mainly on companies' willingness to be open to change and invest in innovation (GS1, 2012).

Implementing the Blockchain-Based Traceability

To understand how blockchain-based traceability could work along the whole supply chain of a product, it is important to analyze the potential uses of blockchain-based traceability at different steps in the food supply chain.

The process starts when supply chain members can register themselves in the system as a user which can provide credentials and a unique identity to the members. After registration, public and private cryptographic key pairs will be generated for each user. The public key can be used to identify the user within the system and the private key can be used to authenticate the user when interacting with the system. This enables each product can be digitally addressed by the users when being updated, added, or exchanged to the next user in the downstream position of the supply chain. In food supply chains, when a user who is in a particular link receives a product, he can add new data into the profile of the product only with its private key. In addition, when the user transfers this product to the next user, both of them have to sign a digital contract to authenticate the exchange (Tian, 2017).

The application process of this technology could be divided into two parts. The first one is related to the standard traceability process and the second one is related to the blockchain, which is correlated to the first one. The traceability process in the agri-food sector is generally structured in five steps, but most of the time it depends on the type of the crops. These processes are indicated in figure 3. Administration or certification authorities could visit the working field at random times, in order to be sure that the rules and regulations are matched or if some data have tampered with.

The immutable nature of blockchain enables us to record the complete chain of custody for every item that is logged to the blockchain from its origin to the point of sale. This chain of custody gives increased confidence and assurance of the authenticity and quality of goods that leads to better sourcing decisions (Deloitte, 2018).

Figure 3. The application process of blockchain-based traceability

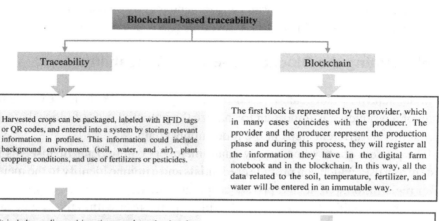

Blockchain-based traceability

Traceability | Blockchain

Production

Harvested crops can be packaged, labeled with RFID tags or QR codes, and entered into a system by storing relevant information in profiles. This information could include background environment (soil, water, and air), plant cropping conditions, and use of fertilizers or pesticides.

The first block is represented by the provider, which in many cases coincides with the producer. The provider and the producer represent the production phase and during this process, they will register all the information they have in the digital farm notebook and in the blockchain. In this way, all the data related to the soil, temperature, fertilizer, and water will be entered in an immutable way.

Processing

It includes reading and inserting new data related to the processes into the product's profile. New information includes the processing environment or the use of the additive.

Distribution

Real-time environmental data for products including temperature and humidity can be added to digital profiles and tags at regular intervals and a monitoring system can be established by setting temperature and humidity sensors in different temperature areas of refrigerated containers. This helps to assure food safety and quality at the distribution stage considering time, temperature, and tolerance. An alarm will be immediately raised if the temperature or humidity exceeds the security standard. In addition, by using GPS technology, a distribution center can implement vehicle positioning for each refrigerated truck and optimize its route to shorten delivery times.

The administrator will create the third and the fourth block to enter all the data related to the processing phase (processing method information) and the distribution phase, such as temperature during transportation or humidity. In this way, the retailer will have all the information about the production phase of the product (Liu and De Giovanni, 2019).

Retailers

Thanks to blockchain technology, all information produced along the supply chain is auditable, with details about the products by inspecting the traceability system in real-time. The system can also be used to monitor the freshness lifetime of products so that retailers can replace them close to their expiry date. In addition, thanks to the traceability inherent in the blockchain, if a food safety incident occurs, the defective products can be immediately located. Reasons, location, and responsible staff can be easily traced, and losses and hazards will be reduced largely, as a result.

With these blocks, the retailer could monitor the expiry date, the freshness lifetime of the products at every moment.

Consumers

They are the final point of the supply chain and they can now trace the information of a product in few seconds, scanning the QR code with their smartphone.

At the end of the process, there will be hypothetically five or six blocks that contain all the sensible information related to the specific product.

Smart contracts are created when the company's employees save the information and data during the product's production phase (De Giovanni, 2021a). A smart contract is a program that runs itself when certain predetermined conditions are met. In addition to this, specific smart contracts will be able to automate various expensive or complicated operations. Through the smart contracts, used on Ethereum or Hyperladger, every action performed along the Food supply chain is recorded in the Blockchain, which is responsible for storing all data uploaded by the participants in the supply chain in an immutable way. The information recorded during each session must be validated by business partners, forming a consensus of all participants. After each block is validated, it is added to the transition chain becoming permanent and unchangeable. With the blockchain and smart contract introduction, the traceability process will be divided into blocks.

Blockchain-Based Traceability Performance

The improvements due to the blockchain-based traceability implementation should be analyzed considering economic and strategic advantages. In addition to the increase in sales and revenues, blockchain is a technology that affects all areas of the company and there will be cost advantages due to digitization and reduction of internal bureaucracy (Digital notebook, quality check improvements). Although implementing this strategy will be expensive at the beginning, it will bring greater benefits by reducing costs, and therefore, it will be economically sustainable for the company over time. In fact, in the business case that we will analyze later, the project implementation of this system has resulted in an ROI higher than that of the entire sector. After starting the sale of the traced products, the company could record in a short time an increase in sales for both the traced bottles (sold at a higher price) and the untraced bottles (standard price).

Regarding the strategic advantages, this solution will give the possibility to monitor information about consumers (age, country of origin, gender), this is crucial information to manage future marketing campaigns and to monitor the brand awareness and recognition of the consumers. In addition, the implementation of blockchain-based traceability is a new and unknown solution that brings the interest of major national and international magazines and newspapers, creating a positive media effect for the product. The implementation of this solution will also involve the interest of foreign consumers which leads to increasing the internationalization process of the company.

CASE STUDY: CANTINA PLACIDO-VOLPONE

Placido Volpone S.r.l., established by the partnership between the families of Domenico Volpone, a well-known winemaker, and Michele Placido, a well-known actor. It is the first winery to adopt blockchain in its product traceability systems. The success of the winery's production is also due to its territorial qualities. In fact, it is located in a hilly area known to be one of the stoniest and windy areas of Italy that provides suitable conditions for the cultivation of vines, giving the wine a unique flavor. Today, the winery company is specialized in the production of some of the most typical red and white Italian wines, like Falanghina, Sangiovese, Nero di Troia, and Aglianico. Bottling, distribution, and marketing processes are provided by the Placido Volpone winery, while farming and winemaking are provided by Azienda Agricola Domenico Volpone.

The proposed company had its maximum development in 2016 when it made new decisions at the strategic and operational levels. A new re-branding policy was introduced; the offer was revolutionized primarily through a re-design of labels and packaging, moving from plastic to glass containers, which resulted in an increase in packaging costs from € 0.20 to € 0.70. The company also made another important decision which was turning to another type of end consumer by moving the target from a lower-middle to a more sought after. This shift was only possible by making changes in the packaging, production process, and providing new sales channels that are better suited to the new target.

Blockchain-Based Traceability at Volpone

Hereby we discuss how Volpone improved traceability by adopting a blockchain-based traceability system. Further innovations were made by the winery in 2016 dictated by the need to meet the tastes of the most demanding consumers as well as to comply with the rules in terms of traceability. The winery suffered damage to its turnover and reputation due to a counterfeit wine made by a representative, as it did not have the appropriate and necessary tools to trace the counterfeit lot and had no evidence to trace it back to the counterfeiter. In order to avoid further inconveniences, the winery decided to implement blockchain-based traceability by the collaboration of EY and EzLabMoreover, this system intensifies the relationship of trust between the consumer and the producer, enhancing the quality of the product. The idea of applying the blockchain system in the wine sector is aimed at removing the obstacles that companies encounter in transmitting the amount of information on what is sold, due to a production chain that is often very complex. Every story can be told to consumers in an easy and intuitive way, all they need is a smartphone with which to scan the QR Code.

With wine blockchain "Cantina Placido-Volpone" had the possibility to give consumers a full account of its wine quality and its DNA's information, through real uneditable data collected during the winemaking process. The blockchain-based traceability, generated by Ernst Young, creates a sort of database containing information at every stage of the winemaking process from cultivation to bottling. It created a detailed shared transparent direct source of information on the entire production process, visible to all the players involved, in order to verify the accuracy of the information stored and to give consumers the true story behind every bottle. The main benefits that the company enjoys thanks to the implementation of this solution are mentioned in figure 4 (based on the information from Placido-Volpone's website).

Figure 4. The main benefits of implementing blockchain solution at Cantina Placido-Volpone

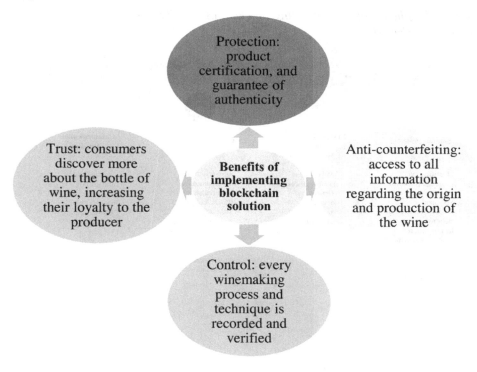

Indeed, Cantina Placido-Volpone could control geolocation data during distribution and storage temperature throughout the entire production process by implementing this technology. Also, the firm can really get to know and profile its consumers by inviting them through the app to share experiences and to geolocalize consumption (Tiscini, 2020). However, being a very early adopter, the company had to address some problems linked to the limited knowledge of this new technology and the resulting employee training costs.

Blockchain-Based Traceability Application Process at Placido-Volpone

In order to understand how Placido-Volpone implemented blockchain-based traceability, it is important to move on to the analysis of the phases and individual activities that made up the project. In total, four different macro phases can be distinguished (E&Y,2019) including Assessment, Data Collection, Development, and Communication which are indicated in figure 5.

Figure 5. The phases of implementing blockchain-based traceability
Source: EY Blockchain Hub, 2019

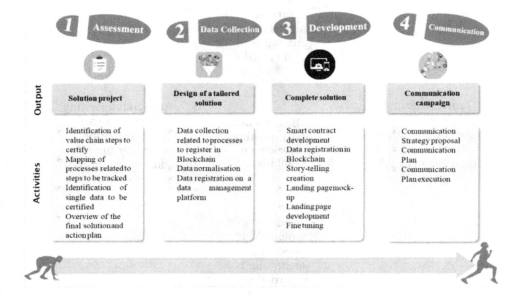

Assessment

During this phase, E&Y in collaboration with Cantina Placido-Volpone had to define the result to be reached and how to achieve it. The assessment phase lasted about two months and they defined their final objective as the perfect recording of all the information contained in the entire life cycle of Cantina Placido-Volpone's Falanghina wine. In other words, the final objective was the recording of all sensitive data in the blockchain, guaranteeing the security and immutability of the data. The secondary objective included environmental sustainability, anti-counterfeiting, and the internationalization of the company. Analyzing precisely the first phase, the actions that have been carried out are as follows:

The actions which are mentioned in figure 5 were carried out through numerous interviews between E&Y officials and employees and managers of the Placido-Volpone winery, where the two parties treated the project in detail without omitting any data. During the interviews it was therefore decided to analyze all the phases of the process, from the cultivation of the soil to the marketing of the bottles, leaving out only the "after-sale" process. Tracing the entire production process of the wine was possible because the Placido-Volpone winery does not rely on third-party companies for any process but all phases of cultivation are "in-house"; this allowed the two companies to have at their disposal all the data needed to complete the project.

Data Collection

The second phase of the project is data collection, a phase in which useful information for the product traceability process is collected. The entire data collection process was manual because the Apulian company had not invested in new technologies or digitization before, but all the information was taken manually on paper notebooks. Therefore, the crucial point of this phase was the beginning of the collaboration between E&Y and Cantina Placido-Volpone with EzLab. Indeed, in order to speed up data recording and to give an innovative boost to the company, AgriOpenData was introduced, an online platform developed by EzLab for the optimization of business management and the recording of information on the Data Management System. This software represented an innovation for the company, being able to support agronomists in crop treatment processes, through the use of OpenData, which are directly integrated with the information processed during field activities. This allowed the company's employees to exchange and share data and information continuously and quickly.

Another advantage of the AgriOpenData software was the replacement of the old *paper campaign notebook* with a digital one. The campaign notebook is obligatory by law for all farms in Italy, until a few years ago it had to be presented once a year, but with the new provisions, it has to be presented once a month. With a digital notebook, writing the campaign notebook becomes much faster, safer, and more reliable because there is no possibility to lose some data or information.

Figure 6. Comparison between old collection of data and AgriOpenData developed by EzLab

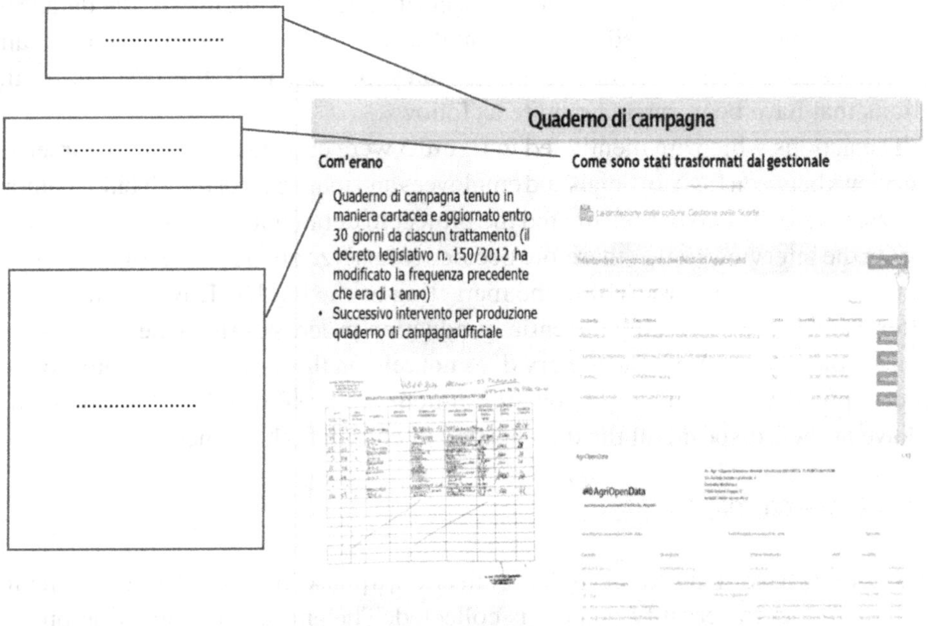

Development

The Development is divided into two steps: the recording of data in the blockchain and the creation of the Landing Page. The first step starts with the structuring and implementation of the Smart Contract that is the basis of Ethereum. During the process, the managers of Cantina Placido-Volpone had to choose which information to trace in clear text on the blockchain and which to hide through encryption. Although transparency is one of the main objectives of the project, some information had to be hidden because it was strategically important.

The second step concerned the creation of the Landing Page, the web page that the end consumer can reach by scanning the QR Code on the label on the back of the bottle. The design of the Landing Page was conducted by NeriWolff, a company belonging to E&Y. The Landing Page as is shown in figure 7 contains all the useful information for the consumer such as the geographical context, the cultivation, the winemaking process, the distribution, and the sale. For each of these areas, the customer has the possibility to consult all the information recorded in the blockchain. In fact, it is necessary for the customer to click on "verification of interventions" to be taken to another web page where all the information relating to that specific area of interest is recorded chronologically. Moreover, for each piece of information (e.g. pruning or grape harvest) it is possible to click on "Certificate register" to be traced back to another Etherscan web page, which represents the Ethereum search engine. By reading the information contained on the Etherscan page the customer can see that all the information has been recorded immutably in the blockchain.

Figure 7. Landing page, conducted by NeriWolff
Source: EY Blockchain Hub, 2019

Communication

The fourth and final phase is the creation of a divulgation plan to present to the world the first wine entirely traced with the Blockchain. In this phase, E&Y and Cantina Placido-Volpone have different goals.

In order to gain new customers, E&Y had a strong interest in publicizing the excellent result to increase the good reputation of the company. In fact, a few months after the completion of the project at Placido-Volpone, E&Y started several projects with blockchain-based traceability with other wineries and with Carrefour.

For Cantina Placido-Volpone, the main goal in this phase was to internationalize its sales, go beyond national borders, and sell its wine abroad. Therefore, it was important that this project be advertised in the best possible way so that it would also be known abroad. At a media-level the project was highly appreciated, having been mentioned by Sole24Ore and Borsa Italiana.

Information Accessibility for Customers

Figure 8. Available information by scanning smart labels
Source: EY Blockchain Hub, 2019

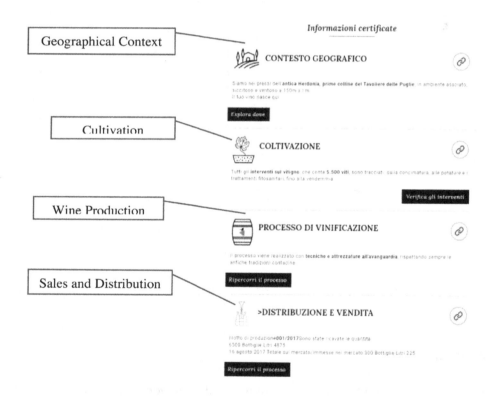

Blockchain-based traceability is important because consumers can find out more about the final product, increase their awareness of what they are drinking and their loyalty to the brand. By scanning the QR Code, consumers will be able to access a web page that offers information mainly about the production process and other different types of information such as:

- Geographical context, which shows all the information related to the geographical area of production of the wine, in particular the vineyard.
- Cultivation, shows detailed information on agro-pharmaceuticals, fertilizers, and plant growth phases, following a specific timeline.
- Wine production, which shows all the steps of wine production with a time tag and a description of the process.
- Sales and distribution, which shows data on the total quantity of wine produced (in liters) and the number of bottles distributed worldwide.

Performance Improvements at Placido-Volpone

The introduction of the blockchain used as an auxiliary tool for the traceability of products has led to numerous economic benefits. Although Cantina Placido-Volpone initially had to spend a large amount of money to implement this new traceability system, this innovation had a positive impact on the company's balance sheet and the main profitability indicators. This analysis was carried out by analyzing Cantina Volpone's balance sheet for 2017 and through interviews with the winery owners.

To implement this technology, the company had to sustain fixed costs of 40.000 €, divided into an up-front fee of 30.000 € at the beginning of the project and 10.000€ at the middle of the project. In addition to the fixed costs, the winery had to incur variable costs equal to € 0.10 for each bottle traced. In this case, the variable costs amounted to 13.000 €, having E&Y and Volpone traced 130.000 bottles. Therefore, in 2017 the total costs amounted to 53.000 €.

It should be noted that as a result of this innovation, the Volpone winery decided to re-brand its bottles, primarily to achieve the canons of beauty that the winery wanted to target and also to justify the premium price applied to the bottles traced. In fact, from 2017, the Falanghina of Cantina Placido-Volpone went from a price of 7 € to 9.20 €, recording a premium price of 2.20 €. According to some analyses carried out by Cantina Placido-Volpone staff, 80% of the premium price was due to rebranding and 20% to the investment made with E&Y. In fact, as one of the Volpone's manager said: "the 20% of premium price allows to neutralize the increase in value due to rebranding with a high level of certainty". In this way, knowing that the 20% of the premium price is 0.44€, multiplying the latter by the number of bottles traced, the benefit of the solution is outlined, which amounted to 57.200€. As a result, in 2016 there was an increase in the cost of bottle production, costs increased by 31.42% and had a significant impact on the company's profits. Production costs thus rose to 100.000 €, but as a result, the blockchain has managed, through its own features, to create additional cost advantages such as:

- Digitization, which amounted to 10% of the production cost, largely due to the reduction of beurocratric tasks and efficiency of the cloud management system (AgriOpenData);
- Quality and Assurance check improvements, which amounted to 25% of production costs;
- Costs of the company related to quality and assurance checks and beurocratic tasks, which amounted to 10% of costs.

Therefore, multiplying the production costs by the sales of the company, the sum of digitization, and quality and assurance improvements, the company estimated saving of 3.500 € in production costs. This result was estimated by the winery.

The total margin of the solution can be calculated by adding 4.200 € (calculated by the difference between the benefits of the solution and the costs of the solution) and 3.500 € (cost advantages), for a total of 7.700 €, due only to the introduction of the blockchain. Now, it is possible to calculate the ROI of the project, comparing the total margin to the cost of the solution (7.700/53.000), which equals 14.53%. Table 2, summarizes the economic-financial analysis.

Table 2. Economic-financial analysis for implementing block-based traceability

Number of Traced bottles	130.000	
Fixed Cost	At the beginning of the project (Euro)	30.000
	At the middle of the project (Euro)	10.000
	Total Fixed Cost (Euro)	40.000
Variable costs	Per bottle (Euro)	0.1
	Total for 130.000 bottles (Euro)	13.000
Total Cost	40.000+13.000=53.000	
The benefit of the solution	57.200	
Cost Advantages	3.500	
Total margin	(57.200-53.000)+3.500=7.700	
ROI	14.53%	

An analysis carried out by Medio Banca, looking at the average ROI in the wine sector in Italy, showed that in 2017 it was 7.9%, and then decreased to 6.7% in 2018.

So even though the initial costs for the introduction of the Blockchain may seem exorbitant, it had a positive effect on the company's profitability, leading to a higher than average market ROI and significant cost advantages. These results are due to the transparency that the Placido Volpone Winery has offered to its consumers. Customers preferred to pay a higher price in exchange for a product that was fully traced and safe for their health. Moreover, traceability has increased sales abroad which led to an increment in earnings.

Analyzing the number of digital label displays and the geographical location of users showed that the project has indeed met with strong interest among consumers. Besides, the geographical analysis has been very useful to outline the guidelines for future marketing strategies. Figure 8 indicates the consumers' nationality who have scanned QR codes until June 12, 2018.

Figure 9. Analyzing consumers' nationality who have scanned QR codes until June 12, 2018
Source: Cantina Placido-Volpone Analytics

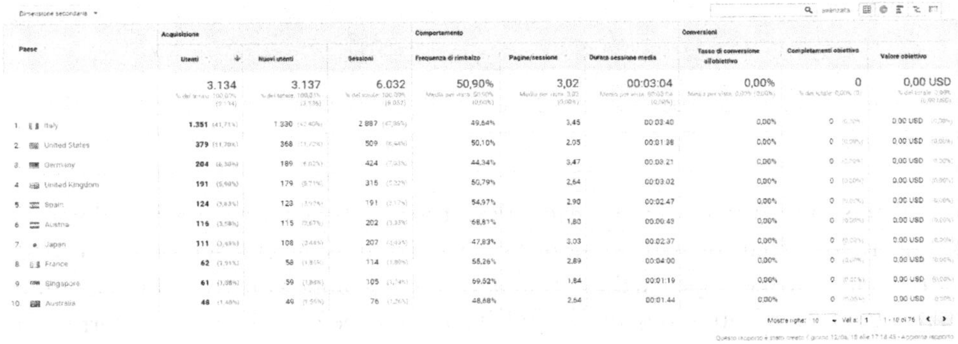

Paese	Acquisizione: Utenti	Nuovi utenti	Sessioni	Comportamento: Frequenza di rimbalzo	Pagine/sessione	Durata sessione media	Conversioni: Tasso di conversione all'obiettivo	Completamenti obiettivo	Valore obiettivo
	3.134	3.137	6.032	50,90%	3,02	00:03:04	0,00%	0	0,00 USD
1. Italy	1.351	1.330	2.887	49,64%	3,45	00:03:40	0,00%	0	0,00 USD
2. United States	379	368	509	50,10%	2,05	00:01:38	0,00%	0	0,00 USD
3. Germany	204	189	424	44,34%	3,47	00:03:21	0,00%	0	0,00 USD
4. United Kingdom	191	179	315	50,79%	2,64	00:03:02	0,00%	0	0,00 USD
5. Spain	124	123	191	54,97%	2,90	00:02:47	0,00%	0	0,00 USD
6. Austria	116	115	202	68,81%	1,80	00:00:49	0,00%	0	0,00 USD
7. Japan	111	108	207	47,83%	3,03	00:02:37	0,00%	0	0,00 USD
8. France	62	58	114	58,26%	2,89	00:04:00	0,00%	0	0,00 USD
9. Singapore	61	59	105	69,52%	1,84	00:01:19	0,00%	0	0,00 USD
10. Australia	48	49	76	48,68%	2,64	00:01:44	0,00%	0	0,00 USD

In June 2018, more than 50% of the visits to the winery's page by scanning the codes were made by European consumers including Germany (6.30%) and the United Kingdom (5.90%). Moreover, it is very useful to point out that the second place in this ranking is occupied by the United States (with 11.70%), whose wine consumers are very sensitive to information about the origin and originality of the product. This shows that through the introduction of Blockchain in its traceability system, Cantina Placido-Volpone is achieving one of the goals set at the beginning of the project, the internationalization of its products. Analyzing the views in Italy in the period between April 5, 2017, and June 11, 2018, Cantina Placido-Volpone received most of the visits to its website from consumers living in Rome, Milan, and other cities in northern Italy. This is a very important result because two of the main objectives after the rebranding were to attract a clientele more interested in the quality of wine and to expand its sales in the major Italian cities. Figure 9 shows the diffusion of the visualizations in the Italian territory.

Figure 10. The geographical location of consumers in Italy
Source: Cantina Placido-Volpone Analytics

Thanks to the use of Google Analytics, it is also possible to combine this type of quantitative analysis with a qualitative evaluation of the characteristics of those individuals who have opened the Blockchain link or scanned the QR code. The study begins with data on the frequency of visits to the page containing the information recorded in the blocks and then identifies the locations in the world where the accesses come from. Figure 10 shows the number of views made during the period from April 5, 2017, to June 11, 2018.

In 2017, there have been 6,032 views since the realization of the project, whose duration was about 3 minutes. This data is very important because it highlights how each user has navigated for a sufficient time to consult all the data available. Moreover, figures 11 and 12 indicate the percentage of visitors based on their gender and age respectively. Based on figure 12, the knowledge of users about new technologies decreases as their age increases.

Figure 11. QR code scanning trend from April 5, 2017, to June 11, 2018
Source: Cantina Placido-Volpone Analytics

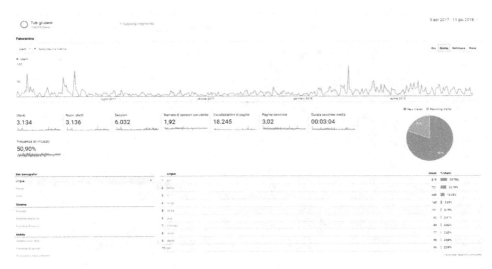

Figure 12. Analyzing gender of consumers who used QR codes
Source: Cantina Placido-Volpone Analytics

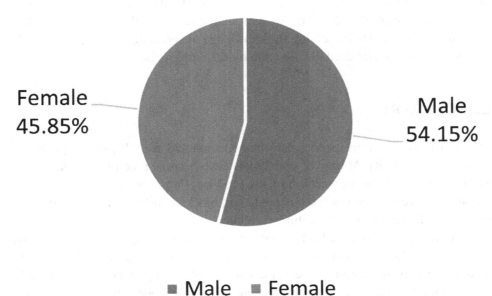

Figure 13. Analyzing the age of consumers who used QR codes
Source: Cantina Placido-Volpone Analytics

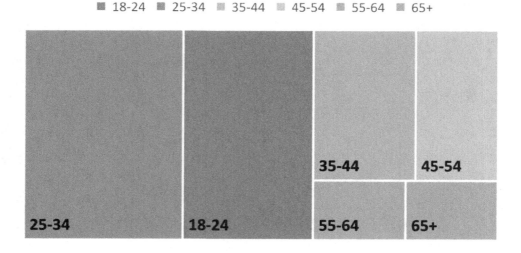

Besides the most important qualitative results, there is an increase in brand awareness. Innovation and transparency are the two fundamental concepts that are now associated with the name of the winery. The winery without a doubt is the one that has made its production process more transparent than all the others in the sector. The introduction of blockchain has also brought changes to the internal system of the winery. It has led to increasing the knowledge of specialized skills in the fields such as agriculture and digitalization among the employees.

CONCLUSION

The agri-food sector in recent years has encountered a multitude of problems related to traceability. Moreover, consumers have become much more demanding and curious about the information of the products they buy. As demonstrated in the literature review and in the business case, blockchain-based traceability is an excellent solution to solve traceability problems.

In this chapter, a technical solution was presented to ensure traceability through blockchain in the agri-food sector. Some aspects of blockchain-based traceability such as the implementation process, the benefits of its implementation especially the economic sustainability of the solution have not yet been studied in previous researches. So, the aim of this chapter was to investigate the viability and desirability of using blockchain technology to improve traceability systems.

Indeed, Cantina Placido-Volpone was the first firm in the world to implement blockchain-based traceability in the wine sector which resulted in protection, trust, control, and anti-counterfeiting. Once the consumer scans the QR code, a web page will open where there will be information like geographical context, cultivation, wine production, distribution, and sales. With this solution, Cantina Placido-Volpone has accelerated its internationalization process. The performance improvements have been analyzed both from an economic and strategic point of view. This solution has generated a 14% ROI in 2017, and the company can monitor its customers' behavior for devising its future marketing campaigns.

Based on what has been analyzed by this work, blockchain-based traceability generates a lot of advantages including economic return. It is not only a source of income for companies but also a source of security for and their brands and consumers.

REFERENCES

Aung, M. M., & Chang, Y. S. (2014). Traceability in a food supply chain: Safety and quality perspectives. *Food Control*, *39*, 172–184. doi:10.1016/j.foodcont.2013.11.007

Banerjee, M., Lee, J., & Choo, K. K. R. (2018). A blockchain future for internet of things security: A position paper. *Digital Communications and Networks*, *4*(3), 149–160. doi:10.1016/j.dcan.2017.10.006

Behnke, K., & Janssen, M. F. W. H. A. (2020). Boundary conditions for traceability in food supply chains using blockchain technology. *International Journal of Information Management*, *52*, 101969. doi:10.1016/j.ijinfomgt.2019.05.025

Beloglazov, A., Abawajy, J., & Buyya, R. (2012). Energy-aware resource allocation heuristics for efficient management of data centers for cloud computing. *Future Generation Computer Systems*, *28*(5), 755–768. doi:10.1016/j.future.2011.04.017

Bhardwaj, S., & Kaushik, M. (2018). Blockchain—technology to drive the future. In *Smart Computing and Informatics* (pp. 263–271). Springer. doi:10.1007/978-981-10-5547-8_28

Bhatt, T., Buckley, G., McEntire, J. C., Lothian, P., Sterling, B., & Hickey, C. (2013). Making traceability work across the entire food supply chain. *Journal of Food Science*, *78*(s2), B21–B27. doi:10.1111/1750-3841.12278 PMID:24138197

Biswas, K., Muthukkumarasamy, V., & Tan, W. L. (2017). Blockchain based wine supply chain traceability system. In *Future Technologies Conference (FTC) 2017* (pp. 56-62). The Science and Information Organization.

Bogdan, R. C., & Biklen, S. K. (1998). *Qualitative Research for Education: An Introduction to Theory and Methods*. Allyn and Bacon.

Buratto, A., Cesaretto, R., & De Giovanni, P. (2019). Consignment contracts with cooperative programs and price discount mechanisms in a dynamic supply chain. *International Journal of Production Economics*, *218*, 72–82. doi:10.1016/j.ijpe.2019.04.027

Caro, M. P., Ali, M. S., Vecchio, M., & Giaffreda, R. (2018, May). Blockchain-based traceability in Agri-Food supply chain management: A practical implementation. In *2018 IoT Vertical and Topical Summit on Agriculture-Tuscany (IOT Tuscany)* (pp. 1-4). IEEE.

Casado-Vara, R., Prieto, J., De la Prieta, F., & Corchado, J. M. (2018). How blockchain improves the supply chain: Case study alimentary supply chain. *Procedia Computer Science*, *134*, 393–398. doi:10.1016/j.procs.2018.07.193

Comunicazione, C. (2017). *La filiera del vino del vino guarda al Blockchain*. https://www.corrierecomunicazioni.it/digital-economy/la-filiera-del-vinoguarda-al-blockchain-in-nome-del-made-in-italy/

Creydt, M., & Fischer, M. (2019). Blockchain and more-Algorithm driven food traceability. *Food Control*, *105*, 45–51. doi:10.1016/j.foodcont.2019.05.019

Crosby, M. (2016). *Blockchain Technology: Beyond Bitcoin*. Giugno.

De Giovanni, P. (2019a). *Eco-Digital Supply Chains Through Blockchains*. Available at SSRN 3488925.

De Giovanni, P. (2019b). Digital Supply Chain through Dynamic Inventory and Smart Contracts. *Mathematics*, *7*(12), 1235. doi:10.3390/math7121235

De Giovanni, P. (2020a). Blockchain and smart contracts in supply chain management: A game theoretic model. *International Journal of Production Economics*, *228*, 107855. doi:10.1016/j.ijpe.2020.107855

De Giovanni, P. (2020b). Smart Contracts and Blockchain for Supply Chain Quality Management. In *Dynamic Quality Models and Games in Digital Supply Chains*. Springer Nature.

De Giovanni, P. (2020c). An optimal control model with defective products and goodwill damages. *Annals of Operations Research*, *289*(2), 419–430. doi:10.100710479-019-03176-4

De Giovanni, P. (2021). Smart Supply Chains with vendor managed inventory, coordination, and environmental performance. *European Journal of Operational Research, 292*(2), 515–531. doi:10.1016/j.ejor.2020.10.049

De Giovanni, P., & Cariola, A. (2020). Process innovation through industry 4.0 technologies, lean practices and green supply chains. *Research in Transportation Economics*, 100869. doi:10.1016/j.retrec.2020.100869

De Giovanni, P., & Ramani, V. (2017). Product cannibalization and the effect of a service strategy. *The Journal of the Operational Research Society*, 1–17.

De Giovanni, P., & Zaccour, G. (2019). Optimal quality improvements and pricing strategies with active and passive product returns. *Omega, 88*, 248–262. doi:10.1016/j.omega.2018.09.007

Duhaylongsod, J. B., & De Giovanni, P. (2019). The impact of innovation strategies on the relationship between supplier integration and operational performance. *International Journal of Physical Distribution & Logistics Management, 49*(2), 156–177. doi:10.1108/IJPDLM-09-2017-0269

Ernst & Young Report. (2019). E&Y Opschain traceability. Author.

European Union Council. (2019). European Parliament, & European Union Council Regulation (EC) No 178/2002 of the European Parliament and of the Council of 28 January 2002 laying down the general principles and requirements of food law, establishing the European Food Safety Authority and laying down procedures in matters of food safety *Official Journal of the European Union*, 02002R0178-EN-26.07.2019-007.001

Feng, H., Wang, X., Duan, Y., Zhang, J., & Zhang, X. (2020). Applying blockchain technology to improve agri-food traceability: A review of development methods, benefits and challenges. *Journal of Cleaner Production, 260*, 121031. doi:10.1016/j.jclepro.2020.121031

GS1. (2010a). *Healthcare supply chain traceability*. Available from: https://www.gs1.org/docs/gdsn/support/20101025_Traceability_White_Paper_final.pdf

GS1. (2012). *GS1 Standards Document*. Business Process and System Requirements for Full Supply Chain Traceability. GS1 Global Traceability Standard.

Galvez, J. F., Mejuto, J. C., & Simal-Gandara, J. (2018). Future challenges on the use of blockchain for food traceability analysis. *Trends in Analytical Chemistry, 107*, 222–232. doi:10.1016/j.trac.2018.08.011

Helo, P., & Hao, Y. (2019). Blockchains in operations and supply chains: A model and reference implementation. *Computers & Industrial Engineering, 136,* 242–251. doi:10.1016/j.cie.2019.07.023

Heyman, H. M., Senejoux, F., Seibert, I., Klimkait, T., Maharaj, V. J., & Meyer, J. J. M. (2015). Identification of anti-HIV active dicaffeoylquinic-and tricaffeoylquinic acids in Helichrysum populifolium by NMR-based metabolomic guided fractionation. *Fitoterapia, 103,* 155–164. doi:10.1016/j.fitote.2015.03.024 PMID:25841639

ISO. (2007). 22005: Traceability in the feed and food chain—General principles and guidance for system design and development. International Organisation for Standardization.

Jansen-Vullers, M. H., van Dorp, C. A., & Beulens, A. J. M. (2003). Managing traceability information in manufacture. *International Journal of Information Management, 23*(5), 395–413. doi:10.1016/S0268-4012(03)00066-5

Kamath, R. (2018). Food traceability on blockchain: Walmart's pork and mango pilots with IBM. *The Journal of the British Blockchain Association, 1*(1), 3712. doi:10.31585/jbba-1-1-(10)2018

Kamble, S. S., Gunasekaran, A., & Sharma, R. (2020). Modeling the blockchain enabled traceability in agriculture supply chain. *International Journal of Information Management, 52,* 101967. doi:10.1016/j.ijinfomgt.2019.05.023

Lin, Q., Wang, H., Pei, X., & Wang, J. (2019). Food safety traceability system based on blockchain and EPCIS. *IEEE Access : Practical Innovations, Open Solutions, 7,* 20698–20707. doi:10.1109/ACCESS.2019.2897792

Liu, B., & De Giovanni, P. (2019). Green process innovation through Industry 4.0 technologies and supply chain coordination. *Annals of Operations Research,* 1–36. doi:10.100710479-019-03498-3

Mishra, N., Mistry, S., Choudhary, S., Kudu, S., & Mishra, R. (2020). Food Traceability System Using Blockchain and QR Code. In *IC-BCT 2019. Blockchain Technologies.* Springer. doi:10.1007/978-981-15-4542-9_4

Ølnes, S., Ubacht, J., & Janssen, M. (2017). *Blockchain in government: Benefits and implications of distributed ledger technology for information sharing.* Academic Press.

Olsen, P., & Borit, M. (2013). How to define traceability. *Trends in Food Science & Technology, 29*(2), 142–150. doi:10.1016/j.tifs.2012.10.003

Pizzuti, T., & Mirabelli, G. (2015). The Global Track & Trace System for food: General framework and functioning principles. *Journal of Food Engineering, 159,* 16–35. doi:10.1016/j.jfoodeng.2015.03.001

Prashar, D., Jha, N., Jha, S., Lee, Y., & Joshi, G. P. (2020). Blockchain-based traceability and visibility for agricultural products: A decentralized way of ensuring food safety in india. *Sustainability, 12*(8), 3497. doi:10.3390u12083497

Preeker, T., & De Giovanni, P. (2018). Coordinating innovation projects with high tech suppliers through contracts. *Research Policy, 47*(6), 1161–1172. doi:10.1016/j.respol.2018.04.003

Raskin. (2017). The law and legality of smart contracts. *Georgetown Law Technol. Rev.,* 305-341.

REGULATION (EC) No 178/2002 of the European parliament and of the council, of 28 January 2002

Deloitte Report. (2018). *When two chains combine Supply chain meets blockchain.* Author.

Salah, K., Nizamuddin, N., Jayaraman, R., & Omar, M. (2019). Blockchain-based soybean traceability in agricultural supply chain. *IEEE Access: Practical Innovations, Open Solutions, 7,* 73295–73305. doi:10.1109/ACCESS.2019.2918000

Schwägele, F. (2005). Traceability from a European perspective. *Meat Science, 71*(1), 164–173. doi:10.1016/j.meatsci.2005.03.002 PMID:22064062

Storøy, J., Thakur, M., & Olsen, P. (2013). The TraceFood Framework–Principles and guidelines for implementing traceability in food value chains. *Journal of Food Engineering, 115*(1), 41–48. doi:10.1016/j.jfoodeng.2012.09.018

Storøy, J., Thakur, M., & Olsen, P. (2013). The TraceFood Framework–Principles and guidelines for implementing traceability in food value chains. *Journal of Food Engineering, 115*(1), 41–48. doi:10.1016/j.jfoodeng.2012.09.018

Tian, F. (2017, June). A supply chain traceability system for food safety based on HACCP, blockchain & Internet of things. In *2017 International conference on service systems and service management* (pp. 1-6). IEEE.

Tiscini, R., Testarmata, S., Ciaburri, M., & Ferrari, E. (2020). The blockchain as a sustainable business model innovation. *Management Decision, 58*(8), 1621–1642. Advance online publication. doi:10.1108/MD-09-2019-1281

Treiblmaier, H. (2018). The impact of the blockchain on the supply chain: A theory-based research framework and a call for action. *Supply Chain Management, 23*(6), 545–559. doi:10.1108/SCM-01-2018-0029

Tsang, Y. P., Choy, K. L., Wu, C. H., Ho, G. T., Lam, C. H., & Koo, P. S. (2018). An Internet of Things (IoT)-based risk monitoring system for managing cold supply chain risks. *Industrial Management & Data Systems, 118*(7), 1432–1462. doi:10.1108/IMDS-09-2017-0384

UNI. (2015). Quality management systems - Fundamentals and vocabulary, Milan. *UNI EN ISO, 9000.*

Wang, F., Cao, R., Ding, W., Qian, H., & Gao, Y. (2011, July). Incentives to enable food traceability and its implication on food traceability system design. In *Proceedings of 2011 IEEE International Conference on Service Operations, Logistics and Informatics* (pp. 32-37). IEEE. 10.1109/SOLI.2011.5986524

Wang, S., Zhang, Y., & Zhang, Y. (2018). A blockchain-based framework for data sharing with fine-grained access control in decentralized storage systems. *IEEE Access : Practical Innovations, Open Solutions, 6,* 38437–38450. doi:10.1109/ACCESS.2018.2851611

Xu, X., Lu, Q., Liu, Y., Zhu, L., Yao, H., & Vasilakos, A. V. (2019). Designing blockchain-based applications a case study for imported product traceability. *Future Generation Computer Systems, 92,* 399–406. doi:10.1016/j.future.2018.10.010

Zhang, J., & Bhatt, T. (2014). A guidance document on the best practices in food traceability. *Comprehensive Reviews in Food Science and Food Safety, 13*(5), 1074–1103. doi:10.1111/1541-4337.12103

Zhao, G., Liu, S., Lopez, C., Lu, H., Elgueta, S., Chen, H., & Boshkoska, B. M. (2019). Blockchain technology in agri-food value chain management: A synthesis of applications, challenges and future research directions. *Computers in Industry, 109,* 83–99. doi:10.1016/j.compind.2019.04.002

Chapter 4

A Milk Blockchain– Enabled Supply Chain:
Evidence From Leading Italian Farms

Marco Francesco Mazzù

(iD) https://orcid.org/0000-0002-8427-9664
Luiss University, Italy

Andrea Benetton
Maccarese S.p.A., Italy & Cirio Agricola, Italy

Angelo Baccelloni
Luiss University, Italy

Ludovico Lavini
Luiss University, Italy

ABSTRACT

Blockchain is proven to support businesses in traceability, data reliability, and data retrieval in all the steps of the supply chain, but still has limited use in the food sector. Through the EU-Horizon 2020-backed example of an Italian regional milk value chain, the chapter describes a real case toward the implementation of such technology in the food sector for the benefit of multiple stakeholders. The case sheds light on the gathering of information concerning the milk production through a network of advanced internet of things sensors, the output of which is employed both for data-driven decision-making and for information certification through blockchain. This trustable and certified information could be shared and employed by other stakeholders to get informed about the status of the production process and, in turn, to potentially deliver an enlarged set of details about the product, progressively up to the end consumers, with implications of technology adoption for food tech-firms and on related impacts on a circular economy.

DOI: 10.4018/978-1-7998-8014-1.ch004

INTRODUCTION

In recent years, supply chain processes have been the recipient of constant innovations (Wong et al., 2013), especially in the aspects of technology and traceability. Traceability, in particular, is a hot topic when talking about food, together with transparency and sustainability in the area of farming. Consumers are more and more interested (Olsen et al., 2018) in knowing where the food they are eating comes from, how it was produced, and what were the ethical principles behind the production chain. Governments and supranational organizations, such as the EU, are also promoting global efforts in that direction, with the aim of increasing food safety and protecting food quality (Badia-Melis et al., 2015). This important information presents a matter of reliability, when considering how consumers, suppliers, and legislators might trust that the details they are reading are correct. This is a relevant topic also when dealing with one of the most recent and discussed topics derived from the "Farm to Fork" strategy, connected to the labelling system of food products (Mazzù et al., 2021a).

Although omnichannel marketing implies the nature and typology of communication channels through which brands interact with customers (Ailawadi et al., 2017), several firms are still struggling with a plethora of issues related to communicating their transparency (Abeyratne et al., 2016). Specifically, a major challenge for firms has been to make their value chain more unambiguous and consistently deliver their brand promise to their external stakeholders (Boukis et al., 2020).

Blockchain technology could be one of the possible solutions to this issue (Galvez et al., 2018). Through it, detailed information about products, sources of materials, and production processes, at every step of the manufacturing and supply chains, can be stored and then made available (Feng et al., 2020). Effects of the intrinsic features of this technology, such as immutability and transparency, can thus be transferred to the data and, thus, to the product (Galvez et al., 2018).

In order to better understand these concepts in a real-world scenario, this chapter analyzes the case of an Italian dairy supply chain. In the scope of the Horizon 2020 European framework, as part of an effort to both increase transparency over the quality of products, and to increase the data-driven approach to decisions in farming. Maccarese S.pA., Ariete Fattoria Latte Sano S.p.A., Engineering Ingegneria Informatica S.p.A., and Ro Technology S.r.L. have deployed a blockchain-based project for the traceability of the entire milk production process and distribution chain. Metrics related to cows such as health state, certifications, medicines, or antibiotics, are progressively tracked through an immutable set of information stored in a dedicated system. Consumers and other actors along the supply chain could leverage this technology to obtain information about the product, all with a de-facto certification that the product that they have in their hands is authentic, healthy, and safe.

The final part is dedicated to exploring potential implications and further streams of research.

BACKGROUND

Authenticity and trust are of paramount importance in the food sector (Bryła, 2015; EU Science Hub, 2021; Reid et al., 2006). Being able to offer something of high quality is relevant, but it is even more relevant to be able to certify this quality, in order to drive the interest of the customer (Grunert, 2005; Verdú Jover et al., 2004). This must be related not only to the customer that finds the product on the shelf, but also when dealing with all the steps of the supply chain, downstream and upstream (Ali et al., 2017a; Ali et al., 2017b; Aung et al., 2014).

Present-day supply chains are faced with many issues related to information reliability: consumer trust, supply chain transparency, product quality, logistic issues, environmental impact, personal consumer data, fraud, food safety, etc. (Ge et al., 2016; Trienekens et al., 2012). These issues go hand in hand with the innovations that are taking place in the sector. Supply chains are increasingly interconnected: Suppliers are tightly related to one another and to customers, internally and externally (Wong et al., 2013), and technology is becoming more and more present (Ayoub et al., 2017). Food supply chains, in particular, are increasingly adopting traceability features that put a spotlight on every detail (Bosona et al., 2013; Francisco et al., 2018), also mirroring the goal of many governmental programs such as the recent "Farm to Fork", with a specific interest on sustainability (Grunert, 2011).

Through the adoption of blockchain technology, consumers can eventually gain better access to more detailed information about products and services (Francisco et al., 2018; Kshetri, 2018), and on the underlying supply chain. Specifically, thanks to blockchain networks, users can gain deep visibility into all the activities, production, and/or service delivery processes that create the product, together with a certification that this information is reliable. As blockchain as a storage system resides on various interconnected devices that retain independence, and keep only a specific intertwined part of the data (Li et al., 2020), no single party in the supply chain can alter existing information (Pun et al., 2018), a situation particularly relevant both to combat counterfeiting and to track with 100% accuracy the life cycle of a product (Zhang et al., 2020). Blockchain can also be used throughout the supply chain to store and share trustable data with other parties, e.g., suppliers, customers, etc. (Bumblauskas et al., 2020).

The continuous, certified sharing of information can be helpful in increasing companies' accountability and transparency (Hwang et al., 2017), as it can help provide information regarding the route of a product from raw materials to manufacturer to distributor to retailer, and finally, to the consumer (Apte et al., 2016; Montecchi et al., 2019). Transparency also reflects on interactions with brands, enabling firms to build consumer trust in the long term (Bengtsson et al., 2010), but also to improve cooperation between all the actors of the supply chain (Aste et al., 2017).

Additional advantages relate to better information sharing, reductions of disputes among business partners and of asymmetries (Lucena et al., 2018), and fraud prevention (Ahmed et al., 2017). In the food sector, blockchain technology could also be used to supplement food traceability in new and existing supply chains. Currently, by contrast, either there is very limited traceability, or there are many siloed solutions, meaning traceability only exists internally for specific stakeholders within the supply chain (De Giovanni, 2021; Bumblauskas et al., 2020).

With regard to this aspect, a relevant factor is that of food information standardization. While offline standards exist, such as the Food Safety Modernization Act (FSMA) (FDA, 2011) in the U.S. and the General Food Law in the EU (European Commission, 2002), they are limited to their respective countries of origin. Moreover, they do not have interoperability in mind, and there is no standardized element that allows for a centralized, holistic, access to the archived data. (Dey et al., 2021). The centralization of existing information systems also creates trust problems, as it is easy by involved actors to tamper with the data.

As mentioned, in the food sector firms can use blockchain-based solutions to monitor their whole production process (Francisco et al., 2018). For example, Carrefour uses blockchain technology to trace the production of free-range chicken. Through the scanning of a special code on the package, consumers can obtain all the information about the chickens independent of the channel that consumers use to finalize their purchases. Barilla, working alongside IBM, is testing blockchain to monitor every step of basil production to guarantee the quality of the "Made in Italy" label (Prandelli et al., 2020). This information will be available to all consumers in all channels in which Barilla's products are present. Another partnership exists between IBM and the Rio Mare brand of the Bolton Food group: Consumers can access information about the entirety of the production process of the cans of tuna in their hand, with elements such as fishing method, the FAO area of origin, and the names of the ship and the production plant (Costa, 2020).

Ease of access to the information stored in the blockchain is also relevant. In the case of end-customers, there are two main ways to grant simple access to the information stored: QR codes, and a link text (Dey et al., 2021; Mishra et al., 2020). A common way to communicate the availability of these elements to the end customer is by placing a QR code on the packaging of the product that, once scanned with a mobile device, opens up a website that allows exploration and retracing of the details stored on it (Bumblauskas et al., 2020; Kennedy et al., 2017). QR codes are traditionally perceived as more effective and easier to use. They can be applied to almost any object at minimal cost (Seino et al., 2004). The other alternative is a simple link placed on the packaging that redirects to a website in which the customer enters a unique ID related to the product, e.g., serial number or lot ID, and can subsequently retrieve the information.

Aside from the traceability aspects, it is also important to evaluate the reasons why adding certified, trustable information about animal welfare and food safety can be beneficial to more sales oriented aspects such as Willingness-to-Buy and Willingness-to-Pay, especially in the space of dairy products (Dickinson et al., 2002), or to increase consumers' flavor and health perceptions (Mazzù et al., 2021b). These elements can set the foundations for a competitive advantage (Kafetzopoulos et al., 2013; Nancarrow et al., 1998). Prior research has demonstrated that customers place a high value on ethical practices during the production of egg, meat, and dairy products, with a specific focus on animal welfare (Spain et al., 2018). The recording of the processes and products that constitute the entire supply chain enables customers to purchase from ethical sources (Saberi et al., 2019).

However, when exposed to technological concepts perceived as distant, consumers might be skeptical about the technology (Davis, 1989) and thus transfer this skepticism and mistrust to the product itself. One of the ideal outputs derived from an investment in implementing a blockchain system in food is thus to reinforce the food quality perception and the trust in both the brand's information and in the product. Highlighting and showcasing in a trustable and certified way elements that contribute to the perception of quality, such as ethical farming and agricultural practices, should improve the perception of the company in the eye of consumers, and thus contribute to value generation (Choe et al., 2009).

MAIN FOCUS OF THE CHAPTER

Data-driven farming is defined as the use of data to augment decision-making in farming systems, and thus improve food system outcomes such as crop yields, profits, environmental sustainability, and food security.

As farming is getting more and more data-driven (Mehrabi et al., 2021), this chapter studies the approach implemented by leading Italian companies in the fields of dairy farming and transformation, to progressively introduce advanced technologies to assess multiple parameters, ranging from animal life signs to derive health, to satellite maps and drone imaging to drive cultivations and cropping. All these parameters are combined in order to provide end consumers (B2C) with information about the product, and to allow business partners (B2B) to improve and optimize production.

The Case of the DEMETER Project Applied to a Regional Milk Value Chain

DEMETER: The Horizon 2020 Project

DEMETER[1] belongs to the *"Industrial Leadership"* pillar of the EU Horizon 2020[2] research project, and focuses on the incorporation of existing technologies in their infant stage into new applications related to the food sector, by also promoting the development of public-private partnerships. It operates on 20 pilot projects located in several European countries, and involves 60 different partners, from farmers and transformation companies to technical and technological players. It embraces 25 distribution sites, 6,000 farmers, and deploys more than 38,000 devices and sensors.

At the base of the project stands the Multi-Actor Approach, a pattern that makes the projects revolve on real problems or opportunities as shared by farmers or service advisors, resulting in a continuous feedback loop of knowledge-sharing and development activity, from scientists and developers to end users. Moreover, end users are de facto co-owners of the project, thus promoting active usage of the solutions developed (European Commission, 2020).

The initiative guides the digital transformation of the European agricultural sector through the rapid adoption of advanced technologies such as IoT, Big Data, and precision agriculture. It guarantees long-term sustainability by promoting interoperability between software systems with the implementation of a common data model, which can help different players share their data in a common format. It also promotes the adoption of enabling technologies, such as Agri-hubs, Artificial Intelligence (AI), and enablers for the security of information and service discovery.

Participating companies can take advantage of technologies such as benchmarking and visualization dashboards in the form of Decision Support Systems, which operate on all the gathered data to help decision processes.

Pilot Project

The case analyzed in this chapter belongs to Pilot 4.2, a project titled "Milk Quality and Animal Welfare Tracking," focused on the development and implementation of a regional food value chain backed by blockchain technology, and built on three main assumptions:

- Milk quality is closely linked to animal welfare; adequate eating and resting of animals is positively correlated with high milk production and quality. Thus, improvements in these factors will lead to increased dairy yields.
- Processing companies have an interest in knowing milk quality levels; the variable premium paid to farmers is based on legally defined quality indicators of milk that revolve around hygiene and welfare of livestock. These factors and the related premiums encourage and push farmers to control and improve the quality of their milk.
- Consumers are interested in knowing about the food they eat, and on the level of transparency granted by the firms that produce it.

The objective is thus to optimize the flow of information among those that are part of the milk value chain, with a focus on animal health and milk quality, and to make all this information transparent and available to the end consumer. Specifically, the information flow optimization focuses on:

- Breeding and milking with a focus on animal welfare and improvement of farm activities.
- Transportation of milk, with a focus on product safety.
- Processing, with a focus on the quality of the final product.
- Labelling, with a focus on information to consumers.

The pilot involves several players, organized in two macro-areas—"Production Operators" and "Technology Providers"—with Coldiretti, the largest agricultural organization in Italy and across Europe, acting as a coordinator.

One of the project's "Production Operators," i.e., the end-user companies that provide the requirements, advise on the development of the technological solution, and that will benefit from the advantages that stem from the implementation of the technological solutions, is Maccarese S.p.A., one of the largest Italian dairy farms, with 1,450 Friesian dairy cows, 600 fattening calves, and 3,240 hectares of land (DEMETER Project, 2021), located in Maccarese (Rome), as the producer of milk. Also included is Ariete Fattoria Latte Sano S.p.A., a milk processing company, located in Rome, the leader within Lazio Region with a daily collection of 200 tons of milk, that distributes milk and dairy products to large retailers and the Ho.Re.Ca. channel.

"Technology providers" comprises two engineering and software development companies that, in accordance with the farming partners, have to implement the backbone of supporting technological solutions. Specifically, Engineering Ingegneria Informatica S.p.A., the first information technology (IT) group in Italy and among the top 10 IT groups in Europe, and Ro Technology S.r.l., a company which designs, develops, and validates applications, tools, firmware, and hardware components for several markets. The final stakeholders in the project are consumers, who, thanks to the availability of information about the quality and history of the dairy products in front of them, in the future will be able to make more informed choices.

Data Gathering

Data about every single step of the value chain processes is then organized in dashboards that can trace milk quality and provide insights to support decision-making. Information is stored on the blockchain, to ensure transparency, certainty, and trust, and is easily reusable and shareable with other players of the agri-food world, to improve their processes and performances as well.

Two kinds of data sources are used: animal welfare-related (collected through sensors which measure the animal's rest, rumination, eating habits, etc.) and milk quality-related (analysis of samples obtained during collection, transportation, and storage). Hardware-wise, the farm has a comprehensive network of legacy sensors that are usually not connected to any network. This sensor network has been augmented by the purchase of smart, connected modern IoT devices that allow for precise and unified health tracking.

Cow health is constantly evaluated through two metabolic sensor devices that are worn by the animal. The first one, AfiCollar, is a cow neck collar that uses motion sensors to monitor rumination and other health parameters. The second one, AfiActII, is a pedometer applied to the cow's leg that monitors locomotor activity and rest behavior. In parallel, temperature control sensors applied to the animal's vagina are employed to monitor the temperature of the animal and to potentially regulate the refrigeration of the animal's living environment. Data is transferred wirelessly to a central system, and can be used to derive animal health through scientific models devised by Maccarese S.p.A.

Crop quality is driven through a combination of satellite and thermal high-precision maps, GPS-guided croppers and harvesters, and advanced soil analyses. In fact, a healthy cow, that eats well, produces better milk.

Milk quality is assessed in two steps: directly at the milking stage, and when the milk is received by the processor. At the milking stage, animals are identified through their unique ID directly by the automatic milking machine, and parameters such as volume and temperature are stored. Moreover, information on electrical conductivity is gathered, as this parameter is correlated with the incidence of mastitis.

Subsequently, the milk passes through AfiLab, a milk analysis laboratory, that by employing NIRS techniques can determine the composition in terms of fat, proteins, lactose, and bacterial load. Instead of using samples as a proxy for the quality of the whole quantity milked, every deciliter of milk that comes through the network is analyzed and evaluated to assess bovine health and milk quality, and to optimize bovine nutrition on the fly (TDM Website, 2021). Through the employment of the Afilab software console, a granular control on milk quality and animal health can be obtained, as farmers can pinpoint data tracing back to a particular animal.

Milk is then transferred from Maccarese S.p.A. to Ariete Fattoria Latte Sano S.p.A. by a special tank truck with insulated walls, thus passively guaranteeing a 4°C temperature for the entirety of the 20-minute transfer time. At the processor stage, a device called Milkbox MKII is employed in the transfer phase from milk truck to reservoir, in order to collect a weighted-average sample of the milk that passes through it (ACRAM, 2021; Milkbox Website, 2021). In addition to certifying that a certain quantity of milk has been transferred between the two parts, elements such as temperature, acidity, and timestamps are recorded. Once all the milk has been moved to Ariete Fattoria Latte Sano S.p.A.'s reservoirs, further laboratory analyses are performed by Milkoscan FT1-NIR on representative samples (see Figure 1).

Figure 1. Data processing
Source: Own Elaboration

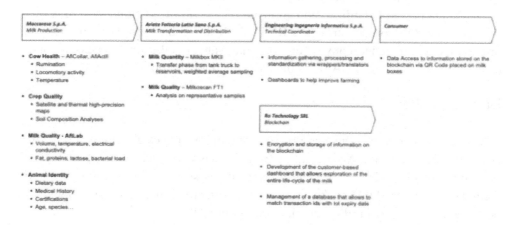

Data Storage

Data points from different providers, machines, and devices are offered in different formats and stored in different locations. Many are closed legacy or proprietary systems, offering data in static formats such as CSV and XLS and that require manual intervention in order to be shared.

One of the core principles of DEMETER's architecture is the mandate to transform and unify this data, as it promotes the development of a shared Agricultural Information Model (AIM).

A custom wrapper/translator has been thus developed by Engineering Ingegneria Informatica S.p.A. in order to transfer and merge the different data points that originate from Maccarese S.p.A. and Ariete Fattoria Latte Sano S.p.A. into a single data model based on the overarching AIM.

The data gathering, transformation, and processing cloud infrastructure is based on the Software-as-a-Service (SaaS) paradigm and implements a micro-services architecture deployed on Docker containers[3]. The data that is processed by the system follows a data-in-motion paradigm, as opposed to data-at-rest, and is thus assessed and transformed in real time.

The underlying data model is based on the JSON-LD. JSON-LD is a lightweight syntax to serialize linked data in JSON (JavaScript Object Notation) [RFC7159]. Its design allows existing JSON to be interpreted as Linked Data with minimal changes. JSON-LD is primarily intended to be a way to use Linked Data in web-based programming environments, to build interoperable web services, and to store Linked Data in JSON-based storage engines (Kellogg et al., 2019). The main advantage is that every data point can be linked to an existing ontology that can be used by different actors to easily interpret the data.

This data now standardized and archived on a centralized cloud system is then fungible in JSON format through a REST API[4]. In addition to that, other farms, processors, and in general any other actor that wants to take advantage of the data produced, can leverage the AIM to interpret the data and build on it.

Data Utilization

Cow health data outputs, once combined, are employed to establish a baseline of a cow's standard behavior. Any deviation from this baseline, such as a sudden increase in activity, can signal status changes such as the onset of a cow's heat to improve fecundation results (TDM Website, 2021). Other factors, such as resting times, can be factored into the overall production quality of milk.

A Decision Support System (DSS) has been developed to integrate all the data, and can help with elements such as decision making, data analysis, acquisition, storage, aggregation and transformation. After these manipulations, everything is displayed on a single dashboard that, in addition to raw and overall parameters, provides algorithmic, literature-driven evaluations on elements such as milking and nutritional value and pathologies (lameness risk, mastitis, ketosis, etc.).

One of the activities under ongoing development is the training of an AI machine learning model that will be able to predict overall milk quality by analyzing some reference parameters.

Moreover, by promoting the adoption of a shared data interoperability model, information on the entire production, transformation, and transportation can be easily shared with other actors in the value chain.

Dashboards and DSSs are developed by Engineering Ingegneria Informatica S.p.A. and based on KNOWAGE, a flexible, professionally developed, self-service and user-oriented Open Source Business Analytics Suite (Knowage, 2021) (see Figure 2).

Figure 2. KNOWAGE decision support system dashboard
Source: Engineering Ingegneria Informatica S.p.A.

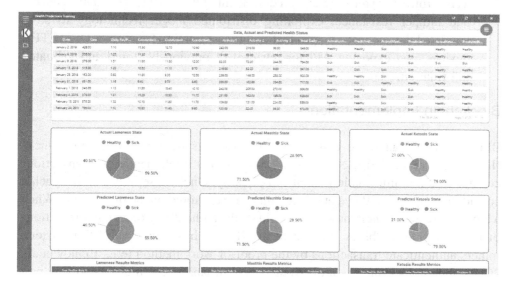

Both farmers and producers could thus leverage these systems:

- **Animal Welfare Decision Support System (DSS):** This DSS aims to provide the breeder with important indicators mainly with respect to animal welfare (i.e., prediction of pathologies) having as input all the data collected in the farm through specific devices. The DSS will have as output a pie chart showing a prediction of the percentage of sick and healthy cows for each pathology, in order to provide integrated insight on animal welfare and suggest corrective actions to the breeding farmer.
- **Estimate Milk Quality Dashboard:** The data points gathered through all the sensors are combined in order to provide farmers with a prediction of the quality of the milk produced.

- **Milk Quality Prediction Dashboard:** Offers a milk quality assessment to the processing company, taking into consideration the analysis of the milk collected from the different farmers and the analysis of the total milk collected in order to highlight tampering or anomalies during transport.
- **Benchmarking System:** Both the farmer and the producer are provided with a short report showing a comparison of a set of the farm's performance indicators (such as milk yield by cow, milk total yield, milk quality, cow health, nutrition, and company productivity) with a set of target values (i.e., average and optimal indicator values from similar/neighboring companies).
- **Traceability System:** Tackles requirements for data integrity, data security, and tamper resistance, exploiting distributed ledger technology to store validated data concerning production process coming from other DEMETER devices, and exposing API for retrieval of previously stored and validated information.

Blockchain Implementation

Blockchain leverages the concepts of transactions between nodes and blocks (Karafiloski et al., 2017; Nakamoto, 2008). In this implementation, transactions contain data and information about milk quality. Once these transactions reach a considerable quantity, they get merged into a block stored on the blockchain. When a block is created, *miners* proceed to validate the authenticity of all the transactions that exist inside the block. Similar to the Bitcoin blockchain validation system, miners authenticate transactions by the proof-of-work method (e.g., Efanov et al., 2018). Since blockchain is a distributed system, and every miner "owns" a part of the chain, information present on it is immutable and cannot be modified, thus ensuring that milk quality data is certain (Ayoade et al., 2018; Huang et al., 2018; Zhaofeng et al., 2020).

All the previously listed timestamped data gathered by hardware sensors during milk production and transformation is processed by a cloud system and transformed into a standardized JSON-LD based data model. It is then processed by a middleware called a *"transaction manager"* that sits between the cloud storage designed by Engineering Ingegneria Informatica S.p.A. and the blockchain nodes owned and managed by Ro Technology S.rR.l., and stored on the actual chain, which for this project is an Ethereum Testnet called Rinkeby.

A blockchain, such as Ethereum, can be divided in mainnets and testnets. A mainnet is the public, production blockchain, the kind usually known by the general public (Ethereum Documentation, 2021), where actual-value transactions occur on the distributed ledger. Transactions on these networks usually have a financial value attached to them. A testnet is instead a test blockchain that can be used by developers to test smart contracts in a production-like environment before deployment to the mainnet. With this aim, the Rinkeby Test Network, created in 2017, provides ether, the cryptocurrency part of the Ethereum protocol, to test applications, as well as in-depth statistics that can be used to track the amount of time a transaction takes to execute (Ranganthan et al., 2018). It is a proof-of-authority network running a specific consensus protocol. A proof-of-authority network relies on trusted nodes designated as "signers" that have the ability to create blocks. A majority of signers on the network are required to validate the chain (Wuehler, 2018).

An overview of the entire project is provided in Figure 3.

Figure 3. Project process overview
Source: Ro Technology S.R.L.

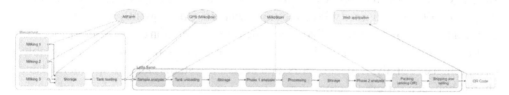

All the information gathered via the sensor network available at Maccarese S.p.A., in the farm, and through the certification of milk transport and transformation phases at Ariete Fattoria Latte Sano S.p.A., could be made available in its entirety to all the supply chain stakeholders. As it is stored on the blockchain, it can be accessed by all the actors in a certified form; they can read it and also add elements pertaining to their respective transformation process.

The B2B traceability aspect is relevant, as downstream suppliers can have certainty about the quality of the product they purchase and transform, and thus make evaluations and informed business decisions.

Aside from being available to the actual "operators" of the blockchain, the details about the products could be shared with the end customers.

A way to make the information stored on the blockchain available in a clean, simple, and easy-to-read format is through a web app, for example, reachable by visiting a specific URL, with a webpage allowing end users to retrieve specific information about their specific milk carton.

Alternatively, a QR code applied on the packaging, once scanned with a mobile phone, could redirect to the aforementioned webpage.

End customers might significantly benefit from all the product information tracked, validated, and made available from the blockchain; elements such as ingredients, animal well-being, nutrition facts, and additives can be related to healthiness, and customers evaluate overall food quality based on this information (Petrescu et al., 2019). Food quality, and its perception, is in fact often seen as a proxy for healthiness and well-being (Mascarello et al., 2015; Sadilek, 2019). In particular, it has been shown that customers show a relatively higher Willingness-to-Pay for elements such as animal welfare and organic production methods (Baltzer, 2004). Organic foods are perceived to be higher quality than traditional food (Loebnitz et al., 2016; Naspetti et al., 2009), and this Willingness-to-Pay concretizes when customers trust the information they receive about quality (Velčovská et al., 2015). More broadly, positive ethical attributes and quality generate a positive effect on customer Willingness-to-Pay (Auger et al., 2008; Homburg et al., 2005; Van Doorn et al., 2011).

Furthermore, the adoption of blockchain could lead to a standardization of the storage of food information in a unique format, thus leading to a convergence of the outputs of different sources within the supplycchain. Consequently, different players could also be incentivized to collaborate and share information to streamline processes and to improve outputs and, since the entire history of the product is available, comprehensive analysis, dashboards, and decision systems can be implemented and shared between different actors.

SOLUTIONS AND RECOMMENDATIONS

The blockchain project implemented by Maccarese S.p.A. and its partners in the supply chain presents clear opportunities for future technological advancements and new research streams.

Additional supporting tools and methods might be introduced to minimize potential issues that stem from the quality of input data. The implementation of automated systems, consensus protocols, and hardened boxes that can not physically be tampered with, which gather and transform the data deriving from the sensors to an incontrovertible, certain input for the blockchain could increase the transparency of the firms and decrease the possibility of unproper usages (Dedeoglu et al., 2019). In fact, the data uploading process implies that the information created by the sensors becomes certified only after it is loaded on the blockchain. Thus, this information could be subject to sensor noises or the intervention of malicious actors both inside and outside the firm. Also, once inserted in the blockchain, mistakes or interventions, such as the aforementioned, cannot be corrected. The implementation of an ecosystem based on blockchain technology would then require high investments both in terms of technological infrastructure and of employee training, to counteract the potential uploading of incorrect data. Processes of data control which analyze the inputs before the upload could then become standardized in the sector.

Moreover, further efforts could be nurtured by institutions to make consumers, supply-chain stakeholders, and consortiums more aware of the blockchain's benefits, to enhance adoption and to make the technology more widespread and familiar. This could generate additional positive effects, countering common objections having to do with the technology's reliability and transparency (Biswas et al., 2017; Kshetri, 2018; Lu et al., 2017), while increasing consumers' trust of blockchain-backed processes. In turn, higher trustworthiness could lower the related barriers encountered by consumers during the decision-making process.

Furthermore, the blockchain technology has relevant implications for adopters as regards to circular economy. Indeed, tracking the product from the early stage to the end customers also allows monitoring of the expired or unusable quantities of milk in each phase of the supply chain, aiding recycling. For example, it could become digestate utilized as a field fertilizer, or biogas employed for electricity production through a bio transformer, such as the one available at Maccarese S.p.A. Thus, the higher the quantity of information available on the product, the higher the likelihood of recovering nonmarketable products and using them to nurture the production process. This could have additional environmental benefits.

Finally, the high costs associated with the connection of multiple actors could be addressed by exploiting the growing funding opportunities made available by the EU (e.g., Horizon 2021–2027). In addition, the initial variable costs should lead to an increase of visibility, transparency, and security (De Giovanni, 2020).

Table 1. Pros and cons of Maccarese S.p.A.'s adoption of blockchain

Pros	Cons
• Enhanced traceability • Supply-chain information availability both for end customers and supply-chain actors • Food information standardization • Collaboration of all the supply-chain actors • Supply-chain information certification • Data visualization and fast interpretation through dashboard systems • Value driver—differentiating element	• Data uploading—The information created by the sensors becomes certified only after being uploaded on the blockchain by an operator • Potential lack of trust by technology-averse stakeholders • Incorrect data is not modifiable once uploaded on the blockchain • High costs associated to the connection of several supply-chain actors

FUTURE RESEARCH DIRECTIONS

Indeed, while blockchain technology can effectively support firms and supply chain processes and information, little is known from a theoretical perspective about the effects on consumer behavior deriving from its adoption. Unmet research questions on this topic are the object of many analyses which have highlighted a lack of trust toward the technology (Dierksmeier et al., 2020; Kouhizadeh et al., 2018; Saberi et al., 2019; Venkatesh et al., 2020). Regarding transparency, some authors (Biswas et al., 2017; Kshetri, 2018; Lu et al., 2017) have discussed the relevance of trust toward blockchain domains and highlighted that consumers tend to be averse toward the technology; as a consequence, they mistrust the information provided. Since transparency is one of the main advantages of implementing the technology, future studies could investigate the proper methods to present the technology and the information it produces, considering the nature of the platform as a way to shed light on the supply chains and the firms.

Also, future research could assess whether food products cued with blockchain information positively alter either their adoption, or the perceived healthiness and tastiness according to the type of information provided on the sources of the end product, as well as the impact on Willingness-to-Buy, Willingness-to-Pay, and Word-of-Mouth intention. Consumers' positive attitudes toward transparent, trustworthy, and socially responsible firms result in a higher intention to engage in positive word of mouth (Maxham et al., 2003). Companies involved in positive practices are also more likely to receive word of mouth from consumers (Handelman et al., 1999). Assuming blockchain as a technology is able to certify and validate supply chain information, consumers will be able to get more reliable messages (Biswas et al., 2017; Lu et al., 2017).

In addition, as concerns about food safety and sustainability-related issues are increasingly dominating the consumer decision-making process (Tian, 2017), consumers are paying much more attention to the authenticity and legitimacy of the products they purchase (Abeyratne et al., 2016). As a consequence, they increasingly demand to know how, when, and where products are sourced and processed. In this vein, while considering the potential effect of perceived social responsibility on consumer behavior, blockchain could emerge as a technology able to ensure the truthfulness, accountability, and transparency of supply chain-related information (Biswas et al., 2017; Kshetri, 2018; Lu et al., 2017).

Moreover, considering that the described project involves different actors in the supply chain, from the producer to the distributor, a further research avenue might explore the adoption of such a blockchain implementation to define differentiating elements of the value proposition and the impact on brand equity. As technological attributes associated with the product could be perceived as something unique and could increase perceptions of the healthiness of the product, it would also be relevant to understand the impact of the disclosure of all the information related to the product itself on the decision-making processes of consumers.

CONCLUSION

Initiatives promoting the implementation of blockchain technology are of paramount importance in the food sector, in order to increase information transparency and support end customers in making healthier food choices. Several initiatives have already been promoted with the goal of progressively introducing this technology to improve food traceability for the benefit of consumers and economies.

To ensure widespread adoption along food supply chains, these initiatives cannot only focus on technology; education is also required. This has to be directed at consumers, who need to develop more trust in blockchain-backed technological as own supporting systems when deciding what to eat; at firms, to help them make data more accessible and understand the importance of contributing to public health by shedding light on their production processes; and to policymakers to encourage them to make adequate funding available for a fast adoption of the technology.

ACKNOWLEDGMENT

The authors thank Matteo Boggian from Maccarese S.p.A. for being the focal point and a collaborative and knowledgeable counterpart in developing the case study, sharing relevant information about the company, the Horizon project, and acting as a liaison with all other participants in the study. They also deeply thank the team of Engineering S.p.A., represented by Antonio Caruso, in illustrating the DEMETER project and the technologies involved. A further thanks goes to Ro Technology S.R.L. in the persons of Diego Grimani, Lorenzo Bortoloni, and Mattia Modugno, for explaining the technical aspects of the blockchain implementation.

Moreover, they recognize Ariete Fattoria Latte Sano S.p.A. for granting access to data/information employed in the development of the research.

The project described in this work has received funding from the European Union's Horizon 2020 research and innovation program under Grant Agreement No. 958205.

The authors also thank MarkTech S.r.L. for providing funds for this research.

REFERENCES

Abeyratne, S., & Monfared, R. (2016). Blockchain Ready Manufacturing Supply Chain Using Distributed Ledger. *International Journal of Research in Engineering and Technology, 5*.

ACRAM. (2021, April 28). *ACRAM - Lattoprelevatori di campioni al ricevimento*. Retrieved from, from https://acram.it/it/prodotti/trattamento-acque/lattoprelevatori-di-campioni-al-ricevimento/

Ahmed, S., & Broek, N. (2017). Blockchain could boost food security. *Nature*, *550*(7674), 43. doi:10.1038/550043e PMID:28980633

Ailawadi, K. L., & Farris, P. W. (2017). Managing Multi- and Omni-Channel Distribution: Metrics and Research Directions. *Journal of Retailing*, *93*(1), 120–135. doi:10.1016/j.jretai.2016.12.003

Ali, M. H., Tan, K. H., & Ismail, M. D. (2017a). A supply chain integrity framework for halal food. *British Food Journal*, *119*(1), 20–38. doi:10.1108/BFJ-07-2016-0345

Ali, M. H., Zhan, Y., Alam, S. S., Tse, Y. K., & Tan, K. H. (2017b). Food supply chain integrity: The need to go beyond certification. *Industrial Management & Data Systems*, *117*(8), 1589–1611. doi:10.1108/IMDS-09-2016-0357

Apte, S., & Petrovsky, N. (2016). Will blockchain technology revolutionize excipient supply chain management? *Journal of Excipients and Food Chemicals*, *7*(3).

Aste, T., Tasca, P., & Di Matteo, T. (2017). Blockchain Technologies: The Foreseeable Impact on Society and Industry. *Computer*, *50*(9), 18–28. doi:10.1109/MC.2017.3571064

Auger, P., Devinney, T. M., Louviere, J. J., & Burke, P. F. (2008). Do social product features have value to consumers? *International Journal of Research in Marketing*, *25*(3), 183–191. doi:10.1016/j.ijresmar.2008.03.005

Aung, M. M., & Chang, Y. S. (2014). Traceability in a food supply chain: Safety and quality perspectives. *Food Control*, *39*(1), 172–184. doi:10.1016/j.foodcont.2013.11.007

Ayoade, G., Karande, V., Khan, L., & Hamlen, K. (2018). Decentralized IoT data management using blockchain and trusted execution environment. *Proceedings - 2018 IEEE 19th International Conference on Information Reuse and Integration for Data Science, IRI 2018*, 15–22. 10.1109/IRI.2018.00011

Ayoub, H. F., Abdallah, A. B., & Suifan, T. S. (2017). The effect of supply chain integration on technical innovation in Jordan: The mediating role of knowledge management. *Benchmarking*, *24*(3), 594–616. doi:10.1108/BIJ-06-2016-0088

Badia-Melis, R., Mishra, P., & Ruiz-García, L. (2015). Food traceability: New trends and recent advances. A review. *Food Control*, *57*, 393–401. doi:10.1016/j.foodcont.2015.05.005

Baltzer, K. (2004). Consumers' willingness to pay for food quality – The case of eggs. *Food Economics - Acta Agriculturae Scandinavica, Section C, 1*(2), 78–90.

Bengtsson, A., Bardhi, F., & Venkatraman, M. (2010). How global brands travel with consumers: An examination of the relationship between brand consistency and meaning across national boundaries. *International Marketing Review, 27*(5), 519–540. doi:10.1108/02651331011076572

Biswas, K., Muthukkumarasamy, V., & Tan, W. L. (2017). Blockchain based wine supply chain traceability system. *Future Technologies Conference (FTC) 2017,* 56–62. Retrieved from https://acuresearchbank.acu.edu.au/item/86y07/blockchain-based-wine-supply-chain-traceability-system

Bosona, T., & Gebresenbet, G. (2013). Food traceability as an integral part of logistics management in food and agricultural supply chain. *Food Control, 33*(1), 32–48. doi:10.1016/j.foodcont.2013.02.004

Boukis, A., & Christodoulides, G. (2020). Investigating Key Antecedents and Outcomes of Employee-based Brand Equity. *European Management Review, 17*(1), 41–55. doi:10.1111/emre.12327

Bryła, P. (2015). The role of appeals to tradition in origin food marketing. A survey among Polish consumers. *Appetite, 91,* 302–310. doi:10.1016/j.appet.2015.04.056 PMID:25916623

Bumblauskas, D., Mann, A., Dugan, B., & Rittmer, J. (2020). A blockchain use case in food distribution: Do you know where your food has been? *International Journal of Information Management, 52,* 102008. doi:10.1016/j.ijinfomgt.2019.09.004

Choe, Y. C., Park, J., Chung, M., & Moon, J. (2009). Effect of the food traceability system for building trust: Price premium and buying behavior. *Information Systems Frontiers, 11*(2), 167–179. doi:10.100710796-008-9134-z

Costa, C. (2020, October 7). *La carta d'identità del tonno Rio Mare grazie al Cloud e a IBM Services - Agrifood.Tech.* Agrifood.Tech. Retrieved from, https://www.agrifood.tech/food-industry/la-carta-didentita-del-tonno-rio-mare-grazie-al-cloud-e-a-ibm-services

Davis, F. D. (1989). Perceived usefulness, perceived ease of use, and user acceptance of information technology. *Management Information Systems Quarterly, 13*(3), 319–340. doi:10.2307/249008

De Giovanni, P. (2020). Blockchain and smart contracts in supply chain management: A game theoretic model. *International Journal of Production Economics*, *228*, 107855. doi:10.1016/j.ijpe.2020.107855

De Giovanni, P. (2021). Smart Contracts and Blockchain for Supply Chain Quality Management. In *Dynamic Quality Models and Games in Digital Supply Chains* (pp. 91–110). Springer. doi:10.1007/978-3-030-66537-1_5

Dedeoglu, V., Jurdak, R., Putra, G. D., Dorri, A., & Kanhere, S. S. (2019, November). A trust architecture for blockchain in IoT. *Proceedings of the 16th EAI International Conference on Mobile and Ubiquitous Systems: Computing, Networking and Services*, 190-199. 10.1145/3360774.3360822

DEMETER Project. (2021, February). *Interview Series: Antonio Caruso from Engineering Ingegneria Informatica S.p.A. (ENG) – Demeter*. Retrieved from https://h2020-demeter.eu/interview-series-antonio-caruso-from-engineering-ingegneria-informatica-s-p-a-eng/

Dey, S., Saha, S., Singh, A. K., & McDonald-Maier, K. (2021). FoodSQRBlock: Digitizing Food Production and the Supply Chain with Blockchain and QR Code in the Cloud. *Sustainability*, *13*(6), 3486. doi:10.3390u13063486

Dickinson, D. L., & Bailey, D. (2002). Meat traceability: Are US consumers willing to pay for it? *Journal of Agricultural and Resource Economics*, 348–364.

Dierksmeier, C., & Seele, P. (2020). Blockchain and business ethics. *Business Ethics (Oxford, England)*, *29*(2), 348–359. doi:10.1111/beer.12259

Efanov, D., & Roschin, P. (2018). The all-pervasiveness of the blockchain technology. *Procedia Computer Science*, *123*, 116–121. doi:10.1016/j.procs.2018.01.019

Ethereum Documentation. (2021). *Networks*. Ethereum. Retrieved from, https://ethereum.org/en/developers/docs/networks/

EU Science Hub. (2021). *Food authenticity and quality | EU Science Hub*. Retrieved from, https://ec.europa.eu/jrc/en/research-topic/food-authenticity-and-quality#

European Commission. (2002). *General Food Law Principles*. Retrieved from, https://ec.europa.eu/food/safety/general_food_law_en

European Commission. (2020). *Horizon 2020 multi-actor projects*. www.eip-agri.eu

FDA. (2011). *Food Safety Modernization Act (FSMA) | FDA*. Retrieved from, https://www.fda.gov/food/food-safety-modernization-act-fsma/full-text-food-safety-modernization-act-fsma

Feng, H., Wang, X., Duan, Y., Zhang, J., & Zhang, X. (2020). Applying blockchain technology to improve agri-food traceability: A review of development methods, benefits and challenges. *Journal of Cleaner Production, 260,* 121031. doi:10.1016/j.jclepro.2020.121031

Francisco, K., & Swanson, D. (2018). The Supply Chain Has No Clothes: Technology Adoption of Blockchain for Supply Chain Transparency. *Logistics, 2*(1), 2. doi:10.3390/logistics2010002

Galvez, J. F., Mejuto, J. C., & Simal-Gandara, J. (2018). Future challenges on the use of blockchain for food traceability analysis. *Trends in Analytical Chemistry, 107,* 222–232. doi:10.1016/j.trac.2018.08.011

Ge, L., Brewster, C. A., Macdonald, B., Termeer, K., Opdam, P., & Soma, K. (2016). Informational institutions in the agrifood sector: Meta-information and meta-governance of environmental sustainability. *Current Opinion in Environmental Sustainability, 18,* 73–81. doi:10.1016/j.cosust.2015.10.002

Grunert, K. G. (2005). Food quality and safety: Consumer perception and demand. *European Review of Agriculture Economics, 32*(3), 369–391. doi:10.1093/eurrag/jbi011

Grunert, K. G. (2011). Sustainability in the Food Sector A Consumer Behaviour Perspective. *International Journal on Food System Dynamics, 2*(3), 207–218.

Handelman, J. M., & Arnold, S. J. (1999). The Role of Marketing Actions with a Social Dimension: Appeals to the Institutional Environment. *Journal of Marketing, 63*(3), 33–48. doi:10.1177/002224299906300303

Homburg, C., Koschate, N., & Hoyer, W. D. (2005). Do Satisfied Customers Really Pay More? A Study of the Relationship between Customer Satisfaction and Willingness to Pay. *Journal of Marketing, 69*(2), 84–96. doi:10.1509/jmkg.69.2.84.60760

Huang, Z., Su, X., Zhang, Y., Shi, C., Zhang, H., & Xie, L. (2018). A decentralized solution for IoT data trusted exchange based-on blockchain. *2017 3rd IEEE International Conference on Computer and Communications, ICCC 2017,* 1180–1184.

Hwang, J., Choi, M. I., Lee, T., Jeon, S., Kim, S., Park, S., & Park, S. (2017). Energy Prosumer Business Model Using Blockchain System to Ensure Transparency and Safety. *Energy Procedia, 141,* 194–198. doi:10.1016/j.egypro.2017.11.037

IBM. (2021). What is a REST API? *IBM Cloud Education.* Retrieved from https://www.ibm.com/cloud/learn/rest-apis

Kafetzopoulos, D., Gotzamani, K., & Psomas, E. (2013). Quality systems and competitive performance of food companies. *Benchmarking*, *20*(4), 463–483. doi:10.1108/BIJ-08-2011-0065

Karafiloski, E., & Mishev, A. (2017). Blockchain solutions for big data challenges: A literature review. *17th IEEE International Conference on Smart Technologies, EUROCON 2017 - Conference Proceedings*, 763–768. 10.1109/EUROCON.2017.8011213

Kellogg, G., Sporny, M., & Longley, D. (2019). *JSON-LD 1.1*. JSON-LD Documentation. Retrieved from, https://json-ld.org/spec/latest/json-ld/#basic-concepts

Kennedy, Z. C., Stephenson, D. E., Christ, J. F., Pope, T. R., Arey, B. W., Barrett, C. A., & Warner, M. G. (2017). Enhanced anti-counterfeiting measures for additive manufacturing: Coupling lanthanide nanomaterial chemical signatures with blockchain technology. *Journal of Materials Chemistry. C, Materials for Optical and Electronic Devices*, *5*(37), 9570–9578. doi:10.1039/C7TC03348F

Knowage. (2021). *The Open Source Business Analytics - Knowage suite*. Retrieved from, https://www.knowage-suite.com/site/

Kouhizadeh, M., & Sarkis, J. (2018). Blockchain Practices, Potentials, and Perspectives in Greening Supply Chains. *Sustainability*, *10*(10), 3652. doi:10.3390u10103652

Kshetri, N. (2018). 1 Blockchain's roles in meeting key supply chain management objectives. *International Journal of Information Management*, *39*, 80–89. doi:10.1016/j.ijinfomgt.2017.12.005

Li, X., Wang, D., & Li, M. (2020). Convenience analysis of sustainable E-agriculture based on blockchain technology. *Journal of Cleaner Production*, *271*, 122503. doi:10.1016/j.jclepro.2020.122503

Loebnitz, N., & Aschemann-Witzel, J. (2016). Communicating organic food quality in China: Consumer perceptions of organic products and the effect of environmental value priming. *Food Quality and Preference*, *50*, 102–108. doi:10.1016/j.foodqual.2016.02.003

Lu, Q., & Xu, X. (2017). Adaptable Blockchain-Based Systems: A Case Study for Product Traceability. *IEEE Software*, *34*(6), 21–27. doi:10.1109/MS.2017.4121227

Lucena, P., Binotto, A. P., Momo, F. D. S., & Kim, H. (2018). *A case study for grain quality assurance tracking based on a Blockchain business network*. arXiv, 1803.07877.

Mascarello, G., Pinto, A., Parise, N., Crovato, S., & Ravarotto, L. (2015). The perception of food quality. Profiling Italian consumers. *Appetite*, *89*, 175–182. doi:10.1016/j.appet.2015.02.014 PMID:25681654

Maxham, J. G. III, & Netemeyer, R. G. (2003). Firms Reap what they Sow: The Effects of Shared Values and Perceived Organizational Justice on Customers' Evaluations of Complaint Handling. *Journal of Marketing*, *67*(1), 46–62. doi:10.1509/jmkg.67.1.46.18591

Mazzù, M. F., Marozzo, V., Baccelloni, A., & de'Pompeis, F. (2021b). Measuring the Effect of Blockchain Extrinsic Cues on Consumers' Perceived Flavor and Healthiness: A Cross-Country Analysis. *Foods*, *10*(6), 1413. doi:10.3390/foods10061413 PMID:34207107

Mazzù, M. F., Romani, S., Baccelloni, A., & Gambicorti, A. (2021a). A cross-country experimental study on consumers' subjective understanding and liking on front-of-pack nutrition labels. *International Journal of Food Sciences and Nutrition*, 1–15. PMID:33657942

Mehrabi, Z., McDowell, M. J., Ricciardi, V., Levers, C., Martinez, J. D., Mehrabi, N., Wittman, H., Ramankutty, N., & Jarvis, A. (2021). The global divide in data-driven farming. *Nature Sustainability*, *4*(2), 154–160. doi:10.103841893-020-00631-0

Milkbox Website. (2021, April 28). *Lattoprelevatore Milk Box - Lattoprelevatore*. Retrieved from, http://www.lattoprelevatore.it/product/lattoprelevatore/

Mishra, N., Mistry, S., Choudhary, S., Kudu, S., & Mishra, R. (2020). Food Traceability System Using Blockchain and QR Code. In *IC-BCT 2019*. Springer. doi:10.1007/978-981-15-4542-9_4

Montecchi, M., Plangger, K., & Etter, M. (2019). It's real, trust me! Establishing supply chain provenance using blockchain. *Business Horizons*, *62*(3), 283–293. doi:10.1016/j.bushor.2019.01.008

Nakamoto, S. (2008). Bitcoin: A peer-to-peer electronic cash system. *Decentralized Business Review*, 21260.

Nancarrow, C., Tiu Wright, L., & Brace, I. (1998). Gaining competitive advantage from packaging and labelling in marketing communications. *British Food Journal*, *100*(2), 110–118. doi:10.1108/00070709810204101

Naspetti, S., & Zanoli, R. (2009). Organic Food Quality and Safety Perception Throughout Europe. *Journal of Food Products Marketing*, *15*(3), 249–266. doi:10.1080/10454440902908019

Olsen, P., & Borit, M. (2018). The components of a food traceability system. *Trends in Food Science & Technology*, *77*, 143–149. doi:10.1016/j.tifs.2018.05.004

Petrescu, D. C., Vermeir, I., & Petrescu-Mag, R. M. (2019). Consumer Understanding of Food Quality, Healthiness, and Environmental Impact: A Cross-National Perspective. *International Journal of Environmental Research and Public Health*, *17*(1), 169. doi:10.3390/ijerph17010169 PMID:31881711

Prandelli, E., & Verona, G. (2020). *Le cinque regole del business in Rete*. Academic Press.

Pun, H., Swaminathan, J. M., & Hou, P. (2018). Blockchain Adoption for Combating Deceptive Counterfeits. SSRN *Electronic Journal*.

Ranganthan, V. P., Dantu, R., Paul, A., Mears, P., & Morozov, K. (2018). A decentralized marketplace application on the ethereum blockchain. *Proceedings - 4th IEEE International Conference on Collaboration and Internet Computing, CIC 2018*, 90–97. 10.1109/CIC.2018.00023

Reid, L. M., O'Donnell, C. P., & Downey, G. (2006). Recent technological advances for the determination of food authenticity. *Trends in Food Science & Technology*, *17*(7), 344–353. doi:10.1016/j.tifs.2006.01.006

Saberi, S., Kouhizadeh, M., Sarkis, J., & Shen, L. (2019). Blockchain technology and its relationships to sustainable supply chain management. *International Journal of Production Research*, *57*(7), 2117–2135. doi:10.1080/00207543.2018.1533261

Sadilek, T. (2019). Perception of food quality by consumers: Literature review. *European Research Studies Journal*, *22*(1), 57–67. doi:10.35808/ersj/1407

Seino, K., Kuwabara, S., Mikami, S., Takahashi, Y., Yoshikawa, M., Narumi, H., Koganezaki, K., Wakabayashi, T., & Nagano, A. (2004). Development of the traceability system which secures the safety of fishery products using the QR code and a digital signature. *Ocean '04 - MTS/IEEE Techno-Ocean '04: Bridges across the Oceans - Conference Proceedings*, *1*, 476–481.

Spain, C., Freund, D., Mohan-Gibbons, H., Meadow, R., & Beacham, L. (2018). Are They Buying It? United States Consumers' Changing Attitudes toward More Humanely Raised Meat, Eggs, and Dairy. *Animals (Basel)*, *8*(8), 128. doi:10.3390/ani8080128 PMID:30044402

TDM Website. (2021a, April 28). *Afiact® | TDM | Total Dairy Management*. Retrieved from https://www.tdm.it/en/project/afiact/

TDM Website. (2021b, April 28). *Afilab® | TDM | Total Dairy Management.* Retrieved from https://www.tdm.it/project/afilab/

Trienekens, J. H., Wognum, P. M., Beulens, A. J. M., & Van Der Vorst, J. G. A. J. (2012). Transparency in complex dynamic food supply chains. *Advanced Engineering Informatics, 26*(1), 55–65. doi:10.1016/j.aei.2011.07.007

Van Doorn, J., & Verhoef, P. C. (2011). Willingness to pay for organic products: Differences between virtue and vice foods. *International Journal of Research in Marketing, 28*(3), 167–180. doi:10.1016/j.ijresmar.2011.02.005

Velčovská, Š., & Del Chiappa, G. (2015). The food quality labels: Awareness and willingness to pay in the context of the Czech Republic. *Acta Universitatis Agriculturae et Silviculturae Mendelianae Brunensis, 63*(2), 647–658. doi:10.11118/actaun201563020647

Venkatesh, V. G., Kang, K., Wang, B., Zhong, R. Y., & Zhang, A. (2020). System architecture for blockchain based transparency of supply chain social sustainability. *Robotics and Computer-integrated Manufacturing, 63,* 101896. doi:10.1016/j.rcim.2019.101896

Verdú Jover, A. J., Lloréns Montes, F. J., & Fuentes Fuentes, M. (2004). Measuring perceptions of quality in food products: The case of red wine. *Food Quality and Preference, 15*(5), 453–469. doi:10.1016/j.foodqual.2003.08.002

Wong, C. W. Y., Wong, C. Y., & Boon-Itt, S. (2013). The combined effects of internal and external supply chain integration on product innovation. *International Journal of Production Economics, 146*(2), 566–574. doi:10.1016/j.ijpe.2013.08.004

Wuehler, M. (2018, September 6). *Rinkeby consensus post-mortem.* Infura Blog. Retrieved from https://blog.infura.io/rinkeby-consensus-post-mortem-4abbcace0539/

Zhang, A., Zhong, R. Y., Farooque, M., Kang, K., & Venkatesh, V. G. (2020). Blockchain-based life cycle assessment: An implementation framework and system architecture. *Resources, Conservation and Recycling, 152,* 104512. doi:10.1016/j.resconrec.2019.104512

Zhaofeng, M., Xiaochang, W., Jain, D. K., Khan, H., Hongmin, G., & Zhen, W. (2020). A Blockchain-Based Trusted Data Management Scheme in Edge Computing. *IEEE Transactions on Industrial Informatics, 16*(3), 2013–2021. doi:10.1109/TII.2019.2933482

ENDNOTES

[1]   Named after Demeter, the Greek goddess of the harvest who presides over grains and fertility of the earth.

[2]   Horizon 2020 is an EU-backed research and innovation project that involves almost €80 billion of funding from 2014 to 2020, with a mix of private and public investments. The main goal of this EU Framework Program is to redefine cooperation in funding and scientific research of the EU countries. It is part of the Innovation Union, a project aiming to increase the mutual effort towards competitiveness of the continent.

[3]   A Docker container is a standard unit of software that packages up code and all its dependencies so the application runs quickly and reliably from one computing environment to another.

[4]   An API (Application Programming Interface) is a set of rules that deterdetermine the way applications or devices interact and communicate with each other. A REST API is an API that operates based on the REST design principles, or Representational State Transfer (Uniform interface, Client-server decoupling, Statelessness, Cacheability, Layered System Architecture, Code on Demand) (IBM, 2021).

Chapter 5

Application of Blockchain in the Saffron Industry:
The Case of Arte Zafferano

Riccardo Zugaro
Luiss University, Italy

Pietro De Giovanni
https://orcid.org/0000-0002-1247-4807
Luiss University, Italy

ABSTRACT

In the era of tech-driven globalization, supply chains are becoming increasingly complex, with an increasing number of stakeholders spread across continents. A complex supply chain requires complex management systems. Supply chain management digitalization and information technology have advanced simultaneously in time, but a more technological and connected society calls for more information, uncovering the limits of supply chain management tools available today, which, while providing efficiency, automation, and organizational capabilities, are quite scarce in providing transparency. Consumer awareness on sensible issues such as climate change, human rights, or counterfeiting is increasing.

INTRODUCTION

In the era of tech-driven globalization, supply chains are becoming increasingly complex, with an increasing number of stakeholders spread across continents (Abeyratne et al., 2016). A worldwide supply chain requires complex management

DOI: 10.4018/978-1-7998-8014-1.ch005

systems, which call for more information to guarantee transparency (Abeyratne et al., 2016). Consumers' awareness of sensible issues such as climate change, human rights, and counterfeiting is increasing. Despite the transparency expected by end-users, companies themselves have very limited visibility on supply chains (Deloitte, 2018). Modern Enterprise Resource Planning (ERP) tools are falling short of current supply chain management requirements and are based on both the quality and the quantity of available information (Li et al., 2006). Information on inputs and processes is very unreliable due to the centralization of data storage, which can be easily accessed and perturbed, leaving space for fraud and falsification; all these issues contribute to lower quality outputs and generally lower customer satisfaction (De Giovanni, 2020a; Eskildsen et al., 2007).

One important solution emerging nowadays for solving these issues is blockchain. The blockchain is a ledger technology that is distributed, decentralized, and public. Because the information blocks are concatenated in a chronological manner, any attempt to change the data stored would require the recalculation of all precedent blocks (Gurtu et al., 2019). Furthermore, with the way the data are distributed, any tampering attempt must be carried out on all network's machines making the data stored on the blockchain practically immutable (De Giovanni, 2020b). This technology is not new since it has been available since 1991. Nevertheless, the focus has primarily hovered around cryptocurrencies and financial transactions (Gurtu et al., 2019). Only relatively recent literature and practical examples have started to implement the tamper-proof distributed ledger concept to the supply chain as a means of replacing non-transparent centralized supply chain management (SCM) tools. The benefits of the technology are relevant, and governments worldwide have started drafting policies to determine an implementation agenda (Suominen et al., 2018). While the blockchain could be a significant step forward for large supply chains to improve current ERP solutions, it may represent a breakthrough for smaller enterprises, lagging behind on digitalization (Buratto et al., 2019) and often taking the hit from non-transparent supply chains (Zimmerman, 2016).

Small and medium enterprises (SMEs) represent a supporting column for the Italian economy, contributing circa 66% to the value added by non-financial businesses (World Bank, 2019). The largest number of SMEs is active in the food sector, which is also the main industry by gross domestic product (GDP) contribution. Despite the large quantity of academic studies and pioneering examples in the application of the blockchain to large-scale supply chains or in the banking industry, studies on the implementation of the technology on small enterprises remains very theoretical. Therefore, this chapter aims to contribute in a practical manner to the discussion on the implementation of the blockchain as an SCM tool for SMEs by answering the following research questions:

1. How can the blockchain be implemented for SMEs?
2. Can the blockchain provide SMEs with the required level of transparency and offer traceability over the supply chain?

We investigate a case study in the saffron industry to track costs and benefits of the blockchain technology and understand if the implementation is economically and operationally viable. The case is based on a small Italian firm affected by the lack of transparency in an industry susceptible to fraud and counterfeiting. In fact, saffron is the most expensive food product in the world, with prices that can reach 30 euros per gram. It ranks in the top 10 most counterfeited Italian food products.

The supply chain processes of the firm were studied in order to understand how each activity would be affected by the blockchain. Our findings reveal that the blockchain can contribute significantly to supply chain management by improving supplier selection processes; increasing harvests, thanks to Internet of Things (IoT) sensors, enabling access to larger retailers; and, ultimately, providing transparency to final consumers. Despite the benefits, the costs analysis highlights that the direct economic advantages obtainable in terms of increased production and higher prices would not explain the investment. Research suggests that an implementation framework similar to the one used by large corporations where the network is built by focus firm and proposed to suppliers is not applicable to SMEs. Due to the lack of internal resources, Italian and European SMEs like the one examined cannot afford the implementation of such technology. The early stage of maturity of blockchain translates into scarce standardization, and the existing out-of-the-box solutions cannot yet fully harvest the benefits of a blockchain-enabled supply chain. The idea brought forward by the Australian government is the development of a unique blockchain infrastructure to which national businesses can connect, exchange goods, and complete transactions while enabling information sharing across companies. Governments, start-ups and larger tech corporations are moving in this direction. However, this line of thought still requires deep research. Future studies aimed at favouring digitalization and transparency for smaller businesses through the use of blockchain shall explore the organizational viability of a central blockchain network as well as creating a solution able to satisfy the numerous different business models of all the SMEs active within a country.

In the next sections, first, the existing literature is reviewed, defining the concepts at stake and understanding how the blockchain technology is implemented nowadays in companies. Secondly, the importance of SMEs' digitalization in the Italian context is explored. A case study will then explore the implementation of the blockchain technology on the Italian agricultural SME producing saffron, with the intent of answering the research questions and participating practically to the discussion.

LITERATURE REVIEW

SCM is a very extensive concept. Digitalization can take different forms across the many layers of the supply chain, and each technology serves a specific purpose in improving the efficiency of the supply chain (De Giovanni, 2021a). From 3D printing to radio-frequency identification (RFID) and cloud computing, the technologies adopted in modern supply chain management are numerous (Agrawal et al., 2018). For the purpose of this chapter, we focus on SCM systems and software, which gather and manage data obtained from all different devices and technologies across the supply chain to gather, elaborate, and share information across partner firms, as are compatible with the utility that the blockchain technology can bring to SCM. Such systems are called ERP software and are management software that, through a suite of applications, track resources, transaction, and contracts (www.sap.com). Such solutions already enable the digitalization of most of SCM processes, from demand forecasting, inventory tracking and management, to order placement and fulfilment, as well as enabling to a certain extent contracts management (De Giovanni, 2016). Systems such as SAP manage well the organizational aspect of the SCM in order to maximize supply chain efficiency. However, issues of transparency and traceability still remain. According to a survey completed by Deloitte, 65% of procurement managers surveyed state they have no visibility beyond tier-1 suppliers (Deloitte, 2018). In systems such as SAP, firms receiving product information must either trust their partners on the contracts signed or carry out a secondary analysis, leading often to loss in efficiency due to double checks or disputes over characteristics of products and services received.

The blockchain technology appears really appealing as a digital SCM solution. Many studies and experiments have been carried out on this technology, and today it is starting to be integrated both in pre-existing ERP software from companies such as IBM (www.ibm.com), as well as completely new solutions being developed. SCM is a broad topic, and it deals with the management of many different areas of the supply chain. Blockchain must be integrated at every level to satisfy the organizational requirement of each department (Van Hoek, 2019). At the same time, the blockchain system must be integrated along the entire supply chain so that customers and peers at the end of the chain have access to information on suppliers, logistics, and so forth, and the other way around. As of today, research on the implementation of blockchain within the supply chain is still at an early stage, and, despite the hype around the technology, the studies are still mostly theoretical (Dobrovnik et al., 2018). While the publications available describe it as a breakthrough, such theories are still based on little implementation and might create unreliable expectations.

Non-financial blockchain adopters often implement the blockchain as the back-end of their ERP software to provide for additional security and validity (Oracle.

com). Large companies with strong supplier bargaining power tend to implement the system for their own processes and then require suppliers to participate to the network (Hyperledger.org). According to a scenario developed by Deloitte, a turnkey blockchain-enabled supply chain today has an estimated annual cost of over 200,000 dollars, highlighting how expensive the technology is at the current stage (Deloitte, 2019).

Large information technology (IT) companies and different academic studies have suggested different designs for a blockchain-enabled SCM, but no optimal design is recognized; as mentioned before, research on the topic is still at an early stage (Wang et al., 2019). Despite that, an important heterogeneity exists, and different models and design have the following elements in common:

A Shared Platform

The implementation starts from the creation a unique platform (database) where each peer can access, view, and add any information Lin et al. (2018). This decentralized platform should be accessible at every stage of the supply chain and by the firms involved at each level to maximize the integration (Duhaylongsod & De Giovanni, 2019). Any stakeholder should be able to access any kind of information regarding the products or transactions. Despite that this model of a transparent and integrated supply chain may represent an advantage in terms of efficiency and quality, managers appear sceptical of sharing strategic information with partners (De Giovanni, 2021b).

These barriers are most likely mitigated through the blockchain partner selection (Wang et al., 2019). Today, many firms have a selection of suppliers that they trust more and are more integrated with. Companies such as Luxottica carry out a continuous supplier evaluation in order to maximize trust in supply chain partners (Luxottica, 2020). Such monitoring of parties might be even easier thanks to the information disclosure of a blockchain system, which would deeply affect the relationships between supply chain partners, and it might require establishing a new governance model to manage the supply chain (Wang et al., 2019).

The Use of Smart Contracts

The key element defining a relationship between any two parties in a supply chain is the contract (De Giovanni, 2019a). Contracts establish trust between counterparts. Any transaction and exchange of resources must be carried out according to pre-agreed and pre-defined terms. In blockchain-enabled SCM, such contracts would be converted into smart contracts. Smart contracts are no more than a digitalized "scripted version" of real-life contracts (Christidis et al., 2016). Just like in the real world, they determine the relationship between two parties. However, smart contracts also act as middlemen; they control the outcome of any transaction, whether monetary or of any exchange of goods and services, according to the pre-defined contractual terms. The clauses of any supply contract can be converted into "if statements," meaning that if the conditions of the transaction between the two parties are infringed, the smart contracts will not approve the normal output of the transaction, impeding it (Christidis et al., 2016). A smart contract is able to avoid any dispute or damages before they happen and be based on both operational and economic terms (Preeker & De Giovanni, 2018). Unless all defined conditions are fulfilled, the transaction between the two parties in the blockchain cannot be executed.

The outcome of a smart contract is always predictable, because if any parameter is not respected the contract rejects the exchange; in contrast, it accepts and confirms the transaction (Christidis et al., 2016). A smart contract is signed at the moment of execution; that is, if the terms are not met the contract does not take place (De Giovanni, 2019b).

Recording Truthful Information: The Use of Sensors and RFID Chips

The benefits of the blockchain (and the smart contracts) are only enabled by the use of sensor and devices that can monitor and write to the ledger any information regarding the state of either a process or a product along the supply chain (Christidis et al., 2016). When dealing with IoT devices and blockchain, a keyword is RFID chips. RFID are thin magnetic tags, similar to the ones present in credit cards, which can store information. Extensive research has been carried out on the implementation of RFID technology to improve supply chain traceability. RFID chips can store more information than simple barcodes. They can be read-only or read-write, meaning that information can be added to an RFID tag as the products advance through manufacturing processes (Angeles, 2005). Moreover, the magnetic nature of the chip allows the tag to be identified at a greater distance, without the need for an optical reader and manual scanning. RFID tags are already widely used in the automotive industry. Both Ford and Chevrolet use RFID to track engine components throughout manufacturing processes (Swedberg, 2015). They can monitor the arrival of raw materials or finished goods at the manufacturing facility or retail store through RFID gates (readers; this allows for automatic inventory management as well as for keeping track of timing, especially for deteriorating goods such as foods. RFID can also confirm an order and communicate its completion to a smart contract. It is possible to know instantaneously the purchase of products and the leftover stock in the warehouse and place replenishment orders to suppliers, automatically enabling a leaner supply chain (Angeles, 2005; De Giovanni and Cariola, 2020).

Beyond RFIDs, other devices such as sensors are fundamental to assure the terms and conditions specified in supply smart contracts. Having sensors measuring characteristics such as temperature, moisture, weight, or, for example, the presence of certain chemicals, is fundamental, especially in the agricultural industry, to assure the maximum level of quality and safety to the final consumers (Kamilaris et al., 2020; Zeto, 2018). For example, the temperature sensors present in meat containers and linked to the blockchain can assure the recipient that the temperature during the transfer never exceeded 4°C (De Giovanni, 2020b). Today, there are a wide variety of sensors available, some directly connected to the Internet and hence able to communicate directly to the blockchain, such as long-term evolution radios; others instead record the data and then transfer it once a connection is reached (Christidis et al., 2016). The main barriers to the implementation of the IoT are of economic in nature. Depending on the level of the technology used, both RFID chips and sensors can represent a significant investment to firms (Angeles, 2005, Tian et al., 2016). The concept is that the investment in such devices is proportional to the value of the good to be traced and the entity of the damages that could arise in case of issues in the supply chain. Read-only RFID chips are already widely used even in retail stores and have a very low cost. Today some stores adopt them as a replacement to barcodes, due to faster checkout times and easier theft-identification (Wright, 2019). Table 1 summarizes the benefits or "enablers" of the blockchain technology as well as the barriers that might slow blockchain adoption.

Table 1. Benefits and barriers to blockchain implementation

Blockchain Enablers	Blockchain Barriers
BE1 – Transparency Information about any product, process, or transaction is stored, and it is auditable by any stakeholder at anytime. This enables enhanced trust and reputation among partners.	**BB 1 – Implementation Costs** Building a blockchain network represents a significant investment due to the scarcity of existing technology and the requirement for skilled developers.
BE2 – Traceability Trusted information can be traced back in time, allowing for the evaluation of the origin of any product or the nature of any activity within the supply chain.	**BB 2 – Spreading BT Across The Supply Chain** A blockchain-oriented supply chain is only beneficial if supply chain stakeholders are connected and share information through it. Difficulties of different natures can arise in convincing partners to adopt the system.
BE2 – Immutability Information stored cannot be tampered by anyone. Falsification of data, certificates, or transactions is impossible.	**BB 3 – Public Strategic Information** Adopting the blockchain signifies making all supply chain transactions and contracts public. This is one of the main sources of scepticism from managers against the implementation of the technology (Van Hoek, 2019).
BE3 – Decentralization The ledger being distributed on numerous devices lowers the risk of losing data due to a damaged database or hacking.	
BE4 – Lower Transaction Costs and Risks The high security of blockchain technology ensures safe transactions, decreasing the need for intermediaries. Moreover, the use of smart contracts reduces transaction risks and possible conflicts among partners.	

Sources: Kamble (2018) and Kamilaris (2020)

RESEARCH METHODOLOGY

For the purpose of this chapter, a small, family-owned agricultural firm active in the saffron industry was selected to answer our research questions and investigate the implementation of blockchain technology. The company studied is Arte Zafferano and operates in the lower area of Latium in Italy.

The saffron supply chain begins with bulbs suppliers. Such companies grow bulbs that are sold to saffron farmers. The Italian saffron industry is very fragmented, with many small or micro companies each producing small quantities. Processors purchase and aggregate similar saffron qualities to then package it or further process it into other products, which are then passed on to resellers. The saffron agriculture industry comprises two different types of organizations: one produces saffron and one makes both saffron and bulbs, acting as bulb suppliers also. Arte Zafferano is part of this second group of firms, and it is active both in the sale of saffron and bulbs. Crocus Sativus is usually planted in the summer, around August, and harvested in autumn, usually in October. Arte Zafferano sells both saffron pistils as well as processed products such as saffron honey and saffron pasta, for which it relies on external processors. The chart below shows Arte Zafferano's supply chain.

Figure 1. Saffron production supply chain

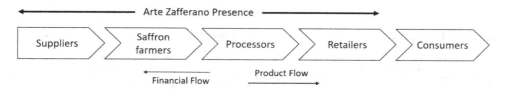

Creating a Blockchain-Enabled Environment

The basis for a blockchain-enabled supply chain begins with the creation or existence of a blockchain platform. The customized platform can be created through existing IT services providers such as IBM or Microsoft Azure. Such interfaces are complex and require the knowledge of an IT professional, which strongly affects the total costs of the implementation. The service of an IT professional is a recurring requirement because beyond the initial implementation, the system will require new smart contracts to be drafted, IoT sensors replaced, and system maintenance carried out. Despite cheaper, readily available solutions already existing, the explored products had a low level of customization, with some offering partial solutions often limited to the smart contracts trade aspects. The blockchain platform is linked directly to IoT sensors, described in the next paragraphs, logging data on a chronological basis. Any information stored on the network will be readily available to any person, including final consumers. Data is accessible through an authenticated web portal. Any information stored is attributable to single saffron or bulbs lots through quick response (QR) codes, in the case of individual saffron packages, and is easily accessible by individuals or RFID chips for bulb boxes, in order to further improve traceability of the bulbs. Regarding the use of smart contracts, according to the Italian legal requirements, any transaction or smart contract executed on the blockchain must comply with the digital signature standards to verify the effective signing of the agreements.

The true advantage of the blockchain is only tangible when it is adopted by stakeholders throughout the supply chain. Suppliers, business customers, and certification institutions should participate in the blockchain network with data from their activities or by emitting quality certificates about products directly on the blockchain in order to avoid possible falsification. In the interviews carried out with Arte Zafferano's suppliers, the owners manifested the interest in greater supply chain traceability, but at the same time, they would not consider adopting a platform developed by Arte Zafferano; rather, they feel that the technology should be developed by a consortium and then adopted by the participant, to maximize collaboration.

Arte Zafferano, being a small company, does not possess enough bargaining power to impose the adoption of the blockchain platform to its suppliers or business customers. Hence, to answer the first research question, smaller enterprises might not be able to implement the blockchain technology by developing a custom solution, as it would be difficult to include supply chain stakeholders within the platform. The main consideration is that the implementation shall be brought forward by a group of SMEs where the larger size of the group leads to greater traceability.

IoT and the Blockchain: More Transparent and Efficient Processes

Despite that blockchain network creation might be out of SMEs hands, the implementation of the technology in the supply chain processes advances by understanding which activities the technology could improve. The saffron and bulbs production requires very transparent processes in order to differentiate authentic Italian saffron and bulbs from lower quality and counterfeit products.

The Bulbs

Saffron plants (Crocus Sativus), beyond producing the flower containing the precious pistils, yield around three bulbs per plant. Each of these parts is sold to other agricultural firms demanding bulbs. In the saffron industry, bulbs characteristics are fundamental, and the prices are strongly affected by their attributes. A larger bulb is always preferred to a smaller bulb. Moreover, the origin of the bulb is what confers the saffron its authenticity. A bulb purchased from the Netherlands and planted in Italy does not produce Italian Saffron. In order to be considered Italian, a bulb must have lived at least two years in Italian soil. Arte Zafferano specifies that such authenticity is usually certified; despite this, the bulbs market offers many "Italian bulbs" lacking certification. The sale of bulbs is an important aspect of the firm's business and accounts for around 40% of yearly revenues. A regional institution demands that saffron nursery companies keep count of the bulbs being harvested, sold, or purchased in order to track the location of the bulbs and certify their origins. Such a bulbs register is on paper, and it is edited manually. The institution verifies such number at the end of the year. Farmers producing top-quality Italian saffron demand such certification, and origin-tracking methods used today are not reliable in guaranteeing the bulbs' origin. Furthermore, bulbs' harvesting time and planting time are offset four months, during which such bulbs must be stored before being delivered to the client. Saffron plants' yield is strongly related to storing conditions. A bulb must not be stocked outside of the soil for more than 90–150 days, as it may dry out. Moreover, to avoid possible infections, it must be stored in a dry place. Lastly, the warehousing temperature is fundamental. According to Arte Zafferano, a bulb stored between 25°C and 27°C will have a greater yield. Today, such storing characteristics cannot be verified by business customers (farmers).

The blockchain could enable for the storage of the bulbs registry on the distributed ledger, giving direct access to the regional institution that, once the numbers are verified, can release such certification directly on the blockchain. Because the blockchain is immutable and accessible to the entire supply chain, bulbs buyers can immediately verify the origin of the bulb, distinguishing them from non-certified bulbs available on the market. Furthermore, IoT sensors that are directly connected to the blockchain network can measure the humidity and temperature of the storing environment on the ledger. Bulbs buyers can then verify how the lot of purchased bulbs was stored, ensuring the maximum yield. RFID chips can play a role in tracking such bulbs lots. Such benefits would translate into a price premium, and would definitely enable Arte Zafferano to label its bulbs as top quality, increasing lot prices (1,000 bulbs) from the current price of 350 euro up to 400 euro, the unitary price for caliber-10, top-quality, guaranteed Italian bulbs. According to Arte Zafferano, an average of 40,000 bulbs are sold per year. A price increase would translate into an increase in revenues of around 2,000€.

The Saffron

There are a variety of factors and processes affecting the final organic properties of the saffron as well as determinants of the fields-yield. Soil preparation before burying the bulbs plays a fundamental role. Soil nutrients, low moisture and a neutral PH are all fundamental characteristics for Crocus Sativus growth. Drought periods can compromise the harvest, as happened in 2017 for Arte Zafferano. Electrochemical sensors can detect soil PH and certain chemicals, while buried moisture sensors can detect soil humidity in different areas of the field. This ensures optimal conditions are present before the bulbs are planted and allows Arte Zafferano to intervene before the yield is compromised. Integrating such sensors into the blockchain network, the firms can store soil analysis data, making it accessible to the entire supply chain and—most importantly—to customers, who can trust there is an absence of chemical fertilizers and check the real cultivation conditions and procedures. Once the planting is complete, the same sensors can ensure correct monitoring activity, noticing when the field might require irrigation.

Once harvested, before being sold to other businesses or final consumers, the saffron must be dried out. Humid saffron is heavier and hence generates more revenues at the expense of quality. In order to be sold, saffron stigmas may contain a maximum of 12% of water. The drying process, if carried out correctly, enhances the taste of the spice, but most importantly prevents the creation of mold in the product. Again, IoT moisture sensors can log saffron stigmas' humidity throughout and after process to guarantee buyers the nature of the drying. Moreover, today Arte Zafferano cultivates saffron on two separate fields, which are located within the same geographical area. Plans to expand to a third and fourth field are limited by available personnel, which cannot be present on the field to monitor saffron growth. The set of soil monitoring IoT sensors could limit the firm's needs to scale up as it can track terrain and field conditions remotely, and hence intervene only in case optimal farming conditions degrade.

From an economic standpoint, a blockchain implementation would not favor a price increase, as Arte Zafferano's saffron stigmas are already sold at the highest price for such quality range. On the other hand, soil monitoring processes through IoT sensors would improve the yearly average yield, which was difficult to perform in 2017, when an in-depth soil analysis would have indicated the need for irrigation. According to Arte Zafferano, low-yield years take place statistically every five years due to drought or poor soil conditions. Over time, it would signify an increase in yearly average production of almost 10%.

Processing and Retailing

In the processing and retailing layers of the saffron supply chain Arte Zafferano relies on external organizations for the production of saffron-tasting products such as honey and pasta. Because Arte Zafferano's business is focused around organic-only products, it selects suppliers according to the certified organic nature of the products. Today, Arte Zafferano relies on two exclusive suppliers: one for honey and one for pasta. Due to the size of the business, Arte Zafferano inspects its supplier processes manually and relies exclusively on local firms. The participation to the blockchain network by supplier firms would allow Arte Zafferano to monitor processes remotely and continuously. Secondly, remote inspections can allow Arte Zafferano to expand suppliers' choice beyond the geographical requirements, with the possibility of increasing its bargaining power and possibly having access to higher quality suppliers. Lastly, Arte Zafferano would be able to share retailing data, allowing for automatic stock replenishment without placing manual orders and leaving such products sold out. On the retail side, saffron consumers, through a simple QR code or even RFID chip, could access a web portal to inspect the entire supply chain processes of the saffron they are purchasing and consuming, guaranteeing the quality and origin of all inputs and the saffron itself. This would allow for the differentiation of superior quality saffron as produced by Arte Zafferano, discouraging consumers from purchasing low-quality saffron or facing counterfeit products.

Digitalizing Relationships

The data gathered from IoT sensors and the information stored on the blockchain offer the transparency of processes to any supply chain stakeholder. To fully harvest the benefits of such large information flows, the supply chain must implement one of the most important items: the smart contracts. Arte Zafferano shall digitalize all relationships with suppliers and customers. In the world of saffron, where quality and origin are essential characteristics, any trade contract provides terms defining the quality of the products. Digitizing such contracts through smart contracts would mean that any exchange between any two partners must be backed by quality guarantees provided by all the information gathered and stored on the blockchain. A smart contract between Arte Zafferano and the pasta supplier would complete the transaction where the organic characteristics are verified and hence an organic certificate is released on the blockchain network by the certification authority. The smart contract allows Arte Zafferano to check the external suppliers without the need for physical inspections, giving access to other companies (as far as they are accessible through the blockchain), increasing negotiation capability, and having the opportunity to improve its products.

The same relationships can be true between Arte Zafferano and its customers. Larger retailers purchase quantities of saffron from the different small producers to then aggregate, pack, and sell the stigmas. Such retailers give a minimum threshold in terms of saffron volumes because purchasing smaller quantities than 1 kg from each single retailer signifies carrying out quality inspections on a very large number of samples. Through the blockchain, Arte Zafferano would have recorded production processes and the obtained certifications on the immutable ledger. Through a smart contract, larger retailers can increase the trust towards smaller producers without the need to carry out singular inspections. This would allow Arte Zafferano to sell saffron wholesale without reaching the minimum threshold. In fact, selling directly to end consumers represents a burden for Arte Zafferano today because they must pack and sell the products to individual consumers, with much higher costs of sales.

Costs and Benefits

Table 2 summarizes how a blockchain-enabled supply chain can improve Arte Zafferano's processes.

Table 2. Enablers for blockchain implementation

Activity	Currently	Blockchain-enabled supply chain	Blockchain Enablers and Barriers
Purchasing Strategy	• Purchasing strategy limited to physically inspections for local suppliers • Reliance on falsifiable certifications	• Access to a wider range of trustable suppliers, thanks to the use of smart contracts • Improved negotiation capability • Continuous audit over suppliers' processes • Improved supplier selection process	Enablers: BE1, BE4 Barriers: BB2, BB3
Production	• Soil preparation takes place in a similar manner every year • Farming on fields only near the farm	• Increased production, thanks to improved soil monitoring • Ability to expand on multiple fields without the need to scale up	Enablers: BE1, BE2 Barriers: BB1, BB3
Inventory Management	• Manual replenishment	• Automatic replenishment of processed products inventory according to sales volumes	Enablers: BE4 Barriers: BE2
Selling Strategy	• Strictly business-to-consumer retailing	• Access to larger business (business-to-business) customers thanks to enhanced trust and information	Enablers: BE1, BE2, BE4 Barriers: BB1, BB2
Customer Relationship Management	• No guarantee of saffron origin or organic faming • Inability to differentiate from counterfeit or lower quality products beyond label information	• Ability for consumers to explore and trace the products' supply chain	Enablers: BE1, BE2, BE4 Barriers: BB1

Many benefits mentioned above are strictly organizational and are quite difficult to quantify in monetary terms. However, certain direct economic benefits have been identified. A possible increase in bulb prices, thanks to the possibility of guaranteeing the highest bulb quality can directly affect revenues. Furthermore, increased saffron production through an improved soil preparation would allow Arte Zafferano to expand its activities on fields located further away from the farm, thanks to IoT devices.

For the cost analysis, the implementation of a customized blockchain network requires the hiring of a freelance IT engineer to develop and maintain the platform throughout the years. Speaking to an IT engineer, the construction of a blockchain network using currently available tools has an asking price of 80,000€ annually. Moreover, the blockchain requires great computational power distributed across different machines (distributed ledger); such services can be purchased from different companies such as IBM or Microsoft for which the cost is estimated in terms of computing hours. A company comparable to Arte Zafferano would require 750 computing hours per month. The implementation and ownership of a blockchain network goes beyond any plausible investment for a firm of Arte Zafferano's size. Indeed, it would be far out of reach for the average European SMEs, which have a digitalization budget that actually covers only circa 20% of the required annual investment.

Table 3 summarizes the direct effect on Arte Zafferano's revenues of the implementation of the blockchain on a short-term timeline (1–3 years since implementation).

Table 3.

Precision Farming Improved soil preparation would allow the company to avoid difficult years in which drought and other causes may compromise the harvest. Considering a 10% increase in average harvest	960€
Fields expansion E monitoring through IoT and Blockchain would allow the company to expand on a field further away from the farm without scaling operations	5.700€
Bulbs Price E monitoring through IoT and Blockchain would allow the company to expand on a field further away from the farm without scaling operations. Bulbs unitary price can increase from 0.30 to 0.35	2.000€
Direct Increase in Annual Revenues	**8.660€**

The table below summarizes instead an estimate of the annual costs of developing a blockchain network for 20 partner firms.

Table 4. Costs for blockchain implementation

Platform hosting costs	1.080€
IT engineer	80.000€
IoT devices	1.000€
Direct Increase in Annual Costs	**82.080€**

The evidence from the above tables suggests that the implementation of the blockchain surely represents a means to improve the process and transparency of SCM, allowing Arte Zafferano to differentiate its product and possibly gain a competitive advantage. The blockchain provided an increase in efficiency in terms of greater production as well as improving organizational capabilities. Despite such benefits, the implementation is quite challenging for small firms. The blockchain enablement of SMEs' supply chain cannot happen individually, as the costs of the technology are still high if compared to the average budget allocated to digitalization.

The early stages of the technology translate into a low level of standardization in the solutions available on the market. The required customization and the complexity of the technology calls for the advice of expensive IT professionals to construct the links between the blockchain members, IoT sensors, and the creation of smart contracts. The cost–benefit analysis only considers the economic advantages received by the focus firm, Arte Zafferano, without considering the benefits extended to the other organization parts of the supply chain.

Certain firms might benefit more from the implementation of the technology, up to the point of explaining the financial investment. Beyond the economic barriers, the implementation and the utility of the technology is limited by the intent of stakeholders to participate. A blockchain with a single participant will lose most of the benefits. In the case study, Arte Zafferano's partners have denied the interest in participating in the construction of the network unless it is a spread practice where their supply chain partners also adopt it. Hence, the implementation should not start from the single company but rather should be planned by a group of partnered SMEs.

Despite positively answering one of the research questions, the case study has demonstrated that investing in the blockchain as a mean of supply chain management may not be economically viable for smaller enterprises due to the current costs of implementing such solutions. Furthermore, the implementation framework used by larger enterprises cannot be currently applied to many SMEs. Contrarily, the numerous benefits analysed and the improvements contributed by the technology cannot be disregarded. The main cost is the construction of the actual blockchain network, the backbone to which firms, part of the same supply chain, are linked in order to transact and share information. This means that for a multiplicity of firms the required blockchain is one, and hence the core investment could well be shared among the participants. It is the role of institutional bodies or consortiums to promote the implementation of such system. Blockchain policies analysed aim exactly at building a central blockchain network to which all SMEs can subscribe and hence trade with one another. While the most complete idea is in the Australian National Blockchain, the project is still far from being realized (Australian Government, 2019). Solutions like We.Trade are also premature, compared to what SMEs might currently need. Future research should aim in the direction of a unified blockchain network provided by an institution, similar to what has been done with unified citizens portals such as the Sistema Pubblico di Identità Digitale (SPID) in Italy, an easy-to-use standardized common platform. Today, Italian SMEs are falling behind in digitalization, and the effect is amplifying as innovation proceeds. A substantial investment in a breakthrough solution could represent a shortcut to increase the competitivity of Italian SMEs on the global market as well as protect the "Made in Italy" label, recovering part of the economic damages. Such direction in future research implies much broader studies, which shall make sense from a technical, economical, and organizational point of view, understanding whether the requirements of individual SMEs can be satisfied by a unique blockchain infrastructure.

Despite the infeasibility of the implementation, considering common implementation frameworks, the advantages that the technology can bring to SMEs is notable. The blockchain can improve trust for consumers in smaller enterprises by providing full transparency of their activities as well as the complete traceability of the supply chain. The blockchain can translate into a significative competitive advantage but most importantly would allow traceable products to be differentiated from lower quality or counterfeit ones. A well-spread adoption of the technology might allow the Italian economy to recover part of the damages inflicted by counterfeiting and other unfair practices. For this purpose, further research must be carried out into the development of a blockchain infrastructure to which individual SMEs can connect to trace their activities and trade among each other to create a unique ecosystem able to guarantee Italian products all around the world.

REFERENCES

Abeyratne, S. A., & Monfared, R. P. (2016). Blockchain ready manufacturing supply chain using distributed ledger. *International Journal of Research in Engineering and Technology*, 5(9), 1–10. doi:10.15623/ijret.2016.0509001

Agrawal, P., & Narain, R. (2018). Digital supply chain management: An Overview. *IOP Conf. Ser.*

Angeles, R. (2005). Rfid Technologies: Supply-Chain Applications and Implementation Issues. *Information Systems Management*, 35(2), 60–64. doi:10.1 201/1078/44912.22.1.20051201/85739.7

Australian Government. (2020). *The national blockchain roadmap.* Author.

Buratto, A., Cesaretto, R., & De Giovanni, P. (2019). Consignment contracts with cooperative programs and price discount mechanisms in a dynamic supply chain. *International Journal of Production Economics*, 218, 72–82. doi:10.1016/j.ijpe.2019.04.027

Christidis, K., & Devetsikiotis, M. (2016). Blockchains and Smart Contracts for the Internet of Things. *IEEE Access: Practical Innovations, Open Solutions*, 4, 2292–2303. doi:10.1109/ACCESS.2016.2566339

Coldiretti. (2020, Sept 2). *Covid: il cibo diventa la prima ricchezza del Paese, vale 538 mln.* Retrieved from Coldiretti: https://www.coldiretti.it/economia/covid-il-cibo-diventa-la-prima-ricchezza-del-paese-vale-538-mln

De Giovanni, P. (2016). Coordination in a distribution channel with decisions on the nature of incentives and share-dependency on pricing. *The Journal of the Operational Research Society*, 67(8), 1034–1049. doi:10.1057/jors.2015.118

De Giovanni, P. (2019a). Digital Supply Chain through Dynamic Inventory and Smart Contracts. *Mathematics*, 7(12), 1235. doi:10.3390/math7121235

De Giovanni, P. (2019b). Eco-Digital Supply Chains Through Blockchains. *International Journal of Business and Management Study*, 6(2).

De Giovanni, P. (2020a). Blockchain and smart contracts in supply chain management: A game theoretic model. *International Journal of Production Economics*, 228.

De Giovanni, P. (2020b). An optimal control model with defective products and goodwill damages. *Annals of Operations Research*, 289(2), 419–430. doi:10.100710479-019-03176-4

De Giovanni, P. (2021). Smart Contracts and Blockchain for Supply Chain Quality Management, in Dynamic Quality Models and Games in Digital Supply Chains. *Springer Nature*.

De Giovanni, P. (2021). Smart Supply Chains with vendor managed inventory, coordination, and environmental performance. *European Journal of Operational Research, 292*(2), 515–531. doi:10.1016/j.ejor.2020.10.049

De Giovanni, P., & Cariola, A. (2020). Process innovation through industry 4.0 technologies, lean practices and green supply chains. *Research in Transportation Economics*, 100869. doi:10.1016/j.retrec.2020.100869

De Giovanni, P., & Ramani, V. (2019). Product cannibalization and the effect of a service strategy. *The Journal of the Operational Research Society*, 1–17.

Deloitte. (2018). *Leadership: Driving innovation and delivering impact*. Deloitte.

Duhaylongsod, J. B., & De Giovanni, P. (2019). The impact of innovation strategies on the relationship between supplier integration and operational performance. *International Journal of Physical Distribution & Logistics Management, 49*(2), 156–177. doi:10.1108/IJPDLM-09-2017-0269

Eskildsen, J., & Kristensen, K. (2007). Customer Satisfaction – The Role of Transparency. *Total Quality Management & Business Excellence, 18*(1-2), 39–47. doi:10.1080/14783360601043047

European Commission. (2019). *2019 EBA Italy Fact Sheet*. European Commission.

European Commission. (2020). *DESI 2020*. Author.

Francisco, K., & Swanson, D. (2017). *The Supply Chain Has No Clothes: Technology Adoption of Blockchain for Supply Chain Transparency*. Department of Marketing & Logistics, University of North Florida.

Gurtu, A., & Johny, J. (2019). Potential of blockchain technology in supply chain management: A literature review. *International Journal of Physical Distribution & Logistics Management, 49*(9), 881–900. doi:10.1108/IJPDLM-11-2018-0371

Hackius, N., & Petersen, M. (2017). Blockchain in Logistics and Supply Chain: Trick or Treat. *Hamburg International Conference of Logistics*.

Hoek, R. (2019). Exploring blockchain implementation in the supply chain. *International Journal of Operations & Production Management, 39*(6/7/8), 829–859. doi:10.1108/IJOPM-01-2019-0022

Hoek, R. v. (2020). Unblocking the chain – findings from an executive workshop on blockchain in the supply chain. *Supply Chain Management*, 255–261.

Iasiniti, M., & Lakhani, K. R. (2017). The Truth About The Blockchain. *Harvard Business Review*.

Kamble, S. S., Gunasekaran, A., & Sharma, R. (2020). Modeling the blockchain enabled traceability in agriculture supply chain. *International Journal of Information Management, 52*, 101967. doi:10.1016/j.ijinfomgt.2019.05.023

Kamilaris, A., Fonti, A., & Prenafeta-Boldú, F. X. (2019). The Rise of Blockchain Technology in Agriculture and Food Supply Chains. *Trends in Food Science & Technology, 91*, 640–652. doi:10.1016/j.tifs.2019.07.034

Kotula, M. (2020, Mar 11). *Can A Supply Chain Be Really Transparent In A Digital World?* Retrieved from Digitalist Magazine: https://www.digitalistmag. com/digital-supply-networks/2020/03/11/can-supply-chain-be-really-transparent-in-digital-world-06202976/

Li, S., & Lin, B. (2006). Accessing information sharing and information quality in supply chain management. *Decision Support Systems, 42*(3), 1641–1656. doi:10.1016/j.dss.2006.02.011

Lin, J., Shen, Z., Zhang, A., & Chai, Y. (2018, July). Blockchain and IoT based food traceability for smart agriculture. In *Proceedings of the 3rd International Conference on Crowd Science and Engineering* (pp. 1-6). 10.1145/3265689.3265692

Martinez, V., Zhao, M., Blujdea, C., Han, X., Neely, A., & Albores, P. (2019). Blockchain-driven customer. *International Journal of Operations and Production Management, 39*(6-8), 993-1022.

Mentzer, J. T., DeWitt, W., Keebler, J. S., Min, S., Nix, N. W., Smith, C. D., & Zacharia, Z. G. (2001). Defining Supply Chain Management. *Journal of Business Logistics, 22*(2), 1–25. doi:10.1002/j.2158-1592.2001.tb00001.x

Oracle. (2019, Feb 28). *Oracle Certified Origins Italia*. Retrieved from Oracle: https://www.oracle.com/it/customers/certified-origins-1-blockchain-story.html

Perona, M., & Miragliotta, G. (2002). Complexity management and supply chain performance assessment. A field study and a conceptual framework. *International Journal of Production Economics*, 103–115.

Preeker, T., & De Giovanni, P. (2018). Coordinating innovation projects with high tech suppliers through contracts. *Research Policy, 47*(6), 1161–1172. doi:10.1016/j.respol.2018.04.003

Pursuing the digital future amid macro-gloom. (2019, Jan 18). Retrieved from Deloitte: https://www2.deloitte.com/us/en/insights/focus/industry-4-0/italy-4-0-digital-future-technology.html

Quillhash. (2020, Jan 28). *Blockchain in Supply of Saffron: A prevention of frauds on the World's most expensive spice*. Retrieved from Quillhash: https://blog.quillhash.com/2020/01/28/blockchain-in-supply-of-saffron-a-prevention-of-frauds-on-the-worlds-most-expensive-spice/

Radovilsky, Z. (n.d.). *Enterprise Resource Planning*. California State University.

SAP. (n.d.). *What Is ERP?* Retrieved from Sap Insights: https://insights.sap.com/what-is-erp/

Suominen, K., Chatzky, A., Reinsch, W., & Robison, J. (2018). *What Should U.S. Blockchain Policy Be?* CSIS.

Swedberg, C. (2015). *Ford Motor Co. Uses Omni-ID 64-kbit Tag to Monitor Engine Production*. RFID Journal.

Tian, F. (2016). *An Agri-food Supply Chain Traceability System for China Based on RFID & Blockchain Technology*. Vienna University of Economics and Business.

World Bank. (2018). *Italy Trade Statistics*. Retrieved from World Bank: https://wits.worldbank.org/CountryProfile/en/ITA

Wright, J. (2019, Aug 1). *Case Study: Decathlon: getting smart with RFID tags*. Retrieved from Internet Retailing: https://internetretailing.net/magazine-articles/magazine-articles/case-study-decathlon-getting-smart-with-rfid-tags

Yli-Huumo, J., Ko, D., Choi, S., Park, S., & Smolander, K. (2016). Where Is Current Research on Blockchain Technology? - A Systematic Review. West Virginia University.

Zimmerman, D. V. (2016). *SMEs and digitalisation: The current position, recent developments and challenges*. KfW Research.

Zimmermann, V. (2018). *SME Digitalisation Report 2018*. kWF Research.

Chapter 6

Blockchain in the Biopharmaceutical Industry:
Conceptual Model on Product Quality Control

Tiziano Volpentesta
Luiss University, Italy

Mario Miozza
Luiss University, Italy

Abhijeet Satwekar
Merck Serono S.p.A., Italy

ABSTRACT

Biopharmaceutical companies and health authorities continuously exchange information to provide safe and effective therapeutics. The interactions between the two require transparency and extensive documentation exchange concerning the processes which extend from the development through the manufacturing phase. The current processes rely on paper documentation, notebooks, and point-to-point electronic data interchange (EDI) for the storage of data. Thereby, generating challenges of data integrity within the internal siloed structures and the traceability of the medicinal products in the pursuit to avoid counterfeiting. With Industry 4.0 and blockchain, the authors envisioned a reinvented workflow that helps to 1) manage data integrity with decentralized trust and 2) improve the track and trace capabilities. Hence, biopharmaceutical companies can manage data in a more trustable manner while maintaining security and privacy, further enabling the external ecosystem with track and trace to ensure complete transparency until the therapeutics reach patients.

DOI: 10.4018/978-1-7998-8014-1.ch006

ORGANIZATION BACKGROUND

Since the 18th century, industrial revolutions transformed the production processes from one leaning around craftsmanship to an economy of industrialized machines and processes. Leading to an exponential rise in Gross Domestic Product (GDP), each of the industrial revolutions (1st Mechanical, 2nd Electrical, 3rd Electronical and 4th Cyber-Physical) revolutionized the technological, socio-economical, and cultural levels of societies. Overall, these revolutions provided increased affordability and accessibility of products, along with an enhanced quality of life. Although each industrial revolution also entailed negative and untended environmental and social consequences, they have improved work through innovations, reducing the demand for physical and repetitive labor activities, as the latter can be executed more efficiently by machines. This has led to the rise of knowledge-intensive labourers, which encouraged the migration of people to industrialized zones (Rafferty, 2018). Nowadays, society is witnessing the fourth industrial revolution, which is characterized by the integration and synergies stemming from a wide range of technologies, such as Artificial Intelligence, the Internet of Things, Big Data Analytics, Distributed Ledger Technologies, Robotics, Augmented, Virtual and Mixed Reality, Additive and Smart Manufacturing, Quantum Computing, the Cloud and Edge Computing. These technologies are empowering important developments in manufacturing industries as a lever for productivity, improving quality processes, expanding product portfolio, understanding customer behaviour, enhancing costs effectiveness, and reducing time to market.

The fourth industrial revolution impacts all industries, and the biopharmaceutical industry is not an exception. Digital emerging technologies are affecting the value chain of the biopharmaceutical industry, from Research & Development to the Commercialization stage. However, the biopharmaceutical industry ranks lowest for the use and adoption of digital technologies in comparison to other industries such as retail, finance, media and insurance (Gopal, Suter-Crazzolara, Toldo, & Eberhardt, 2019), due to a challenging regulatory framework (Cauchon, Oghamian, Hassanpour, & Abernathy, 2019).

The biopharmaceutical industry is a high asset and knowledge-intensive industry that deals with the discovery, development, manufacturing, and distribution of medications towards specific health conditions to provide treatments for underlying disease conditions of patients and improve their quality of life. It has two major categories "small molecules" and "biologics or biopharmaceuticals". Small molecules are produced by chemical synthesis and have a well-defined chemical structure. Instead, biopharmaceuticals are produced from biological sources and consists of a complex and heterogeneous structure (Declerck, 2012). These differences are responsible for a wide gap in the production costs between small molecules and biopharmaceuticals

(Makurvet, 2021). Furthermore, the production of biopharmaceutical drugs has a more stringent regulatory pathway in comparison to small molecules due to their complexities, and this impacts the drug development process and the time to market. Indeed, the annual Food and Drug Administration (FDA) approvals for biopharmaceutical products are less than the small molecules (Torre & Albericio, 2021). Moreover, a decline in the productivity of biopharmaceutical research and development led to increased costs within the past few decades (Farid, Baron, Stamatis, Nie, & Coffman, 2020; Scannell, Blanckley, Boldon, & Warrington, 2012). At the same time, the development and manufacturing of therapeutic drugs necessitate sophisticated instrumentation, human capital, scientific knowledge, and stringent regulatory adherence to bring innovative healthcare products to the market to satisfy patient's needs. Overall, the drug development process takes on an average of 12 years (Van Norman, 2016) and involves costs up to US$2B (Mullard, 2014). In 2019, the Food and Drug Administration approved 48 novel drugs (FDA, 2020b) while pharmaceutical companies worldwide had more than 16 thousand drugs in their Research and Development pipelines (Pharma R&D Annual Review, 2020).

The biopharmaceutical ecosystem consists of a complex and dynamic network of players that interacts with each other and is characterized by a set of interrelated players that gravitate around patients' needs, with the common objective of improving their quality of life. Figure 1 reports the main players that are relevant to the discussion within the chapter, which have been further detailed in Table 1.

Figure 1. The biopharmaceutical ecosystem

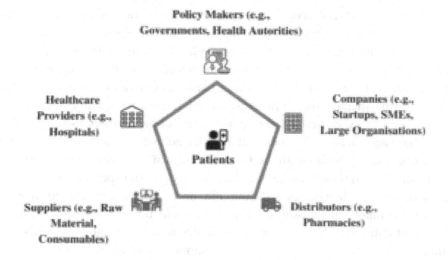

Among the players in the biopharmaceutical ecosystem, a major role in the development, launch, and monitoring of therapeutic products is driven by the interactions between biopharmaceutical companies and health authorities. Indeed, the collaboration among companies and regulators is of utmost importance to bring safe and effective medications towards patient care, cure, and improvement. Health authorities are responsible to authorize the development, manufacturing, and commercialization of biopharmaceuticals products within their legislation power. For example, the Food and Drug Administration (FDA) in the United States, the European Medicines Agency (EMA) in the European Union, the Italian Medicines Agency (AIFA) in Italy, and the Medicines and Healthcare products Regulatory Agency (MHRA) in the United Kingdom. Furthermore, the International Council for Harmonization of Technical Requirements for Pharmaceuticals for Human Use (ICH) is an effort to harmonize guidelines across the globe, given the global scale of operations of modern biopharmaceutical companies. Among other activities, health authorities establish regulations to which biopharmaceuticals companies must comply, such as the Current Good Manufacturing Practices (CGMPs) and the Code of Federal Regulations (CFR), enforced by the Food and Drug Administration.

Biopharmaceutical companies must abide by these guidelines and regulations, and a minimum of one comprehensive CGMPs evaluation is performed on the organization every two years (FDA, 2014). The non-compliance to regulation can result in a loss of company reputation, safety-related risks to patients, expensive fines, or retraction from the market, depending on the nature of the violation. In 2019, CGMPs deviations were the major cause of product recalls in pharmaceutical products in the United States (Stericycle, n.d.). To ensure the highest quality standard, biopharmaceutical companies stringently test the quality of samples from every single batch of produced drugs, to confirm that the therapeutic product is within the specifications of safety and efficacy as defined in the initial drug approval submission to the health authorities. Over time, the drug manufacturing process evolves consistently to exceed the minimum standards with innovative processes and systems that ensure quality by design and operational excellence towards a compliant drug manufacturing process that guarantees the quality of therapeutic products towards excellent therapeutic outcomes for patients across the world.

Biopharmaceutical companies and health authorities continuously exchange information and cooperate with the final objective of providing safe and effective therapeutics. The interactions between the two require transparency and extensive documentation exchanges concerning the processes which extend from the development phase all the way through its manufacturing phase, and at last, on the product data. The data contained in the documentation must be verified and maintained, and this process is resource consuming. Nowadays, thanks to industry 4.0 and the emergence of advanced digital technologies such as blockchain, there is an opportunity to have a lean and smart process that can increase coordination and trust across the various stakeholders in the healthcare ecosystem. Our conceptual proposal is to envision the organization of internal and external ecosystems for positioning the blockchain technology in the healthcare sector with a modular setup. The scope is to allow a leaner technology implementation to address the current challenges of data integrity in the internal siloed structures of the biopharmaceutical company to increase transparency, trust, and coordination. This is to further extend the ecosystem to facilitate the track and trace necessities from regulators and bring this transparency through to the patient. As a conceptual instantiation in this chapter, our concept is designed within one function (actor/stakeholder), i.e., by detailing the use of the blockchain in the biopharmaceutical quality control focusing on the data integrity aspect.

SETTING THE STAGE

Bringing a therapeutic product from its manufacturing to the patients undergoes many complex interactions between the internal functions of the biopharmaceutical company (regarded as an internal ecosystem) and amounts to a large and comprehensive data generation and exchange across multiple internal groups, such as Research & Development, Manufacturing, Quality, Technical Services, Supply Chain, and many others. As the therapeutic product moves outside of the biopharmaceutical company towards the external ecosystem to reach the patients, another set of players is involved that range from suppliers to distributors, health authorities, hospitals, pharmacists etc. (see Figure 2). This involves higher external cross-organizational interactions, the need for transparency and efficient coordination among players.

Figure 2. Internal (left) and external (right) ecosystem

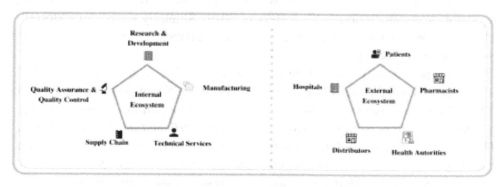

The internal ecosystem within the biopharmaceutical companies is evolving to eliminate the current challenges of data silos, to centralize information and improve communications. All these barriers may affect the process of sharing data and information towards higher regulatory compliance. However, the process has been slow and still many of the workflows rely on paper documentation, notebooks, and point-to-point Electronic Data Interchange (EDI) for the storage of data. At the same time, data integrity is of utmost importance for biopharmaceutical companies. Data integrity refers to the "Completeness, consistency, and accuracy of data" as by Food and Drug Administration Guidance (Food and Drug Administration, 2016) and revolves around the ALCOA principles (Attributable, Legible, Contemporaneous, Originals, Accurate) and Good Documentation Practices (GDP). The former encompasses that *Complete, consistent, and accurate data should be attributable, legible, contemporaneously recorded, original or a true copy, and accurate* (ALCOA) (Food and Drug Administration, 2016). In recent years, Health authorities (e.g., FDA, EMA, MHRA) have issued warning letters, import alerts and consent decrees for the non-compliance involving data integrity, as it is an important element to ensure and monitor safety, efficacy and quality of therapeutic products (EMA, 2016a; Food and Drug Administration, 2016; Medicines & Healthcare products Regulatory Agency, 2018). Hence, data integrity is a critical area within the biopharmaceutical companies for ensuring the therapeutic product to be safe and efficacious. Majorly, data integrity issues are related to inconsistent storage of data, lack of traceability, errors in the data entries (due to typos or fraud) (Morrell, 2017; Rattan, 2018). Thus, generating a lack of trust in the digital data. Therefore, there is an immediate need for a new technological system to provide traceability, data accuracy, visibility, security, and connected real-time data in biopharmaceutical companies. Technological advances as blockchain have been proposed as a potential solution for addressing the data integrity challenges. For example, Steinwandter & Herwig, 2019 have elaborated a workflow based on git control versioning, Ethereum blockchain and smart contracts to guarantee the data integrity in the data storage systems, that can be audited by regulatory agencies (Steinwandter & Herwig, 2019). Similarly, an article by Morrell, 2017 envisions the use of blockchain to capture the data along the life cycle of the pharmaceutical product (Morrell, 2017).

Within the external ecosystem on a particular topic of track and trace of medicinal products; the United States FDA has released the Drug Supply Chain Security Act (DSCSA) that *outlines steps to build an electronic, interoperable system to identify and trace certain prescription drugs as they are distributed in the United States. This will enhance FDA's ability to help protect consumers from exposure to drugs that may be counterfeit, stolen, contaminated, or otherwise harmful. The system will also improve detection and removal of potentially dangerous drugs from the drug supply chain to protect U.S. consumers* (adapted from (Jung & Food, 2014)).

Thus, there would be a necessity of enabling track and trace capability within the pharmaceutical supply chain by 2023. In a similar vein, the European Union released the Falsified Medicines Directive (FMD) to harmonize measures against medicine falsifications, and to ensure drug safety and controls of medicine trade. The directive includes *obligatory safety features a unique identifier and an anti-tampering device on the outer packaging of medicines, a shared, EU wide logo to identify legal online pharmacies, Tougher rules on the import of active pharmaceutical ingredients, strengthened record-keeping requirements for wholesale distributors* (EU, 2021). As a part of the DSCSA Pilot Program under the FDA, several pilot projects were initiated to explore and evaluate the processes and technological areas to enhance the safety and security of the drug supply chain with the blockchain technology (FDA, 2019, 2020a). Specific pilot projects were initiated to address the areas of Interoperability, Processes (serialization, product tracing, verification/notifications, aggregation, exceptions handling…), Data (simulated/real, product/transaction), Systems/Architecture/Databases, Technologies (blockchain, data carriers, barcode readability), Governance and Implementation Challenges. The key purpose is to enhance traceability of the therapeutic product, to ensure that the right patient receives the correct medicinal product at a proper dosage via a correct route of administration at the right time (Klein & Stolk, 2018). The current approaches are focused on the track and trace at the level of batch numbers and the European Medicines Agency (EMA) recommends a *routine bar code scanning at all points in the supply chain*(EMA, 2016b; Klein & Stolk, 2018).

Our visionary concept positions the blockchain technology, firstly within the internal ecosystem of the pharmaceutical companies to address the aspects of data integrity and connect the internal siloed structures of the pharmaceutical company to increase transparency, trust, and coordination, for adherence to regulatory guidelines in an efficient manner. Moreover, the internal blockchain ecosystem would be a trigger to extend and connect with the external ecosystem, to facilitate the track and trace necessities from regulators and bring transparency through to the patient, and to ascertain the distribution of authentic and safe medicinal products. Thus, facilitating the introduction of blockchain with a modular set-up. From the perspective of managing the transformation, the internal ecosystem is partly standardized, and it will be easier to establish the introduction of blockchain technology in a less complex internal ecosystem first, and then extend to a higher level of complexity within the external ecosystem. Indeed, keeping a set of information filters at the merger between the internal and external ecosystem. Thus, sharing externally only the data that is relevant for the track and trace, that verifies the authenticity of the medicinal products.

Our conceptual case in this chapter focuses on the elaboration of a Minimum Viable Ecosystem for a Blockchain workflow specific to the internal context i.e., by detailing the use of blockchain in the biopharmaceutical quality control to assure data integrity, and thereby connecting or extending it later to the external ecosystem towards the track and trace.

CASE DESCRIPTION

Introduction

Our concept focuses on providing a lean and agile approach to formulate the introduction of a blockchain technology in the biopharmaceutical industry and in particular, within a typical Quality Control Laboratories, in order to enhance the data integrity of the operational process. To this aim, the conceptual minimum viable ecosystem (MVE) for the blockchain would be made up of participants categorized as either internal or external, depending on whether they are part of the organization or part of an external unit. This approach will allow the reduction regarding the complexities and provide a favourable environment to initiate the set-up of blockchain within the healthcare sector. As a subset for elaborating a Proof of Concept (PoC) approach towards a minimal viable ecosystem, in Table I, the players specific to the categorization of the internal and external ecosystem have been described.

Table 1. Players in the ecosystem

Ecosystem	Actor	Description
Internal	Suppliers	Suppliers provide raw materials such as chemicals and laboratory consumables, which are used across the medicinal product manufacturing, testing, distribution processes.
	Manufacturing	The manufacturing function is responsible for the processes that transform the raw materials into the final product, which must be tested before the introduction in the market.
	Quality Control	Quality Control is a support function that monitors the features and characteristics of the product by testing samples of manufactured batches according to safety and efficacy standards.
	Quality Assurance	Quality Assurance is a support function that verifies that entire operations are performed by the compliance and health authorities' requirements.
External	Regulators	Regulators audit the product data to ensure compliance towards safety and efficacy.
	Distributors	Distributors manage and deliver the medicinal products at large unit volumes, to retailers/pharmacies or hospitals.
	Retailer	Retailers deliver the medicinal product to the end-users such as patients or hospitals.
	Patients	Patients are the end-users of the medicinal product and are the most fundamental actors in the ecosystem.

Internal Ecosystem: Quality Control (QC)

The pervasiveness of the current Good Manufacturing Practices (CGMPs) requirements is not by itself an assurance of error-free products or processes. To test and monitor the quality of products, specific functions inside a biopharmaceutical company are devoted to the monitoring of the product's features. According to the Food and Drug Administration, *The pharmaceutical quality control laboratory serves one of the most important functions in pharmaceutical production and control* (FDA, 2014). Quality Control activities are of paramount importance in the process of the market release of safe drugs. Quality Control Laboratories (QC) are part of the core activities of the "pharmaceutical quality system" in biopharmaceutical companies for testing the quality of final products, in-process samples and the raw materials used in the manufacturing process. In order to accomplish its mission of monitoring product quality, a typical Quality Control (QC) laboratory is equipped with sophisticated scientific instruments (e.g., microscopes, centrifuges, chromatography systems, sample preparation equipment) managed by knowledgeable operators (e.g., scientists, biologists, and statisticians) that test the quality of samples of every batch of medicinal products, according to a set of standard methods and procedures, to verify the conformity of the product to its specifications and ensure safety and efficacy. The testing allows monitoring of the product quality to ensure the efficacy and safety of the therapeutic product. The Quality Control operations follow Current Good Manufacturing Practices (CGMPs) adhering to regulatory and compliance guidelines with clear and concise documentation. Typically, the product testing is performed as by the standard operating procedures (SOPs), using an analytical method that is specifically developed and validated for quality testing purposes. The sequential steps encountered in the product testing involve sample preparations, analyzing the sample on scientific equipment, data acquisition and processing, interpretation of results, and reporting. The Quality Control operations are under constant pressure to adhere to the schedules and the delivery of test results as right first time being on the critical path for the final product release for commercialization. Thus, minimalizing the margins for manual errors, variabilities, and non-compliances. Hence, these aspects have a higher impact on the business costs and compliance with health regulators. In this context, the need for clear and concise documentation translates into additional efforts, that arise within the biopharmaceutical organization. Currently, the process for assuring data integrity does not rely on a blockchain system, and the process is partially manual with operator checks and using traditional IT systems and databases.

Data Integrity

Health authorities release warning letters related to data integrity issues. In 2018, approximately 40% of warning letters included a data integrity component (Unger, 2019). Examples of data integrity issues sampled from FDA's warning letter range from data signatures that did not match the person who was present on that working day, or the backdating of results to meet requirements or the alteration of original raw data. Within the digitalization drive, the systems need to be integrated and the interconnections defined. However, even the structuring of the data systems, internal to the biopharmaceutical industry, is a complex process involving multiple functional stakeholders and it is prone to data integrity issues. This leads to inconsistencies, multiple sources of data, or accidental errors or typos. Structuring the data of the entire process of developing drugs towards its market release is difficult to manage and retrieving data is challenging and inefficient, often leading to the loss of information. The automatic system facilitates the process, eliminating annoying steps such as that of interpreting incomprehensible notes from scientists or accidental typos, further strengthening the adherence of working in compliance.

The monitoring of compliance and quality of products and processes within the Quality Control function generates data that is crucial to understand the compliance performance and the control of variabilities within the entire lifecycle of the biopharmaceutical product. The generated data is inscribed into documentations as reported in physical and digital archives (i.e., paper, or electronic records), and are stored in various formats from paper-based to digital files that include the processed data, metadata, and raw data. According to the Good Manufacturing Practices requirements, all the activities must be comprehensively documented. The documentations broadly cover the actions of operators such as results of experiments on the test samples, the use and maintenance of equipment (e.g., calibration, cleaning), historical records dealing with the operator's training (confirming that they are qualified and trained to perform the tasks), and environmental data on physical parameters such as temperature. The information is usually stored in the Quality Control laboratory notebooks or instrument logbooks (either paper-based or electronic). Hence, adherence to compliance entails efforts on data related to the generation (e.g., documentation), maintenance (e.g., retention), verification (e.g., the cost for search) and sharing (e.g., with the health authorities and within the organization) of data. Thus, there is high complexity in operating processes and a variety of data is generated throughout the steps of the process. Consequently, the integrity of data inscribed in documentations is of paramount importance in the biopharmaceutical industry. Moreover, the audits carried out when monitoring the status of compliance often rely on document inspections and analysis. To ensure that the data is reliable, its management revolves around the principles of data quality, compliance, and audibility. Indeed, all the data outflows and inflows in the Quality Control labs have to satisfy the principles of Attributability, Legibility, Contemporaneity, Originality, and Accuracy (ALCOA) (PICS/S Secretariat, 2018). To synthesize, the ALCOA principles are reported in Table 2.

Table 2. ALCOA principles

	Pillar	Expectations *(not exhaustive)*
ALCOA	Attributability	The action that led to the creation, modification, deletion of the data entity must be uniquely identifiable in a specific user (i.e., with electronic signature) and with a specific timestamp.
	Legible, traceable, and Permanent	Data must be readable and must show a clear chain of evidence to trace back all the actions at any point of time, during the necessary time length of data storage. Moreover, alterations to the data cannot be saved in a temporal local memory but must be always recorded permanently, and no overwriting must be enabled. Data must be stored in enduring databases with open formats (e.g., PDF, XML, SGML) and backups schedules must allow for disaster recovery.
	Contemporaneity	Data must be recorded at the same time it is generated and observed. Time zones must be synchronized across the global systems and the system must be always reachable.
	Originality	The original source of data or record (which could even be a paper-based document) must be complete, reviewed and retained for the whole retention period.
	Accuracy	Data must be correct, represent the truth, be complete, valid, and reliable. To have the accuracy, systems and processes must be qualified and validated (e.g., calibrating a balance, monitoring the data transmission system).

(WHO 926 - 53rd report Annex 5, 2016)

Solution

Our proposal entails a solution able to integrate the external and internal ecosystem in a lean manner, starting from the Quality Control (QC) function and the specific data integrity (data integrity in the internal siloed structures of the biopharmaceutical company to increase transparency, trust, and coordination) and track and trace capabilities (as requirements from regulators and bring transparency through to the patient). Our concept is designed within one function (actor/stakeholder), i.e., by detailing the use of the blockchain in the biopharmaceutical quality control focusing on data integrity.

The conceptual blockchain-based solution design is focused on the application of a hybrid blockchain. The overall approach is to link the internal ecosystem processes (e.g., data generated within Quality Control labs, manufacturing, supply chain departments etc.) to the external ecosystem (e.g., health authorities, patients, and hospitals) through internal validation mechanisms. Thus, the set-up within the Minimum Viable Ecosystem is to be configured internally as a closed enterprise blockchain, linking different functions within the same organization with a restricted and preapproved group of participants with a specific role and privileges. An internal private blockchain intends to preserve the intellectual property related to the information on the products and their processes. Thus, not fully available for public disclosure. The gateway between the internal and external ecosystem is to be configured to allow the linkage of limited internal information to the product in accordance with the track and trace needs from the regulators. The authors envision the external environment as a second component of the blockchain solution. That is, an external public permissioned blockchain is set up to allow information sharing within the external ecosystem of players (Hewett, Lehmacher, & Wang, 2019). The hybrid blockchain-based solution allows meeting the data integrity for the internal processes to provide traceability, data accuracy, visibility, security, and connected real-time data on the verification of quality parameters within the biopharmaceutical company. Once the internal validation is performed, the blockchain securely shares the relevant information with the external ecosystem. The conceptual solution is shown in Figure 3. However, in the context of this chapter, emphasis is focused on the internal ecosystem in the first phase of the blockchain deployment. Thus, allowing to structure the concept in an agile and lean approach while having reduced complexities.

Figure 3. Envisioned blockchain configuration

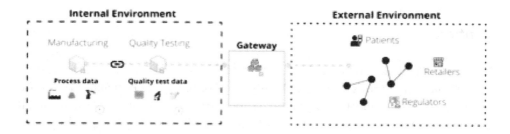

The blockchain technology implementation will help to meet ALCOA requirements with an enhanced adherence to compliance through data verification between parties. Within the internal ecosystem, blockchain technology can streamline the interactions across internal functions (e.g., Manufacturing, Quality Control, Quality Assurance). With the implementation of the blockchain in the internal ecosystem, trust is decentralized. Internally, the blockchain is configured to allow the data to be verified and shared through a validation strategy. Each step of the biopharmaceutical operations will be performed at the specific nodes of the blockchain in accordance with the business logic. Nodes that send data to the blockchain rely on the Proof of Authority (PoA) validation strategy as the internal network is private and nodes are aware of each other and their belonging to the network is pre-specified. Hence, nodes validate transactions based on their unique status inside the network based on the operational business logic. The value from blockchain technology in the biopharmaceutical industry will be driven with smart contracts, that can be set in place to automatize the processes of verification and cross-checking of information based on predefined parameters. It will allow the batches that are proceeding toward the market to be compliant, and at the same time, capture the non-conformance events by triggering the manual root cause analysis and investigation. Smart contracts would define the conformity range of the product and process with enhanced traceability and transparency towards higher compliance. The flow of data in the internal setting is shown in Figure 4. Firstly, the flow covers the internal manufacturing unit operational information, that is transmitted into the blockchain. This information is related to the product in terms of supplier identification codes, corresponding raw material compositions and the linked batch of production. This first block allows an easier and trustable track and trace mechanism and a comprehensive set of information to be added to the blockchain for later inspection from other units. Then, the quality testing phase performed by Quality Control proceeds with the analysis of the sample batches, having its history in terms of composition and adding a second block with information related to the results of the testing activities, including the recording of all the equipment, personnel, and procedures that have to be captured according to the documentation guidelines. In this manner, data alteration is infeasible, and any changes and version history are easy to identify and check. This system enforces the consistency of the shared data by avoiding data manipulation and enhancing the audit verification process (both internally and externally).

Figure 4. Flow of the internal environment (with and without the blockchain)

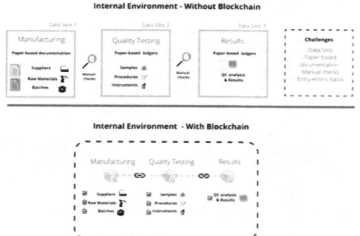

A secure Application Program Interface (API) communication layer connects the internal quality data on products with the external product movements, thus allowing the data integrity along with the track and trace until the product reaches the patient. Hence, on one side, it increases inter-organizational data integrity with selective data privacy, and on the other, it enhances the point-to-point internal coordination. This intra and inter-organizational configuration would allow for enhanced regulatory compliance with reduced costs and efforts for the pharmaceutical companies.

The use of blockchain can reinvent data management in the intra and inter-relationship which occur within the organization and with the regulators. The solution would bring the use of an efficient and effective data exchange process through a ledger that lowers the transaction cost and increases coordination and transparency across the ecosystem. The implementation would majorly exploit the benefit and value of the technology, as reported in Table 3.

Table 3. Blockchain benefits and business challenges

Benefit area	Current Process issues	Improvements	BC Business Challenges
Data Integrity enhancement	Data silos, paper-based documentation and manual checks on electronic data may lead to several kinds of risks (e.g., typos, alteration, data losses, inconsistency, cyberattacks)	The envisioned configuration brings together several units to increase data integrity and consistency, creating a single and unmodifiable source of truth. Data from machines (e.g., status, calibration, location, integrity, versioning), operators (e.g., training path, inspectors) and manufacturing e.g., suppliers, distributors) is validated and added to the distributed database. Moreover, smart contracts can outline the ranges of data and conditions that guarantee the compliance of the system, resulting in increased trust in the inter-organizational processes.	The digitalization of every lab, as well as the upskilling of workers, is a precondition for implementing a blockchain-based solution that entails high resource commitment. Each instrument must be connected to the blockchain and able to produce digital output, as well as the operator, must understand the functioning of the new process. Moreover, to avoid data silos, global companies must set a standard and common policies across functions.
Audit trail	Currently, as soon as an observation or trigger event emerges, the organization must trace back, verify, and collect all the relevant information on the event. For example, by inspecting notes (digital or paper-based) and performing analysis on audit trials, leading to an increasing engagement of resources.	The chain of blocks enhances the visibility and tracing of the process, fostering more reliable and consistent workflows. All the sample composition, movements, quality checks, and market release can be tracked with a single and immutable audit trail that captures the who, what, where, and when. Thus, augmenting data traceability and accountability to construct the product lifecycle and to have a reliable and consistent quality management system as per the Current Good Manufacturing Practices (GMP) needs.	The audit trail has to integrate data from multiple sources; hence, data inconsistencies challenges may arise if rules and policies regarding the role of each unit in the system are not given the correct priority and rights.
Cybersecurity and data security	Currently, companies strive to carefully share information to avoid accidental (e.g., errors) or unintended (e.g., attacks) data leaks or breaches that can result in major consequences for the protection of intellectual property or loss of company reputation.	Blockchain can help to maintain data security and confidentiality. In particular, the hybrid configuration as discussed in this chapter allows the sharing of specific data only after the internal validation of the company with a limited level of information to meet the exact needs of the regulators. Moreover, the distributed ledger is resistant to attacks and single point failures due to the distributed storage.	New IT systems that require new capabilities for their development and maintenance have to be set in place. The gaps in competencies might slow down the diffusion process.

CURRENT CHALLENGES FACING THE ORGANIZATION

Through the years, several companies, have shown their intention to commit to Blockchain. However, due to the complexities of the operational processes in the biopharmaceutical companies and the interactions involved in the distribution of medicinal products to finally reach patients, there are numerous challenges. From a broader perspective, several implementation challenges are related to the immature state-of-the-art of blockchain technology and the competitive based approach of companies. One major challenge is related to the lack of interoperability among different blockchain networks, which in most cases, retain standalone protocols, coding languages, consensus mechanisms and privacy measures in disagreement with each other. With the purpose to avoid this problem, a potential solution would relate to the setting of universal standards enabling different networks to communicate and allow companies to collaborate on the application development, validate proof of concept and share blockchain solutions. From a managerial point of view, a shift in organizational thinking is needed, as companies are only focused on developing their own networks to overcome competitors, implying the consequent creation of multiple blockchain standards with multiple differences.

Concerning our conceptual case, the blockchain creates multiple opportunities to primarily benefit the biopharmaceutical Quality Control function and thereby internally extending it transversely to the various stakeholders. However, companies tend to struggle with the adoption of emerging technological paradigms: Some of the limiting factors for the blockchain adoption range from the immaturity and costs of the technology to the need of reaching an industry standard, and to the organizational readiness (Toufaily, Zalan, & Dhaou, 2021). Moreover, before blockchain adoption within the organization, the Information Technology backbone needs to be well-built in order to allow the intended benefits from the blockchain. Indeed, it is possible that some companies still rely on paper-based archives or are equipped with stand-alone and old generation machines that are not interconnected or produce analog data. Hence, the first step is to digitize and digitalize all the necessary steps to avoid bottlenecks due to the coexistence of digital and non-digital data. Connected instruments, Internet of Things (IoT) and similar industry 4.0 related investments must be sustained, prior to generating flows of data within all company laboratories and processes within the blockchain. An effective blockchain solution would thrive on such a technological ecosystem and unlock all the benefits intended by the technology. Digitally enabled QC laboratories would generally provide significant cost reductions. Just the reduction of paper usage by 80% provides an important tangible benefit to the Quality Control laboratories of the biopharmaceutical companies (Han, Makarova, Ringel, & Telpis, 2019), and have a positive impact on the environment towards the sustainability drivers. The current process sometimes involves manual data transcription and requires a second operator to validate the data. With the advent of blockchain, a fully automatic digital-enabled system would be set. Such change is crucial both in terms of productive efficiency, and to achieve sustainable performances and significant long-run cost reductions. On average, an automated Quality Control laboratory can cut costs by 25 to 45 per cent, but still, there is a low tendency to approach new paths, also because of old paradigms retention among employees (Han et al., 2019).

Nevertheless, before an organization can respond to any type of technology disruption, it is important to understand the nature of that disruption. Digitally maturing companies are reimagining structures, resetting strategies, encouraging cross-sector collaborations, and opening new ways of working and doing businesses. Whereas, the remaining others that are mainly waiting at the window, would tend to lose huge opportunities (Deloitte, 2018). To overcome the technical and organizational challenges, the managers must plan and consider specific change management approaches to facilitate the transition to new technological paradigms such as the blockchain. The biopharmaceutical industry technology gap is not likely to immediately disappear because of a positive trend. In order to eliminate it, the organisation need to aim for future strategies by looking at the new organizational structures and cultural changes among all organizational members. Transformation is not only a problem of technology but above all, it concerns the ability of the organization and individuals to include innovative cultures in the mindset of each employee, i.e., from the top management level to the scientists and at the shop floor. Almost certainly, employees are attached to previous working success routines and may be reluctant to change in the future. Bringing blockchain technologies in the biopharmaceutical industry needs a change not only in terms of acquiring the technology, and its related competencies, but also a change in the management culture and its operational processes. Therefore, the introduction of a new technology into the day-to-day operations entails a company and industry-wide process of change, where collaboration among industry players and regulators is essential. To lead the company-wide changes, there is a need for structured managerial approaches. New technologies are disrupting the manner of doing business in many manufacturing industries, enhancing paces and overall requiring new cultural attitudes and change in the employee's mindset. The organizations need to acknowledge this shift within the environment in order to build a sustainable future.

The majority of biopharmaceutical companies lack high investments commitment to automation and distributed Quality Control (Han et al., 2019). The top management may argue that not all operational processes have sufficient volumes to justify such investments; in this context, there would be a probability to lose benefit opportunities within the long-run perspective (Han et al., 2019). In order to monitor the benefit brought on by the implementation of the solution, specific benefit areas are selected and reported in Table 4. These indicators allow us to focus the attention and quantify the benefit expected from the application of the blockchain in this context. Most of the benefits configured under efficiency, as the output of compliance and quality, are the main concerns of the biopharmaceutical companies and quality control commitment The framework is useful to align sponsors on the expected benefits and related impacts and provide a guideline to monitor the expected benefits after the implementation.

Table 4. Blockchain implementation indicators and analytics

Drivers	Benefits						Estimate on AS-IS Cost
Efficiency	Reduction in data processing timelines	Peak time accommodation	Reduction in human error	Increased adherence to standards	Auditability of the process	Improved quality of output	50-60%
	Operator time saving (or overtime) calculated as AS-IS minus TO BE hours		Historical frequency of errors in AS-IS process minus TO BE process; Standard Cost for rework & mitigation process				
Innovation & Technology	Boosting innovation – new business area	Agility and forward-looking focus	Fostering an innovation and data culture	Improved data maturity	Competitive advantage from improved operations		10-15%
			Time savings by reusing existing data		-		
People	Up-skilling of workforce with digital skills	Redeploy operators to high-value tasks	Boosting engagement by focusing on creative, intellectual, and social tasks		Improved training and knowledge documentation		10%
					Reduction in training time from AS-IS process minus TO BE process AS-IS training hours		
Sustainability	Minimize use of paper-based archives	Improved utilization of resources by load balancing	-		-		10%
	Potential Reduction in Carbon footprint as contributed by AS-IS minus TO BE process				-		

SOLUTIONS AND RECOMMENDATIONS

Our conceptual proposal is to envision the internal and external organizational ecosystems for the positioning of the blockchain technology in the healthcare sector using a modular setup. The scope is to allow a leaner technology implementation in order to address the current data integrity challenges in the internal siloed structures of the pharmaceutical company in order to increase transparency, trust, and coordination.

This is to further extend the ecosystem to facilitate the track and trace necessities from regulators and bring this transparency through the patient. As a conceptual instantiation in this chapter, our concept is designed within one function (actor/ stakeholder), i.e., by detailing the use of the blockchain in the biopharmaceutical quality control focusing on the data integrity aspect.

In this chapter, the authors have presented the blockchain opportunity within the biopharmaceutical quality control operations as a conceptual case. The intention is to initiate the use of blockchain technology within the healthcare sector, even though much of the focus on the use of blockchain has been on the supply chain and distribution of medicinal products, due to the emerging regulatory guidelines. The paradigm of deploying the blockchain technology across multiple external stakeholders is highly challenging. Therefore, our concept focuses on a modular approach to address two important areas of the biopharmaceutical industry and healthcare system i.e. data integrity to increase transparency, trust, and coordination within the internal ecosystem of the biopharmaceutical company, and track and trace to facilitate transparency and authenticity of the medicinal products for the patients.

As the authors have elaborated the conceptual application of blockchain towards ensuring data integrity within the internal ecosystem, there is the need to open the stage to a more important question which is: "How can the biopharmaceutical industry achieve a well-performing blockchain-based traceability system?" This question is addressed by reviewing the main benefit that the blockchain-based traceability could create for a company such as the authenticity of the data, efficiency, transparency, and security. The time perspective for the blockchain pursual will be important to have technology structuring, and its implementation leading to the tangible benefits at the right time. In the long run, the introduction of the Blockchain is all about enhancing trust. Currently, the biopharmaceutical industry suffers from an absence of trust between different participants (Han et al., 2019). Blockchain allows the decentralization of trust with a process that is immutable and highly reliable. The dependency of an intermediatory third party is eliminated, and the entire system is self-validating. Thus, reinvents the data management with a decentralized approach.

The deployment of our visionary blockchain concept within the biopharmaceutical industry will require an adequate strategy, that involves a phase appropriate management approach. Here, the digital innovation of introducing the blockchain is phase appropriately structured via a hybrid model that combines traditional Stage-Gated approaches - characterized by incremental phases (in terms of scale, costs, and resources with reduced risks) and Go-No/Go gates to evaluate the progress and have the option to disengage resources if the outcomes are not achieved or allow changing the scopes as by the evolving nature of benefits. The use of Agility Based approaches is to favour rapid sprints of development and frequent feedback on the product deliverable as a continuous adaptation to needs and contingencies arising during the innovation process. This practical strategy allows the pursuing of the change starting from a Proof-of-Concept phase, entailing the experimentation and development of a Minimum Viable Product, in order to prove the conceptual application of the blockchain in a sandboxed approach and gain confidence that the solution meets the intended business objectives. Thus, the Proof of Concept (PoC) phase sets the visionary forecast of the expected benefits envisioned as a justification to pursue the investment, for the second phase. Following the PoC, the Proof of Feasibility has the objective to develop the minimum viable product according to requirements and needs gathered more closely to the day-to-day working environment and testing it on a rolling basis. This phase is crucial to emphasize with the employee who will need to interact with the solution, so as to build, for example, all the peripheral features that are necessary to move the solution toward the full integration with the legacy IT system and gain acceptance from other employees and alignment with the legacy operational processes in the organization. In this second phase, the engagement of resources is increased in order to cover additional features following the needs of all the stakeholders. Proof of Feasibility provides real-world metrics on the benefit and performances of the solution, that can be monitored on an evolving basis and benchmarked with the initially envisioned benefits from PoC. The last and concluding phase is the Proof of Value phase, which seeks to bring the solution into routine operation and to fully integrate it into the business operations of the organization. This is just a visionary overview of the approach, that could be used to build digital innovations, such as the envisioned blockchain concept by strategically managing the systemic barriers. Of note, the cultural maturity towards the implementation of the blockchain is a vast topic on its own and relevant management strategies are needed to be planned specifically for the organization.

ACKNOWLEDGMENT

The authors wish to thank Mara Rossi and Tobias Haas from Merck for supporting the review of the content, that has greatly assisted us to understand the process and structure of the arguments. Furthermore, the authors extend our thanks to Laura Fumei for the English language proof reading of the article.

REFERENCES

Cauchon, N. S., Oghamian, S., Hassanpour, S., & Abernathy, M. (2019, July 1). Innovation in Chemistry, Manufacturing, and Controls—A Regulatory Perspective From Industry. *Journal of Pharmaceutical Sciences*. doi:10.1016/j.xphs.2019.02.007

Declerck, P. J. (2012). Biologicals and biosimilars: A review of the science and its implications. *GaBi Journal, 1*(1), 13–16. doi:10.5639/gabij.2012.0101.005

Deloitte. (2018). *Survey finds biopharma companies lag in digital transformation It is time for a sea change in strategy.* Retrieved from https://www2.deloitte.com/content/dam/Deloitte/de/Documents/life-sciences-health-care/DI_CHS-MIT-survey_Final.pdf

EMA. (2016a). *Guidance on good manufacturing practice and good distribution practice: Questions and answers.* European Medicines Agency. Retrieved from https://www.ema.europa.eu/en/human-regulatory/research-development/compliance/good-manufacturing-practice/guidance-good-manufacturing-practice-good-distribution-practice-questions-answers

EMA. (2016b). *Track-change version following public consultation Guideline on good pharmacovigilance practices (GVP) Product-or Population-Specific Considerations II: Biological medicinal products.* Retrieved from https://www.ema.europa.eu/en/documents/scientific-guideline/guideline-good-pharmacovigilance-practices-gvp-product-population-specific-considerations-ii_en-0.pdf

EU. (2021). *Falsified medicines.* Retrieved January 4, 2021, from https://ec.europa.eu/health/human-use/falsified_medicines_en

Farid, S. S., Baron, M., Stamatis, C., Nie, W., & Coffman, J. (2020). Benchmarking biopharmaceutical process development and manufacturing cost contributions to R&D. *mAbs, 12*(1), 1754999. doi:10.1080/19420862.2020.1754999 PMID:32449439

FDA. (2014). *Pharmaceutical Quality Control Labs (7/93).* Retrieved June 11, 2021, from https://www.fda.gov/inspections-compliance-enforcement-and-criminal-investigations/inspection-guides/pharmaceutical-quality-control-labs-793

FDA. (2019). *DSCSA Pilot Project Program.* Retrieved from https://www.fda.gov/drugs/drug-supply-chain-security-act-dscsa/dscsa-pilot-project-program

FDA. (2020a). *Drug Supply Chain Security Act pilot project program and enhanced drug distribution security.* Retrieved from https://www.fda.gov/drugs/news-events-human-drugs/drug-supply-chain-security-act-pilot-project-program-and-enhanced-drug-distribution-security

FDA. (2020b). *New Drug Therapy Approvals.* Retrieved from https://www.fda.gov/media/133911/download

Food and Drug Administration. (2016). *Data Integrity and Compliance With CGMP Guidance for Industry*. Retrieved from https://www.fda.gov/files/drugs/published/Data-Integrity-and-Compliance-With-Current-Good-Manufacturing-Practice-Guidance-for-Industry.pdf

Gopal, G., Suter-Crazzolara, C., Toldo, L., & Eberhardt, W. (2019). Digital transformation in healthcare - Architectures of present and future information technologies. In *Clinical Chemistry and Laboratory Medicine* (Vol. 57, pp. 328–335). De Gruyter. doi:10.1515/cclm-2018-0658

Han, Y., Makarova, E., Ringel, M., & Telpis, V. (2019). *Industry 4.0, innovation, and pharmaceutical quality control*. Retrieved May 28, 2021, from https://www.mckinsey.com/industries/pharmaceuticals-and-medical-products/our-insights/digitization-automation-and-online-testing-the-future-of-pharma-quality-control

Hewett, N., Lehmacher, W., & Wang, Y. (2019). *Inclusive Deployment of Blockchain for Supply Chains: Part 1 – Introduction*. World Economic Forum.

Jung, C., & Food, U. S. (2014). *Drug Supply Chain Security Act*. Retrieved January 4, 2021, from https://www.fda.gov/Drugs/DrugSafety/DrugIntegrityandSupplyChainSecurity/DrugSupplyChainSecurityAct/

Klein, K., & Stolk, P. (2018). Challenges and Opportunities for the Traceability of (Biological) Medicinal Products. *Drug Safety, 41*(10), 911–918. doi:10.100740264-018-0678-7 PMID:29721822

la Torre, B. G., & Albericio, F. (2021). The Pharmaceutical Industry in 2020. An Analysis of FDA Drug Approvals from the Perspective of Molecules. *Molecules (Basel, Switzerland), 26*(3), 627. Advance online publication. doi:10.3390/molecules26030627 PMID:33504104

Makurvet, F. D. (2021). Biologics vs. small molecules: Drug costs and patient access. *Medicine in Drug Discovery, 9*, 100075. doi:10.1016/j.medidd.2020.100075

Medicines & Healthcare products Regulatory Agency. (2018). *Medicines & Healthcare products Regulatory Agency (MHRA) "GXP" Data Integrity Guidance and Definitions*. Author.

Morrell, B. (2017). *How to strengthen product life cycle management using blockchain*. Retrieved June 11, 2021, from https://www.ey.com/en_gl/life-sciences/how-to-strengthen-product-life-cycle-management-using-blockchain

Mullard, A. (2014). New drugs cost US$2.6 billion to develop. *Nature Reviews. Drug Discovery, 13*(12), 877–877. doi:10.1038/nrd4507 PMID:25435204

Pharma R&D Annual Review. (2020). Retrieved from https://pharmaintelligence. informa.com/~/media/informa-shop-window/pharma/2020/files/whitepapers/rd-review-2020-whitepaper.pdf

PICS/S Secretariat. (2018). *Guidance on Data Integrity.* Retrieved from https://picscheme.org/users_uploads/news_news_documents/PI_041_1_Draft_3_Guidance_on_Data_Integrity.pdf

Rafferty, J. P. (2018). *The Rise of the Machines: Pros and Cons of the Industrial Revolution.* Retrieved January 4, 2021, from https://www.britannica.com/story/the-rise-of-the-machines-pros-and-cons-of-the-industrial-revolution

Rattan, A. K. (2018, March). Data integrity: History, issues, and remediation of issues. *PDA Journal of Pharmaceutical Science and Technology.* doi:10.5731/pdajpst.2017.007765

Scannell, J. W., Blanckley, A., Boldon, H., & Warrington, B. (2012, March). Diagnosing the decline in pharmaceutical R&D efficiency. *Nature Reviews. Drug Discovery, 11*(3), 191–200. Advance online publication. doi:10.1038/nrd3681 PMID:22378269

Steinwandter, V., & Herwig, C. (2019). Provable data integrity in the pharmaceutical industry based on version control systems and the blockchain. *PDA Journal of Pharmaceutical Science and Technology, 73*(4), 373–390. doi:10.5731/pdajpst.2018.009407 PMID:30770485

Stericycle. (n.d.). *Recall Index.* Retrieved June 11, 2021, from https://pages.stericycleexpertsolutions.co.uk/2020-q3-recall-index-ous

Toufaily, E., Zalan, T., & Ben Dhaou, S. (2021). A framework of blockchain technology adoption: An investigation of challenges and expected value. *Information & Management, 58*(3), 103444. doi:10.1016/j.im.2021.103444

Unger, B. (2019). *An Analysis Of 2018 FDA Warning Letters Citing Data Integrity Failures.* Retrieved June 1, 2021, from https://www.pharmaceuticalonline.com/doc/an-analysis-of-fda-warning-letters-on-data-integrity-0003

Van Norman, G. A. (2016). Drugs, Devices, and the FDA: Part 1: An Overview of Approval Processes for Drugs. *JACC. Basic to Translational Science, 1*(3), 170–179. Advance online publication. doi:10.1016/j.jacbts.2016.03.002 PMID:30167510

WHO. (2016). *Annex 5 Guidance on good data and record management practices. WHO Technical Report Series.* Retrieved from https://www.who.int/medicines/publications/pharmprep/WHO_TRS_996_annex05.pdf

Chapter 7
Blockchain Tokenisation in Grant Management

Conrad Kraft
University of Nicosia, Cyprus

Mariana Carmona
University of Nicosia, Cyprus

ABSTRACT

Grant management is a vital process that enables organisations to successfully deliver programmes that address social, economic, environmental, and other challenges. Globally, grant transfers represent significant sums, and their management is fraught with deficiencies that undermine the impact of the donated funds. Among the most urgent challenges in grant management are to improve transparency and reduce high administration costs. Digital transformation has done much to enhance efficiency, transparency, and accountability in grant administration; however, numerous shortcomings still exist. Blockchain, smart contracts, and tokenisation can be combined to achieve greater levels of efficiency and control in grant management than is currently possible. Through the study of fundamental blockchain concepts, the authors propose a grant-management solution that tokenises every expenditure item and uses smart contracts to automate payments, reporting, and budgetary compliance.

INTRODUCTION

Populations living in poverty across the world suffer from social ills ranging from a lack of basic social infrastructure (water, sanitation, electricity, healthcare access,

DOI: 10.4018/978-1-7998-8014-1.ch007

etc.) to discrimination and hunger. These challenges severely jeopardise the futures of people in countless communities who are desperate to escape the cycles of hopelessness that these social ills create. Governments, multilateral organisations, foundations, and philanthropists attempt to address these issues by developing and funding programs to the tune of trillions of US dollars annually.

Unfortunately, shortcomings in the management of grant programs, such as the misappropriation of funds and poor oversight of administration, prevent many people from benefiting from the assistance they desperately need. To address these deficiencies, a number of different grant management systems have been developed over time. These systems have sought to incorporate new tools to update their capabilities in accordance with the latest technological advances. Still, much inefficiency in grant management persists.

Since 2008, blockchain technology has shaken up the financial world and the Internet at large. With unprecedented automation capabilities, enhanced security, and real-time auditability, it holds great promise to significantly address current inefficiencies in grant management.

This chapter explores the use of blockchain in grant management by paying particular attention to the core features of blockchain and blockchain tokenisation that are relevant to the administration of grants. Through an exploration of a case study, significant challenges in current grant management systems are highlighted and a blockchain-based solution is proposed while further expounding on the lesser-known features of blockchain tokenisation.

BACKGROUND

Blockchain and Smart Contracts: The Basics

Since the release of Satoshi Nakamoto's white paper (2008), where the first cryptocurrency—bitcoin—was unveiled, blockchain, the underlying technology of bitcoin, has gained traction in applications beyond finance and payment systems. Blockchains, as the name suggests, consist of a chain of blocks that enable peer-to-peer transactions in an append-only distributed database, with tamper-proof, time-stamped transactions that are secured by cryptographically distributed trust and incentivised consensus (Cong & He, 2019, p. 8). Its novel feature set includes decentralisation, immutability, real-time traceability, auditability, security, and privacy.

Decentralisation in blockchain technology refers to the distributed validation of transactions without reliance on a central authority. Distributed nodes validate transactions according to a consensus mechanism that combines cryptography with economic incentives (Narayanan et al., 2016). Decentralisation safeguards data contained on a blockchain against a single point of failure, a shortcoming of centralised systems (Kraft & Carmona, 2020).

Immutability refers to the unalterable nature of blockchain records. Each block is chronologically ordered and inextricably tied to each other using a hash pointer, which references all other blocks in the blockchain. Therefore, if a malicious actor wanted to modify transactions within a block, they would have to alter all preceding transactions back to the genesis (first) block of the blockchain (Kraft & Carmona, 2020). In this way, no record can be reasonably reversed, or modified, establishing the reliability and credibility of records. Although transactions cannot be reasonably altered, the manipulation of transactions is possible; however, it requires an inordinate amount of resources, which is economically and computationally prohibitive.

Blockchains further ensure sound, real-time, traceability with the use of a search-engine-like tool called a block explorer. Block explorers enable any individual to view all transactions that have taken place on a blockchain. Moreover, since transactions and blocks are immutable, transparent, and traceable, a blockchain ledger provides an inherent level of assurance towards fulfilling audit assertions—completeness, occurrence, accuracy, existence, valuation, and cut-off (Kraft & Carmona, 2020).

Smart Contracts

Since Bitcoin, other blockchains have rapidly emerged and expanded upon Bitcoin's features. One such blockchain is Ethereum, most widely utilised for decentralised applications (dApps). Unlike the Bitcoin blockchain, Ethereum introduced greater functionality with the development of smart contracts.

Smart contracts are generally understood as machine-readable programmes, written in code, that self-execute when a set of predetermined conditions is met. New technical advances in blockchain have enabled truly autonomous smart contracts that are capable of self-execution and self-enforcement (Lausati et al., 2017).

There is no single smart contract protocol. Hewa et al. (2020) analysed smart contracts in the Ethereum, Corda, Hyperledger Fabric, Stellar, and Waves blockchain environments. By comparing features such as privacy, security, interoperability, and transaction costs, Hewa et al. (2020) outlined advantages and disadvantages of different smart contract design environments. Further illustrated in Table 1 are inescapable trade-offs that exist in smart contract design. For instance, in a permissioned blockchain such as Hyperledger, the ability to integrate various consensus mechanisms provide greater flexibility for users, whereas in public blockchains that do not support customized consensus mechanisms, there is reduced flexibility but a greater level of security (2021, p. 5). Since no blockchain can excel in all facets of smart contract design, each blockchain optimizes their smart contract design environment for the features required by the community of developers who utilize their platform.

Table 1. Advantages and disadvantages of smart contract design environments

Blockchain	Smart Contract	
	Advantages	Disadvantages
Ethereum	• Open-source system • Worldwide developer community • Availability of private and public modes	• Public ledger storage overhead • Variation in transaction approval times (seconds to minutes) • Transaction costs (gas fees) • Single programming language (Solidity) • Integration limitation
Hyperledger	• Permissioned operational capability • Different consensus modes • No transaction costs • Different programming language support • Microservice adopted architecture	• No native cryptocurrency • Complexities in deployment • Number of proven use cases is relatively low
Corda	• Extended privacy • Broad industrial compatibility • Contractual enforcement capability • Multiple consensus mechanism support	• No native cryptocurrency • Verification only occurs through trusted notaries
Stellar	• Cryptocurrency support (Lumen) • No overhead on mining • Fast transaction processing • Enhanced security with non-Turing complete smart contract	• Regulatory difficulties especially in banking and financial applications
Waves	• Custom token creation capability • Enhanced security with non-Turing complete smart contract	• High volatility of custom tokens

Source: Author's elaboration based on Hewa et al. (2020)

Since a smart contract is only able to access data that is on its native blockchain, external data must be fed to a smart contract via a special type of smart contract called an *Oracle*. Oracles verify, authenticate, and send off-chain data to smart contracts, allowing them to execute as programmed. Oracles exist in many forms, such as the following (Kraft, 2020):

• **Software**: Provide data from online sources to smart contracts and, due to their online nature, can provide information in near-real time (i.e., website data, stock prices, flight information, etc.).

- **Hardware**: Provide data from physical devices, such as sensors, and translate this information for the smart contract.
- **Wetware (human)**: People, usually experts in a certain field, appointed and trusted by smart-contract creators, who provide information to an Oracle.
- **Inbound and Outbound**: Oracles can provide data from off-chain sources to smart contracts as well as provide smart-contract data to the off-chain.

Oracles are instrumental to the functioning of smart contracts, especially since most data (identity, attestation, tax, financial data, etc.) are not yet contained on a blockchain.

Tokenisation

Tokenisation is a process whereby a token (i.e., a symbol) represents an underlying asset or function. For instance, casino chips represent money within a casino ecosystem, as they enable patrons to play games and can also be exchanged for money. Money itself is a token that symbolises legal tender backed by the state, and is recognised as able to extinguish a public or private debt. Digital tokenisation has its origins in data security within the payments industry, where sensitive credit-card data is converted to a random string that is non-sensitive, enhancing security of confidential user information and reducing security burdens on merchants.

In the blockchain context, tokenisation is the process of converting physical and non-physical assets, collectibles, identity, and other information (Antonopoulos & Wood, 2018, p. 222) into data that transfers ownership or rights. Tokens inherit the functionalities and characteristics of the blockchain protocol (Fisher et al., 2020) upon which it is created, such as immutability, traceability, decentralisation, and others. Tokens can also represent a set of instructions used to effect change on a blockchain through smart contracts. Many developers believe tokenisation to be the "killer-app" for blockchain mass adoption (Elliot, 2020).

An Introductory Taxonomy of Tokens

Tokens broadly fall into two categories: fungible and non-fungible. Fungible tokens are *interchangeable*, meaning that they can be exchanged for another token of the same type; *identical*, that is, they are uniform in nature and specification; and *divisible*, meaning that they can be divided into smaller units without difference to the user (Oxcert, 2018).

On the other hand, non-fungible tokens (NFTs) represent digital assets that are not equal in value, even though they can be of the same type. Each NFT is *unique*, *not interchangeable* (unlike fungible tokens), and *non-identical* (Elliot, 2020; Oxcert, 2018).

Financial authorities, such as the Swiss Financial Market Supervisory Authority (FINMA) and the Financial Conduct Authority (FCA) in the United Kingdom, have classified fungible tokens according to their various functions in a move towards setting a basis for regulation. In their respective guidelines (FCA, 2019; FINMA, 2018), tokens are grouped into three categories:

1 *Payment tokens*, also called *exchange tokens*, are decentralised crypto assets used as a means of payment for the acquisition of goods and services. Payment tokens are usually not regulated.
2 *Utility tokens* provide access to a blockchain-based product or service (Elliot, 2020). These tokens are not regulated.
3 *Asset tokens*, also named *security tokens*, are regulated tokens that represent assets, debt (e.g. bonds), or equity claims (e.g. shares) on the issuer and are used to bind physical assets promising to share profits.

Hybrids of these token types are also possible; that is, tokens can have overlapping functions (e.g., payment and utility tokens, utility, and security tokens) (Antonopoulos & Wood, 2018, p. 222; Lo & Medda, 2020).

Each blockchain has its own protocol and standards for issuing tokens. For instance, the Ethereum blockchain has the ERC-20 standard for creating fungible tokens, the ERC-721 standard for creating NFTs, and the ERC-1404 token standard that allows token issuers to enforce transfer restrictions on their tokens, determining to whom and under what conditions tokens may be assigned (TokenSoft, 2018). Token standards outline the minimum specifications and rules that govern functions and behaviours of a token. A token standard is not a fixed rule as developers are at liberty to add new features that were not part of the initial standard, increasing the application spectrum (Antonopoulos & Wood 2018, p. 249).

Blockchain tokenisation is an emerging field under constant development; as such, the above classifications are not exhaustive and do not cover the full scope of the token landscape.

Tokenisation and the Evolution of Money as Data

In monetary and financial economics, money is understood to have three primary purposes. It is a store of value, a medium of exchange, and a unit of account. As a unit of account, money can be thought of as data, particularly as money becomes increasingly digital. Westermeier (2020) notes that, as societies shift from using traditional financial infrastructure towards digital platforms, money is increasingly used as data, "By embedding money as a form of data deeply into the platform, money is levelled with other kinds of data" (Westermeier, 2020, p. 2054).

Money primarily exists as an entry on a ledger within the banking sector. This ledger is almost always external to the transactions or context in which the money is being transacted. For instance, an online purchase is a transaction between a seller and a buyer; however, the payment stage of the transaction requires engaging third parties (the issuing and merchant banks, the merchant acquirer, card network, etc.) to conclude the purchase. In part, these numerous intermediaries are a consequence of the "low-data" characteristic of money.

Traditionally, money contains very little information. A digital transaction, on average, contains only four pieces of information, including the amount transacted, the payer, the payee, and the date transacted. Physical fiat money contains even less data (value only).

Unlike cash or current digital payment systems, blockchain adds functionality to money (funds) by sophisticating and enhancing the data contained in money when it is tokenised. By tokenizing money, permission, condition, and restriction requirements can be embedded within money itself. The exchange of money will, therefore, no longer be separate to the set of contractual obligations and conditions of a transaction but will now be inextricably part of it. Related to grant management, blockchain tokenization can improve all processes of grant administration, since tokenisation merges a grant's conditions and its funds.

THE GRANT MANAGEMENT PROCESS

An Overview

The granting process involves an organisation or a donor distributing funds to another organisation or recipient for the purpose of achieving predetermined objectives (Weiss, 1973). Grants from governments, multilateral organisations, global funds, private philanthropy, and international cooperation agencies amount to trillions of US dollars every year. According to the Organisation for Economic Co-operation and Development (OECD, 2021), in 2020, official development assistance (ODA) from OECD countries to developing and low-income countries accounted for US$ 161.2 billion. On average, 90% of ODA measured by the OECD is a subsidy (Keeley, 2012, p. 49); that is, the recipient does not have to reimburse the amount. Grants, at a high level, follow a process that can be outlined in five major steps illustrated in Figure 1.

Figure 1. High-level overview of a grant process

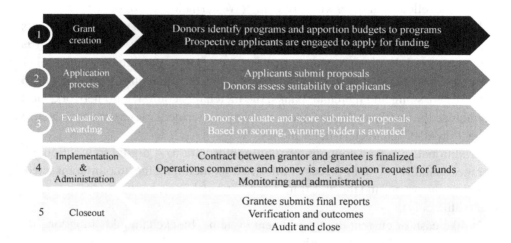

Grant projects have varying purposes. Some grants fund research, others support infrastructure development, subsidise training, transfer cash to vulnerable populations, etc. Each grant project includes a series of activities that aim to achieve a specified purpose. Grant projects have either a sole executor or adopt a multi-tiered system with grantees and sub-grantees. Some grant funding is unconditional, while other grant funding is based on stringent conditions (e.g. subject to the delivery of research findings or other outcomes). Grants are thus multi-dimensional, and the complexity of their management is influenced by several factors, including the number of grantees and intermediaries, activities, and conditionalities, among others.

Grant management starts once an applicant is awarded and signs a contract with the donor (step 4 in Figure 1). Grant contracts include items such as activities, expenditure budgets, intermediaries, milestones, and timeframes. Usually, donors require that grantees provide regular updates via reports, as to the progress of a grant project's implementation (monitoring). These reports assist donors in determining whether a project is achieving its predetermined milestones in accordance with the project plan (administration). Key to this reporting is the financial assessment, which compares the budgeted forecast expenditure to amounts expended within a given period. This process requires reconciliation of progress reports with bank statements, payment vouchers, and contract conditions to ensure that amounts were spent in line with grant contract stipulations (step 5 in Figure 1).

In the management of grants, the transfer of funds generates several flows of information between executors, grantors, auditors, suppliers, banks, and grantees, among others (Figure 2) that must be monitored, reported on, and accounted for. This level of complexity, if not well managed, leads to an untold number of challenges and often, undesirable consequences.

Figure 2. Grant execution in legacy systems
Source: Author's elaboration

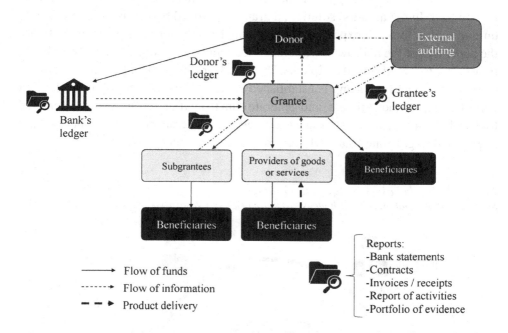

TOKENISING GRANT MANAGEMENT

It is possible to incorporate blockchain technology in every step of the grant management process (Figure 1); however, the authors will focus on the "implementation and administration" and "closeout" steps for which blockchain-based applications have already emerged. In this regard, IBM has developed a proof of concept for the use of blockchain to facilitate a more seamless process to apply for natural disaster relief funds, and make it easier for applicants to prove that they are truly victims (Delaney, 2020). In 2017, the Office of Financial Innovation and Transformation (FIT), in partnership with Deloitte and the National Science Foundation, developed a proof of concept to analyse how blockchain could improve grant-payment processes and increase transparency in multi-tiered grant-payment projects (Fisher et al., 2020, p. 26). The project also highlighted how grant recipients could use tokens to transfer and redeem grant payments (Bureau of the Fiscal Service, n. d.). A finalised application is not yet available, and research efforts continue. A similar application is Disberse, a fund-management platform on the blockchain that allows donors, governments, and other types of grantors, to transfer and trace funds from donors to intermediaries and from the latter to final beneficiaries. Disberse further facilitates cash transfers via mobile or vouchers for vulnerable populations (Marke, 2018).

In this section, a conceptual model of grant tokenization using smart contracts is proposed. In the authors' solution, a grant's approved budget is used to generate unique tokens for each expenditure line item. These tokens are programmed with the addresses of the approved, whitelisted recipients, preventing tokens from being transferred to unauthorised recipients. Drawing from the work of Dai and Vasarhelyi (2017), automated reporting is established (Figure 3), consisting of a set of smart contracts that extract, process, and generate data from transactions using the created tokens. In so doing, information at various levels of the grant process may be instantly aggregated to generate financial, managerial, and operational reports.

Figure 3. Blockchain-based grant management
Source: Author's elaboration, with ideas taken from Dai and Vasarhelyi (2017) and MITRE (2019)

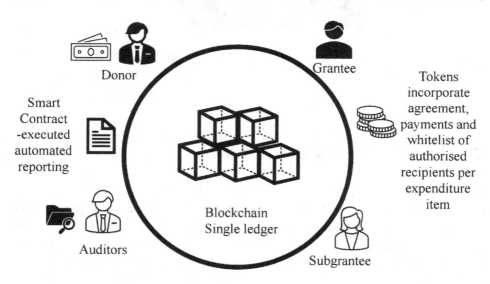

First, fungible tokens are created in an amount equal to the budgeted fiat money allocated to each category of expenditure (e.g. human resources, supplies, equipment, operation, finance—such as taxation, fees—etc.). Each token is backed by fiat currency in a traditional bank account. For example, suppose wages (W), supplies

(S), and equipment (E) are expenditure items with a budgeted fiat value of US$ 1,000 each. These expenditure items will therefore each be assigned 1,000 tokens. Following the example, (W) tokens, (S) tokens, and (E) tokens will be created as payment tokens since they are used to settle debt obligations, in this case, with suppliers and employees; however, they also perform functions such as triggering smart contracts that automate reporting.

Thereafter tokens are created, and operational mode commences (Figure 4). A comprehensive set of sophisticated smart contracts controls the flow of tokens from approved expenditure budget line items to whitelisted suppliers in accordance with the embedded code logic. Smart contracts execute only after all necessary supply-chain management conditions are met. This information is transmitted to the smart contracts by Oracles from approved data sources (e.g. IoT data). Once the tokens are transferred to whitelisted-supplier wallets, a second set of smart contracts—those responsible for the swap from tokens to fiat currency—is triggered.

The associated fiat currency is transferred from the bank account to the supplier's bank account as per the values determined by the smart contracts.

Figure 4. Blockchain-based grant management: the operational scheme
Source: Author's elaboration

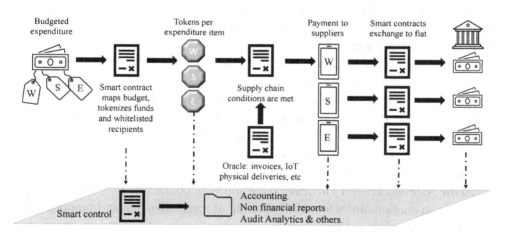

Leveraging from Dai and Vasarhelyi (2017), detailed reporting can be manually requested or automatically sent to donors and administrators alike. Such reports of unalterable transaction data may be as comprehensive as required and automatically generated at intervals suitable for the users of such information.

GRANT MANAGEMENT CHALLENGES AND BLOCKCHAIN SOLUTIONS: A CASE STUDY

Through explication of the following case study, the common challenges of current grant management systems will be highlighted, and potential blockchain-based remedies outlined.

Municipal Grants Used in Bank Heist - South Africa (2018)

In 2018, several South African municipalities illegally transferred various grant funding received from the National and Provincial governments, which was meant to reduce basic service infrastructure (water, sanitation, etc.) backlogs in poor communities to a little-known VBS mutual bank. These funds were subsequently redirected to fraudsters' bank accounts and stolen (SAHRC, 2019). Investigations by curators found that municipalities had actively disregarded the Municipal Finance Management Act (MFMA) (which prohibited municipalities from transferring funds to mutual banks) by making deposits with the VBS mutual bank to the tune of billions of rands. Once the fraud was identified by the National Treasury of South Africa, R2 billion (approximately US$ 140 million) had already been embezzled by banking staff, the bank's auditors, and senior government officials, leaving complicit municipalities in severe financial distress. The worst affected were rural municipalities where the misappropriated funds represented as much as 50% of their annual operating revenue.

Fifteen municipalities were impacted, and their funding was frozen. These municipalities faced political tensions due to ensuing cash flow shortages and associated non-delivery of services because of the heist. Despite municipalities being required to report their monthly financial performance to the National Treasury in terms of Section 71 of the MFMA, the VBS bank heist revealed the weaknesses in this monitoring mechanism and highlighted the need to revise the public sector granting system. The South African Local Government Association (SALGA, 2018) urged the National Treasury to develop the ability to obtain real-time data and other reports from municipalities towards better monitoring, advisory, and support. They further lobbied provincial treasuries to strengthen Council oversight structures, and most importantly, to revise monitoring instruments in Section 71 of MFMA.

This case study highlights how safeguards such as Section 71 of the MFMA are implemented, but are insufficient to ensure the efficient and transparent execution of grants. Beyond a robust legal framework, the sound execution of grants in local government is dependent on the enforcement of procedures and controls during day-to-day operations, such that fraud is prevented rather than regretted.

Grant Management Challenge I: The Misappropriation of Funds

The ability to transfer funds to unsuitable service providers or altogether illegitimate persons is a primary shortcoming of the grant management system in the case study. Since fiat and digital money do not possess intrinsic safeguards against unauthorised transfers, spending is at the discretion of administrators who are not always trustworthy. Additionally, theft is only detected after an audit, long after funds have been stolen.

The flagrant misappropriation of public funds by municipalities resulted in far-reaching consequences for both themselves and their residents. Despite complicit municipalities not being able to pay staff salaries for months and experiencing severe cash flow shortages, many citizens were once again deprived of desperately needed access to water and electricity.

The VBS bank heist is but one example of such plundering of public coffers worldwide. The Organized Crime and Corruption Reporting Project has reported a number of similar instances where billions of US dollars of COVID-19 relief have been unscrupulously embezzled worldwide. In one of the reports, the procurement of equipment to fight the COVID-19 pandemic, valued at US$ 30.18 million, was contracted to a service provider of digital infrastructure who had no experience in health care (OCCRP, 2020).

Tokenised Grant Management Alternative

It is possible to address the misappropriation that is so prevalent in current grant management systems using blockchain-based equivalents. A key feature of the proposed blockchain-based solution is the ability to stipulate who may possess a token.

Through account whitelisting, grantors can restrict the transfer of tokens to unauthorized parties who have not been vetted. Additionally, payment conditions, budget limits, and other contractual stipulations are programmatically contained within tokens, strengthening internal controls against subversion.

Furthermore, real-time traceability at blockchains ensures that any untoward activity may be timeously identified and investigated with the use of block-explorers and heuristic software. While the proposed solution does not totally remove the possibility of misappropriation, it does significantly deter would-be fraudsters from attempting to commit crime through early detection, unprecedented traceability, and high incidence of fund recovery.

Grant Management Challenge II: Reporting and Monitoring Inefficiencies

Although the implicated municipalities submitted monthly financial performance reports to the National Treasury detailing how monies were being spent, they were clearly ineffective at adequately and timeously detecting the large-scale maladministration. In a National Parliament Committee debriefing to discuss the economic impact on municipal finances of the VBS fraud, it was noted that the "veracity of the information coming from municipalities had been challenging in terms of accuracy, timeliness, and completeness" (Mdakane, 2018).

Grantors too, through their legacy oversight mechanisms, contribute to grant management inefficiencies. When a significant amount of time elapses between the occurrence of a transaction and the reporting thereof, reports are rendered ineffectual. In October 2016, two years before the allegations of fraud at the VBS emerged, the District Attorney raised concern as to the activities of municipalities with the National Treasury. A subsequent National Treasury warning to municipalities only went out in August 2017, almost a year later. This delay was caused by inefficiencies in obtaining supporting information. To issue a warning to a municipality, the National South African authorities had to gather, verify, aggregate, and reconcile information that was siloed in third-party ledgers such as bank statements and municipal financial systems. The Parliamentary Monitoring Group refers to this problem as follows: "If it (i.e., National Treasury) had that insight (i.e., to the municipal information in real-time), then probably its early warning and monitoring systems would have picked things up [...]" (Mdakane, 2018).

Moreover, even if reports are timeously drafted and submitted, there is no guarantee as to the veracity of their contents. As such, extensive resources are expended to validate municipal information. In the case study, the detection of fraud and financial inaccuracies appeared only after audits by SALGA and KPMG. The US Fiscal Office of Financial Innovation and Transformation (FIT), while studying the use of blockchain for the numerous US grant programs, noted that on average, each payment request from grantees takes two hours to be reconciled, grant managers spend 40% of their time on compliance, and almost US$ 20 billion are returned due to overpayments (Fisher et al., 2020).

Tokenised Grant Management Alternative

When grant funds are tokenised, compliance is automated and certain, allowing for efficient and credible reporting. Compliance-related data, such as the payee, payment type, amount, purpose, location, recipient details, satisfying conditions, and whitelist information are embedded within tokens. All this information is attached to funds and tracked from a project's budget to its outcomes, in a truly end-to-end fashion within the smart control layer (Figure 4).

Furthermore, data that exists in silos may be aggregated by Oracles and smart contracts. If all relevant reporting data (bank statements, municipal records, etc.) were contained on a blockchain, authorized oracles and smart contracts could instantly aggregate such data to generate any level of required reporting. Such a solution would have allowed the National Treasury of South Africa to promptly confirm the level of non-compliance and issue timeous warnings or remedies.

Further Challenges of Grant Management: Over and Under Expenditure

Although unrelated to the case study, the over and under expenditure of grant funds are serious challenges experienced in current grant management systems.

Over-expenditure on projects results from poor budgetary control during its implementation. To compensate for this shortfall, administrators source funds allocated to other line items or, perhaps more worryingly, supply inferior goods or services to compensate for the shortfall. For example, overspending on employee costs could reduce goods or services provided to beneficiaries or impact their quality, as well as cause delays in project completion.

Prevention of Over-Expenditure

Often grantees do not judiciously remain within budget limits and spending occurs at the discretion of administrators. Over-expenditure is only detected at the reporting stage, after funds have been spent or when a grantee has already created an obligation with suppliers. By creating tokens equivalent to approved budgeted expenditure values, fiscal discipline is enforced. The opportunity to illegally cross-subsidize one expenditure item for another is eliminated since tokens can only be utilised for their intended purpose. Additionally, account whitelisting restricts the transfer of funds to recipients in excess of the budgeted amount set by grantors. Should additional funds be required, this may be facilitated by the reprogramming of smart contracts after the express approval of grantors.

Under-Expenditure and the Recovery of Unspent Funds

Under-expenditure of grant funds is just as damaging as over-expenditure since this indicates that the objectives of a grant have not been met within a prescribed time frame. As such, when under-spending occurs the outcomes of grants (aid, relief, service delivery, etc.) remain unfulfilled. While there may be legitimate reasons for not fully spending funds within allotted timeframes, the process of recovering unspent funds from non-performing grantees is not without significant administrative effort.

Grant tokenisation can alleviate these administrative challenges since grantors may program tokens to self-destruct should tokens (funds) not be appropriately spent within agreed-upon timeframes.

Advantages and Disadvantages of Tokenising Grant Management Processes

While blockchain technology has great potential to enhance grant management, it is important to consider the limitations and disadvantages of this transformative technology. In the realm of social processes, no technological solution is a panacea. While tokens inherit the benefits of their associated blockchains, they also bear their limitations. In Table 2 (below) a few of the pros and cons of the proposed solution are outlined.

Table 2. Advantages and disadvantages of applying blockchain technology in the grant sector

Advantages	Disadvantages
1. Blockchain allows for unprecedented levels of automation and reduces misappropriation of funds and inefficiencies related to inaccurate reporting and ineffective monitoring.	1. Blockchain cannot eliminate the challenges in grant management that depend on human input, such as policy design and implementation (i.e., the quality and quantity of goods and services that are provided to the beneficiaries of a grant), cultural and societal factors, or last mile delivery problems.
2. Blockchains with smart contracts and oracles allow for the automation of effective and timely reports, reducing administrative costs and thereby potentially enhancing the available funds for grantees to implement projects.	2. Most data required by smart contracts currently reside outside of blockchain (identities, tax, invoices, etc.) therefore the proposed application is still reliant on off-chain data (information) that could be subject to manipulation. Nonetheless, projects that aim to enhance the reach of smart contracts (e.g. Chainlink and Balancer) are steadily making great strides towards incorporating off-chain data onto the blockchain. It is envisioned that, in the future, a global blockchain standard similar to TCP/IP and ASCII will emerge. This standard will make it possible for smart contracts to access data outside of the blockchain and on blockchains other than the one upon which they are developed, essentially removing the need for Oracles (Kraft, 2020).
3. Tokenisation per item of expenditure reduces and prevents administrators from deviating from the approved scope of the budget during execution.	3. When adopting blockchain technology, it is prudent to consider the cost vs. benefit of its implementation. The derived benefits of blockchain technology must be weighed against the development and maintenance costs of such a system. At present, blockchain development fees could be prohibitive to small and medium enterprises looking to add this technology to their management toolkit.
4. The proposed solution using tokens and smart contracts result in high levels of automation by incorporating data with money, which eliminates middlemen. Accountability is more transparent and immediate.	4. Organizational resistance to the introduction of a technology, which could potentially reduce staff due to automation.
5. Compliance and enforcement are guaranteed since requirements are embedded/programmed within tokens.	5. There is reduced flexibility to respond to unforeseen circumstances during the implementation of grant projects. Since grant conditions and outcomes are determined and programmed at the outset of projects, it is necessary to reprogram tokens to accommodate changes. This can result in delays in responding to deviations from grant plans promptly.

FUTURE RESEARCH DIRECTIONS

Grants and other support management is an area of great interest, particularly since the COVID-19 pandemic, for countries and multinationals alike. All donors seek to amplify the efficacy of their projects while reducing wastage and inefficiencies. Future research may consider exploring the most suitable blockchain architecture (permissioned environment or a hybrid permissioned and permission-less environment) on which a grant management solution may be tailored and consider the real-world efficiency savings of such a system.

Furthermore, the study of the solution requires decisions regarding information storage in or off blockchain, while keeping it private and secure. Tokenisation is creating new business models, such as innovative crowdfunding models, multiple world models, and decentralised autonomous organisations. Foundations or donor organisations can leverage these new business models to raise funds that are allocated in relief projects.

With the introduction of new technologies, user behaviour is altered. Similarly, this new method of grant management will influence user behaviour, and it is worth exploring how the relationship between grantors, grantees, and users of such systems will change accordingly.

CONCLUSION

This chapter presents a comprehensive overview of the basic blockchain, smart contracts, and tokenisation concepts while emphasising their characteristics and appeal. Blockchain technology as a whole is being used for the digital representation of assets and more abstract value representation, such as intellectual property rights, liabilities, facilitating contract underwriting, and value accrual, as is the case with shares or securities. Other better-known applications of blockchain include its use in supply-chain management, health care recording, and energy provision. The authors have envisioned the use of blockchain tokenisation in grant management since a great need exists for local and international grantors to ensure that their funds are utilised in accordance with agreements and towards achieving expected outcomes.

Current research on blockchain-based grant projects is primarily focused on real-time tracking and reporting of projects. The authors, however, expand upon this research by focusing on reducing the grant tracking and reporting burden, and the misappropriation of funds. The proposed model further outlines a smart contract layer to aggregate data for report generation in the frequency and with the detail required by the various stakeholders in a grant project (donors, fiscal authorities, grantees, beneficiaries, etc.).

It is important to consider that the solution presented has broader applicability, not only for the management of public funds, but also for once-off specific projects.

Finally, the proposed solution is particularly relevant in countries with poor budgetary controls and transparency, and with high levels of corruption. These countries are often among the poorest, those who can least afford the misappropriation of vital funding, and whose citizens need grant funding the most.

FUNDING

This research received no specific grant from any funding agency in the public, commercial, or not-for-profit sectors.

REFERENCES

Antonopoulos, A. M., & Wood, G. (2018). *Mastering Ethereum - Building smart contracts and apps*. O'Reilly Media, Inc.

Bureau of the Fiscal Service. (n. d.). *DEEE blockchain fit update*. FIT: Financial Innovation & Transformation. https://www.fiscal.treasury.gov/fit/updates/deee-blockchain-fit-update.html

Cong, L. W., & He, Z. (2019). Blockchain disruption and smart contracts. *Review of Financial Studies*, *32*(5), 1754–1797. doi:10.1093/rfs/hhz007

Dai, J., & Vasarhelyi, M. A. (2017). Toward blockchain-based accounting and assurance. *Journal of Information Systems*, *31*(3), 5–21. doi:10.2308/isys-51804

Delaney, C. (2020, January). *Bonds of trust: Blockchain and disaster relief*. Blockchain Pulse: IBM Blockchain Blog. https://www.ibm.com/blogs/blockchain/2020/01/bonds-of-trust-blockchain-and-disaster-relief/

Elliot, H. (2020, September) *An introduction of tokenization*. Cardano Foundation. https://medium.com/cardanorss/an-introduction-to-tokenization-5ce087a7b6c3

FCA. (2019). *Guidance on cryptoassets* (Policy Statement PS19/22). https://www.fca.org.uk/ publication/policy/ps19-22.pdf

FINMA. (2018). *FINMA publishes ICO guidelines*. https://www.finma.ch/en/news/2018/02/20180216-mm-ico-wegleitung

Fisher, C., Poll, J., & Wetklow, M. (2020). The benefits of blockchain to tokenize grants payments. *Journal of Government Financial Management*, *69*(2), 24–29.

Hewa, T., Ylianttila, M., & Liyanage, M. (2020). Survey on blockchain-based smart contracts: Applications, opportunities and challenges. *Journal of Network and Computer Applications, 102857.* Advance online publication. doi:10.1016/j. jnca.2020.102857

Keeley, B. (2012). *From aid to development: the global fight against poverty.* OECD Publishing. doi:10.1787/9789264123571-4-en

Kraft, C. (2020). *Future smart contracts, loosed of oracles.* LinkedIn. https://www. linkedin.com/pulse/future-mart-contracts-loosed-oracles-conrad-kraft/?trackingId= s1Dog16USrCmLRnGVrGqow%3D%3D

Kraft, C., & Carmona, M. (2020, April). *How blockchain spells the end of corruption in public sector procurement.* LinkedIn. https://www.linkedin.com/pulse/how-blockchain-spells-end-corruption-public-sector-mariana-carmona/

Lauslahti, K., Mattila, J., & Seppälä, T. (2017). Smart contracts – how will blockchain technology affect contractual practices? *ETLA Reports,* (68). https://pub.etla.fi/ ETLA-Raportit-Reports-68.pdf

Lo, Y. C., & Medda, F. (2020). Assets on the blockchain: An empirical study of tokenomics. *Information Economics and Policy, 53,* 100881. doi:10.1016/j. infoecopol.2020.100881

Marke, A. (Ed.). (2018). *Transforming Climate Finance and Green Investment with Blockchains.* Academic Press.

Mdakane, R. (2018). *VBS Bank impact on municipalities' finances; Municipal Councillors Pension Fund.* Parliamentary Monitoring Group. https://pmg.org.za/ committee-meeting/26233/

MITRE. (2019, June). *Assessing the potential to improve grants management using blockchain technology.* MITRE Grants Management Blockchain Supply. https:// www.mitre.org/sites/default/files/publications/PR-19-1654-MITRE%20Grants%20 Mgt%20Blockchain%20 Study%20Report.pdf

Nakamoto, S. (2008). *Bitcoin: a peer-to-peer electronic cash system.* Bitcoin. *Decentralized Business Review, 21260.* https://bitcoin.org/bitcoin.pdf

Narayanan, A., Bonneau, J., Felten, E., Miller, A., & Goldfeder, S. (2016). *Bitcoin and cryptocurrency technologies: A comprehensive introduction.* Princeton University Press.

OCCRP. (2020). *Crime, corruption and coronavirus.* https://www.occrp.org/en/ coronavirus/

OECD. (2021, April). *COVID-19 spending helped to lift foreign aid to an all-time high in 2020. Detailed Note.* https://www.oecd.org/dac/financing-sustainable-development/development-finance-data/ODA-2020-detailed-summary.pdf

Oxcert. (2018, April). *Fungible vs non-fungible tokens on the blockchain.* Oxcert. https://medium.com/0xcert/fungible-vs-non-fungible-tokens-on-the-blockchain-ab4b12e0181a

SAHRC. (2019, March). *Who will save us when governance decays?* South African Human Rights Commission. https://www.sahrc.org.za/index.php/sahrc-media/opinion-pieces/item/1855-who-will-save-us-when-governance-decays

SALGA. (2018, April). *VBS: VBS Bank impact on municipalities' finances; Municipal Councillors Pension Fund.* Parliamentary Monitoring Group. https://pmg.org.za/committee-meeting/26233/

TokenSoft. (2018). *ERC-1404: Simple restricted token standard.* Medium. https://medium.com/erc1404/erc-1404-simple-restricted-token-standard-f71290a48faa

Weiss, E. H. (1973). Grants management: A systems approach. *Socio-Economic Planning Sciences, 7*(5), 457–470. doi:10.1016/0038-0121(73)90042-6

Westermeier, C. (2020). Money is data–the platformization of financial transactions. *Information Communication and Society, 23*(14), 2047–2063. doi:10.1080/1369118X.2020.1770833

ADDITIONAL READING

Antonopoulos, A. M. (2017). *Mastering bitcoin: Programming the open blockchain.* O'Reilly Media, Inc.

Bonsón, E., & Bednárová, M. (2019). *Blockchain and its implications for accounting and auditing.* Meditari Accountancy Research. https:www.emeraldinsight.com/2019-372X.htm

Lee, J. Y. (2019). A decentralized token economy: How blockchain and cryptocurrency can revolutionize business. *Business Horizons, 62*(6), 773–784. doi:10.1016/j.bushor.2019.08.003

Voshmgir, S. (2020). *Token economy–how the Web3 reinvents the Internet* (Vol. 2). Token Kitchen.

KEY TERMS AND DEFINITIONS

Blockchain: A decentralised ledger that enables peer-to-peer transactions with time-stamped and tamper-proof registries that utilises cryptography and consensus algorithms to validate transactions and solve the double-spending problem.

Consensus Mechanism: A method by which parties in a network reach an agreement about the correctness of transactions in a shared ledger.

Cryptocurrency: A digital currency programmed on a blockchain using cryptography and a consensus algorithm to secure and validate transactions. Cryptocurrencies can be used to buy goods and services.

Double-Spending Problem: When the same digital token is spent more than once.

Smart Contract: An encoded set of rules typically programmed in high-level computer languages. A smart contract executes upon the fulfilment of certain conditions with clauses that are binding, unstoppable, and automatic, without the involvement of third parties.

Token: In a blockchain, tokens are crypto assets that can be programmed with various functions such as to facilitate transactions, represent other assets, to provide access to decentralised applications, as governance or reputation, or to validate transactions in a blockchain.

Token Standard: Minimum specifications that encourage interoperability between smart contracts and other infrastructure components such as wallets, exchanges, and user interfaces with predictability. Standards allow token trading without the need to upgrade or additional programming efforts.

Turing Complete Computer Language: A programming language that is capable of running any possible algorithm.

Wallet: Software applications that are used as user interfaces with a blockchain. They are applications used to store, track, and manage a user's keys to transact with cryptocurrencies.

Chapter 8

How ENI Can Improve Procurement Through Blockchain Technology

Audet Victoire Malonga Bibila
Luiss University, Italy

Pietro De Giovanni
 https://orcid.org/0000-0002-1247-4807
Luiss University, Italy

ABSTRACT

The study aims at investigating the potential use of blockchain technology in procurement processes. To better understand how the procurement process works, the case study of Eni is analyzed. Eni seeks to decarburize all its products by 2050, and its fight towards the energy transition is committed to working with suppliers ready to support it in this vision. After understanding the procurement process within Eni and identifying the potential uses of blockchain within these processes, the chapter proves that blockchain could be a powerful tool for the procurement process, especially for supplier qualification.

INTRODUCTION

The energy transition has been trending over recent years all over the world and particularly in Europe, fast-tracking the fusion of many technologies and shaping the new industrial environment (De Giovanni, 2021a). The energy sector is of the highest economic importance with a turnover of around EUR 1.9 trillion along the

DOI: 10.4018/978-1-7998-8014-1.ch008

supply chain in the EU (Eurostat, 2018). This shows the significant impact the sector has on countries' GDPs and how efficient the transition process should be to avoid massive capital and job losses.

Alongside the European Union as well as the European Commission, which have pledged in their 2030 framework on climate and energy to move gradually green (EEA, 2019), many companies in the energy sector have set up a clear roadmap, implemented many projects in different world regions and incorporated the 17 United Nations 2030 Agenda Sustainable Development Goals (SDGs) in order to comply with the new related regulations that are being implemented.

To this end, they are committed to working with suppliers who meet specific criteria in line with sustainability. A careful selection and evaluation of suppliers are the initial steps to ensure the sustainability of supply chains (Wenyan S., 2017). This endeavor is carried out by the procurement department, which includes procuring goods, raw materials, services, infrastructure, and maintenance in exchange for financial assets (Preeker and De Giovanni, 2018). It is part of the upstream supply chain that has the most profound influence on the overall supply chain and can affect its resilience (Sarkis J., 2019). Green procurement, however, consists of considering environmental sustainability practices in the most traditional procurement activities, from supplier selection to equipment or service delivery (De Giovanni and Cariola, 2020).

Studies show that almost 14% of the GDP expenditure in the European Union is dedicated to public procurement simply because a robust procurement system fosters development and brings economic growth to a country (Sanchez, 2019). Following the same trend, procurement in the private sector represents one of the most significant expenses. A report on best practices in procurement, written by the Aberdeen Group, an international marketing company, explained that the procurement of goods and services not directly involved in the production processes usually constitutes thirty to sixty percent of its total expenditures (Orr, 2002). Being part of the upstream supply chain, procurement has a high level of influence on the remaining part of the supply chain and, this is true even in terms of sustainability.

A survey carried out in Western European firms reveals that sustainable supplier cooperation generally positively affects firm performance across social, green, and economic dimensions. It adds that investments in sustainability result in sufficient returns (Hollos D., 2012). Therefore, supplier cooperation is one of the strategic points that can influence a company's plans to go green.

Vendor selection is also viewed by industry and academia as a critical issue for the long-term success of supply chains (Wenyan S., 2017). The choice of suitable suppliers is then made through a qualification process based on the information provided by potential suppliers. However, qualifying and evaluating suppliers in a sustainability context is a multi-dimensional and complex activity depending on information. Indeed, information is critical in improving relationships between suppliers. Increased coordination between supply chain actors could reduce risks, costs and improve a supply chains' overall competitiveness (Badzar, 2016).

When environmental information on suppliers is available, the qualification and selection of suppliers having high environmental performance can be facilitated (Sarkis J., 2019). Unfortunately, this information is not always accessible, and when it is, it is not easily certifiable or auditable. Furthermore, in order to be awarded lucrative contracts, suppliers tendering for a contract provide information on relevant environmental issues not necessarily accurate.

Since supplier qualification in a sustainability context relies on data verification or auditable information, organizations must double-check all data provided in order to qualify the right supplier in line with the organization's vision on sustainability. They should also implement more transparency in their procurement and qualification processes to counteract this imbalance due to asymmetric information (Badzar, 2016). For doing so, they have to access, certify and audit information available on suppliers. With technological advancements, these procurement practices are being revisited because companies are looking to new technologies for help (De Giovanni, 2021b). And, currently, one of the best technologies able to handle this significant sustainable information limitation barrier is Blockchain.

In a report presented in April 2016, the European Commission emphasized that the Blockchain can radically change the traditional business models (Laurent Probst, 2016). In recent years, the Blockchain has attracted much attention from practitioners. To date, an increasing number of businesses embrace it since it promises a plethora of benefits, including increased transparency, time savings, cost savings, increased trust in the system, reduced tampering, reduced human error due to manual processes, and others (Torres de Oliveira, 2017). It is an innovative solution, and to date, various businesses from all sectors want to benefit from its advantages.

Blockchain is a decentralized digital payment system based on cryptography and a public ledger, containing information on every transaction made within a system (Bettina Warburg, 2019). It seems to be an up-and-coming solution that could enhance transparency, security, speed of work, and privacy (De Giovanni, 2020a). Blockchain offers the benefits like traceability, immutability, and security. This new technology, the main issues and challenges organizations face in procurement, could find an effective and sustainable solution and fix information certification issues (Fin., 2020).

In this regard, Eni is embarking on blockchain technology notably as a procurement evaluation tool to efficiently tackle and address the footprint reduction from its suppliers. Hence, this work aims to assist Eni in enhancing its procurement system's efficiency with the relevant stakeholders.

This research would be of great importance for managers, researchers, and practitioners wanting to know and further evaluate the potential contribution of Blockchain in business and, more specifically, for procurement to improve sustainability. Procurement encompasses direct and indirect procurement. This chapter will focus on indirect procurement related to purchasing goods, services, or works not directly involved in but supporting an organization's primary activity. We will also focus on operational and sustainability criteria in procurement.

To date, many researchers have worked on the blockchain application in the procurement processes; however, most articles discuss the use of the Blockchain in public procurement, and just a few discuss the use of the Blockchain in procurement processes for sustainability improvement. Some articles also discuss the green supply chain or challenges faced by companies willing to move on green procurement (Santosh, 2019) and how Blockchain can achieve this. Some others discuss information certification in the academic, art, and media sectors, but very few articles discuss blockchain technology's use to certify supplier information related to sustainability for the procurement process. Therefore, further research is required to fully explore how blockchain technology can be used on procurement for sustainability purposes. In approaching the subject, the research questions to be answered would be:

RQ: How does Blockchain impact the efficiency and performance of procurement processes?

With the sub-questions:

- How could Eni's procurement processes benefit from blockchain adoption?
- What are the different challenges faced with the Blockchain implementation?

To investigate the impact of Blockchain in procurement processes, the Eni case study will be discussed. Data used has been collected from different meetings with the Eni team, Eni documentation, and the literature. After the introduction, we introduce the case study, the challenges, as well as recommendations and conclusions.

THE CASE OF ENI

Eni - formerly known as Ente Nazionale Idrocarburi, for Italian National Hydrocarbons Company - is a private Italian hydrocarbon company founded in 1953 under the presidency of Enrico Mattei (Bloomberg). It was privatized in 1998; still, the Italian state retains a minority shareholding. It is active in the oil, natural gas, petrochemical, power generation, and engineering sectors. It is present in 68 countries and has approximately 31,400 employees. Its revenues amounted to 43 billion euros in 2020. Eni's business model is based on operational excellence, carbon neutrality (2050), and alliances for development. Sustainability is an essential part of its business and is integrated into all its operations.

The energy supply in Europe is still dominated by fossil fuels even if renewable energy sources in the primary energy supply have more than tripled since 1990 (EEA, 2019). One of the most important goals of Eni is to achieve the total decarburization of its products and processes by 2050. It also wants to contribute to achieving the Sustainable Development Goals of the United Nations 2030 Agenda. Eni then translates its commitment to tangible actions by incorporating the UNSDGs in its mission and supporting the just energy transition. The energy transition aims to respond to different climate change challenges with economically sustainable solutions.

Eni's activities are exploration, development, and extraction of oil and natural gas, generation of electricity from cogeneration and renewable sources, traditional and biorefining and chemicals, and circular economy processes. Eni is also an innovation-oriented company that looks forwards to innovative technologies and the digitization of processes.

The biggest challenge in the energy sector is balancing full access to energy with the climate change fight. This is why Eni wants to reduce its impact on the planet by integrating sustainability in all its operations, from reducing GHG emissions to respect for the environment.

Eni has many sustainable projects and has a clearly defined road to get to its project by 2050, as displayed in Figures 1 and 2.

Figure 1. Carbon neutral results in 2020
Source: Eni website

Figure 2. Carbon neutral road by 2050
Source: Eni's website

To support suppliers who want to join in this energy transition, Eni has implemented tools like EniSpace and Open-es. Open-es is the new digital platform dedicated to sustainability in industrial supply chains and open to all companies involved in the energy transition process. It is an innovative, inclusive, and open tool for all companies engaged in the energy transition process (Eni website, 2021). The platform is open to all companies willing to play a leading role in enhancing the industrial ecosystem on sustainability aspects in Italy and worldwide. It results from the partnership between Eni, Boston Consulting Group (BCG), and Google Cloud.

One thousand companies on average have already joined the community in a collaborative, non-competitive process for common growth on four pillars that are fundamental to our present and future: the Planet, People, Economic Prosperity and, The Principles of Corporate Governance. Thanks to this initiative, the synergy between the transition towards decarburization targets and digital transformation is fully realized, enabling the exploitation of sustainability experiences and best practices throughout the industrial chain. In order to promote the dissemination of sustainability culture, other companies have joined the spirit of the initiative. Rina and Techedge Group provide their expertise and play a key role in validating the data and the platform's evolution, ensuring its reliability and scalability (Eni website, 2021).

EniSpace, on the other hand, is Eni's supplier collaboration platform. The platform was created to develop a shared 'space' with suppliers and involve them in Eni's energy transition path. The interactive platform becomes a showcase dedicated to those who work or want to work with Eni. On this platform, maximum attention is paid to the user-friendly nature of the navigation experience, which is more direct, immediate, and intuitive, with the possibility of being updated on the candidature or qualification, on the status of a competition, or for self-service management of one's data, or specific channels in which to share experiences and compare notes. EniSpace is divided into four macro sections:

- "JUST": suppliers at the heart of Eni's energy transition
- A continuous update on "Business Opportunities."
- "Innovation Match": to share innovative, virtuous, and sustainable ideas and solutions
- "Agora': a virtual marketplace for sharing best experiences

In this way, current and prospective suppliers will be able to stay up-to-date and actively participate in Eni's Innovation journey, having an overview of all the areas of study addressed. Eni also organizes workshops with suppliers to discuss sustainable subjects. Each workshop addresses a specific topic with suppliers concerned by that topic. During the workshop, suppliers explain what their companies have achieved concerning sustainability. This is a support measure for suppliers implemented by Eni in addition to the tools already available.

THE PROCUREMENT PROCESS AT ENI

As already mentioned above, Eni's operations range from exploration, development, and extraction of oil and natural gas to circular economy processes. As an energy company, its procurement service is much more indirect than direct.

Upstream of the procurement process, we have both the supplier qualification process and the activation of the procurement process that can be carried out concurrently.

- **The activation of the procurement process** defines the activities, roles, and responsibilities of all the parties involved.

This is the preparation or the planning phase of the procurement process at Eni. Based on the requirements planning, the requesting units identify their needs. Afterward, they meet with the procurement unit, and the requesting unit issue the purchase requisition, which is the act that finalizes the activation of the procurement process. The Purchasing requisition must contain specific minimum requirements before being processed; otherwise, it can be rejected. For instance, the request should be consistent with the approved budgets, contain all the information/documentation necessary for the procurement unit to accept the purchase requisition, and be approved by an authorized internal officer with the appropriate authority. However, sending the purchase order by the requesting units must also consider the time required to complete the procurement activity. The information between the requesting units and the procurement units must be documented and traceable.

- **The vendor qualification process**

The qualification process identifies suppliers who can be potential candidates for the vendor list. It is based on several criteria, from technical aspects to sustainability, that suppliers must meet before being qualified as Eni suppliers. During this process, the procurement unit asks a set of questions to all prospective suppliers. The answers to these questions and the documentation provided will determine who is eligible and who is not. The answers provided by the prospective suppliers are data that should be certified and validated in order to be reliable and be used as competitive lever (Sacco and De Giovanni, 2019).

- **Contract preparation and award framework**

After the activation of the procurement process, the procurement unit prepares the contract. It defines the best contract solution to be used and the type of contract to be assigned based on the purchasing requisition contents. It also defines the number of contracts to be awarded and the tender evaluation criteria.

- **The vendor selection**

The vendors to be invited to the bidding process shall be selected from the Eni list of qualified vendors. The selection depends on the product group or commodity class of the scope of the contract to be assigned. Criteria used to select a short vendor list shall be objective, not discriminatory, and relevant to the scope of the contract to be awarded.

- **Invitation to tender**

Bid management or preparation of the invitation to tender is the responsibility of the procurement unit, using the available contract standards, according to the approved contractual strategy, and in full respect of the principles of transparency and equal treatment of all the tenderers

- **Bid evaluation:** Tenders are usually composed of three separate sections: The administrative, technical, and economic sections (priced tender).

Bid evaluation phases:

1. Notice of the beginning of the evaluation activities (Tenderers in the vendor selection list, date, and place of the first session, technical evaluation subcommittee)
2. Opening of envelopes
3. Opening and evaluating the administrative section: The administrative section contains all those documents/self-certifications provided by the bidders related to legal obligations and requested by Eni regulations.
4. Opening and evaluating the technical section: Evaluate the tender according to the criteria indicated in the contract strategy and the invitation to tender. The evaluation criteria and formulas cannot be changed after opening the envelopes.

Figure 3 summarizes the Eni procurement process

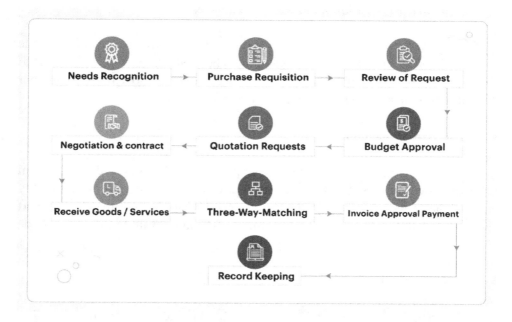

Figure 4. Steps involved in the procurement process
Source: Procurement cloud, 2021

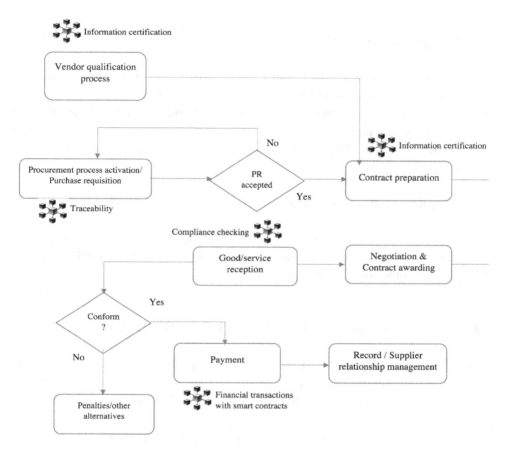

The final results of the technical evaluation are communicated to the procurement unit.

5. Opening and evaluation of the economic section: Check the consistency of the economic value of the bid and define the final ranking.

- **Contract award:** after a series of activities, the procurement unit awards the contract. The appointed managers examine the Contract Award Memorandum and the contract award proposal for approval or rejection.

Contract finalization and handover: The procurement unit sends the contract proposal to the awarded tenderer, receives and records the acceptance form from the tenderer, Manages the handover activity following the "Post-award Contract Management."

- **Equipment/ service delivery process**

After the contract award, the supplier should deliver the equipment or the service requested by the procurement unit. The equipment or service should comply with the specifications provided by the supplier during the tendering process. Information certification is also needed for equipment compliance checking. It is required to validate the compliance between the information provided during the bidding and supplied products.

- **Supplier relationship management**

After the contract, the organization and the suppliers should keep a good relationship. Eni does so by managing a good relationship with its suppliers through platforms and other tools available.

IMPROVEMENT OPPORTUNITIES THROUGH BLOCKCHAIN

Following an in-depth analysis of the procurement process at Eni, and the literature related to the benefits of Blockchain in the supply chain and procurement, we identified a list of blockchain-based applications to improve the Eni's procurement process.

- The use of Blockchain between the procurement department and the other departments of the company:

Eni is a big company with many departments sending purchase requisitions to the procurement department. The information between these departments must be documented and traceable. Furthermore, the procurement department needs to validate the required documents. For traceability and recordkeeping reasons, Blockchain can be used. However, less costly platforms and technologies could efficiently address this kind of situation.

- The use of Blockchain during the bid evaluation process to reduce fraud and increase confidentiality, to allow the team evaluating the bids to crosscheck the information provided by the suppliers.

Procurement fraud is classified as one of the most reported types of crime in the economy (Kamali, 2019). Researchers claim corruption, unfair, and not transparent practices in public procurement. Given that buyers are usually involved directly with vendors or suppliers, procurement fraud is likely to occur in this department, mainly during tendering, and using traditional methods to eradicate this phenomenon would not be effective (Buratto et al., 2019). Therefore, using Blockchain would reduce fraud and unfair practices by rendering the process auditable, transparent, and confidential.

- The use of smart contracts for the qualification and selection of suppliers before issuing invitations to tender.

Before selecting suppliers, they should be qualified. The qualification process identifies potential Eni suppliers, who later would be short-listed in the vendor selection list. The information and documentation related to sustainability and provided during the qualification process could be certified, and the criteria required evaluated using smart contracts.

Vendors invited to tender are selected from the Eni list of qualified vendors. The procurement unit checks any potential third-party risk to all vendors who may be selected for the tender. Any anomaly or inconsistency between commodity classes shall be immediately notified to the relevant vendor management unit. Any cancellation from the preliminary vendor list shall be traced, justified, and registered. In this case, smart contracts can be used to select only the suppliers who meet the required criteria and to whom the invitation should be sent.

- The use of smart contracts to validate transactions between the organization and the suppliers without the intervention of third parties.

Based on the agreements between both parties, smart contracts can execute the contract conditions and trigger the bill payments if all conditions are met.

- The use of Blockchain for compliance checking of the delivered equipment.

Suppliers selected for contracts must deliver equipment that complies with the information provided in the bid proposal.

Based on the description of the procurement process at Eni and the applications described in the previous section, Figure 4 shows how Blockchain can be potentially used by Eni.

For Eni, some of these potential blockchain applications are not all feasible at the moment.

- Eni already has a reliable system for internal communication between the procurement department and the requesting units. Moreover, Eni is a vast company, so once a system is set up, it is more beneficial for the company to make updates rather than completely overhauling the current system in use.
- The way the tender management system is designed considerably minimizes fraud and tampering. Blockchain could be an innovative tool but not necessarily required at the time.
- The use of smart contracts for the validation of transactions: Eni awards nearly 3000 contracts per year. Each contract has its complexity and does not always concern the same type of supplier. In addition, several financial procedures and approvals must be completed before a transaction can be validated, which requires a certain amount of bureaucracy that the smart contract is far from replacing.

However, the vendor management unit spends much time analyzing and validating data from suppliers before their qualification. This task becomes particularly challenging when it comes to analyzing data related to sustainability, which remains one of the significant challenges Eni is trying to overcome.

DATA PROCESSING AND BLOCKCHAIN

Data collection based on incomplete, inaccurate, or erroneous information prevents an organization from monitoring its partners' accurate data and leads to a disaster because the risk of making wrong decisions is high. Therefore, while having information is one of the main objectives of an organization, a practical, robust validation process is crucial to ensure that the given data is reliable. An in-depth analysis of the questions asked to the suppliers, the type of information requested by Eni, and the procedure followed during the qualification process shows that sustainability takes an essential place in Eni processes, so the information and documentation provided must be exact and accurate.

Since Eni expects accurate and truthful information to identify and qualify the adequate supplier, it is essential to take the time to validate internally or by the third party the information provided by the different companies during the qualification process. However, the data verification in the supply chain has always been a complex task.

According to Thomas Burke, supply chain actors in sustainability and human rights have a significant incentive to conceal practices that may compromise their ability to continue to sell their products to their customers (De Giovanni, 2016). In the same way, to be awarded lucrative contracts, suppliers participating in the qualification process may intend to withhold information that would prevent them from being qualified and submit only the one favorable to the qualification process.

To overcome this challenge, organizations monitor or audit suppliers' practices and processes. Auditing is a widely used tool for product and process verification. The British Standards Institution defines it as a documented and independent process and helps obtain proofs of statements of facts and determine to which extent requirements or policies, on which are based auditing criteria, are fulfilled (ISO 9001, 2015). The auditee's activities, products, or processes are systematically examined to check their conformity to audit criteria. Although the method has proven to be effective and is still relevant, it would be costly and time-consuming for Eni if it were to audit all potential suppliers in the qualification process.

Another way of checking information validity is through certification by a third party. Certification can be defined as the process through which an accredited organization delivers a written certificate with the audit report or a scoring system grade, guaranteeing that an organization complies with the requirements of a given standard (Global Standard, 2021). Certification companies are third parties that work with organizations to issue and check the validity of certificates for compliance with environmental regulations. Therefore, a company can refer to these accredited certification agencies to verify the authenticity of the information or documents provided by its partners. The method is also practical since accredited certification agencies are reliable; still, current methods for certifying and validating documents depend on third parties, generally requiring longer processing times, a lot of man work, phone calls, and emails (Trong, 2018).

At Eni, there has been no change in the way organizations conduct document processing for over 20 years. In fact, the verification procedure of required documentation involves important physical work and must be performed by several departments, which seems costly for the company. However strong the procurement team is finding suitable suppliers to meet the company's needs in compliance with sustainability goals is time-consuming and costly. Besides, the increasing number of potential suppliers adds complexity to managing their information, especially when using more basic tools. Existing solutions currently in use are relatively slow, costly, hard to trace, and prone to fraudulence.

Nowadays, Eni should solve the following issues:

1. How can we be sure that the data received is authentic?
2. How could we reduce the long processing times required for document certification?

Manipulating data, regardless of whether it is unintended or due to scientific fraud, may be challenging to identify in the absence of a robust data asset management infrastructure. One technology that mainly handles data authentication and verification is Blockchain. Although enhancing data acquisition and analysis transparency requires a many-sided approach, using Blockchain can mitigate the risk of data manipulation. Blockchain is a promising technology that can improve data integrity. It is one of the means that facilitates verification thanks to a permanent record and a potential solution to the trust problem in many use cases (Hao, Arsyad, et al., 2019).

Blockchain through smart contracts is an adequate tool for certification process improvement (De Giovanni, 2020a). Smart contracts can facilitate, execute and enforce the negotiation or performance of an agreement using blockchain technology. It is verifiable and signed and would help maintain the authenticity. While checking the accuracy of data or documentation, the company seeks to know who is responsible, the entity sourcing the information, where and when actions occurred, what inputs, and which process (how).

By implementing blockchain technology, certifying and validating digital assets (documents) will eliminate unfavorable factors and drawbacks. Executing these transactions in a blockchain ensures the authenticity and security of the information and fast processing.

POTENTIAL USE OF BLOCKCHAIN TECHNOLOGY

The solution would be to create a decentralized blockchain application; it is tampered proof, traceable and encrypted. Then, smart contracts program can be used at the backend to interact with the Blockchain, and the encrypted hash value of each data will be stored in Blockchain and verified against the supplier's documents.

Four main entities will be involved in the system: suppliers, the company (Eni), the blockchain service provider for maintaining the system, and the external database or third parties. The platform would bring together potential suppliers and the Eni procurement unit. The vendor management unit will submit the questionnaire and the qualification criteria on the Blockchain platform. Suppliers wishing to be qualified as Eni suppliers will access the platform and provide the information required by the organization. The suppliers running for the qualification process are added on the platform as members and have the responsibility of providing their information on sustainability aspects.

Usually, the vendor management department and other departments related to specific suppliers' categories control documents and information data collected. Nevertheless, with smart contracts, information data is encrypted. Similar to a person's unique fingerprint, digital assets likewise possess their own specific "fingerprint." The fingerprint of a digital asset can be generated using cryptographic hash functions. Such a function can take any file as an input parameter to generate a sequence of letters and characters as an output; this sequence is considered its unique "fingerprint" or its hash value. Each data will then have a hash function before being stored on the Blockchain (Stellnberger, 2016).

Blockchain-based hash validation may be applied in several diverse use cases, notably validating published scientific results, validating audit trail data, and validating other data shared between various parties (Kalis, 2018).

When suppliers issue data, all the details are sent to the smart contract. Smart contract checks if the information originates from an accredited agency and verifies its validity.

The use of a permissioned Blockchain would be better in this case so that only the authorized persons (i.e., procurement unit) will have access to the information entered by potential suppliers. These authorized persons will see discrepancies and any changes made.

If the information is accurate and one supplier meets the criteria requested by Eni, a notification would be sent to the vendor management unit with the company's name to be considered for the next step. Alternatively, if the information provided by one potential supplier is not accurate, the following actions will not be executed. In this case, penalties could also be applied to prevent from providing inappropriate information. However, if the information is accurate, but one supplier does not meet the requested criteria, a report should be sent to the vendor management unit to evaluate where that supplier failed. The report could also be part of the feedback the procurement unit will send to the supplier when the qualification process ends. In this way, suppliers could know why they are unqualified and improve themselves next time.

To facilitate the Blockchain platform utilization, a Web or Admin interface can be used. Eni's procurement unit could be checking data with external sources on cloud computing outside the Blockchain network. So the Blockchain would connect the company with external sources which are not integrated into the current system.

Compliance checking encompasses the techniques to verify that the process or a product fulfills constraints representing regulations, guidelines, policies, and laws. It differs from conformance checking, which is more technical. Here, constraints focus on process rules rather than on entire process runs (Wattana, 2019).

After qualifying, suppliers who are awarded contracts are required to fulfill them, providing the products or services for which they were selected and awarded a contract. When a supplier delivers a specific order, the company will check whether the information the supplier has declared in the tender process complies with what the equipment can achieve in terms of sustainability, whether it is carbon emission, energy consumption, or another criterion.

If the information provided matches the reality, then the order reaches the next step with the validation and initiation of the payment procedure. If the requirements are not met, then there would be either the cancellation of the order, penalty fees to be paid, or another outcome elaborated by both parties.

In this case, the Blockchain can also be used through smart contracts to check information compliance to reality. Use the Blockchain to compare if the technical information provided by the supplier in the tender is the same as the reality when the equipment arrives.

BLOCKCHAINS PLATFORMS CHOICE

Choosing the appropriate Blockchain platform for a specific business application may be challenging. Blockchain offers a wide range of technical features. Therefore, the choice will depend on characteristics such as the technological maturity of the platform, expected transaction speed, technical features such as smart contract compatibility, type of Blockchain (public or private), energy consumption, implementation costs, and many others. A company will choose the platform according to its objectives and its budget.

Bitcoin and Ethereum are famous and still the most prominent players in the blockchain market. Popularity in the Blockchain environment is associated with technical maturity and a large community for ensuring future maintenance. Therefore, these two platforms are old with a low average of transactions per second but more valued. However, newer platforms like Cardano are faster and generally have lower power consumption. In the Figure 5 and Table 1, data are showing the existing difference between various blockchain platforms.

Figure 5. Transactions per second for blockchain platforms
Source: Pradip S., Sign's

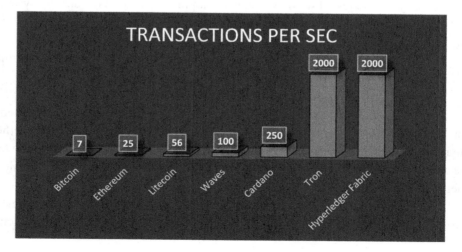

Each platform has a different number of transactions per second. However, even the lowest transaction speed blockchain would execute transactions faster than traditional systems. Therefore, implementing Blockchain would result in substantial time savings. Referring to the supplier qualification process, Blockchain would reduce the execution time from weeks to days.

Table 1. Comparison of some blockchain platforms

Types	Bitcoin	Ethereum	Waves	Hyperledger
Data can be stored	Cryptocurrency	Cryptocurrency, digital assets, smart contracts		Chain code, smart contracts
Support smart contracts?	No	Yes	Yes	Yes
Energy consumption	Very high (110TWh)	Medium (49TWh)		-
Governance	Decentralized (Bitcoin community)	Decentralized (Ethereum community)		Linux foundation
Ledger type	No permission	No permission		Permission
Industry focus		Cross-industry		Cross-industry

(Source: BitcoinEnergyConsumption.com, Forbes, EthereumEnergyConsumption.com)

BLOCKCHAIN IMPLEMENTATION COSTS ESTIMATION

The cost of blockchain implementation depends on various factors. Usually, it depends on the blockchain application needed (i.e., financial transactions), the complexity, the blockchain type, the blockchain platform, the number of users to interact on the platform, and many other technology-related features. A company specializing in developing software and digital solutions using emerging technologies estimates the cost of implementing the Blockchain as shown in Table 2.

One should consider consultant fees, prototype development, and white paper costs in the consulting and design phases. In the quality assurance phase, security or legal costs should be considered (De Giovanni, 2020b). The costs estimated in Table 2 are more related to the implementation process of the Blockchain, spent on various phases of the project. However, the blockchain implementation costs also involve project management costs and resource costs for hiring a software development team. There are also costs associated with the creation of the framework. Indeed, to deploy a contract on the Blockchain, Blockchain platforms must contribute a certain fee. For instance, a minimum fee of 32000 gas + 200 gas/byte of the source code is charged while deploying a contract on the Ethereum platform (Takyar, 2019). This cost is also part of the implementation costs of blockchain technology.

Table 2. Cost estimation of blockchain implementation

Phases of Blockchain implementation	Cost estimation (% of the overall project cost
Consulting	10%
Designing	15%
Development	50%
Quality assurance	25%
Deployment, maintenance, and third party costs (15% to 25%)	Private Blockchain - $1500/month Public Blockchain - $750 for the third party

(Source: LeewayHertz, 2019)

It is noteworthy that organizations willing to implement Blockchain technology partner with Blockchain developing companies or start-ups in some cases. In this case, the implementing costs would not necessarily be the same as those mentioned above.

BLOCKCHAIN BENEFITS AND CHALLENGES

However strong the procurement team is, the process of finding suitable suppliers to meet the company's needs is time-consuming and costly. Blockchain-based solutions are game-changing for the identification and management of qualified suppliers. Some benefits are:

- Shortening process time: Procurement officers and buyers spend much time assimilating data from their suppliers, validating that data, and understanding what is happening in their supply chain. Blockchain can validate data in the fastest possible manner with high transaction speed, which considerably reduces the time spent on the qualification process.
- Procurement officers would reduce the suppliers''compliance risks by having access, through the Blockchain and smart contracts, to accurate data about suppliers' sustainability performances and ratings, certifications, and more. Most trusted providers of business sustainability ratings and other third parties will validate supplier records that will be helpful to fill in the missing information not provided by suppliers.

- Costs reduction in the supplier qualification process: Thanks to Blockchain, the time spent for the vendor qualification is optimized, the information provided by suppliers is directly checked and validated. Consequently, expenses related to this process, labor and procurement operation costs are significantly lowered. Blockchain could also help avoid documentation errors and reduce compliance costs.

To summarize, Blockchain facilitates access to information, improves data accuracy, reduces cost and document processing time, and can easily detect fraud. Researchers highlight that the implementation and usage of Blockchain are costly since it may require costly new infrastructure. However, some industrials ensure that Blockchain's implementation costs will progressively decrease over time, making it even more attractive. Nevertheless, the promising technology still faces some limitations:

- **Environmental issues**

Adopting Blockchain would consume too much energy and has a negative impact on carbon emissions; this is the leading environmental risk related to Blockchain (STOA, 2020). For instance, the energy consumption of the "proof of work" consensus used in Bitcoin is evaluated at 110TWh per year as of May 2021. However, the "proof of stake" used in Ethereum is less consuming and other less famous but more sustainable blockchain platforms. Therefore, Blockchain energy consumption depends on the Blockchain platform used.

- **The Oracle problem**

An oracle software helps the blockchain environment integrate with other systems (Wattana, 2019). Blockchain ensures the security of the information it stores, but nothing can be confirmed regarding the information security before entering the Blockchain (or after leaving it). This problem becomes more serious when using smart contracts since they act alone based on the data provided by the third parties. The inputs to the Blockchain should then be verified to solve this problem.

- **Smart contracts**

Smart contracts execute various processes autonomously; still, using these automated solutions could raise other technical issues. A malicious compromise or an error on the program code can allow unauthorized transactions or lead to critical financial consequences. Therefore, the developer team should ensure that the quality of the software code used for smart contracts is reliable.

- **Social issues**

As with all new technologies, Blockchain also has social consequences. Adopting and expanding Blockchain could create an uneven distribution of benefits and costs in social groups. The cost reduction of data validity might create winners, but eliminating current intermediaries might create losers.

- **Skepticism around Blockchain**

Sometimes, the technology is quite complex for new users, and the implementation might be less feasible in some fields (Sanchez, 2019). An additional aspect worth addressing is credibility: the technology is promising, but since it is a nascent and immature technology, there is skepticism about Blockchain's real potential. Currently, it is difficult to assess all blockchain drawbacks because of the lack of experience.

- **Legal issues**

Significant concerns exist relative to the enforcement of smart contracts. Stakeholders should agree on general principles of good governance, applicable law, conflict resolution, and privacy. All technologies involving extensive data and transaction sharing will undoubtedly create legal challenges like governance, privacy, and regulatory recognition (STOA, 2020). It is therefore vital to ensure that Blockchain is interoperable with the complex set of existing regulations.

RECOMMENDATIONS

Procurement officers and buyers spend much time assimilating data from their suppliers, validating that data, and understanding what is happening in their supply chain. A Blockchain-based solution would effectively automate all of that data ingestion into the company. The data will be validated, automatically ingested into the system, and updated by suppliers and third parties on the network. This will have massing savings for Chief Procurement Officers as they are trying to manage an ever-increasing number of suppliers.

As the oldest Blockchain platform, Bitcoin has proved to be more resilient than other platforms. However, the transactions per second are low on this platform, it is smart contracts compatible, and the proof of work consensus consumes too much energy, which is environmentally unfriendly. So, platforms such as Ethereum or Hyperledger Fabric would be preferable to Bitcoin in terms of energy consumption and transaction speed. Regarding the technical aspects, many organizations are still lacking the technological assets to adopt Blockchain. On the other hand, its implementation and infrastructure may be costly for the implementing company. One way of overcoming this challenge is to partner with Blockchain developing companies to increase the implementing company's knowledge and enable faster and cost-effective implementation of the technology. Such is the case of Amazon Managed Blockchain, which partners with industrials to implement blockchain-based solutions implementation. IBM also provides a cross-industry blockchain-based platform used by suppliers to efficiently manage the validation, qualification, and suppliers' maintenance.

Table 3. The blockchain's benefits and challenges in procurement

Benefits of Blockchain	Emerging challenges due to Blockchain
Saving time comparatively to traditional qualification systems	New relationships with specialized operators for implementing and handling the blockchain platform
Lower supplier risk and need for compliance	Energy consumption harming sustainability
Matching the smart contract with the legal issues	Transaction time comparatively to VISA transactions
Suppliers are incentivized to perform to receive the payment by the smart contract	Coding the smart contract can be subject to errors
	Records depend on several parties, also the oracles
	Increasing risks to exclude good suppliers
	Culture of blockchain over the supply chain

CONCLUSION

In this chapter, the Eni's procurement process has been analyzed to understand better how the procurement process works, and areas for improvements have been found for potential Blockchain applications. The study proves that the blockchain has many opportunities and benefits for procurement management and could improve procurement processes through smart contracts. Table 3 summarizes the business opportunites and the emerging challenges linked to Blockchain in procurement. Indeed, Blockchain has the capacity of considerably enhancing trust and transparency in procurement, from tracking inventory to payments. It can also reduce operating costs and processing times. The main potential usages of the blockchain in procurement processes found in the literature reveal that Blockchain can be used:

- Internally to assess each department's needs and the certification and validation of documents provided during the pre-tendering process for multinationals.
- As an interface between the company and the suppliers during the tendering process, from the invitation to tender, supplier bids, to contract negotiations while maintaining traceability, anonymity, and confidentiality.

It can also be used for supplier selection and data validation, carbon emission tracking, monitoring and trading, waste management, and suppliers' performance measurement tracking and compliance checking after delivery.

However, although the theory supports these Blockchain applications throughout the procurement process, it was less straightforward in reality. Looking at the case of Eni, it is obvious to notice that the Blockchain in this company cannot be used for the internal communication between the procurement department and the other departments, nor as an interface for the tender process. In contrast, Blockchain proves to be very useful for Eni when dealing with information validation problems to facilitate suppliers' qualifications. Therefore, investigating the supplier qualification process help to understand this process and find Blockchain technology applications. The article shows that one of the most prominent blockchain applications in the supplier qualification process is data processing and certification.

To be qualified as an Eni supplier, questions are asked to the supplier. The answers to these questions must be submitted with supporting documents. To confirm the authenticity of these information and documentation, this study suggests using a Blockchain-based platform and smart contracts that would bring together Eni, its potential suppliers, and a third party to certify the information provided by the suppliers. In this way, the quality of the information collected is guaranteed, the vendor management unit wastes less time in processing the information, and the procurement department reduces the cost of its operations.

Regarding the choice of platform to use, it should be noted that, although Bitcoin is one of the most mature technologies, its low speed (7 TPS) and high energy consumption make it unattractive. However, Hyperledger Fabric seems to be very fast and consumes less energy than other platforms, making it an attractive choice. On the other hand, although the Blockchain brings many benefits, its implementation costs are pretty high, starting from consulting costs, deployment costs, maintenance costs, and project management and resources costs. Consequently, companies need to evaluate the long-term benefits of blockchain before committing to its implementation. However, some other companies implement Blockchain, choosing to partner with start-ups or companies specializing in the field of Blockchain to ensure the success of their projects and gain experience. Blockchain also faces some other challenges from the social, environmental, technical, and legal perspectives.

Later on, other more profound aspects of the use of blockchain in procurement processes could be examined, such as the monitoring of sustainability parameters, including the monitoring of carbon emissions or the exact energy consumption of the different actors in the supply chain to enable the supplier qualification service, with sustainability-based criteria, to be able to collect this kind of data directly from the source. As the Blockchain is immutable, this data could be permanently recorded, and this information could be used for supplier selection in the bidding process.

REFERENCES

Badzar, A. (2016). *An explorative study of blockchain technology in logistics*. Master.

Bettina Warburg, B. W. (2019). *The Basics of Blockchain*. Animal Ventures LLC.

BRC Global Standard. (2021). Retrieved from www.brcglobalstandards.com

Buratto, A., Cesaretto, R., & De Giovanni, P. (2019). Consignment contracts with cooperative programs and price discount mechanisms in a dynamic supply chain. *International Journal of Production Economics*, *218*, 72–82. doi:10.1016/j.ijpe.2019.04.027

De Giovanni, P. (2016). Coordination in a distribution channel with decisions on the nature of incentives and share-dependency on pricing. *The Journal of the Operational Research Society*, *67*(8), 1034–1049. doi:10.1057/jors.2015.118

De Giovanni, P. (2019). Digital supply chain through dynamic inventory and smart contracts. *Mathematics*, *7*(12), 1235. doi:10.3390/math7121235

De Giovanni, P. (2020a). Blockchain and smart contracts in supply chain management: A game theoretic model. *International Journal of Production Economics*, *228*, 107855. doi:10.1016/j.ijpe.2020.107855

De Giovanni, P. (2020b). An optimal control model with defective products and goodwill damages. *Annals of Operations Research*, *289*(2), 419–430. doi:10.100710479-019-03176-4

De Giovanni, P. (2021a). *Dynamic Quality Models and Games in Digital Supply Chains: How Digital Transformation Impacts Supply Chain Quality Management*. Springer Nature.

De Giovanni, P. (2021b). Smart Supply Chains with vendor managed inventory, coordination, and environmental performance. *European Journal of Operational Research*, 292(2), 515–531. doi:10.1016/j.ejor.2020.10.049

De Giovanni, P., & Cariola, A. (2020). Process innovation through industry 4.0 technologies, lean practices and green supply chains. *Research in Transportation Economics*, 100869. doi:10.1016/j.retrec.2020.100869

EEA. (2019). Adaptation challenges and opportunities for the European energy system. Luxembourg: Publications Office of the European Union.

Eni. (2021, February 27). *Eni, Abiut us*. Retrieved from Eni corporation website: https://www.eni.com/en

Eni. (2021, March). *Media press*. Retrieved from Eni website: www.eni.com

Eurostat. (2018). *EU energy in figures: statistical pocketbook*. Author.

Hao, D. P. (n.d.). *TrialChain: A Blockchain-Based Platform to Validate Data Integrity in Large*. Biomedical Research Studies.

Hollos, D. C. B., Blome, C., & Foerstl, K. (2012). Does sustainable supplier co-operation affect performance? Examining implications for the triple bottom line. *International Journal of Production Research*, 50(11), 2968–2986. doi:10.1080/00207543.2011.582184

ISO 9001. (2015). *Quality Management Systems: Requirements*. London: BS EN ISO 9001.

Kalis, R. B. (2018). Validating Data Integrity with Blockchain. In *2018 IEEE International Conference on Cloud Computing Technology and Science* (pp. 272-277). IEEE.

Kamali, A. (2019). Blockchain's Potential to Combat Procurement Frauds. *International Journal of Biometrics and Bioinformatics*, 101 - 107.

Laurent Probst, L. F.-D. (2016). *Blockchain applications and services*. European Union: European Commission.

Orr, B. (2002). The case for web-based procurement. *ABA Banking Journal*, 59.

Pradip, S. M. (2018). *Performance Analysis of Blockchain Platforms* (Thesis). The University of Nevada, Las Vegas, NV.

Preeker, T., & De Giovanni, P. (2018). Coordinating innovation projects with high tech suppliers through contracts. *Research Policy, 47*(6), 1161–1172. doi:10.1016/j. respol.2018.04.003

Sacco, A., & De Giovanni, P. (2019). Channel coordination with a manufacturer controlling the price and the effect of competition. *Journal of Business Research, 96*, 97–114. doi:10.1016/j.jbusres.2018.09.001

Sanchez, S. N. (2019). The Implementation of Decentralized Ledger Technologies for Public Procurement. *European Procurement and Public Private Partnership Law Review*, 180 - 196.

Santosh, B., & Rane, S. V. (2019). Green procurement process model based on blockchain–IoT. *Management of Environmental Quality*, 741–763.

Sarkis, J. M. K. (2019). Blockchain Practices, Potentials, and Perspectives in Greening Supply Chains. *Sustainability*.

STOA. (2020). Blockchain for supply chain and international trade. Brussels: European Union.

Takyar, A. (2019). Retrieved from LeewayHertz: https://www.leewayhertz.com/cost-of-blockchain-implementation/

Torres de Oliveira, R. (2017). *Institutions, middleman, and blockchains. Shuffle and re-start*. Academic Press.

Trong, T. D. (2018). Issuing and Verifying Digital Certificates with Blockchain. *International Conference on Advanced Technologies for Communications*.

Wattana, V. D. (2019). Blockchain characteristics and consensus in modern business processes. *Journal of Industrial Information Integration*, 32 - 39.

Wenyan,, S., & Z., X.-C. (2017). Developing sustainable supplier selection criteria for solar air-conditioner manufacturer: An integrated approach. *Renewable & Sustainable Energy Reviews*, 1461–1471.

Chapter 9
Smart Metering Systems:
A Blockchain Application for Sustainable Procurement

Bernardo Nicoletti
Temple University, Italy

Andrea Appolloni
University of Rome Tor Vergata, Italy

ABSTRACT

Blockchain technology is one of the most vital and exciting technologies available today. It can transform the business world and the organizations' functions. It offers several possibilities to flourish existing businesses, grow entirely new ones, and severely disrupt traditional organizations. This chapter aims to study the applications of blockchain in procurement, to improve at the same time effectiveness and sustainability, and to define its critical success factors. The chapter presents a model and then describes its application in a real business case. It highlights the critical challenges in this blockchain implementation and the potentials of blockchain in managing sustainable procurement in support of utilities. This blockchain application is for smart metering. The blockchain solution contributes to the three bottom lines: economic, social, and sustainable. It can help support sustainable procurement, reduce errors, improve organizational functions and procedures, and prevent fraud. The chapter includes some challenges and their possible remediations.

DOI: 10.4018/978-1-7998-8014-1.ch009

INTRODUCTION

A blockchain is a ledger filled with a time-stamped series of immutable data records managed by a cluster of servers not normally owned by any single entity. Each of these blocks of data is secured and bound to each other using cryptography. The three main properties of a blockchain solution are:

- Decentralization. Everyone can interact with someone else directly and is the owner or in charge of his/her assets (money, sensitive data) and can manage them.
- Transparency. Through the public address of an actual entity, it is possible to look at all the transactions he/she has engaged in.
- Immutability. Once something has been entered into the blockchain, it cannot be tampered with, and the transmission is fully encrypted.

Blockchain also supports the so-called smart contracts (Vacca, A. et al. 2020). They are computer programs that automatically execute a contract or part of it. Technically, they are code stored on a blockchain solution, triggered by blockchain transactions, and read and write data in that blockchain database. Smart contracts, based on blockchain technology, could reduce infrastructure costs of financial institutions from 13.8 to 18.4 billion euros annually by 2022 (Probst et al., 2016). They could save time and reduce costs in standard transactions. Smart contracts ease, verify or enforce a digital agreement. These programs potentially replace notaries, lawyers, and financial institutions when handling some legal and business transactions.

This chapter reviews and presents an innovative blockchain solution in support of procurement and its critical success factors. The perspective is for the organizations to obtain customers' delight by using blockchain solutions to support an agile, effective, efficient, ethical, and economically sustainable procurement.

Sustainability has become a global corporate mandate, with implementation affected by two key trends. The first is the availability of innovative solutions, such as blockchain, robust, affordable, and flexible. The second is the recognition that procurement strongly impacts sustainability and supports greening the entire supply network.

The business case presented in this paper is relative to an innovative solution for smart metering in an electric network. There are still problems in the quality data collection of smart meters, such as incomplete data collection, quality data loss, and difficulty in data sharing (Yan, L. et al., 2021). This chapter presents a solution for collecting and processing smart quality data using smart meters, blockchain, and smart contract platforms. The solution is designed to realize the automation of data collection and improve the reliability of collected data (Nicoletti, B. et al., 2020). The business case analyzed is very promising from the point of view of the Three Bottom Lines (TBL) of sustainability: ergonomic, financial, and social. Particular attention is devoted to assure also security of the data entered in the blockchain. A thorough analysis and proofs of concept have proved these benefits.

LITERATURE REVIEW AND METHODOLOGY USED

Sustainability as a concept in the corporate world appeared formally in the 1960s as concerns towards the degrading environment and poor resource management began growing (McKenzie, S., 2004). Stakeholders are now becoming more aware of social and environmental sustainability. Thanks to this awareness, organizations are making efforts to adapt and become more responsible and sustainable. These efforts imply that sustainability should become a significant part of the organization's processes, including procurement (Meehan, J. et al., 2011).

The old thinking was that sustainability would increase the costs of the organizations. Sustainability can improve profitability considering the three pillars: social, society, and environment. This chapter's starting point is acquiring an appropriate amount of knowledge on sustainable procurement.

Blockchain is an application layer running on top of internet protocols that enable economic transactions between actors without relying on one third party (Wang, Y. et al., 2019). Literature about the procurement process exists on a large scale. Sustainability and its role in procurement is a more recent topic in scientific literature. According to Millington, A. (2008), social and environmental sustainability in corporations is a 21st-century phenomenon. Many researchers have explored the impact of blockchain technology on supply chain management (Treiblmaver, H. 2018; Saberi, S. et al., 2019), including supply chain coordination (Tian, F. 2016). Blockchain's potential applications could enhance the sustainability of the supply chain since this technology can precisely and securely identify, verify, exchange, and store data. Blockchain solutions can bring supply chain transparency to a new level and expose incorrect practices (Tian, F., 2016). Saberi, S. et al. (2019) investigated activities across and within a supply chain and then provided valuable insights into the diversified sustainability-oriented opportunities connected with blockchain solutions.

The current energy transition from a fossil-fuel-based economy to a zero-carbon has significantly accelerated in recent years, as the largest emitters have committed to achieving carbon-neutral goals in the next 20-30 years (Saraj, S. et al. 2021).

Modernization through digital technologies increases renewable energy generation, and environmental sustainability also characterizes the energy industry. Blockchain technology can play a significant role in providing secure digital distributed platforms. This solution facilitates digitization, decarbonization, and decentralization of the energy systems. Several promising blockchain applications in the energy sector are under research and development, including peer-to-peer energy trading, carbon monitoring, management, trading, and IoT-enabled electric grid management. Several challenges are slowing down the implementation of these applications on a large scale, including outdated legislation and regulations, slow pace of adaptation from the traditional energy industry, and risks associated with the new, untested technology.

Blockchain systems allow managing decentralized electrical energy consumption/ production transactions- It is ideal for managing transactive energy systems, where prosumers can exchange energy widely. Olivares-Rojas, J. C. et al. (2021) present a transactional model of electrical energy using the infrastructure of smart metering and blockchain systems to allow the commercialization of electrical energy by prosumers. The results show that they can be good alternatives for the Mexican electricity market by reducing subsidies and being more profitable than at the current rates.

Adeyemi, A. et al. (2020) studied how blockchains can work and enhance the operation of power distribution systems. Their paper discusses multiple scenarios considering the use of blockchain technologies in power distribution systems. Their paper also discusses challenges for applying blockchain technologies to power distribution systems and how to manage these challenges.

Abdo, J. B. et al. (2020) presented a peer-to-peer multi-utility trading platform that solves the shortcomings of existing utility frameworks.

The impact on sustainable procurement of blockchain solutions has not been analyzed in-depth and is the aim of this chapter. This chapter analyzes answers to two questions whose answers are not available in the literature:

Q1: Which are the critical success factors for blockchain solutions to improve the triple Bottom lines from the procurement point of view?
Q2: How can blockchain solutions support sustainability along the electricity metering process?

BLOCKCHAIN IN SUPPORT OF THE THREE BOTTOM LINES

Procurement during the pandemic seemed incapable of satisfying its primary function: providing organizations with the supplies they needed (Folliot Lalliot, L. et al., 2020). The pandemic has shown the fragility of global ICT procurements systems, with organizations finding that they had little transparency into second-, third-, and fourth-party operations within their overall delivery mechanisms. Providing goods and services at the correct times and the right place should not lose the importance of ensuring the correct quality (Lysons, K. et al., 2006).

Elkington, J: introduced the idea of the Three Bottom Lines (TBL) in 1994. Since then, he and other researchers have written on it (Weber, I. et al. 1991; Carter, C. et al. 2008). TBL includes three performance components: social, environmental, and financial. The TBL dimensions are the three Ps: people, planet, and profits, to which some authors add another P: Principle of Governance (Niskala, M. et al., 2015).

- Economic sustainability is often thought only to be how profitable the business is, its added value to the customers and its different stakeholders. Economic sustainability should also include how financially sound the organization is and its competitiveness.
- Social responsibility summarizes concerns on the efficient and economical use of natural resources, such as water, air, and soil, safeguarding the diversity of nature and tackling climate change. When producing a product or service, the organization is responsible for its climate footprint (Zink, K., 2008).
- Social sustainability covers taking care and improving the personnel and their skills, respecting and acting according to human rights, responsibly managing labor contracts and corporate policies. The organization's strategy should include implementing these sustainability measures above the minimum legislation and regulations imposed by the community, national, and international authorities.

Blockchain solutions can help procurement in terms of sustainability. It is possible to analyze this support within the framework of the TBL. It is interesting how blockchain could contribute to satisfying all three Bottom lines:

- From an economic point of view, blockchain solutions can help in satisfying the need for trust. An application as smart contracts can significantly help assure stakeholders of compliance with the agreements and the regulations governing them. The sustainable economic aspects of the technology found in the reviewed literature are mostly the transformational potentials of blockchain solutions and their capabilities to drive new disintermediated business models, higher operational efficiencies, cost benefits, and added sources of value creation. Thanks to its decentralized nature, blockchain solutions can decrease costs and transaction times for economic sustainability, reducing waste in manufacturing and operational processes (Le, T. V., et al., 2021). Blockchain solutions also provide real-time communications, fast payment with reduced transaction fees, low product/service costs, and faster delivery times. It builds an innovative business model and contributes to a sustainable economy.

- The social empowerment of procurement assures through blockchain solutions the creation of trustful relationships among procurement stakeholders, the increase of perishable product safety, the support to humanitarian logistics, and the promotion of social equity. From a social point of view, the new normal requires doing everything possible remotely. Blockchain solutions can help such distributed models. Blockchain solutions could solve the inequality by guaranteeing human rights and ethical acts (Le, T. V., et al., 2021). For instance, blockchain solutions can enable fairness by immutably recording all the products collected for a specific payment period.

- From an environmental point of view, blockchain solutions contribute to better resilience. Resilience has an old conceptual and analytic presence in ecology. Ecological systems can adapt to change without disruption and continue their services (Folke, C. 2006). More recently, innovative ideas describe global environmental systems functioning in the face of extreme changes, such as those caused by changes in climate or a pandemic. Organizations trying to move forward in their environmental policies and strategies can use blockchain to improve their environmental practices across the procurement, reduce the strain on energy and natural resources, and offer environmentally friendly products. Blockchain solutions can have a positive ecological impact when adopted by procurement, especially in connection with international trade. Due to the irreversible data recorded in a blockchain solution, it is possible to find the transportation with the best level of greenhouse gases (Le, T. V., et al., 2021). In addition, blockchain solutions and smart contracts can constantly check drivers from driving faster (which increases emissions and fuel consumption) and saving energy resources. Blockchain solutions also support finding materials and products/services that use significantly less non-renewable resources. In this way, it is possible to safeguard the environment preservation processes.

CRITICAL SUCCESS FACTORS

Critical success factors in the use of blockchain solutions to support sustainable procurement are:

- Stakeholder Management refers to effective governance to enable communication, risk reduction, and trust among all involved parties. The role of procurement in the future will change. The relationships with partners are essential for the success of the organizations. It is important not to refer to a linear supply chain but to a value network (Nicoletti, B. 2018). The procurement goal is not simply delivering products or services but adding value to customers and the organization. In this vision, the procurement needs to work as a coordinator of the network of partners. The ecosystem must work as one team. Access to the same data in a blockchain solution from all the parties involved can help in improving the reciprocal trust within an ecosystem.

- Transparency means clarity in the choices and actions of the transactions carried out internally and externally by the organization. Blockchain solutions in procurement management can improve visibility and transparency based on record-keeping functionalities (Ivanov, D. et al., 2018). This result depends on the data-driven capability of the organizations. This capability includes the ability of the organizations to capture correct data, store them, analyze them, and have decision-making based on facts in real-time. Traceability across procurement is one of the most compelling use cases for blockchain technology (Kehoe, I. et al., 2017). Traceability also allows respecting compliance since the blockchain solutions refer to standards and controls to supply evidence that regulatory conditions are respected and internalized.

These factors (Stakeholder management and traceability) are not specific to some industries. They are common across different sectors and should help organizations unlock the hidden sustainable-adding capability in their procurement.

To define how much and on what blockchain solutions could help, it is possible to build a graph with the critical success factors mentioned before for the successful use of blockchain solutions in procurement management. The stakeholder management is on the abscissa axis. The incidence of transparency is on the ordinate axis. The function in one of the quadrants shows how blockchain solutions can help those critical success factors (Figure 1):

- Functions with high transparency and a high impact on stakeholder management are "strategic functions." To manage them, the organizations usually develop integration strategies that result in co-makership relationships, that is, the involvement (quasi-integration) of the partners in innovative and operational processes.
- Functions characterized by high importance of transparency but with minimal impact on the relevance of the stakeholder management are defined as "inside functions." To manage them, organizations usually aim at strategies oriented towards the relationship's stability to guarantee the components/services

necessary for their production cycle and minimize the internal risks of interruption of the production flow.

- Functions characterized by a high impact on stakeholder management and without transparency requirements are "external functions." These are functions where any improvement in the connections with stakeholders can significantly affect procurement effectiveness, efficiency, and economics.
- Functions with low importance of transparency in the procurement market and a minimal impact on the relevance of the stakeholder management are "non-critical functions."

Figure 1. Sustainable procurement critical success factors

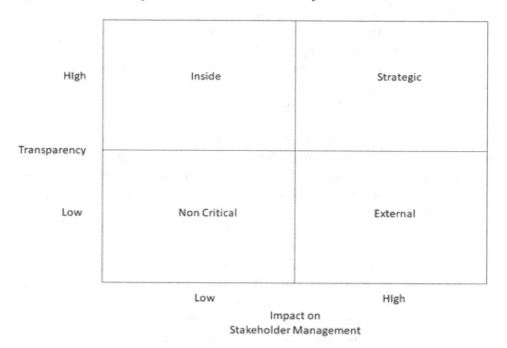

BUSINESS CASE: SMART METERING SYSTEMS

Solution

Smart Metering Systems (SMS) are a fundamental area in the smart utility initiatives (Piatek, K. et al., 2021). The smart utility meters (for instance, for measuring electric electrical consumptions) allow continuous monitoring of utility consumption and report to the vendor company's facilities without an operator's need. Outages, reconnections, and other services can be dynamically automated.

End-users are starting to stop being passive consumers of electricity generated by utilities. They are beginning to install and use renewable energy sources such as photovoltaic panels and wind turbines. Smart meters can measure this local electrical energy production to integrate into the electrical grid.

It is possible to add more functionalities to SMS, such as measuring electrical power quality events, integrating demand response systems, and electrical energy management. Smart meters can support various pricing schema such as a flat rate or based on time intervals of connection with the utility consumption.

Metering is a function with high transparency and a high impact on the customer. It is a "strategic function" in the classification introduced in the previous section.

The Italian telecommunication company, TIM, has proposed an innovative metering solution. In this solution, blockchain and smart contracts are at the base of managing electric energy supply to a device by a vendor (Bellifemine, F. I. et al., 2017). This solution presents several benefits. It also aims to support the best use of energy, increasing the sustainability of the grid system.

The method proposed by TIM includes:

- A certifier system defining a reference electric power profile of each device.
- A certifier system supplying a device couplable to the electric device and a socket delivering electric energy provided by the energy vendor. This device is univocally associated with the electric device through a reference power profile of the electric device.
- A user of the electric device, coupling, through the device, the electric device to the socket for using electrical energy.
- A device checking if the device coupled to the socket is the device it should univocally be associated with. The check compares a measured electric power profile of the device with the reference electric power profile. If the check has a positive outcome, the device collects measures of the electric power absorbed and certifies them as energy consumptions corresponding to the device it should be univocally associates.

The method includes storing the encrypted and certified collected measures into a blockchain distributed data structure. According to the standard implementation, the vendor catalog may be on a blockchain, while a smart contract can manage the legal and economic relationships with the user.

The integrated SMS can connect the distributor and the third party/parties by acting as an intelligent network node. Smart meters can forward encrypted requests for temporary higher power to active nodes on the network using blockchain technology.

SMS can detect underutilization or foresee an underutilization during the time range of the energy required by the regulated system and take into account this situation in its energy grid management.

There is a recording of the entire process on an electronic register. This recording takes place according to the procedure provided by the blockchain so that there is no need for a central authority that keeps a separate register.

Benefits

A blockchain solution applied to smart meters arises from the need for security and transparency of the data processed and the protection of the personal data of individual users and businesses that use these tools (Figure 2). Blockchain can be considered a "certification machine" of transactions in the virtual world. When applying the blockchain to the physical world (for instance, smart grid, stack, food supply chains, and so on), it is necessary to make sure that the information from the real world is "true" before writing it in the blockchain. As part of the regular activity of providing its metering services, SMS can guarantee that certain information originates from a specific Subscriber Identity/Identification Module (SIM), a specific terminal, at a specific time, and a specific location (Cell), assuring complete security of the solution.

The application of smart contracts, in particular, allows to remove barriers between distribution vendors and users, thus saving in management and transaction costs, making the latter more secure. In addition, when a transaction occurs, the data is recorded on new blocks used for future operations. By doing so, vendors can rely on a set of collected data to charge their customers correctly.

Technically speaking, the impact of a blockchain solution derives mainly from the possibility of offering a secure decentralized system, where the nodes can work independently without referring to a central system.

The benefits connected with the Three Bottom lines are as follows.

- From the economic sustainability point of view, the virtual integrated smart meters provide data communication functions. They allow remote control and diagnostics to the energy vendor and the customers and enable smart contracts functions based on blockchain technologies. Through a detailed study of the needs of their customers, utility vendors can offer *ad hoc* proposals aimed at improving the contract and the customer relationship. The proposed solution provides total control by the energy vendors, leaving little need for users to check and verify the actual data.
- From an environmental point of view, the possibility of integrating new technological solutions, such as IoT and blockchain, into the energy ecosystem introduces flexibility relative to the electricity consumption profiles without

necessarily modifying the current contracts. A significant benefit for the utility vendors is the possibility of directing their resources towards specific users: In fact, electricity vendors often balance the needs of their customers for which a particular power profile should be available. If all customers make use of the maximum capacity, the system might collapse. Thanks to using blockchain solutions and controlling the actual usage data, the service provider could know what their users require, minimizing waste, and working to avoid overloads.

- From the social responsibility point of view, smart meters guarantee transparency to the customers by sharing data with them. Smart meters have specific functions that allow generating a large amount of data, thus covering every variation and sending them correctly in real-time or within minutes. Users who acquire more knowledge of their consumption and potential waste can modify their behavior, improve energy savings, and reduce pollution. Currently, the most used process for data exchange takes place with Integrated Information Systems (IIS). These systems take care of collecting and processing data coming from the meters centrally. These systems receive the validated data, while the users do not have access to validated data. Subsequently, IIS will transmit some data to the users. The current process relies on the data flow provided by the utility vendors. The application of blockchain solutions could allow a different approach, no longer based on the information provided by the electricity vendors, which hold control of the data, but on an automatic, immediate, and effective sharing of information with the users, which could be prosumers of electricity.

It could be possible to use smart meters, with the support of integrated virtual systems, to measure all user consumption sources such as water, electricity, gas, and even internet data usage (Hong, Y. et al., 2021). The data input sources can be direct, as in electricity measurement, or derived as in gas and water, which, usually, are measured by independent meters upstream of the smart meters. Third parties that act as verifiers and certifiers of consumption measures should introduce IoT and blockchain. Thanks to the control given by the blockchain, a connection guaranteed by the IoT, and guaranteed work in the authentication of data by third parties, there could be a transfer of the benefits of this flexibility to customers, leaving the contractual form unchanged.

Challenges

Blockchain solutions can offer considerable opportunities and benefits. Since blockchain is a new technology, it has limits and issues that could impose restrictions on SMSs. Among these restrictions, blockchain solutions present time intervals in which transactions and processes can occur. Having a limit to the calculation of data could create a deterrent for their adoption. This problem is found mainly in a public blockchain, characterized by more centralization. For this reason, there is a preference for private blockchains since they are decentralized. It is appropriate to consider the pros and cons of adopting blockchain solutions using a public or a private system. The latter, even if more secure, requires more time to perform transactions.

Security is always a challenge on an open network like a public blockchain. The consideration of security can be in terms of the CIA properties (Dhillon, G. et al., 2000):

- Confidentiality is low in a distributed system that replicates all data over its network. Targeted encryption can help resolve this issue (Kosba, A. et al., 2016).
- Integrity is a vital characteristic of blockchains, albeit challenges exist (Eyal, I. et al., 2014; Gervais, A. et al., 2016).
- Availability can be considered high in terms of reads from blockchain due to the wide replication, but it is less favorable in write availability (Weber, I. et al., 2017).

New attack vectors exist around forking, for instance, through network segregation (Natoli, C. et al., 2017). These are particularly relevant in private or consortium blockchains.

Blockchain solutions require high computing capacity. SMS would allow savings in identifying waste, but it consumes energy to process the blockchain's operations. High consumption of resources, particularly electricity, depends on the blockchain consensus mechanism, where miners constantly compete to mine the next block for a high reward (Weber, I. et al., 2017). This approach can be seen as wasteful, but it is just a slight indication of the vast duplication of effort in proof-of-work mechanisms. Alternatives to the proof-of-work, like proof-of-stake, have been discussed for a while and would be much more efficient (Bentov, I. et al. 2016). At the time of writing, they remain an unproven but exciting alternative. Proof-of-work makes prevalent assumptions in trusting other participants, which is well suited for an open network managing digital assets, like in the smart metering case examined, especially thanks to the SIMs used in this solution.

Blockchain solutions have scalability issues. It is necessary to validate the high number of smart-meter transactions and operations (Mollah, M. B., et al. 2020).

Figure 2. Benefits and challenges of smart metering system

Benefits	Challenges
Security of information entered in the blockshain	Need of strong Security measures for: Confidentiality, Integrity, and Availability
Application of Smart Contracts:	Limits and issues that could impose restrictions on SMSs
Secure decentralized system	High computing capacity with related energy consumptions
Respect of the three bottom line	Scalability
Expandability to other utilities	

FINDINGS

This chapter aims to answer two questions:

Q1: Which are the critical success factors for blockchain solutions to improve the triple Bottom lines from the procurement point of view?

Q2: How can blockchain solutions support sustainability along the electricity metering process?

The chapter has presented a model for the critical success factors in implementing sustainable procurement in response to the first question.

Relatively to the second question, the business case presented for smart metering services shows the benefits and challenges of blockchain solutions supporting responsible procurement and their remarkable impact on sustainability also in terms of electricity consumption. Utility vendors can successfully implement blockchain to ensure transparency to customers and end-users, remove potential problems linked to frauds, human errors, abuses, and other issues, and guarantee a secure traceability of goods and services, especially their processing, at the origin.

CONCLUSIONS

The application of blockchain solutions and smart contracts to smart metering systems represents a step forward in using cutting-edge systems in data collection.

The solution presented in this chapter overcomes the traditional metering model's limitation. The chapter defines its characteristics and limits. In some countries, there is still a need for a technological push that allows adequate instruments to reach the standards of more advanced countries. There is still minor sensitivity of data exchange and sustainability issues.

Blockchain solutions support the integration of smart meters with a system suitable for exchanging data transparently and securely, thanks to the decentralized characteristics of the blockchain nodes and the security that this helps to provide. Through the automatic exchange of large quantities of data, it is possible to control and evaluate when waste occurs and, based on this information, to use *ad hoc* solutions that compensate customers' needs, avoiding the waste of resources.

SMS use blockchain solutions to exchange and analyze customers' data on consumption. The organizations providing the meters would have a register to keep all the necessary information to avoid short circuits and manage customer relationships more effectively.

Despite the opportunities provided, blockchain solutions still have challenges, such as scalability and the cost of managing multiple operations. A private blockchain can overcome or at least mitigate these problems through more advanced blockchain solutions.

FUTURE RESEARCH DIRECTIONS

The interest of researchers is increasing in the application of blockchain solutions to procurement. Blockchain is an effective technology for supplying economy security and privacy in procurement. However, it is essential in future research to find better solutions for scalability, lack of expertise, and high transactional costs of blockchain solutions. A lack of international standards is another significant obstacle to the widespread adoption of these innovative solutions.

Another challenge using blockchain solutions is the energy consumption of the mining process in the case of proof of work (Vukolić, M., 2015). A new wave of blockchain methods will appear in the future, where different mining algorithms will be combined depending on the specific use case. Blockchain solutions introduction will improve sustainability, traceability, support transparency, and increase sustainable products' market share, leading to less CO_2 and NO_x emissions for the involved products.

The more exciting use of blockchain in procurement supports a fundamental change in the organizations' structures (Nicoletti, 2017), a value network makes up an organization's operations in which the different paths allow advanced customization of the product. The aim of digital procurement is not simply delivering products or services to add value to customers and the organization. In this new vision, the procurement needs to work as a coordinator of the network of partners. The ecosystem must work as one team. More research into this new role of procurement is necessary.

It would be interesting to analyze the SMS solution proposed in more depth in support of the new profile of a prosumer. This profile is possible thanks to the new scenario of lowering the cost of electricity generation technologies thanks to renewable energy. This new scenario changes the role of end-users from being simple consumers to producers of energy (Olivares-Rojas, J, C, et al., 2021). This new role has been called a prosumer and has contributed to modifying electricity markets by allowing prosumers merchandizing the energy surplus to electricity companies and other prosumers. Smart meters systems support this new scenario. It is interesting to analyze a distributed energy management algorithm taking full advantage of blockchain technology. It serves as a one-day-ahead energy schedule that allows each networked entity to make peer-to-peer (P2P) secure power trades with the other microgrid agents to develop sustainable solutions (Sivianes, M. et al. 2021). Smart meters can help in peer-to-peer energy trading supporting market auctions. Mengelkamp et al. (2018) constructed an auction mechanism where smart meters can measure and predict each user's demand and production capacity and subsequently broadcast this information. Based on this information, it would be possible to compute excess demand or supply and send this information to the corresponding blockchain account of the agent. Hahn et al. (2017) presented a distributed auction system where a seller with excess power can launch a new auction and publish his/her available power in the blockchain. Bidders in need of electricity can bid after receiving this information. Smart contracts automate the auction and payment processes, and smart meters detect and report the flow of electricity during the transaction, verifying the completion of the transaction.

ACKNOWLEDGMENT

The authors thanks Danilo Gotta of TIM for pointing out this application.

REFERENCES

Abdo, J. B., & Zeadally, S. (2020). Multi-utility framework: Blockchain exchange platform for sustainable development. *International Journal of Pervasive Computing and Communications*.

Adeyemi, A., Yan, M., Shahidehpour, M., Botero, C., Guerra, A. V., Gurung, N., Zhang, L. C., & Paaso, A. (2020). Blockchain technology applications in power distribution systems. *The Electricity Journal*, *33*(8), 106817. doi:10.1016/j.tej.2020.106817

Appolloni, A., & Cheng, W. (2021). *Sustainable Procurement: knowledge and practice towards sustainable development*. Giappichelli.

Bellifemine, F. L., Gotta, D., & Trucco, T. (2017). *System and method for managing supply of electric energy through certified measures*. patents.google.com/patent/WO2019081298A1/en

Bentov, I., Gabizon, A., & Mizrahi, A. (2016, February). Cryptocurrencies without proof of work. In *International conference on financial cryptography and data security*, (pp. 142-157). Springer.

Carter, C., & Rogers, D. (2008). A framework of sustainable supply chain management: Moving toward new theory. *International Journal of Physical Distribution & Logistics Management*, *38*(5), 360–387. doi:10.1108/09600030810882816

Dhillon, G., & Backhouse, J. (2000). Technical opinion: Information system security management in the new millennium. *Communications of the ACM*, *43*(7), 125–128. doi:10.1145/341852.341877

Elkington, J. (1994). Towards the Sustainable Corporation: Win-Win-Win Business Strategies for Sustainable Development. *California Management Review*, *36*(2), 90–100. doi:10.2307/41165746

Eyal, I., & Sirer, E. G. (2014, March). Majority is not enough: Bitcoin mining is vulnerable. In *International conference on financial cryptography and data security* (pp. 436-454). Springer. 10.1007/978-3-662-45472-5_28

Folke, C. (2006). Resilience: The emergence of a perspective for social–ecological systems analyses. *Global Environmental Change*, *16*(3), 253–267. doi:10.1016/j.gloenvcha.2006.04.002

Folliot Lalliot, L., & Yukins, C. R. (2020). COVID-19: Lessons Learned in Public Procurement. Time for a New Normal? *Time for a New Normal*, 46-58.

Gervais, A., Karame, G. O., Wüst, K., Glykantzis, V., Ritzdorf, H., & Capkun, S. (2016, October). On the security and performance of proof of work blockchains. *Proceedings of the 2016 ACM SIGSAC conference on computer and communications security*, 3-16. 10.1145/2976749.2978341

Hahn, A., Singh, R., Liu, C. C., & Chen, S. (2017). Smart contract-based campus demonstration of decentralized transactive energy auctions. *IEEE Power & Energy Society Innovative Smart Grid Technologies Conference*, 1–5.

Hong, Y., Yoon, S., Kim, Y. S., & Jang, H. (2021). System-level virtual sensing method in building energy systems using autoencoder: Under the limited sensors and operational datasets. *Applied Energy*, *301*, 117458. doi:10.1016/j.apenergy.2021.117458

Ivanov, D., Dolgui, A., & Sokolov, B. (2018). Scheduling of recovery actions in the supply chain with resilience analysis considerations. *International Journal of Production Research*, *56*(19), 6473–6490. doi:10.1080/00207543.2017.1401747

Kehoe, L. (2017). *When two chains combine: Supply chain meets blockchain*. Deloitte.

Kosba, A., Miller, A., Shi, E., Wen, Z., & Papamanthou, C. (2016, May). Hawk: The blockchain model of cryptography and privacy-preserving smart contracts. In 2016 IEEE symposium on security and privacy (SP), 839-858. IEEE.

Le, T. V., & Hsu, C. L. (2021, April). A Systematic Literature Review of Blockchain Technology: Security Properties, Applications and Challenges. *Journal of Internet Technology*.

Lysons, K., & Farrington, B. (2006). *Purchasing and supply chain management*. Pearson Education.

McKenzie, S. (2004). *Social Sustainability: Towards Some Definitions*. Hawke Research Institute.

Meehan, J., & Bryde, D. (2011). Sustainable procurement practice. *Business Strategy and the Environment*, *20*(2), 94–106. doi:10.1002/bse.678

Mengelkamp, E., Notheisen, B., Beer, C., Dauer, D., & Weinhardt, C. (2018). A blockchain-based smart grid: Towards sustainable local energy markets. *Computer Science -. Research for Development*, *33*(1–2), 207–214.

Millington, A. (2008). *Responsible Supply Chain Management - The Oxford Handbook of Corporate Social Responsibility*. Oxford University Press.

Mollah, M. B., Zhao, J., Niyato, D., Lam, K. Y., Zhang, X., Ghias, A. M., Koh, L. H., & Yang, L. (2020). Blockchain for future smart grid: A comprehensive survey. *IEEE Internet of Things Journal, 8*(1), 18–43. doi:10.1109/JIOT.2020.2993601

Natoli, C., & Gramoli, V. (2017, June). The balance attack or why forkable blockchains are ill-suited for consortium. In *2017 47th Annual IEEE/IFIP International Conference on Dependable Systems and Networks (DSN)*, (pp. 579-590). IEEE. 10.1109/DSN.2017.44

Nicoletti, B. (2017). Agile Procurement. Volume I: Adding Value with Lean Processes. Springer International Publishing.

Nicoletti, B. (2018). *Procurement Finance*. Springer International Publishing. doi:10.1007/978-3-030-02140-5

Nicoletti, B., & Appolloni, A. (2020). Big Data Analytics in Supply Chain Management: Theory and Applications. In *Big Data Analytics in Supply Chain Management: Theory and Applications*. CRC Press.

Niskala, M., Pajunen, T., & Tarna-Mani, K. (2015). *Yritysvastuu: Raportointi- ja laskentaperiaatteet*. ST-Akatemia Oy.

Olivares-Rojas, J. C., Reyes-Archundia, E., Gutiérrez-Gnecchi, J. A., Molina-Moreno, I., Cerda-Jacobo, J., & Méndez-Patiño, A. (2021). *A transactive energy model for smart metering systems using blockchain*. CSEE Journal of Power and Energy Systems.

Piatek, K., Firlit, A., Chmielowiec, K., Dutka, M., Barczentewicz, S., & Hanzelka, Z. (2021). Optimal selection of metering points for power quality measurements in distribution system. *Energies, 14*(4), 1202. doi:10.3390/en14041202

Probst, L., Frideres, L., Cambier, B., & Martinez-Diaz, C. (2016). Blockchain Applications and Services, Directorate-General for Internal Market, Industry, Entrepreneurship and SMEs. European Union.

Saberi, S., Kouhizadeh, M., Sarkis, J., & Shen, L. (2019). Blockchain technology and its relationships to sustainable supply chain management. *International Journal of Production Research, 57*(7), 2117–2135. doi:10.1080/00207543.2018.1533261

Saraj, S., & Khalaf, C. (2021). Blockchain Applications in the Energy Industry. In *Regulatory Aspects of Artificial Intelligence on Blockchain*. IGI Global.

Sivianes, M., & Bordons, C. (2021, October). Application of Blockchain to Peer-to-Peer Energy Trading in Microgrids. In *International Congress on Blockchain and Applications*, (pp. 138-148). Springer.

Tian, F. (2016, June). An agri-food supply chain traceability system for China based on RFID & blockchain technology. In *2016 13th international conference on service systems and service management* (ICSSSM), (pp. 1-6). IEEE.

Treiblmaier, H. (2018). The impact of the blockchain on the supply chain: A theory-based research framework and a call for action. *Supply Chain Management, 23*(6), 545–559. doi:10.1108/SCM-01-2018-0029

Vacca, A., Di Sorbo, A., Visaggio, C. A., & Canfora, G. (2020). A systematic literature review of blockchain and smart contract development: Techniques, tools, and open challenges. *Journal of Systems and Software*, 110891.

Vukolić, M. (2015, October). The quest for scalable blockchain fabric: Proof-of-work vs. BFT replication. In *International workshop on open problems in network security*, (pp. 112-125). Springer.

Wang, Y., Singgih, M., Wang, J., & Rit, M. (2019). Making sense of blockchain technology: How will it transform supply chains? *International Journal of Production Economics, 211*, 221–236. doi:10.1016/j.ijpe.2019.02.002

Weber, I., Gramoli, V., Staples, M., & Ponomarev, A. (2017). On Availability for Blockchain-Based Systems. *SRDS'17: IEEE International Symposium on Reliable Distributed Systems*.

Yan, L., Angang, Z., Huaiying, S., Lingda, K., Guang, S., & Shuming, S. (2021, July). Blockchain-Based Reliable Collection Mechanism for Smart Meter Quality Data. In *International Conference on Artificial Intelligence and Security*, (pp. 476-487). Springer. 10.1007/978-3-030-78612-0_38

Yukins, C. R. (2006). A Case Study in Comparative Procurement Law: Assessing UNCITRAL's Lessons for US Procurement. *Public Contract Law Journal*, 457-484.

Zink, K. (2008). *Corporate Sustainability as a Challenge for Comprehensive Management*. Physica-Verlag. doi:10.1007/978-3-7908-2046-1

ADDITIONAL READING

Appolloni, A., & Cheng, W. (2021). *Sustainable Procurement: knowledge and practice towards sustainable development*. Giappichelli.

De Giovanni, P. (2020). Blockchain and smart contracts in supply chain management: A game theoretic model. *International Journal of Production Economics, 228*, 107855. doi:10.1016/j.ijpe.2020.107855

Nicoletti, B. (2020). *Procurement 4.0 and the Fourth Industrial Revolution.* Springer International Publishing. doi:10.1007/978-3-030-35979-9

KEY TERMS AND DEFINITIONS

Blockchain: A ledger filled with a time-stamped series of immutable data records managed by a cluster of servers not normally owned by any single entity. Each of these blocks of data is secured and bound to each other using cryptography. The primary distinction between the public and private blockchains is that private blockchains control who can participate in the network, execute the consensus protocol that decides the mining rights and rewards, and maintain the shared ledger.

Energy Grid: An interconnected network for delivering electricity from producers to consumers.

IoT (Internet of Things): Group of infrastructures interconnecting objects and allowing their management, data mining, and access to their generated data.

Prosumer: A consumer who is also a producer of the service or good.

Smart Contract: It is a self-executing contract with the terms of the agreement between buyer and vendor being directly coded into a program. The code controls the execution, and transactions are trackable and irreversible.

Smart Meter: An electronic device that records electricity consumption and communicates information to the electricity vendor for monitoring and billing.

Stakeholder Management: The process of maintaining good relationships with the people who have most impact on the specific work.

Sustainable Procurement: The act of adopting social, economic, and environmental factors alongside the typical price and quality considerations into the organization handling of procurement processes and procedures.

Transparency: Anyone authorized can join the network and, as a result, view all information on that network.

Triple Bottom Lines (TBL): The management framework of three parts: social, environmental, and financial. Some organizations have adopted the TBL framework to evaluate their performance in a broader perspective to create a more excellent value.

Chapter 10
Trends in Blockchain Technologies:
A Bibliometric Analysis

Mariacarmela Passarelli
Università della Calabria, Italy

Alfio Cariola
Università della Calabria, Italy

Giuseppe Bongiorno
Università della Calabria, Italy

ABSTRACT

The aim of this work is to investigate emerging research trends and propose an evidence-based roadmap for encouraging further research into the management of blockchain technology. A bibliometric analysis is proposed, with a focus on intellectual property (IP) issues, in the field of blockchain technology. Then, the study highlights the main benefits that blockchain provides as well as the main difficulties, barriers, and challenges that emerge from the literature. The present study provides a reference for scientific communities to understand the current state of blockchain technology, thereby contributing to future research in the area. Moreover, it offers industrial implications and recommendations for entrepreneurs, managers, and practitioners.

DOI: 10.4018/978-1-7998-8014-1.ch010

INTRODUCTION

In the past few years, blockchain technology has been receiving considerable attention from academics, industry practitioners, and governments. Blockchain technology, particularly the digital payment system Bitcoin, first attracted the public's attention in 2008. It started to be applied in different fields and to stimulate digital innovation. The main advantage of blockchain technology is its ability to verify a multitude of attributes simultaneously (e.g., identity, author/creatorship, property, time, or order). It allows the distribution of correct information across networks by preventing its manipulation. Information can be kept safe and untouched by unauthorised third parties; this is particularly relevant in company and industrial contexts.

Several scholars have conducted reviews on scientific research into blockchain technology (Yu & Pan, 2021), but few are focused on the patent production and on the main possible future trends. Thus, the present study uses bibliometric analysis in order to investigate emerging research trends of intellectual property activity on blockchain. The study is organised as follows. The first section focuses on the literature related to blockchain technology. This is followed by a bibliometric analysis section on the main scientific studies that focus on intellectual property (IP) issues, in the field of blockchain technology. Then, the study highlights the main benefits that blockchain provides as well as the main difficulties, barriers, and challenges that emerge from the literature review of each cluster. Implications, recommendations and further research are reported in the final section.

LITERATURE BACKGROUND

Both academics and industry practitioners have paid attention to the wide range of blockchain applications, but the development of the associated technology has not been thoroughly studied. Some reviews have examined the specific role of blockchain in different sectors: the Internet of Things (IoT; Conoscenti et al., 2016, Christidis & Devetsikiotis, 2016); big data (Karafiloski and Mishev, 2017a); security (Khan & Salah, 2017; Li et al., 2017; Meng et al., 2018); service systems (Seebacher et al., 2017); and peer-to-peer (P2P) platforms (Hawlitschek et al., 2018). Other studies (Bonneau et al., 2015; Tsukerman, 2015; Mukhopadhyay et al., 2016; Khalilov & Levi, 2018; Conti et al., 2018) were focused on privacy. Yli-Huumo et al. (2016) analysed 41 blockchain papers on technology and concluded that there were at that point no reasonable solutions to challenges such as latency and hard forks. Hölbl et al. (2018) examined 33 studies in health care and stated that current research on blockchain applications in the field was still at the framework design stage. Firdaus et al. (2019) carried out a statistical analysis of 1,119 papers and found that the United

States, China, and Germany were the countries with the most published papers on blockchain technologies and that the IoT and medical care were the most popular areas for researchers. Dabbagh, Sookhak, and Safa's (2019) review several papers revealing that computers, engineering, economics, and telecommunications were the main blockchain research areas. Casino et al. (2019) undertook a structured, systematic review and thematic content analysis of the literature and presented a comprehensive classification of blockchain-enabled applications across diverse sectors such as supply chains, business, healthcare, IoT, privacy, and data management. Meanwhile, Hu and Pan (2021) identified the paths of blockchain technology through the examination of relevant patents. However, these have been under-researched. A large amount of investment is flowing into the blockchain space to support inventions and new blockchain's applications in precision medicine, financial transactions, energy waste reduction, digital rights management, and so on. Companies have an interest in staking a claim to their inventions by filing patent applications. This area could become a "land grab" for intellectual property in the next future. Thus, the present study attempts to understand which a*re the main trends in blockchain literature that concentrates on patent activities? Which are the main practices in the field? Which are the main benefits and the future possible challenges?* Through an analysis of 286 papers, it is possible to get an overall picture of the development of blockchain from a technological perspective. Then, a focus on the specific management field is proposed, by selecting 57 papers. The present study provides a reference for scientific communities to understand the current state of blockchain technology, thereby contributing to future research in the area.

PATENT ACTIVITY ON BLOCKCHAIN TECHNOLOGY: A BIBLIOMETRIC ANALYSIS

Several scholars in the field of management (Akbari et al., 2020; Gaviria-Marin et al., 2019; McMillan, 2008; Skute et al., 2019); entrepreneurship (Albort-Morant & Ribeiro-Soriano, 2016; Ferreira, 2018; Gartner et al., 2006; Lampe et al., 2019; Verma & Gustafsson, 2020); social sciences (Ho, 2014); and medical sciences (Cheng & Zhang, 2013) have recognised the importance of bibliometric analysis. This is a tool that complements systematic literature reviews. It supports systematic analysis through objective techniques and allows us to identify influential authors and reveal their interrelationships (Ferreira, 2018). This approach is based on the statistical analysis of scientific documents and relative citations. This can be used to identify the degree of expansion in specific research fields.

Two different methods of citation analysis are used to identify publications in particular areas. The first method is bibliographic coupling analysis, which is used when two documents refer to a third common document in their bibliographic graphs, indicating the probability that these documents are linked through the topic(s) being discussed. The "coupling strength" of two given documents is determined by the number of citations they share with other documents (Ferreira, 2018; Kessler, 1963; Martyn, 1964). The second method is co-citation analysis, which is employed when two documents are cited independently in one or more documents (Small, 1973). In a database where links are restricted, bibliographic coupling analysis clusters the latest documents and only a limited number of very old papers, while co-citation analysis clusters the oldest documents and not newer documents that have yet to be cited. The present study employs coupling analysis.

Data Collection

In this section, the authors present a literature review of papers that examine intellectual property (IP) issues in the field of blockchain technology. An ad hoc protocol was developed to perform bibliometric analysis (Ferriera, 2018). The selection of the relevant articles involved three stages. First, a specific type of query was chosen. The search strategy was based on a structured query and implemented using an extensive citation database. Second, the Elsevier Scopus database was chosen because: (a) it is one of the largest citation databases in the world; (b) it has indexed around 70 million documents (the greatest number of any database) from 1788; and (c) it covers subject areas ranging from biological sciences to management and social sciences (Cavallone & Palumbo, 2020). Moreover, it includes data on academic publications, including affiliations and citations. Finally, the following query was adapted to the certain attributes of the search engines for each database. It was as follows: (TITLE-ABS-KEY (blockchain* AND patent*) OR TITLE-ABS-KEY (block AND chain* AND patent*) OR TITLE-ABS-KEY (intellectual AND property AND blockchain*) OR TITLE-ABS-KEY (intellectual AND property AND block AND chain*). The search was conducted in May 2021 and returned 286 papers. In the following section, the authors describe the papers in more detail. The first was published in 1961, but most were published in 2016 (Figure 1).

Our bibliometric analysis was based on Ferreira (2018). The authors aimed to identify (a) the main articles relating to blockchain; (b) the most influential players in the sector; (c) the respective networks of authors; and (c) possible future research developments in the field of management.

Figure 1. Documents by year

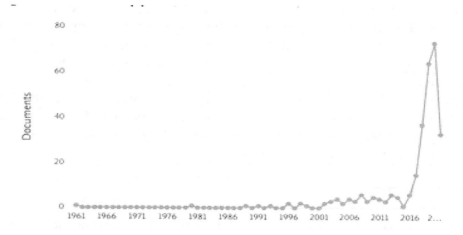

DATA ANALYSIS

The authors used VOSviewer software (www.vosviewer.com) to lead the coupling analysis. VOSviewer allows the construction and visualisation of bibliometric networks, incorporating magazines, researchers based on common citations, bibliographic couplings, and paternity relationships (Van Eck et al., 2010). VOSviewer builds a map based on a three-phase recurrence matrix: (a) a "similarity matrix" applying a mapping method (Waltman et al., 2010) using the strength of the association; (b) a map that reflects the extent of similarity between objects (Van Eck et al., 2010); and (c) translation, rotation, and reflection, to correct the optimisation problem described in the literature (O'Connell et al., 1999).

A bibliographic coupling analysis were performed. Studies show that bibliographic coupling techniques can be used to identify hot research topics and can be an aid to future research directions (Glänzel & Czerwon, 1996). The minimum number of citations of a document was selected as two. Of 286 documents, 119 documents met the threshold. For each of these, the total strength of the bibliographic coupling links with other documents was calculated. The authors omitted the papers that had a total link strength of zero, which then left only 54 items.

Findings

From the coupling analysis, we get **four clusters** (a cluster had to have a minimum number of five citations). The results show that there were four "hot" research topics

(Glänzel & Czerwon, 1996). Figure 2 provides a detailed description of research trends.

Figure 2. Main trends

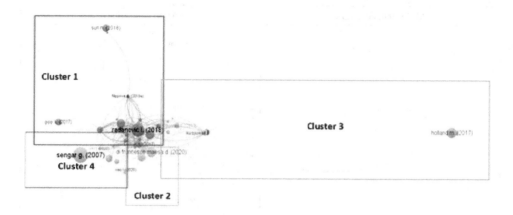

Table 1 provides a summary of the main references related to each cluster.

The clusters that came out from the coupling analysis are described below. In the discussion of each cluster we propose also the highlight of some practices, the related benefits and the possible challenges.

Cluster 1: Technological and Social Sustainability Applications (Red)

The first cluster shows the adaptability of blockchain technology to various aspects of social and working life. **Possible practices** of blockchain applications can be of great interest to social economy enterprises, including the followings:

- **Practice in Energy.** Due to the sustainability trends in recent years, the management of the energy sector has become essential in every part of the world. The application of blockchain technology can make energy supply systems decentralized, simplifying transactions at all levels and straight connecting energy producers, suppliers and distribution systems to consumers. It mainly can concentrate on building platforms for energy exchange and creating distributed energy systems. Through blockchain and smart contracts, energy networks can also be effectively controlled by monitoring consumption, both on bills and through electric vehicle recharges (Filippova et al. 2019; Brilliantova & Thurner, 2019).

Table 1. References by cluster

Main fields/clusters	Main references
Technological and social applications of blockchain	• Radanović, I. & Likić, R. (2018) • Drobyazko, S., Makedon, V., Zhuravlov, D., Buglak, Y., & Stetsenko, V. (2019) • Zeilinger, M. (2018) • Sun, H., Wang, X., & Wang, X. (2018) • Tsai, W., Feng, L., Zhang, H., You, Y., Wang, L., & Zhong, Y. (2017) • Truong, N. B., Um, T., Zhou, B., & Lee, G. M. (2018) • Ito K., O'Dair, M. (2019) • Li, P., Xu, H., Ma, T., & Mu, Y. (2018) • Steinwandter, V. & Herwig, C. (2019) • Filippova E. (2019) • Feng, L., Zhang, H., Tsai, W.T., et al. (2019 • Low, K. & Mik, E. (2020) • Filippova E., Scharl A., & Filippov P. (2019) • O'Leary, K., O'Reilly, P., Feller, J., Gleasure, R., Li, S., & Cristoforo, J. (2017) • O'Dwyer, R. (2020) • Alkhudary, R., Brusset, X., & Fenies, P. (2020) • Yang, Y. J. & Hwang, J. C. (2020) • Alkhudary, R., Brusset, X., & Fenies, P. (2020) • Dong, X. (2018) • Coeckelbergh, M., DuPont, Q., & Reijers, W. (2018)
Market applications and strategic adoption of blockchain	• Maesa, D. D. F. & Mori, P. (2020) • Yang, F., Zhou, W., Wu, Q., Long, R., Xiong, N. N., & Zhou, M. (2019) • Rahmanzadeh, S., Pishvaee, M. S., & Rasouli, M. R. (2020) • Gipp, B., Breitinger, C., Meuschke, N., & Beel, J. (2017) • Wang, J., Wang, S., Guo, J., Du, Y., Cheng, S., & Li, X. (2019) • Huang, Y., Bian, R., Li, J., Zhao, L., & Shi, P. (2019) • Dos Santos, R. B., Torrisi, N. M., Yamada, E. R. K., & Pantoni, R. P. (2019) • Yang, F. et al. (2019) • Alnafrah, I., Bogdanova, E., & Maximova, T. (2019) • Somin, S., Altshuler, Y., Gordon, G., & Shmueli, E. (2020) • Bai, Y. et al. (2018) • Schönhals, A., Hepp, T., & Gipp, B. (2018) • Daim, T., Lai, K. K., Yalcin, H., Alsoubie, F., & Kumar, V. (2020) • Yang J. (2018) • Holland, M., Nigischer, C., & Stjepandic, J. (2017)
Blockchain's management and new emerging business model	• Holland, M., Stjepandić, J., & Nigischer, C. (2018) • Kurpjuweit, S., Schmidt, C. G., Klöckner, M., & Wagner, S. M. (2021) • Papakostas, N., Newell, A., & Hargaden, V. (2019) • Engelmann, F., Holland, M., Nigischer, C., & Stjepandić, J. (2018) • Duy, P. T., Hien, D. T. T., Hien, D. H., & Pham, V. H. (2018) • Klöckner, M., Kurpjuweit, S., Velu, C., & Wagner, S. M. (2020) • Modic, D., Hafner, A., Damij, N., & Cehovin Zajc, L. (2019) • Clarke, N. S., Jürgens, B., & Herrero-Solana, V. (2020) • Lin, J., Long, W., Zhang, A., & Chai, Y. (2019)
Blockchain security and traceability	• Sengar, G., Mukhopadhyay, D., & Chowdhury, D. R. (2007) • Bhuiyan, M. Z. A., Zaman, A., Wang, T., Wang, G., Tao, H., & Hassan, M. M. (2018) • McLoone, M. & McCanny, J. V. (2003) • Jing, N., Liu, Q., & Sugumaran, V. (2021) • Rathor, M. & Sengupta, A. (2020) • Xiao, L., Huang, W., Xie, Y., Xiao, W., & Li, K. (2020b) • Chi, J., Lee, J., Kim, N., Choi, J., & Park, S. (2020) • Bhat, M. & Vijayal, S. (2017) • Grieco, G., Song, W., Cygan, A., Feist, J., & Groce, A. (2020)

Source: (authors' elaboration)

- **Practice in Health.** There are several problems related to healthcare such as the lack of proper management of personal health information of individual patients, as well as the real control of data access, origin and integrity. All this can be bypassed with the application of blockchain technology, in order to make digital medical records secure and immutable. Referring to the pharmaceutical industry and to the quality of medicines, through blockchain, it could be possible, to eliminate counterfeit medicines while protecting public health. (Radanovic & Likić, 2018; Steinwandter & Herwig, 2019; Bhuiyan et al., 2018).

- **Practices for sustainability.** The world's resources are in a state of scarcity and, with reference to the 17 sustainable development goals, there is a need for a sustainable and smart platform to manage these resources as smart as possible. In this context, blockchain can be applied to water quality monitoring and especially stormwater management. (Thejaswini & Ranjitha, 2021; Willrich et al., 2019; Alcarria et al., 2018). For example, possible applications on garbage can be implemented. In fact, by leveraging the features of blockchain technology, the life cycle of garbage can be monitored efficiently. The transparency of recycling systems and all the garbage can be tracked with reference to different characteristics (disposable, recyclable, special, chemical and others) (França et al., 2020; Gupta & Bedi, 2018).

- **Practices in Art.** Normally, artists and rights holders cannot have access to detailed information about the life of their work and therefore do not know where and how their work is being used. (Zeilinger, 2018; O'Dwyer, 2020). Blockchain can help them to track their works. Moreover, visibility of digital art and its ownership can be achieved using blockchain technology as part of a broader solution for the identification, attribution, and also payment for digital work (McConaghy et al., 2017).

- **Practices in Education.** Through this application, it is possible to upload information about pupils' academic results, manage certifications or upload all academic credentials. This creates a collaborative and secure environment where teachers, administrators, and students can safely perform their duties and know that no information will be lost (Sun, Wang & Wang, 2018; Chen et al., 2018)

- **Practice in tracing donations and fundraising.** Through this application, donors are the opportunity to follow the flow and destination of money donated to NGOs. NGOs on the other hand could report in detail on each expenditure stream, ensuring that money invested is actually used for its intended purpose

Some examples of technological and social sustainability applications have shown in BOX 1.

Table 2. Pills of case studies

uPort is an emerging open-source identity management system providing sovereign identity to users, organisations, and other entities. (Lundkvist et al., 2017).
TUDocChain. It is a platform that authorize the academic certificates on public ledger in a reliable and sustainable format. It is a practical solution for issuing, validating and sharing of certificate. (Budhiraja & Rani, 2020).

The applications highlighted in Cluster 1 can also offer some possible **benefits**. Specifically:

- **Secure telemedicine and e-care systems**. A huge number of social economy organisations are involved in health care and social assistance located in proximity to the people needing them, including in decentralised areas where this application could have a considerable impact on people's quality of life.
- The opportunity to **assimilate digital art into the high-end commercial art market.**
- **The security of skill certification** through the applications of blockchain to education with the qualifications and diplomas in digital format.
- **Improvement in waste sector** will enable reliable, transparent and secure recording of all waste movements, thus enabling waste to be traced from source to treatment and disposal (Laouar, Hamad & Eom, 2019).

Different **challenges** come out from the analysis of the literature belonging to cluster 1.

- The application of blockchain in **humanitarian programs** presents a lot of barriers; however, one possible challenge could be for example, the incorporation of blockchain into digital food voucher programs for refugees. Rather than providing physical vouchers to purchase food items with blockchain, technology allows refugees to scan their iris into machines, placed at designated grocery stores, digitally deducting their voucher balance when they make purchases.
- Blockchain application can be applied at private and public level. However, up now, only 25 governments around the world are actively running blockchain

pilot projects. Thus, another challenge could be **to achieve public-sector** applications.

Cluster 2: Market Applications and Strategic Adoptions of Blockchain (Yellow)

Internet allows now marketers to penetrate deeper into their existing markets, to create new online marketplaces and to generate new demand. This dynamic market engagement uses new technologies to target consumers more effectively and to manage payments. **Several practices** related to Market applications and strategic adoptions can be identified. Specifically:

- **Practices in Finance.** The financial sector is perhaps one of the most suited to blockchain technology (Bitcoin, a cryptocurrency created in 2008, has a blockchain system). There are also other applications *(,)* such recording and validating the ownership of digital currency or to execute, validate and record payments made with digital currency, but also with reference to credit securities, derivatives and other financial instruments, credit registers, transactions for the payment of traditional goods and others. Some of these are already a reality, while others are technologically feasible, but encounter legislative and bureaucratic problems (Coeckelbergh, DuPont & Reijers 2018; Yang et al., 2019; Varma, 2019).
- **Practices in Voting.** Another important application regards voting mechanism, used both for the election of presidents and heads of state and for smaller ones, or in the private sphere. With a voting process based on a blockchain network, the preferences are directly executed, and it provides the impossibility of manipulation of the results. It is possible to think about a paradigm shift from traditional voting methods (centralized) to electronic ones (decentralized) based on trust, transparency and confidentiality with the security of breaking down the possible tampering (Maesa & Mori, 2020; Taş & Tanrıöver, 2020).
- **Practices in Insurance.** The traditional insurance marketplace requires several manual transactions involving multiple parties from policy submission to customer purchase. In addition, it might provide the presence of intermediaries that can lengthen the time and increase administration costs. (Duy, et al., 2018; Brophy, 2019).
- **Practices in Food chain.** The food sector involves various subjects (farmers, processors, traders, wholesalers, retailers, restaurants and consumers) that require certain quality standards also in compliance with the regulations. By taking advantage of the features of the blockchain, it is possible to manage

the agri-food supply chain in an innovative way, by uploading information for each entity that enters the field in the supply chain in order to establish provenance, sustainability and other attributes of the product (Dos Santos et al., 2019; Antonucci et al., 2019).

- **Practices in Marketing applications**. Given the characteristics of transparency and trust of the blockchain, different practical marketing implication are emerging. In fact, customers and components of the supply chains can control the goods contained, which for the adopting company can turn into an image improvement that has implications in customer loyalty but also in the general reputation of the company. (Maesa & Mori, 2020; Ertemel, 2018).

Some examples related to Market applications and strategic adoptions are listed in **BOX 2.**

Table 3. Pills of case studies

• **Wave** is a decentralized blockchain hybrid crypto asset exchange platform. It ia a Blockchain revolution in Trade Finance.
• **E-voting** is an application used as a smart contract for the Ethereum blockchain network (Yavuz et al., 2018).
• **NYIAX** (New York Interactive Advertising Exchange) demonstrates the role of blockchain technology to promote a transparent marketplace where a matching engine ensures a fair exchange of future premium advertising inventory as guaranteed contracts (Epstein, 2017).
• **Keybase.io** is a blockchain platform which has been developed to check the integrity of social media users' signature chains and to identify malicious rollbacks (Keybase.io., 2019).

The practices analysed in cluster 2 can offer some possible benefits:

- Blockchain technology fosters **disintermediation aids** in combatting click fraud, reinforces trust and transparency, enables enhanced privacy protection, empowers security, and enables creative loyalty programs.
- Blockchain technology makes consultation of members and **voting more secure and traceable,** facilitating participation even where members are spread out geographically or too numerous to hold traditional general meetings.
- In insurance processes, it becomes **easier to detect fraud**, given the records within the archive, and there is also a strong level of privacy since sensitive data are only accessible with authorization. From the reduction in overhead

costs, insurance companies could offer services and policies at **lower prices** than before.

Possible **challenges** in the field of marketing and strategies can be identified, in particular,

- **The use of blockchain can encourage the exploitation strategies** related to patents, copyrights, trademarks, industrial design, trade dress, handcrafted works, trade secrets, and plant variety rights.
- **The use of blockchain can reduce the number of necessary intermediaries** across the financial services' core functions.

Cluster 3: Blockchain's Management and New Emerging Business Models (Green)

The third cluster examines the blockchain management and business model. In these perspectives, the literature analysed in cluster 3 highlights some interesting practices.

- **Practices in Supply chain.** In the new era, conventional supply chains are replaced by value-added networks (Holland et al., 2018). The product and shipment can be collected through various technologies (sensors, tags and others) and validated before becoming a permanent record on the blockchain network (Casado-Vara et al. 2018). Thus, new supply chain models can emerge, by improving the economic performance of supply chains, in terms of efficiency, flexibility and responsiveness (Alkhudary, Brusset & Fenies, 2020; Rahmanzadeh, Pishvaee & Rasouli, 2020; Kurpjuweit et al., 2021).
- **Practices for Business Processes.** Emerging blockchain technology has the potential to radically change the environment in which inter-organizational processes are able to operate. Blockchain offers a new way to implement processes in a trustworthy manner even in a network without any mutual trust between nodes. Specialized algorithms lead to consensus among the nodes and market mechanisms that motivate the nodes to progress the network.

Some examples related to **Blockchain's management and new business model** are listed in **BOX 3**

Table 4. Pills of case studies

• **IBM and Maersk Line** are establishing a joint venture to bring to market a blockchain trade platform. The platform's aim is to provide the users and actors involved in global shipping transactions with a secure, real-time exchange of supply-chain data and paperwork.
• Individuals wanting to buy or sell real estate in Sweden can use a blockchain technology pilot project powered by **ChromaWay.**
• **Everest,** is a firm that uses a private and permissioned Ethereum-based protocol, provides a decentralized distributed ledger technology that incorporates a payment solution, a multicurrency wallet, and a biometric identity system, to facilitate microfinance transactions, land claims, and medical records to customer segments in developing countries (Everest group, 2016).
• **Centbee**, in South Africa, enables the users of its mobile app to send bitcoin to users' contact lists. The users can move money simply and cheaply across borders to support family and friends without incurring exorbitant currency exchange fees.

Different benefits emerge from the analysis of the main papers belonging to cluster 4:

- Blockchain can **facilitate local manufacturing** and can lay the groundwork for new business models, such as secure design marketplaces and shared factories. Companies could also enhance their value proposition by offering additional services.
- **The application of blockchain to the automation** of business processes helps the reduction of costs and time. (Alkhudary, Brusset & Fenies, 2020; Rahmanzadeh, Pishvaee & Rasouli, 2020). Moreover, the ability of blockchain to connect to existing ERP systems, has the potential to make processes in a company more efficient and transparent (Tönnissen & Teuteberg, 2018).

For the next future, two main *challenges* could be proposed:

- The **interaction of Blockchain** with other enabling technologies across different industries (Lin et al., 2019);
- The use of blockchain technology **for managing** new models based on co-developing processes, in order to transform the way innovative firms create, deliver, and capture value (Passarelli et al., 2020; Holland et al., 2018Klöckner et al., 2020).

Cluster 4: Blockchain Security and Traceability (Blue)

Figure 2 highlights the closed relation of cluster 4 with cluster 1 and cluster 2. This is because, the use of Blockchain to improve **security and traceability** is common to various industries and public practices. Which are the main field where of security and traceability are crucial and which are the main implemented practices?

- **Practice in Anti-theft.** High-value hardware devices are often victims of theft and fraudulent exchanging. Thus, for each part of a devise, a unique ID can be managed by Blockchain. In the assembling line, each worker can verify and update the status of the component or device promptly with their private key. In this way, businesses can tightly control their components with detailed levels to individual items through information systems (Chi et al., 2020; Xiao et al., 2020).
- **Practice in Warranty service.** By having Blockchain traceability, warranty service operators can access to Blockchain system and track back the history of producing, using, and repairing of an item needed to warranty. These data are truthful and cannot be faked.
- **Practice in Empowering Digital Marketing Security**. The power of blockchain security is based on its distributed and decentralized storage of data (Yanik and Kiliç, 2018). Besides, the usage of several security mechanisms, such as asymmetric encryption, digital signatures and access control can secure the appropriate storage, transmission, and retrieval of large amounts of consumer information (Zhang, Xue & Liu, 2019; Mohanta, 2020; Scholl, Pomeshchikov & Rodríguez Bolívar, 2020).
- **Practices in manufacturing:** Through this feature it is possible to have information on products such as components, locations, conformity and originality, throughout all stages of production and distribution. (Schönhals, Hepp & Gipp, 2018; Bhuiyan et al., 2018; Xiao et al., 2020; Xu et al. 2019).

Some examples related to Blockchain security and traceability are listed in **BOX 4**

Table 5. Pills of case studies

• **AgriBlockIoT** is a fully decentralized, blockchain-based traceability solution for Agri-Food supply chain management, able to seamless integrate IoT devices producing and consuming digital data along the chain. (Caro et al. 2020)
• **Gilgamesh** is a knowledge-sharing social platform powered by blockchain technology. Using the Gilgamesh platform, users can gain and transfer knowledge in a protected environment. The network shifts the way readers, critics, and authors communicate and connect with one another.
• **DealBox** is a blockchain business accelerator and crowdfunding platform. It provides a crowdfunding ecosystem with a token (DLBX) that acts as a discounted voucher for exchange on presale tokens of projects launched on the platform. DealBox provides capitalization services, advisory support, marketing and technical executables.
• **SECORA**™ Blockchain in a recycling and warranty & service process for electric vehicles and portable batteries.

Some benefits emerge from the application of blockchain in terms of security and traceability. Specifically:

- With blockchain, an organization can create a **complete decentralized network** where there is no need for a centralized authority, improving the system's transparency.
- Traceability enhances **operational efficiency** by giving the stakeholders a strong tool for tracking and controlling their operations, inventories, and products.
- Shared information across parties in the supply chain would provide **auditors and operators with greater visibility** into all activities along the value chain.
- The supply chain becomes **more transparent** than ever. It enables every party to trace the goods and ensure that it is not being replaced or misused during the supply chain process.

In this cluster, one main challenge can be highlighted. Blockchain is a new and immature technology, even if it can be considered disruptive. However, there are no regulations or laws for the adoption of blockchain technology. Thus, there is a need for serious and clear regulatory approaches by outlining possible development trajectories (Fulmer, 2018).

SOLUTIONS AND RECOMMENDATIONS

The previous sections highlighted the main trends in the applications of blockchain, that arise from the scientific literature. However, to follow these trends and to get positive performance, some fundamental upgrades are required. In particular:

- **The institution of specific laws and regulations,** where regulators must balance the entrepreneurial opportunities of blockchain tech with the imperative to protect human participants.
- **The development of blockchain ethics,** that can consider certain trade-offs, such as efficiency versus security, accountability versus privacy, or permanence versus flexibility.
- **The "cultivation" of future talent for blockchain solutions**. Like it happened for ICT some decades ago, in this new era, there is the need of blockchain technology's experts and talents. Educational programs and also start-ups' competitions could be focused on this new field.

FUTURE RESEARCH DIRECTIONS

Future studies can undertake specific qualitative and quantitative analyses of blockchain technology and applications, with an emphasis on innovation, new ventures, and exploitation strategies. Future researches need to explore and to analyse the barriers to blockchain adoption across different firms' perspectives.

CONCLUSION

The purpose of the present study was to provide a representative picture of blockchain technology and possible growth trajectories using the scientific literature. Four clusters emerged from the bibliometric analysis. The first refers to the adaptability of blockchain technology to various aspects of social and working life. The second cluster refers to the applications and strategic adoptions of blockchain. The third cluster highlights the emerging business model while the fourth focuses on two main blockchain's characteristics: security and traceability. Blockchain applications are possible both in the public and private sectors. To address social impact and governance challenges, innovators must consider potential synergies between blockchain and other emerging technologies (such as artificial intelligence, internet of things, quantum computing, etc). Moreover, there is the need of specific laws and regulations.

REFERENCES

Akbari, M., Khodayari, M., Khaleghi, A., Danesh, M., & Padash, H. (2020). Technological innovation research in the last six decades: A bibliometric analysis. *European Journal of Innovation Management*. Advance online publication. doi:10.1108/EJIM-05-2020-0166

Albort-Morant, G., & Ribeiro-Soriano, D. (2016). A bibliometric analysis of international impact of business incubators. *Journal of Business Research*, 69(5), 1775–1779. doi:10.1016/j.jbusres.2015.10.054

Alcarria, R., Bordel, B., Robles, T., Martín, D., & Manso-Callejo, M. Á. (2018). A blockchain-based authorization system for trustworthy resource monitoring and trading in smart communities. *Sensors (Basel)*, 18(10), 3561. doi:10.339018103561 PMID:30347844

Alkhudary, R., Brusset, X., & Fenies, P. (2020). Blockchain in general management and economics: A systematic literature review. *European Business Review, 32*(4), 765–783. doi:10.1108/EBR-11-2019-0297

Alnafrah, I., Bogdanova, E., & Maximova, T. (2019). Text mining as a facilitating tool for deploying blockchain technology in the intellectual property rights system. *International Journal of Intellectual Property Management, 9*(2), 120–135. doi:10.1504/IJIPM.2019.100207

Antonucci, F., Figorilli, S., Costa, C., Pallottino, F., Raso, L., & Menesatti, P. (2019). A Review on blockchain applications in the agri-food sector. *Journal of the Science of Food and Agriculture, 99*(14), 6129–6138. doi:10.1002/jsfa.9912 PMID:31273793

Bai, Y. (2018). Researchain: Union Blockchain Based Scientific Research Project Management System. *Chinese Automation Congress (CAC)*, 4206-4209. 10.1109/CAC.2018.8623571

Bhat, M., & Vijayal, S. (2017). A Probabilistic Analysis on Crypto-Currencies Based on Blockchain. *International Conference on Next Generation Computing and Information Systems (ICNGCIS)*, 69-74. 10.1109/ICNGCIS.2017.37

Bhuiyan, M. Z. A., Zaman, A., Wang, T., Wang, G., Tao, H., & Hassan, M. M. (2018). Blockchain and big data to transform the healthcare. *Proceedings of the International Conference on Data Processing and Applications*, 62-68. 10.1145/3224207.3224220

Bonneau, J., Miller, A., Clark, J., Narayanan, A., Kroll, J. A., & Felten, E. W. (2015). *Sok: Research perspectives and challenges for bitcoin and cryptocurrencies. In 2015 IEEE symposium on security and privacy*. IEEE. doi:10.1109/SP.2015.14

Brilliantova, V., & Thurner, T. W. (2019). Blockchain and the future of energy. *Technology in Society, 57*, 38–45. doi:10.1016/j.techsoc.2018.11.001

Brophy, R. (2019). Blockchain and insurance: A review for operations and regulation. *Journal of Financial Regulation and Compliance.*

Budhiraja, S., & Rani, R. (2020). TUDoc Chain-Securing Academic Certificate Digitally on Blockchain. Inventive Computation Technologies. ICICIT. *Lecture Notes in Networks and Systems., 98*, 150–160. doi:10.1007/978-3-030-33846-6_17

Caro, M.P., Ali, M.S., Vecchio, M., & Giaffreda, R. (2020). Blockchain-based traceability in agri-food supply chain management: a practical implementation. In *IoT Vertical and Topical Summit on Agriculture-Tuscany (IOT Tuscany)*. IEEE.

Casado-Vara, R., Prieto, J., De la Prieta, F., & Corchado, J. M. (2018). How blockchain improves the supply chain: Case study alimentary supply chain. *Procedia Computer Science, 134,* 393–398. doi:10.1016/j.procs.2018.07.193

Casino, F., Dasaklis, T. K., & Patsakis, C. (2019). A systematic literature review of blockchain-based applications: Current status, classification and open issues. *Telematics and Informatics, 36,* 55–81. doi:10.1016/j.tele.2018.11.006

Cavallone, M., & Palumbo, R. (2020). Debunking the myth of industry 4.0 in health care: Insights from a systematic literature review. *The TQM Journal, 32*(4), 849–868. doi:10.1108/TQM-10-2019-0245

Cesaroni, F., & Baglieri, D. (2012). Technology intelligence: New challenges from patent information. In *Information systems: crossroads for organization, management, accounting and engineering* (pp. 267–274). Physica. doi:10.1007/978-3-7908-2789-7_30

Chang, P. L., Wu, C. C., & Leu, H. J. (2010). Using patent analyses to monitor the technological trends in an emerging field of technology: A case of carbon nanotube field emission display. *Scientometrics, 82*(1), 5–19. doi:10.100711192-009-0033-y

Chen, G., Xu, B., Lu, M., & Chen, N. S. (2018). Exploring blockchain technology and its potential applications for education. *Smart Learning Environments, 5*(1), 1–10. doi:10.118640561-017-0050-x

Chen, M. A., Wu, Q., & Yang, B. (2019). How valuable is FinTech innovation? *Review of Financial Studies, 32*(5), 2062–2106. doi:10.1093/rfs/hhy130

Cheng, T., & Zhang, G. (2013). Worldwide research productivity in the field of rheumatology from 1996 to 2010: A bibliometric analysis. *Rheumatology, 52*(9), 1630–1634. doi:10.1093/rheumatology/ket008 PMID:23502075

Chi, J., Lee, J., Kim, N., Choi, J., & Park, S. (2020). Secure and reliable blockchain-based eBook transaction system for self-published eBook trading. *PLoS One, 15*(2). doi:10.1371/journal.pone.0228418

Chohan U. W. (2017). Blockchain and Securities Exchanges: Australian Case Study. *Available at* SSRN 3085631. doi:10.2139/ssrn.3085631

Christidis, K., & Devetsikiotis, M. (2016). Blockchains and smart contracts for the internet of things. *IEEE Access: Practical Innovations, Open Solutions, 4,* 2292–2303. doi:10.1109/ACCESS.2016.2566339

Clarke, N. S., Jürgens, B., & Herrero-Solana, V. (2020). Blockchain patent landscaping: An expert based methodology and search query. *World Patent Information, 61,* 101964. doi:10.1016/j.wpi.2020.101964

Coeckelbergh, M., DuPont, Q., & Reijers, W. (2018). Towards a Philosophy of Financial Technologies. *Philosophy & Technology, 31*(1), 9–14. doi:10.100713347-017-0261-7

Conoscenti, M., Vetro, A., & De Martin, J. C. (2016). Blockchain for the Internet of Things: A systematic literature review. In *2016 IEEE/ACS 13th International Conference of Computer Systems and Applications (AICCSA)* (pp. 1-6). IEEE. 10.1109/AICCSA.2016.7945805

Conti, M., Kumar, E. S., Lal, C., & Ruj, S. (2018). A survey on security and privacy issues of bitcoin. *IEEE Communications Surveys and Tutorials, 20*(4), 3416–3452. doi:10.1109/COMST.2018.2842460

Dabbagh, M., Sookhak, M., & Safa, N. S. (2019). The evolution of blockchain: A bibliometric study. *IEEE Access: Practical Innovations, Open Solutions, 7,* 19212–19221. doi:10.1109/ACCESS.2019.2895646

Daim, T., Lai, K. K., Yalcin, H., Alsoubie, F., & Kumar, V. (2020). Forecasting technological positioning through technology knowledge redundancy: Patent citation analysis of IoT, cybersecurity, and Blockchain. *Technological Forecasting and Social Change, 161,* 120329. doi:10.1016/j.techfore.2020.120329

Dong, X. (2018). A method of image privacy protection based on blockchain technology. *International Conference on Cloud Computing, Big Data and Blockchain (ICCBB),* 1-4. 10.1109/ICCBB.2018.8756447

Dos Santos, R. B., Torrisi, N. M., Yamada, E. R. K., & Pantoni, R. P. (2019). IGR Token-Raw Material and Ingredient Certification of Recipe Based Foods Using Smart Contracts. *Informatics (MDPI), 6*(1), 11. doi:10.3390/informatics6010011

Drobyazko, S., Makedon, V., Zhuravlov, D., Buglak, Y., & Stetsenko, V. (2019). Ethical, technological and patent aspects of technology blockchain distribution. *Journal of Legal, Ethical and Regulatory Issues, 22,* 1-6. https://www.proquest.com/openview/f0773b7791a9063857d02fe4659a9329/1?pq-origsite=gscholar&cbl=38868

Duan, B., Zhong, Y., & Liu, D. (2017). Education application of blockchain technology: Learning outcome and meta-diploma. In *2017 IEEE 23rd International Conference on Parallel and Distributed Systems (ICPADS)* (pp. 814-817). IEEE.10.1109/ICPADS.2017.00114

Duy, P. T., Hien, D. T. T., Hien, D. H., & Pham, V. H. (2018). A survey on opportunities and challenges of Blockchain technology adoption for revolutionary innovation. *Proceedings of the Ninth International Symposium on Information and Communication Technology*, 200-207. 10.1145/3287921.3287978

Economist, T. (2015). The promise of the blockchain: the trust machine. *The Economist, 31*, 27. https://www.economist.com/leaders/2015/10/31/the-trust-machine.

Engelmann, F., Holland, M., Nigischer, C., & Stjepandić, J. (2018). Intellectual property protection and licensing of 3d print with blockchain technology. *Transdisciplinary Engineering Methods for Social Innovation of Industry, 4*, 103–112. doi:10.3233/978-1-61499-898-3-103

Enk, A. J. (1967). *U.S. Patent No. 3,340,636*. Washington, DC: U.S. Patent and Trademark Office.

Epstein, J. (2017). *Blockchain and the CMO*. Whitepaper. Available online at: https://s3.us-east-2.amazonaws.com/brightline-website/downloads/reports/Brightline_Epstein_Blockchain-and-the-CMO_Blockchain-Research-Institute.pdf?utm_source=resource-page&utm_medium=skip-link

Ertemel, A. V. (2018). Implications of blockchain technology on marketing. *Journal of International Trade, Logistics and Law, 4*(2), 35-44.

Everest Group. (2016). *Smart contracts on a distributed ledger – life in the smart lane*. Available at: www2.everestgrp.com/Files/previews/Smart%20Contracts%20on%20Distributed%20Ledger%20-%20Life%20in%20the%20Smart%20Lane.pdf

Eyassu, S. E. (2019). Overview of blockchain legislation and adoption: Status and challenges. *Issues in Information Systems*, 20(1).

Feng, L., Zhang, H., Tsai, W. T., & Sun, S. (2019). System architecture for high-performance permissioned blockchains. *Frontiers of Computer Science, 13*(6), 1151–1165. doi:10.100711704-018-6345-4

Ferreira, F. A. (2018). Mapping the field of arts-based management: Bibliographic coupling and co-citation analyses. *Journal of Business Research, 85*, 348–357. doi:10.1016/j.jbusres.2017.03.026

Ferreira, J. J., Fernandes, C. I., & Kraus, S. (2019). Entrepreneurship research: Mapping intellectual structures and research trends. *Review of Managerial Science, 13*(1), 181–205. doi:10.100711846-017-0242-3

Filippova, E. (2019). *Empirical Evidence and Economic Implications of Blockchain as a General Purpose Technology. In IEEE Technology & Engineering Management Conference.* TEMSCON. doi:10.1109/TEMSCON.2019.8813748

Filippova, E., Scharl, A., & Filippov, P. (2019). Blockchain: An Empirical Investigation of Its Scope for Improvement. In J. Joshi, S. Nepal, Q. Zhang, & L. J. Zhang (Eds.), Lecture Notes in Computer Science: Vol. 11521. *Blockchain – ICBC 2019. ICBC 2019.* Springer. doi:10.1007/978-3-030-23404-1_1

Firdaus, A., Ab Razak, M. F., Feizollah, A., Hashem, I. A. T., Hazim, M., & Anuar, N. B. (2019). The rise of "blockchain": Bibliometric analysis of blockchain study. *Scientometrics, 120*(3), 1289–1331. doi:10.100711192-019-03170-4

Fisch, C. (2019). Initial coin offerings (ICOs) to finance new ventures. *Journal of Business Venturing, 34*(1), 1–22. doi:10.1016/j.jbusvent.2018.09.007

França, A. S. L., Neto, J. A., Gonçalves, R. F., & Almeida, C. M. V. B. (2020). Proposing the use of blockchain to improve the solid waste management in small municipalities. *Journal of Cleaner Production, 244,* 118529. doi:10.1016/j.jclepro.2019.118529Fulmer, N. (2018). Exploring the legal issues of blockchain applications. *Akron Law Review, 52,* 161.

Gartner, W. B., Davidsson, P., & Zahra, S. A. (2006). Are you talking to me? The nature of community in entrepreneurship scholarship. *Entrepreneurship Theory and Practice, 30*(3), 321–331. doi:10.1111/j.1540-6520.2006.00123.x

Gaviria-Marin, M., Merigó, J. M., & Baier-Fuentes, H. (2019). Knowledge management: A global examination based on bibliometric analysis. *Technological Forecasting and Social Change, 140,* 194–220. doi:10.1016/j.techfore.2018.07.006

Gilgamesh Platform. (n.d.). static.gilgameshplatform.com/pdf/whitepaper.pdf

Gipp, Breitinger, Meuschke, & Beel. (2017). CryptSubmit: Introducing Securely Timestamped Manuscript Submission and Peer Review Feedback Using the Blockchain. *ACM/IEEE Joint Conference on Digital Libraries (JCDL),* 1-4. 10.1109/JCDL.2017.7991588

Glänzel, W., & Czerwon, H. J. (1996). A new methodological approach to bibliographic coupling and its application to the national, regional and institutional level. *Scientometrics, 37*(2), 195–221. doi:10.1007/BF02093621

Grieco, G., Song, W., Cygan, A., Feist, J., & Groce, A. (2020). Echidna: effective, usable, and fast fuzzing for smart contracts. *Proceedings of the 29th ACM SIGSOFT International Symposium on Software Testing and Analysis*, 557-560. 10.1145/3395363.3404366

Guo, J., Li, C., Zhang, G., Sun, Y., & Bie, R. (2019). Blockchain-enabled digital rights management for multimedia resources of online education. *Multimedia Tools and Applications*, 1–21. doi:10.100711042-019-08059-1

Gupta, N., & Bedi, P. (2018). E-waste management using blockchain based smart contracts. In *2018 International Conference on Advances in Computing, Communications and Informatics (ICACCI)* (pp. 915-921). IEEE. 10.1109/ICACCI.2018.8554912

Gürkaynak, G., Yılmaz, İ., Yeşilaltay, B., & Bengi, B. (2018). Intellectual property law and practice in the blockchain realm. *Computer Law & Security Review, 34*(4), 847–862. doi:10.1016/j.clsr.2018.05.027

Hassani, H., Huang, X., & Silva, E. (2018). Banking with blockchain-ed big data. *Journal of Management Analytics, 5*(4), 256–275. doi:10.1080/23270012.2018.1 528900

Hawlitschek, F., Notheisen, B., & Teubner, T. (2018). The limits of trust-free systems: A literature review on blockchain technology and trust in the sharing economy. *Electronic Commerce Research and Applications, 29*, 50–63. doi:10.1016/j.elerap.2018.03.005

Ho, Y. S. (2014). Classic articles on social work field in Social Science Citation Index: A bibliometric analysis. *Scientometrics, 98*(1), 137–155. doi:10.100711192-013-1014-8

Hölbl, M., Kompara, M., Kamišalić, A., & Nemec Zlatolas, L. (2018). A systematic review of the use of blockchain in healthcare. *Symmetry, 10*(10), 470. doi:10.3390ym10100470

Holland, M., Nigischer, C., & Stjepandic, J. (2017). Copyright protection in additive manufacturing with blockchain approach. *Transdisciplinary Engineering: A Paradigm Shift, 5*, 914-921. doi:10.3233/978-1-61499-779-5-914

Holland, M., Stjepandić, J., & Nigischer, C. (2018). Intellectual property protection of 3D print supply chain with blockchain technology. In *2018 IEEE International conference on engineering, technology and innovation (ICE/ITMC)* (pp. 1-8). IEEE. 10.1109/ICE.2018.8436315

Holland, M. J. S., & Nigischer, C. (2018). Intellectual Property Protection of 3D Print Supply Chain with Blockchain Technology. *IEEE International Conference on Engineering, Technology and Innovation (ICE/ITMC)*, 1-8. 10.1109/ICE.2018.8436315

Hou, H. (2017). The application of blockchain technology in E-government in China. In *2017 26th International Conference on Computer Communication and Networks (ICCCN)* (pp. 1-4). IEEE. 10.1109/ICCCN.2017.8038519

Hu, D., Li, Y., Pan, L., Li, M., & Zheng, S. (2021). A blockchain-based trading system for big data. *Computer Networks*, *191*, 107994. doi:10.1016/j.comnet.2021.107994

Huang, Bian, Li, Zhao, & Shi. (2019). Smart Contract Security: A Software Lifecycle Perspective. IEEE Access, 7, 150184-150202. doi:10.1109/ACCESS.2019.2946988

Hughes, L., Dwivedi, Y. K., Misra, S. K., Rana, N. P., Raghavan, V., & Akella, V. (2019). Blockchain research, practice and policy: Applications, benefits, limitations, emerging research themes and research agenda. *International Journal of Information Management*, *49*, 114–129. doi:10.1016/j.ijinfomgt.2019.02.005

Ito, K., & O'Dair, M. (2019). A Critical Examination of the Application of Blockchain Technology to Intellectual Property Management. In *Business transformation through blockchain* (pp. 317–335). Palgrave Macmillan. doi:10.1007/978-3-319-99058-3_12

Jing, N., Liu, Q., & Sugumaran, V. (2021). A blockchain-based code copyright management system. *Information Processing & Management*, *58*(3), 102518. doi:10.1016/j.ipm.2021.102518

KaneE. (2017). Is Blockchain a General Purpose Technology? *Available at* SSRN 2932585. doi:10.2139/ssrn.2932585

Kang, J., Yu, R., Huang, X., Maharjan, S., Zhang, Y., & Hossain, E. (2017). Enabling localized peer-to-peer electricity trading among plug-in hybrid electric vehicles using consortium blockchains. *IEEE Transactions on Industrial Informatics*, *13*(6), 3154–3164. doi:10.1109/TII.2017.2709784

Karafiloski, E., & Mishev, A. (2017). Blockchain solutions for big data challenges: A literature review. In *IEEE EUROCON 2017-17th International Conference on Smart Technologies* (pp. 763-768). IEEE. 10.1109/EUROCON.2017.8011213

Kessler, M. M. (1963). Bibliographic coupling extended in time: Ten case histories. *Information Storage and Retrieval, 1*(4), pp. 169-187. doi:10.1016/0020-0271(63)90016-0

Keybase.io. (2019). *Keybase*. Available online at: https://keybase.io/docs/server_security

Khalilov, M. C. K., & Levi, A. (2018). A survey on anonymity and privacy in bitcoin-like digital cash systems. *IEEE Communications Surveys and Tutorials, 20*(3), 2543–2585. doi:10.1109/COMST.2018.2818623

Khan, M. A., & Salah, K. (2018). IoT security: Review, blockchain solutions, and open challenges. *Future Generation Computer Systems, 82*, 395–411. doi:10.1016/j.future.2017.11.022

Klöckner, M., Kurpjuweit, S., Velu, C., & Wagner, S. M. (2020). Does Blockchain for 3D Printing Offer Opportunities for Business Model Innovation? *Research Technology Management, 63*(4), 18–27. doi:10.1080/08956308.2020.1762444

Kurpjuweit, S., Schmidt, C. G., Klöckner, M., & Wagner, S. M. (2021). Blockchain in additive manufacturing and its impact on supply chains. *Journal of Business Logistics, 42*(1), 46–70. doi:10.1111/jbl.12231

Lacity, M. C. (2018). Addressing key challenges to making enterprise blockchain applications a reality. *MIS Quarterly Executive, 17*(3), 201-222. https://aisel.aisnet.org/misqe/vol17/iss3/3

Lakhani, K. R., & Iansiti, M. (2017). The truth about blockchain. *Harvard Business Review, 95*(1), 119-127. https://hbr.org/2017/01/the-truth-about-blockchain

Lampe, J., Kraft, P. S., & Bausch, A. (2019). Mapping the field of research on entrepreneurial organizations (1937–2016): A bibliometric analysis and research agenda. *Entrepreneurship Theory and Practice, 44*(4), 784–816. doi:10.1177/1042258719851217

Laouar, M. R., Hamad, Z. T., & Eom, S. (2019). Towards blockchain-based urban planning: Application for waste collection management. In *Proceedings of the 9th International Conference on Information Systems and Technologies* (pp. 1-6). 10.1145/3361570.3361619

Li, P., Xu, H., Ma, T., & Mu, Y. (2018). Research on fault-correcting blockchain technology. *Journal of Cryptologic Research, 5*(5), 501–509.

Li, X., Pak, C., & Bi, K. (2020). Analysis of the development trends and innovation characteristics of Internet of Things technology–based on patentometrics and bibliometrics. *Technology Analysis and Strategic Management, 32*(1), 104–118. doi:10.1080/09537325.2019.1636960

Li, Z., Kang, J., Yu, R., Ye, D., Deng, Q., & Zhang, Y. (2017). Consortium blockchain for secure energy trading in industrial internet of things. *IEEE Transactions on Industrial Informatics, 14*(8), 3690–3700. doi:10.1109/TII.2017.2786307

Lin, J., Long, W., Zhang, A., & Chai, Y. (2019). Using Blockchain and IoT Technologies to Enhance Intellectual Property Protection. In *Proceedings of the 4th International Conference on Crowd Science and Engineering* (pp. 44-49). 10.1145/3371238.3371246

Liu, S. H., Liao, H. L., Pi, S. M., & Hu, J. W. (2011). Development of a Patent Retrieval and Analysis Platform–A hybrid approach. *Expert Systems with Applications, 38*(6), 7864–7868. doi:10.1016/j.eswa.2010.12.114

Low, K., & Mik, E. (2020). Pause the blockchain legal revolution. *The International and Comparative Law Quarterly, 69*(1), 135–175. doi:10.1017/S0020589319000502

Lundkvist, C., Heck, R., Torstensson, J., Mitton, Z., & Sena, M. (2017). *Uport: A platform for self-sovereign identity.* https://whitepaper.uport.me/uPort_whitepaper_DRAFT20170221.pdf

Macrinici, D., Cartofeanu, C., & Gao, S. (2018). Smart contract applications within blockchain technology: A systematic mapping study. *Telematics and Informatics, 35*(8), 2337–2354. doi:10.1016/j.tele.2018.10.004

Maesa, D. D. F., & Mori, P. (2020). Blockchain 3.0 applications survey. *Journal of Parallel and Distributed Computing, 138*, 99–114. doi:10.1016/j.jpdc.2019.12.019

Martyn, J. (1964). Bibliographic coupling. *The Journal of Documentation, 20*(4), 236. doi:10.1108/eb026352

McConaghy, M., McMullen, G., Parry, G., McConaghy, T., & Holtzman, D. (2017). Visibility and digital art: Blockchain as an ownership layer on the Internet. *Strategic Change, 26*(5), 461–470. doi:10.1002/jsc.2146

McLoone, M., & McCanny, J. V. (2003). Generic architecture and semiconductor intellectual property cores for advanced encryption standard cryptography. *IEE Proceedings. Computers and Digital Techniques, 150*(4), 239–244. doi:10.1049/ip-cdt:20030499

McMillan, G. S. (2008). Mapping the invisible colleges of R&D Management. *Research Management, 38*(1), 69–83. doi:10.1111/j.1467-9310.2007.00495.x

Mehrwald, P., Treffers, T., Titze, M., & Welpe, I. (2019). *Blockchain technology application in the sharing economy: A proposed model of effects on trust and intermediation.* doi:10.24251/HICSS.2019.555

Meng, W., Tischhauser, E. W., Wang, Q., Wang, Y., & Han, J. (2018). When intrusion detection meets blockchain technology: A review. *IEEE Access: Practical Innovations, Open Solutions, 6*, 10179–10188. doi:10.1109/ACCESS.2018.2799854

Miau, S., & Yang, J. M. (2018). Bibliometrics-based evaluation of the Blockchain research trend: 2008–March 2017. *Technology Analysis and Strategic Management, 30*(9), 1029–1045. doi:10.1080/09537325.2018.1434138

Miau, S., & Yang, J. M. (2018). Bibliometrics-based evaluation of the Blockchain research trend: 2008–March 2017. *Technology Analysis and Strategic Management, 30*(9), 1029–1045. doi:10.1080/09537325.2018.1434138

Modic, D., Hafner, A., Damij, N., & Cehovin Zajc, L. (2019). Innovations in intellectual property rights management: Their potential benefits and limitations. *European Journal of Management and Business Economics, 28*(2), 189–203. doi:10.1108/EJMBE-12-2018-0139

Mohanta, B. K., Jena, D., Ramasubbareddy, S., Daneshmand, M., & Gandomi, A. H. (2020). Addressing security and privacy issues of IoT using blockchain technology. *IEEE Internet of Things Journal, 8*(2), 881–888. doi:10.1109/JIOT.2020.3008906

Moll, O., Heun, J., Eising, R., Gersemsky, U., Norpoth, B., Appel, E., . . . Walloshek, T. (2005). *U.S. Patent Application No. 10/909,660.* US Patent Office.

Mukhopadhyay, U., Skjellum, A., Hambolu, O., Oakley, J., Yu, L., & Brooks, R. (2016). A brief survey of cryptocurrency systems. In *2016 14th annual conference on privacy, security and trust (PST)* (pp. 745-752). IEEE. 10.1109/PST.2016.7906988

Mun, C., Yoon, S., & Park, H. (2019). Structural decomposition of technological domain using patent co-classification and classification hierarchy. *Scientometrics, 121*(2), 633–652. doi:10.100711192-019-03223-8

Nakamoto, S., & Bitcoin, A. (2008). *A peer-to-peer electronic cash system. Bitcoin.* https://bitcoin. org/bitcoin. pdf

Narayanan, A., Bonneau, J., Felten, E., Miller, A., & Goldfeder, S. (2016). *Bitcoin and cryptocurrency technologies: a comprehensive introduction.* Princeton University Press. https://scholar.google.com/scholar_lookup?title=Bitcoin+and+cryptocurrency+technologies%3A+A+comprehensive+introduction&author=Narayanan+A.&author=Bonneau+J.&author=Felten+E.&author=Miller+A.&author=Goldfeder+S&publication+year=2016

Notheisen, B., Cholewa, J. B., & Shanmugam, A. P. (2017). Trading real-world assets on blockchain. *Business & Information Systems Engineering*, *59*(6), 425–440. doi:10.100712599-017-0499-8

O'Connell, A. A., Borg, I., & Groenen, P. (1999). Modern multidimensional scaling: Theory and applications. *Journal of the American Statistical Association*, *94*(445), 338–339. doi:10.2307/2669710

O'Dwyer, R. (2020). Limited edition: Producing artificial scarcity for digital art on the blockchain and its implications for the cultural industries. *Convergence.*, *26*(4), 874–894. doi:10.1177/1354856518795097

O'Leary, K., O'Reilly, P., Feller, J., Gleasure, R., Li, S., & Cristoforo, J. (2017). Exploring the application of blockchain technology to combat the effects of social loafing in cross functional group projects. In *Proceedings of the 13th International Symposium on Open Collaboration* (pp. 1-8). 10.1145/3125433.3125464

Ozcan, S., & Unalan, S. (2020). Blockchain as a General-Purpose Technology: Patentometric Evidence of Science, Technologies, and Actors. *IEEE Transactions on Engineering Management*, 1–18. Advance online publication. doi:10.1109/TEM.2020.3008859

Papakostas, N., Newell, A., & Hargaden, V. (2019). A novel paradigm for managing the product development process utilising blockchain technology principles. *CIRP Annals*, *68*(1), 137-140. doi:10.1016/j.cirp.2019.04.039

Passarelli, M., Landi, G. C., Cariola, A., & Sciarelli, M. (2020). Open innovation in the new context of proof of concepts: Evidence from Italy. *European Journal of Innovation Management*, *24*(3), 735–755. Advance online publication. doi:10.1108/EJIM-02-2020-0052

Patole, D., Borse, Y., Jain, J., & Maher, S. (2020). Personal Identity on Blockchain. In *Advances in Computing and Intelligent Systems* (pp. 439–446). Springer. doi:10.1007/978-981-15-0222-4_41

Radanović, I., & Likić, R. (2018). Opportunities for Use of Blockchain Technology in Medicine. *Applied Health Economics and Health Policy*, *16*(5), 583–590. doi:10.100740258-018-0412-8 PMID:30022440

Rahmanzadeh, S., Pishvaee, M. S., & Rasouli, M. R. (2020). Integrated innovative product design and supply chain tactical planning within a blockchain platform. *International Journal of Production Research*, *58*(7), 2242–2262. doi:10.1080/00207543.2019.1651947

Rahmanzadeh, S., Pishvaee, M. S., & Rasouli, M. R. (2020). Integrated innovative product design and supply chain tactical planning within a blockchain platform. *International Journal of Production Research, 58*(7), 2242–2262. doi:10.1080/00 207543.2019.1651947

Rathor, M., & Sengupta, A. (2020). IP Core Steganography Using Switch Based Key-Driven Hash-Chaining and Encoding for Securing DSP Kernels Used in CE Systems. *IEEE Transactions on Consumer Electronics, 66*(3), 251–260. doi:10.1109/ TCE.2020.3006050

SaterS. (2018). Blockchain transforming healthcare data flows. *Available at* SSRN 3171005. doi:10.2139/ssrn.3171005

Scholl, H. J., Pomeshchikov, R., & Rodríguez Bolívar, M. P. (2020). Early regulations of distributed ledger technology/blockchain providers: A comparative case study. *Proceedings of the 53rd Hawaii International Conference on System Sciences.* 10.24251/HICSS.2020.218

Schönhals, A., Hepp, T., & Gipp, B. (2018). Design thinking using the blockchain: enable traceability of intellectual property in problem-solving processes for open innovation. In *Proceedings of the 1st Workshop on Cryptocurrencies and Blockchains for Distributed Systems* (pp. 105-110). 10.1145/3211933.3211952

Seebacher, S., & Schüritz, R. (2017). Blockchain technology as an enabler of service systems: A structured literature review. In *International Conference on Exploring Services Science* (pp. 12-23). Springer. 10.1007/978-3-319-56925-3_2

Sengar, G. D. M., & Chowdhury, D. R. (2007). Secured Flipped Scan-Chain Model for Crypto-Architecture. *IEEE Transactions on Computer-Aided Design of Integrated Circuits and Systems, 26*(11), 2080–2084. doi:10.1109/TCAD.2007.906483

Skute, I., Zalewska-Kurek, K., Hatak, I., & de Weerd-Nederhof, P. (2019). Mapping the field: A bibliometric analysis of the literature on university–industry collaborations. *The Journal of Technology Transfer, 44*(3), 916–947. doi:10.100710961-017-9637-1

Small, H. (1973). Co-citation in the scientific literature: A new measure of the relationship between two documents. *Journal of the American Society for Information Science, 24*(4), 265–269. doi:10.1002/asi.4630240406

Somin, S., Altshuler, Y., Gordon, G., & Shmueli, E. (2020). network Dynamics of a financial ecosystem. *Scientific Reports, 10*(1), 1–10. doi:10.103841598-020-61346-y PMID:32165674

Steinwandter, V., & Herwig, C. (2019). Provable data integrity in the pharmaceutical industry based on version control systems and the blockchain. *PDA Journal of Pharmaceutical Science and Technology*, *73*(4), 373–390. doi:10.5731/pdajpst.2018.009407 PMID:30770485

Sun, H., Wang, X., & Wang, X. (2018). Application of Blockchain Technology in Online Education. *International Journal of Emerging Technologies in Learning*, *13*(10), 252. doi:10.3991/ijet.v13i10.9455

Taş, R., & Tanrıöver, Ö. Ö. (2020). A systematic review of challenges and opportunities of blockchain for E-voting. *Symmetry*, *12*(8), 1328. doi:10.3390ym12081328

Thejaswini, S., & Ranjitha, K. R. (2021). Blockchain for Management of Natural Resources Using Energy Trading as a Platform. In *International Conference on Communication, Computing and Electronics Systems: Proceedings of ICCCES 2020* (*Vol. 733*, p. 475). Springer Nature. 10.1007/978-981-33-4909-4_36

Tönnissen, S., & Teuteberg, F. (2018). Using blockchain technology for business processes in purchasing– concept and case study-based evidence. In *International Conference on Business Information Systems* (pp. 253-264). Springer. 10.1007/978-3-319-93931-5_18

Trees, M., & Storage, D. F. (2014). *A next-generation smart contract and decentralized application platform.* https://ethereum.org/en/whitepaper/

Truong, Um, Zhou, & Lee. (2018). Strengthening the Blockchain-Based Internet of Value with Trust. *IEEE International Conference on Communications (ICC)*, 1-7. 10.1109/ICC.2018.8423014

Tsai, Feng, Zhang, You, Wang, & Zhong. (2017). Intellectual-Property Blockchain-Based Protection Model for Microfilms. *2017 IEEE Symposium on Service-Oriented System Engineering (SOSE)*, 174-178. 10.1109/SOSE.2017.35

Tse, D., Zhang, B., Yang, Y., Cheng, C., & Mu, H. (2017). Blockchain application in food supply information security. In 2017 IEEE international conference on industrial engineering and engineering management (IEEM) (pp. 1357-1361). IEEE. doi:10.1109/IEEM.2017.8290114

Tsukerman, M. (2015). The block is hot: A survey of the state of Bitcoin regulation and suggestions for the future. *Berkeley Technology Law Journal*, *30*(4), 1127–1170. https://www.jstor.org/stable/26377750

Underwood, S. (2016). Blockchain beyond bitcoin. *Communications of the ACM*, *59*(11), 15–17. doi:10.1145/2994581

Van Eck, N. J., Waltman, L., Dekker, R., & van den Berg, J. (2010). A comparison of two techniques for bibliometric mapping: Multidimensional scaling and VOS. *Journal of the American Society for Information Science and Technology, 61*(12), 2405-2416. doi:10.1002/asi.21421

Varma, J. R. (2019). Blockchain in finance. *Vikalpa, 44*(1), 1–11. doi:10.1177/0256090919839897

Verma, S., & Gustafsson, A. (2020). Investigating the emerging COVID-19 research trends in the field of business and management: A bibliometric analysis approach. *Journal of Business Research, 118*, 253–261. doi:10.1016/j.jbusres.2020.06.057 PMID:32834211

Waltman, L., Van Eck, N. J., & Noyons, E. C. (2010). A unified approach to mapping and clustering of bibliometric networks. *Journal of Informetrics, 4*(4), 629–635. doi:10.1016/j.joi.2010.07.002

Wang, J., Wang, S., Guo, J., Du, Y., Cheng, S., & Li, X. (2019). A summary of research on blockchain in the field of intellectual property. *Procedia Computer Science, 147*, 191–197. doi:10.1016/j.procs.2019.01.220

Willrich, S., Melcher, F., Straub, T., & Weinhardt, C. (2019). Towards More Sustainability: A Literature Review Where Bioeconomy Meets Blockchain. In ICETE (vol. 1, pp. 113-120). doi:10.5220/0007786301070114

Xiao, L. W., Huang, W., Xie, Y., Xiao, W., & Li, K.-C. (2020). A Blockchain-Based Traceable IP Copyright Protection Algorithm. *IEEE Access: Practical Innovations, Open Solutions, 8*, 49532–49542. doi:10.1109/ACCESS.2020.2969990

Xu, X., Lu, Q., Liu, Y., Zhu, L., Yao, H., & Vasilakos, A. V. (2019). Designing blockchain-based applications a case study for imported product traceability. *Future Generation Computer Systems, 92*, 399–406. doi:10.1016/j.future.2018.10.010

Yalcin, H., & Daim, T. (2021). Mining research and invention activity for innovation trends: Case of blockchain technology. *Scientometrics, 126*(5), 3775–3806. doi:10.100711192-021-03876-4

Yang, F. (2019). The Survey on Intellectual Property Based on Blockchain Technology. *2019 IEEE International Conference on Industrial Cyber Physical Systems (ICPS)*, 743-748. 10.1109/ICPHYS.2019.8780125

Yang, F., Zhou, W., Wu, Q., Long, R., Xiong, N. N., & Zhou, M. (2019). Delegated Proof of Stake With Downgrade: A Secure and Efficient Blockchain Consensus Algorithm With Downgrade Mechanism. *IEEE Access: Practical Innovations, Open Solutions*, *7*, 118541–118555. doi:10.1109/ACCESS.2019.2935149

Yang, Y. J., & Hwang, J. C. (2020). Recent development trend of blockchain technologies: A patent analysis. *International Journal of Electronic Commerce Studies*, *11*(1), 1–12. doi:10.7903/ijecs.1931

Yang & Li. (2016). Research framework and anticipated results of cyberspace digital virtual asset protection. *Advanced Engineering Science*, *50*(4), 1–11. doi:10.15961/j.jsuese.20180066

Yanik, S., & Kiliç, A. S. (2018). A framework for the performance evaluation of an energy blockchain. In *Energy Management—Collective and Computational Intelligence with Theory and Applications* (pp. 521–543). Springer. doi:10.1007/978-3-319-75690-5_23

Yavuz, E., Koç, A. K., Çabuk, U. C., & Dalkılıç, G. (2018). Towards secure e-voting using ethereum blockchain. In *2018 6th International Symposium on Digital Forensic and Security (ISDFS)* (pp. 1-7). IEEE. Available: https://followmyvote.com/online-voting-platform-benefits/open-source-code/

Yin, R. K. (2011). *Applications of case study research*. Sage. doi:10.3138/cjpe.30.1.108

Yli-Huumo, J., Ko, D., Choi, S., Park, S., & Smolander, K. (2016). Where is current research on blockchain technology?—A systematic review. *PLoS One*, *11*(10), e0163477. doi:10.1371/journal.pone.0163477 PMID:27695049

Yu, D., & Pan, T. (2021). Tracing the main path of interdisciplinary research considering citation preference: A case from blockchain domain. *Journal of Informetrics*, *15*(2), 101136. doi:10.1016/j.joi.2021.101136

Yu, D., & Sheng, L. (2020). Knowledge diffusion paths of blockchain domain: The main path analysis. *Scientometrics*, *125*(1), 471–497. doi:10.100711192-020-03650-y

Zeilinger, M. (2018). Digital Art as 'Monetised Graphics': Enforcing Intellectual Property on the Blockchain. *Philosophy & Technology*, *31*(1), 15–41. doi:10.100713347-016-0243-1

Zhang, R., Xue, R., & Liu, L. (2019). Security and privacy on blockchain. *ACM Computing Surveys*, *52*(3), 1–34. doi:10.1145/3316481

Chapter 11
Beyond Scattered Applications:
A Taxonomy of Blockchain Outcomes in the Public Domain

Esli Spahiu
Luiss University, Italy

Paolo Spagnoletti
iD https://orcid.org/0000-0003-1950-368X
Luiss University, Italy

Tommaso Federici
iD https://orcid.org/0000-0001-6016-5868
University of Tuscia, Italy

ABSTRACT

As a decentralised digital ledger, blockchain has become a buzzword in the recent years, due to its advantageous characteristics. The application of blockchain has been associated with different implications, ranging from trust generator to increased efficiency. Recently, blockchain application has gained momentum by being implemented by different governments and public bodies, as a solution for tackling different issues, with the intent of providing more efficient public policies. Different blockchain-based systems and platforms have been increasingly introduced as a more secure and orderly alternative of delivering various public functions and services. Given the expansion of use cases in different countries and the scattered information in this regard, this chapter develops a taxonomy of blockchain outcomes in the public domain by identifying the emerging patterns and subcategories. The proposed taxonomy can support decision makers and researchers to better identify the various blockchain applications, alongside their benefits, implications, and possible associated risks.

DOI: 10.4018/978-1-7998-8014-1.ch011

INTRODUCTION

Blockchain is a decentralized data management technology that, through a distributed ledger, provides new ways of managing, governing, storing, and distributing information (Iansiti and Lakhami, 2017; Sun Yin et al, 2019). At the core of blockchain, there is a computer protocol acting as an automatic contract enforcing exchanges between parties by means of irreversible and secure transactions (Cong et al., 2017). Blockchain's novel technology also presents a new way of establishing trust through its different consensus protocols and cryptography that make transactions verifiable and fault tolerant (Beck et al.,2016; Shin, 2019). The advantage of blockchain is that it also has different architectural configurations allowing for better fitting the application of blockchain to different objectives. The different architectural dispositions, such as network access, type of consensus mechanism, data control and network type, offer the opportunity to allow or restrict access while also offering elevated security (Zhang and Lee, 2020).

The current body of knowledge has shifted into disseminating the potential of blockchain into numerous different applications and sectors that go beyond the financial sector and cryptocurrency (Alharby and Moorsel, 2017). The diversity of blockchain applications in terms of scope is not only related to the multi-purpose nature of such technology, but also to various needs. Governments today continue to face the need to be more open and transparent in the eyes of the society (Hollyer et al., 2011). In turn, openness and transparency are considered to be the main components that lead to building strong accountability and trust in a society (Gaventa, 2013; Johnston, 2001). Considering that the root to most of the public policies failure is due to incompetence, corruption, or inefficient governance (Mueller, 2020), this gives reason to explore blockchain as a possible solution to such issues (Hyvarinen, 2017). In fact, blockchain has been adopted in the public domain to enforce existing or new policies through a digital transformation process that offers a rapid accomplishment to multiple societal goals by different governmental bodies (Berryhill, 2018).

Given the dispersive nature of the applications, we find it important to understand the digital transformation rationale behind the adoption of blockchain in public domain, and secondly, to provide a classification of what blockchain outcomes derive from different applications. In this regard, we believe that, under specific conditions, blockchain can be an enabler of digital transformation (Vial, 2019), since it is a technology that creates disruption. Additionally, we agree that digital transformation is more often than ever a byproduct of the need to address different societal challenges (Majchrzak et al., 2016). By highlighting the value created by digital transformation processes when societal challenges are addressed, we are interested in looking at the blockchain applications in the public domain that demonstrate to have achieved improvements that go beyond the efficiency of a specific service. Therefore, we develop a taxonomy (Nickerson et al., 2013) that answers the following research question: *"What are the observed dimensions of blockchain initiatives in the public domain?"*.

We expect this research to draw various contributions in the study of blockchain. By creating a map of successful applications and the various public functions that blockchain could be taken advantage of, we expect to create a better overview for decision-makers in the sector who may be interested in blockchain adoption or organizations seeking to improve their performances through digital transformation. Also, considering the lack of blockchain studies the process of adoption of this technology, we expect our findings to identify new research perspectives that could pave the way to future studies on blockchain-based systems design and implementation.

BACKGROUND

Blockchain in the Public Domain

In recent years, blockchain has gained popularity in the public domain due to successful implementations ranging from public administration to public policy and from public offices to supporting whole e-government transformation. For the purpose of this study, we incorporate such blockchain applications under the term "public domain". According to OECD, the public domain includes services owned or controlled by the government in addition to services that, despite being private, are funded by the government or similar authorities (Pilichowski and Turkisch, 2018).

As regards the wide range of blockchain applications in public domain, from notary services to voting (Alketbi et al., 2019; European Commission, 2018), an important role has been played by the introduction of smart contracts, a main feature of the blockchain technology, as a guarantor of full automation of process without the need of intermediaries or even human interaction (Qi et al, 2017). A particular area where blockchain has gained momentum is digital government or e-government (Hou, 2018; Terzi et al.,2019). Sobolewski and Allesie (2021) show that Europe in particular has been quick in exploring and pioneering different projects in this regard, but real-life applications have been on the rise even in other countries, such as in India, China, UK, and Brazil, etc. (Hou, 2017; Ojo and Adebayo, 2017; Deloitte, 2018).

Public administrations as an operational unit in the public domain have proven to be a good basis for the application of blockchain, since the very nature of their practices is based on data certification, traceability, and transparency (Rot et al, 2020), and blockchain does not change the nature of services, rather it is expected to facilitate the way in which they are provided (Casino et al., 2019). Distinctive features such as citizen trust, privacy and record keeping make blockchain a potentially pervasive technology that can be adopted at different levels in public administrations (Carter and Ubacht, 2014). Subsequently, studies have gone so far as to look at blockchain as the initiator of new governance models in the public administration (Olnes, 2016; Hou, 2017; Konashevyc, 2017).

While some papers focus on specific cases where blockchain has been already implemented in the public domain, most of them continue to be hypothetical in nature about how blockchain can contribute and its potential in various services. Additionally, most of these paper focus on individual cases and do not offer a generalized overview of the outcomes. In order for policy makers to have a better overview of what to expect from blockchain in the light of their needs, it would be important to classify the blockchain applications and link them to different dimensions and implications by looking at various initiatives. This would also allow for the emergence of the societal challenges that this technology is inherited to face.

Blockchain Taxonomies

The versatility of blockchain technology, the application domains of blockchain and the different types of blockchain that could be associated with each application, have offered a good opportunity for various studies contributing to the classification of blockchain and the creation of a diversity of taxonomies. Each taxonomy is considered to be a separate category and would provide a way of structuring knowledge in a particular field (Glass and Vessey, 1995). Sarkitundu et al., (2016) are among the first to study the possibility of creating a taxonomy on the basis of blockchain platforms, as a first step into creating a wider taxonomy that would encompass the whole cryptocurrency ecosystem. Other early studies, such as Xu et al (2017) and Tasca and Tessone (2018), focus on a way of classifying, different blockchains on the basis of their architectural design. Wieninger et al. (2019) develop a blockchain taxonomy based on blockchain characteristics and how different types of blockchain interact. Weking et al. (2019) study the impact of blockchain technology on business models by either affecting existing ones or creating new ones altogether. Labazova et al. (2019) highlight the importance of developing a taxonomy of blockchain applications that categorize all blockchain characteristics across different applications and create a taxonomy encompassing the main technical components of various blockchains. Recently, Alkhalifah et al. (2020) propose a taxonomy based on cybersecurity threats and the possible vulnerabilities, as a way of classifying certain aspects of blockchain.

Despite the increase of blockchain studies aiming at classifying it, it is worth mentioning that, so far, the resulting taxonomies mainly focus on the technical characteristics of blockchain and its various architectural settings. Also, the purpose of any taxonomy is based on its intended use, thus with a concrete idea of the users to be addressed. From the extensively technical nature of the aforementioned studies, it could be inherited that the focus so far has been on technology experts and developers. There is a shortcoming in current literature regarding blockchain with regard to implications, which makes it important classifying blockchain applications adopting this new lens, addressing decision-makers.

The users we mainly expect consist of policy makers, head of institutions of various nature in the public domain and even managers who are primarily concerned with the expected benefits that can be gained from a successful implementation. Our taxonomy's user pool also includes researchers and scholars wishing to underpin the advantages and limits of blockchain as assessed from real cases: this could be the starting point of further research in managerial and governmental studies regarding blockchain. Thus, the objective of our study is to classify the effects of blockchain applications in public domain: consequently, the meta-characteristics in our study relate to consequences and implications, with minimal interference to the characteristics of applied blockchain.

METHODOLOGY

Taxonomy Development Method

From a technical and performing perspective, blockchain has been considered from the very beginning as an evolutionary step towards a new way of thinking about information systems (Brando, 2016; Beck et al., 2017). Research continues to draw comparisons between blockchain and traditional information systems (Rossi et al., 2019), and goes as far as to consider blockchain as a new infrastructure and platform in information systems research (Costantinides et al., 2018). Under this perspective, we adopt the Nickerson et al. (2013) taxonomy development method especially designed for studies concerning Information Systems. This method proposes a process starting with presenting as a first step the meta-characteristics, followed by the determination of ending conditions and the approach as summarized in Figure 1.

We opted for an empirical-to-conceptual approach given that the main objective of the research is to look at observations and evidence coming from real-life case studies. The taxonomy was developed through two inductive iterations. For the first iteration, we compiled the list of dimensions, characteristics and applications that resulted from the list of publications we reviewed from SCOPUS. In the second iteration we did the same thing, this time analyzing the national and international governmental reports, which were identified through the first literature review. Since no dimension was added following this new iteration, the method was not repeated.

Figure 1. Taxonomy development method

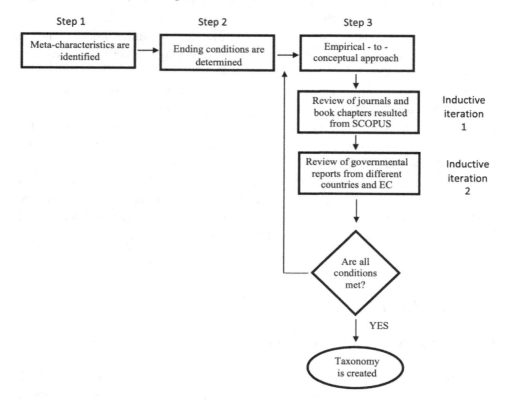

Eventually, the taxonomy is concluded, since also the ending conditions enlisted by Nickerson et al., (2013) are fulfilled. Each dimension highlights the main features of interest in the taxonomy: they are mutually exclusive and there were no dimensions added or merged/split in the last iteration. There is no cell duplication and at least one object is classified under each characteristic. Additionally, all the application cases in our domain of interest can be classified in the taxonomy making it comprehensive, and if a new application case would arise, the taxonomy is extensible enough for a new dimension to be added.

Search Strategy

For the purpose of this study, taking into consideration that the application of blockchain in the public domain could be very multidimensional, we focused on SCOPUS as our main database of research because of its multi-disciplinarity. To fully grasp the application of blockchain in our domain of interest, we made sure to include all words which would interrelate with "public domain" and "blockchain". The final search record included the words "public policy" or "public sector" or "government" or "public governance" and "blockchain" or "bitcoin" or "Ethereum" or "cryptocurrency" or "distributed ledger" or "smart contract".

At first, we included peer-reviewed journal articles, conference papers and the book chapters which resulted to match our criteria on SCOPUS. Eventually, considering the scope of our study, we found it useful to also add country reports and reports from the European Commission, which detailed any implications and outcomes resulting from the application of blockchain in any member country.

Selection Criteria

The search on SCOPUS resulted in 1,175 document documents to be reviewed. During the first screening process, the abstract of each document was investigated to match our selection criteria:

- Only case studies, reports on blockchain applications or literature reviews concerning the former which have already been implemented as a pilot phase or as full scope implementation have been considered
- Implementation had to be promoted by a government institution, whether local or national, and/or by a public administration body and/or related to government policy
- Not including any hypothetical or potential case studies, to make sure that the reflections of the output would be more reliable
- Written in English language
- No restriction applied about the field of study: included publications come from social sciences and engineering.

Subsequently, after the first screening based on the aforementioned criteria, and after the removal of any duplicate, a second screening consisted of reading the full document. This resulted in a total of 79 records from SCOPUS. Based on a snowball effect, some of the important government reports or press releases, which did not result from our initial database, were considered, and eventually 13 reports were added.

Data Organization and Coding

For the purpose of our study, we used NVivo 13 as a data management tool considering the number of articles under review. Considering the exploratory nature of our research, we applied open and axial coding to associate descriptive labels to the emerging themes and identify the connection between these themes.

BLOCKCHAIN INITIATIVES

Considering the objective of this research and the focus on policy makers, it was important to also showcase some of the most distinctive blockchain initiatives in the public domain observed during the investigation. Table 1. presents a summary of 22 of such initiatives that vary in nature and scope. In the later section we match these initiatives which consist of pilot projects or full-scale implementations with each of the dimensions emerging from the taxonomy.

TAXONOMY OF BLOCKCHAIN OUTCOMES

The final taxonomy of blockchain outcomes comprises of 5 dimensions: Use cases, Organizational Extensions, Type of Users, Benefits, Risks and Challenges, Public Value. Two dimensions comprise subdimensions that we have compiled to better label all the items identified from the coding. Figure 2 gives an overview of the identified dimensions and subsets.

Figure 2. Taxonomy dimensions

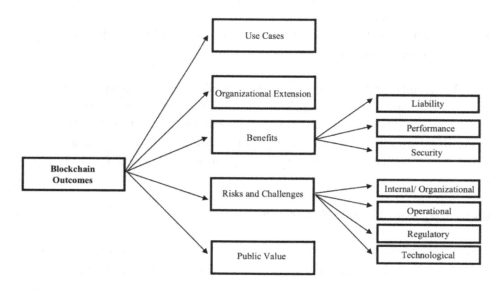

Table 1. Blockchain initiatives

	Blockchain Initiative	Description
B1	UN Joint Staff Pension Fund	Update of manual procedures and creation of an automated solution through a blockchain unchangeable process for delivering the annual Pension Fund Certificate of Entitlement to retired beneficiaries (Lacheca, 2021)
B2	Chancheng - China	Considered as the first blockchain initiative in e-government in China for managing digital identities and for using them as a one stop service by various government institutions (Hou, 2017; Al-Megren et al., 2018)
B3	X-Road - Estonia	Regarded as the backbone of e-Estonia, it allows for different public and private e-service information systems to collaborate and share information (Adeodato and Pournouri, 2020; Rana et al., 2021)
B4	The British National Archives Archangel Project - UK	Identified as an initiative to safeguard archives by fingerprinting documents at their receipt, it ensures the proof of provenance and integrity of each file (Bui et al., 2020; Bhatia and De Hernandez, 2019)
B5	Exonum land title registry - Georgia	Release of digital certificates attesting land titles and checking of property claims legitimacy (Goderdzishvili et al., 2018; Sobolewski and Allesie, 2021)
B6	Blockcerts academic records - Malta	Verifying academic credentials, academic records, and certificates (Sobolewski and Allesie, 2021)
B7	Chromaway property transactions - Sweden	Implementation of blockchain infrastructure for real estate transactions, mortgage contracts and related activities (Thakur et al., 2019; Sobolewski and Allesie, 2021)
B8	uPort decentralized identity - Switzerland	Providing a new automated data management and confirmation for e-government services (Sobolewski and Allesie, 2021)
B9	Infrachain governance framework - Luxemburg	Bringing together blockchain and regulatory and legal requirements through a governance model supplementing current technologies (Sobolewski and Allesie, 2021)
B10	Pension Infrastructure – the Netherlands	Implementing blockchain to the Pension Infrastructure for lowering costs and providing more transparent services to citizens (Sobolewski and Allesie, 2021)
B11	Stjaderpas smart vouchers – the Netherlands	Transfer into a blockchain infrastructure of the voucher system providing various discount services for low-income systems Stjaderpas (Sobolewski and Allesie, 2021)
B12	Delaware Public archives - USA	Pilot project aiming at making public records more accessible, also incorporating the retention and destruction of documents in compliance with law (Warketing and Orgeron, 2019)
B13	Electronic voting - South Korea	Casting votes, both online and offline on various issues such as regarding various community projects that would eventually get funded, etc. (Ojo and Adebayo, 2017; Jagrat and Channegowda, 2020)
B14	Factom Land registry - Honduras	Land registry to better protect local farmers' livelihoods and invest in diversifying their agricultural production (Alketbi et al., 2020)
B15	Vehicle wallet partnership - Denmark	Incorporating blockchain as the infrastructure of a digital asset management of vehicle's life cycle process (Chellasamy, 2019)
B16	Syddjurs municipality - Denmark	Prototype attaching smart contracts to the governmental processes to test the efficiency of blockchain in day-to-day processes (Krogsboll et al., 2020)
B17	Bengal birth certificate - India	Automated system of records based on blockchain when issuing birth certificates (Bhatia and De Hernandez, 2019)
B18	Smart City Dubai - UAE	Leveraging blockchain technology in various applications for transforming the United Arab Emirates into a blockchain haven (Al-Barguthi et al., 2019; World Economic Forum, 2020).
B19	Asylum Procedure - Germany	Pilot use of blockchain to coordinate processes across different authorities in the asylum procedure of migrants and refugees (Rieger et al., 2021)
B20	Illinois Blockchain Initiative	Series of use-case pilot programs aimed at exploring the potential of blockchain (Sullivan, 2021)
B21	Project Jasper – Bank of Canada	Four-phase project to explore blockchain and digital ledger technology in the central bank environment for determining technologies' capabilities and feasibility (Reddick, 2021)
B22	Food Standards Agency - UK	Pilot project implemented by the Food Standards Agency for tracking meat to provide higher transparency in the food sector

The next section will detail each dimension, providing an explanatory description of each category identified under each dimension. Additionally, each category is matched with a third column listing the examples of blockchain initiatives summarized above which identified from our literature review and coding, presented the characteristics of that same category.

Use Cases

We refer to use cases to describe the various blockchain application domains that have been identified across all industries. Through use cases, we aim at specifying the main purposes that blockchain has been explored for. Table 2 presents the identified seven use cases that encompass the reviewed applications in the public domain.

Table 2. Use cases

Use Cases	Description	Initiatives
Digital records	Application for records sharing and storing, registry services, securing information integrity	B2, B3, B4, B5, B7, B10, B12, B14, B18, B19, B20, B22
Supply chain	Tamper-proof and time stamped end-to-end tracing of the supply network distributing any product from the supplier to the final receiver that also replaces manual processes	B15, B22
Identity management	Application for providing a decentralized proof of identity by implementing smart contracts to manage data disclosure through explicit user consent	B1, B6, B8
Bills and Payments	Automating transactions involving payments that meet the regulations, through the smart contract protocol	B3, B10, B16, B18, B21
Welfare distribution	Application to various transformative ways of supporting social welfare, such as through secure e-vouchers, distribution of funds or monitoring of welfare expenditures	B11
E-voting	Application to any process involving the casting or counting of votes done electronically	B13
Legal enforcement	Applications that aid the fight against financial crimes, tracing criminality, securing the change of custody for evidence, etc.	B12, B19

Organizational Extension

The concept of organizational extension denominates the extent that the blockchain has been applied to. More specifically, it relates to whether blockchain has been applied to only a local application that can be a municipality, single administration unit, small local voting, or to a wider application. The latter can be for instance a nationwide blockchain initiative for various institutions or even transnational in the case where the same blockchain is the backbone of an initiative undertaken by different countries that cooperate with each other, such as in the case for instance of the European Union. Table 3 shows a summary of the three types of organizational extension and a brief description of each of them.

Table 3. Organizational extension

Organizational Extension	Description	Initiatives
Local	Applications by a single organizational unit or institution and intended for local use	B2, B8, B11, B12, B13 B16, B17, B18, B20
National	Applications for nationwide services	B3, B5, B6, B7, B9, B10, B14, B15, B19, B21, B14, B22
Transnational	Applications extended to different nations	B1, B3, B4

Benefits

For the purpose of our taxonomy development, we consider benefits as the advantages perceived or the measured profit gained after the successful application of blockchain. In this regard, we were able to identify altogether 13 benefits, which we grouped into three main categories for interpretation purposes. The first set of benefits regards the fact that blockchain features offer new ways for achieving transparency, accountability, and authenticity at every transaction. The second set of benefits concern the advantages that regard the performance aspect of processes, while the last set highlights the successful implications of blockchain in terms of elevated security and risk management. Table 4 describes in detail each of the benefits identified and the distinction between them.

Table 4. Benefits

Benefits		Description	Initiatives
Liability	Transparency	Possibility of viewing at any time any transaction occurring on the chain	B2, B3, B5, B9, B10, B13, B15, B19, B21, B16
	Accountability	Availability of audit trail that can showcase by whom and when any transaction was made	B1, B11, B18, B19, B20
	Authenticity	Quality of data that remains unaltered and legitimate	B2, B5, B9, B14, B15
Performance	Efficiency gains	Efficiency gains due to the automation of the operations	B1, B2, B3, B5, B6, B7, B8, B10, B11, B12, B15, B18, B19, B21
	Cost reduction	Reduced cost and cost saving resulting from removal of intermediaries, faster operations, lower capital requirements	B1, B5, B6, B7, B8, B10, B11, B12, B15, B16, B21, B22
	Time reduction	Reduction of time in performing different various processes	B1, B7, B18, B22
	Fault tolerance	Ability of a system to continue to reach consensus despite malicious activity	B5
	Reduction of human and procedural errors	Removal of interfaces where human errors could have an impact upon	B12, B16, B21, B22
	Streamline of Procedures	Reduction of long bureaucratic procedures and operations	B3, B16, B18
	Interoperability	Capability to share and exchange information easily through various blockchain systems	B2, B3, B19
Security	Immutability	Capability of information and transactions stored in blockchain to remain unalterable and private if needed	B1, B2, B4, B7, B12, B13, B14, B18, B19, B20, B21
	Compliance	Capability to operate under complex and stringent regulatory environments	B3, B10, B16, B19
	Resiliency	Capability to operate as a decentralized network without a single point of failure	B7, B8, B9, B10, B15, B20

Risks and Challenges

We identify the risks and challenges as the issues and constraints observed in association with the application of blockchain in various pilots or full functioning projects. We show a classification of the 16 different challenges identified into four main categories. Internal organizational constraints regard the issues related to the people or policies of the organization where blockchain has been applied to. Operational constraints regard the limitations observed from an operational perspective, while regulatory constraints related to laws and regulations, or a/the lack thereof of proper legislation concerning blockchain. Lastly, technological constraints regard the restrictions related to the technology itself, either due to its architecture or other individual features that are perceived as problematic. The risks and challenges are indicated in Table 5.

Table 5. Risks and challenges

Risks and Challenges		Description	Initiatives
Internal Organizational Constraints	High transaction / running cost	Any fees regarding the development, maintenance and running of blockchain	B2, B3, B10, B12, B16
	Distrusting organizational culture	Lack of trust in adopting blockchain and/or changing the way of doing things	B1, B6
	Lack of proper understanding	Lack of proper information on how blockchain functions or negative public perception regarding blockchain	B1, B3, B18
Operational Constraints	Lack of expertise	Limited knowledge and experience with blockchain and need of new resources	B3, B10, B18, B14
	Infrastructure immaturity	Lack of infrastructure to maintain the network and nodes and avoiding interruptions at any time	B9, B14, B22
	Scalability	Lack of capability to process very large amount of transaction data in a short amount of time	B4, B7, B8, B10, B19, B20
Regulatory Constraints	Regulatory uncertainty	Lack of regulations, especially related to information sharing and reporting	B8, B16, B22
	Law volatility	Uncertainty of how to manage smart contracts in the light of changes in law, considering their immutability feature	B16
	Lack of frameworks	Absence of frameworks regulating governance, control, and risk management	B2
Technological Constraints	Premature technology	Lack of stable, proper development of blockchain	B20, B21
	Data confidentiality	Concerns over privacy, the long-term preservation of data, concurrence with existing rules	B2, B5, B20, B21, B14, B22
	Security concerns	Various security risks and vulnerabilities associated with a still new technology	B2, B16, B20, B14
	Immutability	Difficulties in changing the records if a mistake has been made or if a law changed	B11, B16
	Reliability	Unreliability of records due to various threats, such as third parties or minimal control over nodes	B14
	No added value	Stance on traditional IT systems suffice to integrate processes without the need of introducing blockchain	B16, B21
	High energy consumption	Huge power consumption by blockchain	B5, B20

Public Value

The last dimension identified in our taxonomy regards public value, defined as the value that a successful blockchain application may contribute to the society. It could be considered as a benefit with a wider scope. Differently from Cledou et al. (2018) who simply link public value to different benefits perceived by users through smart mobility services but do not consider it a taxonomy dimension of its own, we consider public value as a separate dimension according to the high presence in the application cases and literature reviewed. Table 6 depicts the five different public values identified by this study.

Table 6. Public value

Public Value	Description	Initiatives
Trust	Establishment or increase of public trust in the public organizations or public services and policies	B2, B3, B4, B5, B6, B7, B9, B15, B16, B17, B22
Democracy	Enforcement of democratic values including, but not limited to, equality, social justice, diversity	B13
Legitimacy	Conformity to law or accordance with rules and regulations	B19
Multilateralism	Stimulation of public administrations to foster collaboration between countries	B3
Efficiency	Increased efficiency of public services	B1, B2, B8, B10, B11, B12, B18, B20, B21
Anti-Fraud	Prevention of fraudulent behavior and corruption	B5, B6, B13, B14, B18

Findings per Case Study

Based on the results emerging from the taxonomy, a comprehensive summary of the categories per dimension that each case study is associated with is depicted in Table 7. As is portrayed from the table, each blockchain initiative alongside its distinctive characteristics, has been noted to offer a series of distinctive benefits, while also facing various challenges during implementation.

Table 7. Summary of findings per case study

Blockchain Initiative	Use Cases	Org. Extension	Benefits	Risks & Challenges	Public Value
UN Joint Staff Pension Fund	Identity management	Transnational	• Accountability • Cost reduction • Efficiency gains • Time reduction • Immutability	• Distrusting organizational culture • Lack of proper understanding	Efficiency
Chancheng - China	Digital records	Local	• Transparency • Authenticity • Efficiency gains • Interoperability • Immutability	• High transaction / running cost • Lack of frameworks • Data confidentiality • Security concerns	Trust, Efficiency
X-Road - Estonia	Digital records, Bills and payments	National Transnational	• Transparency • Efficiency gains • Streamline of Procedures • Interoperability • Compliance	• Lack of expertise • High transaction / running cost • Lack of proper understanding	Trust, Multilateralism
The British National Archives Archangel Project - UK	Digital records	Transnational	• Immutability	• Scalability	Trust
Exonum land title registry - Georgia	Digital records	National	• Transparency • Authenticity • Efficiency gains • Cost reduction • Fault tolerance	• High energy consumption • Data confidentiality	Trust, Anti-Fraud
Blockcerts academic records - Malta	Identity management	National	• Efficiency gains • Cost reduction	• Distrusting organizational culture	Trust, Anti-Fraud
Chromaway property transactions - Sweden	Digital records	National	• Efficiency gains • Cost reduction • Time reduction • Immutability • Resiliency	• Scalability	Trust
uPort decentralized identity - Switzerland	Identity management	Local	• Efficiency gains • Cost reduction • Resiliency	• Regulatory uncertainty • Scalability	Efficiency
Infrachain governance framework - Luxemburg		National	• Transparency • Authenticity • Resiliency	• Infrastructure immaturity	Trust
Pension Infrastructure – the Netherlands	Digital records, Bills and payments	National	• Transparency • Efficiency gains • Cost reduction • Compliance • Resiliency	• Scalability • High transaction / running cost • Lack of expertise	Efficiency
Stjaderpas smart vouchers – the Netherlands	Welfare distribution	Local	• Accountability • Efficiency gains • Cost reduction	• Immutability	Efficiency
Delaware Public archives - USA	Digital records, Legal enforcement	Local	• Efficiency gains • Cost reduction • Reduction of human and procedural errors • Immutability	• High transaction / running cost	Efficiency
Electronic voting - South Korea	E-voting	Local	• Transparency • Immutability • Authenticity	• Regulatory uncertainty	Democracy, Anti-Fraud
Factom Land registry - Honduras	Digital records	National	• Immutability	• Lack of expertise • Infrastructure immaturity • Data confidentiality • Security concerns • Reliability	Anti-Fraud

Continued on following page   253

Table 7. Continued

Blockchain Initiative	Use Cases	Org. Extension	Benefits	Risks & Challenges	Public Value
Vehicle wallet partnership - Denmark	Supply chain	National	• Efficiency gains • Resiliency • Authenticity • Transparency • Cost reduction	N/A	Trust
Syddjurs municipality - Denmark	Bills and payments	Local	• Cost reduction • Reduction of human and procedural errors • Streamline of Procedures • Compliance	• High transaction / running cost • Regulatory uncertainty • Law volatility • Security concerns • Immutability • No added value	Trust
Bengal birth certificate - India	Digital records	Local	• Immutability • Authenticity	• Lack of expertise • High transaction/ running cost	Trust
Smart City Dubai - UAE	Digital records, Bills and payments	Local	• Accountability • Efficiency gains • Time reduction • Streamline of Procedures • Immutability	• Lack of proper understanding • Lack of expertise	Anti-Fraud, Efficiency
Asylum Procedure - Germany	Digital records, Legal enforcement	National	• Transparency • Accountability • Efficiency gains • Interoperability • Immutability • Compliance	• Scalability	Legitimacy
Illinois Blockchain Initiative	Digital records	Local	• Transparency • Accountability • Immutability • Resiliency	• Scalability • Premature technology • Data confidentiality • Security concerns • High energy consumption	Efficiency
Project Jasper – Bank of Canada	Bills and payments	National	• Efficiency gains • Cost reduction • Reduction of human and procedural errors • Immutability	• Premature technology • Data confidentiality • No added value	Efficiency
Food Standards Agency - UK	Supply chain	National	• Time reduction • Cost reduction • Reduction of human and procedural errors	• Data confidentiality • Regulatory uncertainty • Infrastructure immaturity	Trust

DISCUSSION AND IMPLICATIONS

The diffusion of an emergent technology, especially until there is a high uncertainty around it, is always associated with comparing incremental benefits that would come with a successful adoption and the cost attached to such a move (Hall and Khan, 2003). Similarly, two main dimensions emerging in our taxonomy are benefits and risks. Comprehending the various gains witnessed in different initiatives around the world would aid in an easier acceptance of the technology. As regards benefits, it should be specified though that the benefits, despite being generalized and coming from different sources, should not be taken at face value. De Giovanni (2019) in his study regarding the application of blockchain in eco-digital supply chains makes a point in stating that advantages of implementing blockchain, despite being theoretically evident, should be accompanied by detailed analysis in terms of the involved costs or the real convenience.

Similarly, the second important emerging dimension are the constraints and challenges coming along with this technology. Risk identification is considered the first step in managing risks and minimizing any hiccups that may arise (Tchankova, 2002). This makes it possible for some risk to be mitigated and addressed already at a pre-implementation phase. In addition, considering that some risks recognized in literature are associated with technical aspects of blockchain, their identification should also motivate developers at looking into blockchain to recognize possible improvements. This would elevate the status of blockchain and help further applications of blockchain, not only in the public domain.

Public value is another important dimension considering the domain under consideration. For Moore (1995), public value is one of the main components of his famous triangle depicting the main elements for a strategic management in the public sector. Similarly, Meynhardt et al., (2017) states that the value of public administrations is closely connected to the public value they provide through their services. It should be also underlined that any system change aimed at public service transformation should put public value at the top of the change process in the public domain (Tonurist et al., 2019). Therefore, by evidencing the various public values that blockchain is able to contribute to could be expected to help in delineating the importance of this technology in the public domain.

This taxonomy aims to establish a better understanding of blockchain applications and facilitate the sharing of knowledge about blockchain initiatives and their outcomes. We expect its main findings and classifications to support both decision-makers and academic researchers wishing to explore the topic. The implications are both for practice and research and can be summarized as following.

For policy makers in the public domain interested in implementing blockchain in their practices and institutions, this taxonomy is a starting point for understanding the variety of scopes a blockchain adoption relate to, also through several use cases presented. Also, it aids policy makers to consider the benefits and risks associated with its application, and the possible.

We believe this taxonomy to have important implications for academic research. Considering that the taxonomies created around blockchain have predominantly focused on the technical characteristics, an outcome-based taxonomy defines a new mapping and standardization of information regarding blockchain. In addition, this study bridges the need for investigation of blockchain in public domain and the limited research encompassing different areas of the public domain.

CHALLENGES, LIMITATIONS AND FUTURE RESEARCH DIRECTIONS

The main challenge observed during this study refers to the scarcity of detailed data on the results of the blockchain applications in the various sectors provided in most studies. Very often, the blockchain application is associated with what can be considered as expected benefits and implications, yet not supplemented with empirical findings certifying the claims. Another challenge regards the lack of a repository regarding blockchain initiatives per country. Some countries have indeed written reports on some of their initiatives, but such reports are still impaired due to different reasons. The first reason being that they are not yearly reports, thus do not offer a follow-up on important initiatives. Additionally, such reports mostly aim at studying successful cases: despite their importance, they do not cover pilot projects or prototypes that, albeit having failed, would offer an insightful view on the reasons behind such failures.

In terms of possible limitations, this study focuses on applications undertaken in the public domain. Being the blockchain adopted in many fields, it is important to consider that results could differentiate based on the domain of study. Furthermore, new blockchain applications are being deployed every day, which may raise the need to extend the taxonomy or compress it in case some of the issues have been addressed. Still referring to the need of progressing research on blockchain, this study creates the opportunity for further investigations looking more specifically to possible connections between our taxonomy and technical values researched by previous studies. This would shed light on possible links between blockchain outcomes and some technical characteristic, such as type of blockchain, consensus mechanisms, encryption.

Additionally, it would be interesting a similar study adapted to the private sector, to see whether there exist differentiations based on the nature of the industry blockchain is applied to. Also, considering that most research on blockchain today aims at improving the limitations of the technology from an architecture and security point, future studies could shift the attention on challenges going beyond the technical perspective.

CONCLUSION

Since its introduction, blockchain has become an ever-growing topic of interest and has seen a surge in applications in various domains. There has been an increase in governmental initiatives around the world to explore further this technology, with many institutions and organizations in the public domain already having started to implement blockchain for various scopes and purposes.

In this paper we propose a taxonomy able of classifying the outcomes of the aforementioned initiatives in the public domain. Different from previous taxonomies, our study shifts the focus from the technical characteristics of blockchain to the implications regarding its adoption. Along the process, we recognized six different dimensions, each with its own characteristics and features. In addition, through extensive literature research, this study provides a list of some important initiatives in public domain and matches these initiatives with the dimensions recognized in the taxonomy.

This study contributes to the current state of research on blockchain by providing a new way of classifying blockchain applications and, more specifically, by focusing on the public domain where such studies lack. The proposed taxonomy offers valuable insight to policy makers considering adopting blockchain, by offering an overview of the lessons learned from previous applications. It also enables decision makers to understand the possible challenges, offering the opportunity of tackling potential constraints in an initial phase.

REFERENCES

Adeodato, R., & Pournouri, S. (2020). Secure Implementation of E-Governance: A Case Study About Estonia. In *Cyber Defence in the Age of AI, Smart Societies and Augmented Humanity* (pp. 397–429). Springer. doi:10.1007/978-3-030-35746-7_18

Al Barghuthi, N. B., Ncube, C., & Said, H. (2019, November). State of Art of the Effectiveness in Adopting Blockchain Technology-UAE Survey Study. In 2019 Sixth HCT Information Technology Trends (ITT) (pp. 54-59). IEEE. doi:10.1109/ITT48889.2019.9075108

Alharby, M., & Van Moorsel, A. (2017). *Blockchain-based smart contracts: A systematic mapping study.* arXiv preprint arXiv:1710.06372. doi:10.5121/csit.2017.71011

Alkhalifah, A., Ng, A., Kayes, A. S. M., Chowdhury, J., Alazab, M., & Watters, P. A. (2020). A taxonomy of blockchain threats and vulnerabilities. In *Blockchain for Cybersecurity and Privacy* (pp. 3–28). CRC Press. doi:10.1201/9780429324932-2

Alketbi, A., Nasir, Q., & Talib, M. A. (2020). Novel blockchain reference model for government services: Dubai government case study. *International Journal of System Assurance Engineering and Management, 11*(6), 1170–1191.

Al-Megren, S., Alsalamah, S., Altoaimy, L., Alsalamah, H., Soltanisehat, L., & Almutairi, E. (2018, July). Blockchain use cases in digital sectors: A review of the literature. In *2018 IEEE International Conference on Internet of Things (iThings) and IEEE Green Computing and Communications (GreenCom) and IEEE Cyber, Physical and Social Computing (CPSCom) and IEEE Smart Data (SmartData)* (pp. 1417-1424). IEEE. 10.1109/Cybermatics_2018.2018.00242

Beck, R., Stenum Czepluch, J., Lollike, N., & Malone, S. (2016). *Blockchain–the gateway to trust-free cryptographic transactions*. Academic Press.

Beck, R., Avital, M., Rossi, M., & Thatcher, J. B. (2017). *Blockchain technology in business and information systems research*. Academic Press.

Berryhill, J., Bourgery, T., & Hanson, A. (2018). *Blockchains unchained: Blockchain technology and its use in the public sector*. Academic Press.

Bhatia, S., & Wright de Hernandez, A. D. (2019). Blockchain is already here. What does that mean for records management and archives? *Journal of Archival Organization*, *16*(1), 75–84. doi:10.1080/15332748.2019.1655614

Brandon, D. (2016). The blockchain: The future of business information systems. *International Journal of the Academic Business World*, *10*(2), 33–40.

Bui, T., Cooper, D., Collomosse, J., Bell, M., Green, A., Sheridan, J., Higgins, J., Das, A., Keller, J. R., & Thereaux, O. (2020). Tamper-proofing video with hierarchical attention autoencoder hashing on blockchain. *IEEE Transactions on Multimedia*, *22*(11), 2858–2872. doi:10.1109/TMM.2020.2967640

Carter, L., & Ubacht, J. (2018, May). Blockchain applications in government. In *Proceedings of the 19th Annual International Conference on Digital Government Research: governance in the data age* (pp. 1-2). 10.1145/3209281.3209329

Casino, F., Dasaklis, T. K., & Patsakis, C. (2019). A systematic literature review of blockchain-based applications: Current status, classification and open issues. *Telematics and Informatics*, *36*, 55–81. doi:10.1016/j.tele.2018.11.006

Chellasamy, A., & N, A. (2019). An Outlook in Blockchain Technology- Architecture, Applications and Challenges. *International Journal of Engineering Research & Technology (Ahmedabad)*, *12*(12), 1–5.

Cledou, G., Estevez, E., & Barbosa, L. S. (2018). A taxonomy for planning and designing smart mobility services. *Government Information Quarterly*, *35*(1), 61–76. doi:10.1016/j.giq.2017.11.008

Cong, L. W., & He, Z. (2019). Blockchain disruption and smart contracts. *Review of Financial Studies, 32*(5), 1754–1797. doi:10.1093/rfs/hhz007

Constantinides, P., Henfridsson, O., & Parker, G. G. (2018). *Introduction—platforms and infrastructures in the digital age.* Academic Press.

De GiovanniP. (2019). Eco-Digital Supply Chains Through Blockchains. Available at SSRN 3488925.

Deloitte. (2018). *Blockchain in Public Sector Transforming government services through exponential technologies.* Retrieved from https://www2.deloitte.com/content/dam/Deloitte/in/Documents/public-sector/in-ps-blockchain-noexp.pdf

European Commission. (2018). *Case Study Report e-Estonia.* Retrieved from https://jiip.eu/mop/wp/wp-content/uploads/2018/10/EE_e-Estonia_Castanos.pdf

European Commission. (2019). *Blockchain for digital government.* Retrieved from https://joinup.ec.europa.eu/sites/default/files/document/2019-04/JRC115049%20blockchain%20for%20digital%20government.pdf

Glass, R. L., & Vessey, I. (1995). Contemporary application-domain taxonomies. *IEEE Software, 12*(4), 63–76. doi:10.1109/52.391837

Goderdzishvili, N., Gordadze, E., & Gagnidze, N. (2018, April). Georgia's Blockchain-powered Property Registration: Never blocked, Always Secured: Ownership Data Kept Best! In *Proceedings of the 11th International Conference on Theory and Practice of Electronic Governance* (pp. 673-675). 10.1145/3209415.3209437

Hall, B. H., & Khan, B. (2003). *Adoption of new technology* (No. w9730). National Bureau of Economic Research.

Hollyer, J. R., Rosendorff, B. P., & Vreeland, J. R. (2011). Democracy and transparency. *The Journal of Politics, 73*(4), 1191–1205. doi:10.1017/S0022381611000880

Hou, H. (2017, July). The application of blockchain technology in E-government in China. In *2017 26th International Conference on Computer Communication and Networks (ICCCN)* (pp. 1-4). IEEE. 10.1109/ICCCN.2017.8038519

Hyvärinen, H., Risius, M., & Friis, G. (2017). A blockchain-based approach towards overcoming financial fraud in public sector services. *Business & Information Systems Engineering, 59*(6), 441–456. doi:10.100712599-017-0502-4

Iansiti, M., & Lakhami, K. (2017). The Truth About Blockchain. *Harvard Business Review.* Retrieved 1 June 2021, from https://hbr.org/2017/01/the-truth-about-blockchain

Jagrat, C. P., & Channegowda, J. (2020, February). A Survey of Blockchain Based Government Infrastructure Information. In *2020 International Conference on Mainstreaming Block Chain Implementation (ICOMBI)* (pp. 1-5). IEEE. 10.23919/ ICOMBI48604.2020.9203152

Konashevych, O. (2017, June). The concept of the blockchain-based governing: Current issues and general vision. In *Proceedings of 17th European Conference on Digital Government ECDG* (p. 79). Academic Press.

Krogsbøll, M., Borre, L. H., Slaats, T., & Debois, S. (2020, February). Smart Contracts for Government Processes: Case Study and Prototype Implementation (Short Paper). In *International Conference on Financial Cryptography and Data Security* (pp. 676-684). Springer. 10.1007/978-3-030-51280-4_36

Labazova, O., Dehling, T., & Sunyaev, A. (2019, January). From hype to reality: A taxonomy of blockchain applications. *Proceedings of the 52nd Hawaii International Conference on System Sciences (HICSS 2019)*. 10.24251/HICSS.2019.552

Lacheca, D. (2021). *Case Study: Digital Transformation of a Legacy Paper-Based Process (U.N. Joint Staff Pension Fund)*. Gartner. Retrieved from https://www. gartner.com/en/documents/3996055/case-study-digital-transformation-of-a-legacy-paper-base

Lemieux, V. L. (2016). Trusting records: Is Blockchain technology the answer? *Records Management Journal, 26*(2), 110–139. doi:10.1108/RMJ-12-2015-0042

Majchrzak, A., Markus, M. L., & Wareham, J. (2016). Designing for digital transformation: Lessons for information systems research from the study of ICT and societal challenges. *Management Information Systems Quarterly, 40*(2), 267–277. doi:10.25300/MISQ/2016/40:2.03

Meynhardt, T., Brieger, S. A., Strathoff, P., Anderer, S., Bäro, A., Hermann, C., & Gomez, P. (2017). Public value performance: What does it mean to create value in the public sector? In *Public sector management in a globalized world* (pp. 135–160). Springer Gabler. doi:10.1007/978-3-658-16112-5_8

Moore, M. H. (1995). *Creating public value: Strategic management in government*. Harvard university press.

Mueller, B. (2020). Why public policies fail: Policymaking under complexity. *Economía, 21*(2), 311–323. doi:10.1016/j.econ.2019.11.002

Nickerson, R. C., Varshney, U., & Muntermann, J. (2013). A method for taxonomy development and its application in information systems. *European Journal of Information Systems*, *22*(3), 336–359. doi:10.1057/ejis.2012.26

Ojo, A., & Adebayo, S. (2017). Blockchain as a next generation government information infrastructure: A review of initiatives in D5 countries. *Government 3.0–Next Generation Government Technology Infrastructure and Services*, 283-298.

Ølnes, S. (2016, September). Beyond bitcoin enabling smart government using blockchain technology. In *International conference on electronic government* (pp. 253-264). Springer. 10.1007/978-3-319-44421-5_20

Pilichowski, E., & Turkisch, E. (2008). *Employment in Government in the Perspective of the Production Costs of Goods and Services in the Public Domain*. OECD Working Papers On Public Governance. doi:10.1787/19934351

Qi, R., Feng, C., Liu, Z., & Mrad, N. (2017). Blockchain-powered internet of things, e-governance and e-democracy. In *E-Democracy for Smart Cities* (pp. 509–520). Springer. doi:10.1007/978-981-10-4035-1_17

Rana, N. P., Dwivedi, Y. K., & Hughes, D. L. (2021). Analysis of challenges for blockchain adoption within the Indian public sector: An interpretive structural modelling approach. *Information Technology & People*. Advance online publication. doi:10.1108/ITP-07-2020-0460

Reddick, C. G. (2021). Analyzing the Case for Adopting Distributed Ledger Technology in the Bank of Canada. In *Blockchain and the Public Sector* (pp. 219–238). Springer. doi:10.1007/978-3-030-55746-1_10

Rieger, A., Stohr, A., Wenninger, A., & Fridgen, G. (2021). Reconciling Blockchain with the GDPR: Insights from the German Asylum Procedure. In *Blockchain and the Public Sector* (pp. 73–95). Springer. doi:10.1007/978-3-030-55746-1_4

Rossi, M., Mueller-Bloch, C., Thatcher, J. B., & Beck, R. (2019). Blockchain research in information systems: Current trends and an inclusive future research agenda. *Journal of the Association for Information Systems*, *20*(9), 14. doi:10.17705/1jais.00571

Rot, A., Sobińska, M., Hernes, M., & Franczyk, B. (2020). Digital Transformation of Public Administration Through Blockchain Technology. In *Towards Industry 4.0—Current Challenges in Information Systems* (pp. 111–126). Springer. doi:10.1007/978-3-030-40417-8_7

Sarkintudu, S. M., Ibrahim, H. H., & Abdwahab, A. B. (2018, September). Taxonomy development of blockchain platforms: Information systems perspectives. In. AIP Conference Proceedings: Vol. 2016. *No. 1* (p. 020130). AIP Publishing LLC. doi:10.1063/1.5055532

Shin, D. D. (2019). Blockchain: The emerging technology of digital trust. *Telematics and Informatics, 45,* 101278. doi:10.1016/j.tele.2019.101278

Sobolewski, M., & Allessie, D. (2021). Blockchain Applications in the Public Sector: Investigating Seven Real-Life Blockchain Deployments and Their Benefits. In *Blockchain and the Public Sector* (pp. 97–126). Springer. doi:10.1007/978-3-030-55746-1_5

Sullivan, C. (2021). Blockchain-Based Identity: The Advantages and Disadvantages. In *Blockchain and the Public Sector* (pp. 197–218). Springer. doi:10.1007/978-3-030-55746-1_9

Sun Yin, H. H., Langenheldt, K., Harlev, M., Mukkamala, R. R., & Vatrapu, R. (2019). Regulating cryptocurrencies: A supervised machine learning approach to de-anonymizing the bitcoin blockchain. *Journal of Management Information Systems, 36*(1), 37–73. doi:10.1080/07421222.2018.1550550

Tasca, P., & Tessone, C. (2019). A Taxonomy of Blockchain Technologies: Principles of Identification and Classification. *Ledger, 4.* Advance online publication. doi:10.5195/ledger.2019.140

Tchankova, L. (2002). Risk identification–basic stage in risk management. *Environmental Management and Health, 13*(3), 290–297. doi:10.1108/09566160210431088

Thakur, V., Doja, M. N., Dwivedi, Y. K., Ahmad, T., & Khadanga, G. (2020). Land records on blockchain for implementation of land titling in India. *International Journal of Information Management, 52,* 101940. doi:10.1016/j.ijinfomgt.2019.04.013

Tonurist, P., & Cook, J. (2019). *Public Value in Public Service Transformation Working with Change.* OECD. Retrieved from https://www.oecd.org/governance/public-value-in-public-service-transformation-47c17892-en.htm

Vial, G. (2019). Understanding digital transformation: A review and a research agenda. *The Journal of Strategic Information Systems, 28*(2), 118–144. doi:10.1016/j.jsis.2019.01.003

Warkentin, M., & Orgeron, C. (2020). Using the security triad to assess blockchain technology in public sector applications. *International Journal of Information Management, 52,* 102090. doi:10.1016/j.ijinfomgt.2020.102090

Weking, J., Mandalenakis, M., Hein, A., Hermes, S., Böhm, M., & Krcmar, H. (2019). The impact of blockchain technology on business models–a taxonomy and archetypal patterns. *Electronic Markets*, 1–21.

Wieninger, S., Schuh, G., & Fischer, V. (2019, June). Development of a Blockchain Taxonomy. In *2019 IEEE International Conference on Engineering, Technology and Innovation (ICE/ITMC)* (pp. 1-9). IEEE.

World Economic Forum. (2020). *Inclusive Deployment of Blockchain: Case Studies and Learnings from the United Arab Emirates*. Retrieved from https://www3. weforum.org/docs/WEF_Inclusive_Deployment_of_Blockchain_Case_Studies_ and_Learnings_from_the_United_Emirates.pdf

Xu, X., Weber, I., Staples, M., Zhu, L., Bosch, J., Bass, L., . . . Rimba, P. (2017, April). A taxonomy of blockchain-based systems for architecture design. In 2017 IEEE international conference on software architecture (ICSA) (pp. 243-252). IEEE. doi:10.1109/ICSA.2017.33

Zhang, S., & Lee, J. H. (2020). Analysis of the main consensus protocols of blockchain. *ICT Express, 6*(2), 93-97.

ADDITIONAL READING

Batubara, F. R., Ubacht, J., & Janssen, M. (2018, May). Challenges of blockchain technology adoption for e-government: a systematic literature review. In *Proceedings of the 19th Annual International Conference on Digital Government Research: Governance in the Data Age* (pp. 1-9). 10.1145/3209281.3209317

Bolívar, M. P. R., Scholl, H. J., & Pomeshchikov, R. (2021). Stakeholders' Perspectives on Benefits and Challenges in Blockchain Regulatory Frameworks. In *Blockchain and the Public Sector* (pp. 1–18). Springer. doi:10.1007/978-3-030-55746-1_1

Datta, A. (2021). Blockchain Enabled Digital Government and Public Sector Services: A Survey. In Blockchain and the Public Sector (pp. 175-195). Springer.

Ølnes, S., & Jansen, A. (2018, May). Blockchain technology as infrastructure in public sector: an analytical framework. In *Proceedings of the 19th Annual International Conference on Digital Government Research: Governance in the Data Age* (pp. 1-10).

Salnikova, O., Lagodiienko, V., Ivanchenkova, L., Kopytko, V., Kulak, N., & Usachenko, O. (2019). Evaluation of the effectiveness of implementation blockchain technology in public administration.

Spagnoletti, P., Kazemargi, N., Constantinides, P., & Prencipe, P. (2022). Data control coordination in cloud-based ecosystems. In C. Cennamo, G. B. Dagnino, & F. Zhu (Eds.), *Handbook of Research on Digital Strategy*.

Sujatha, R., Navaneethan, C., Kaluri, R., & Prasanna, S. (2020). Optimized Digital Transformation in Government Services with Blockchain. *Blockchain Technology and Applications*, 79-100.

Wessel, L., Baiyere, A., Ologeanu-Taddei, R., Cha, J., & Blegind-Jensen, T. (2021). Unpacking the difference between digital transformation and IT-enabled organizational transformation. *Journal of the Association for Information Systems*, *22*(1), 102–129. doi:10.17705/1jais.00655

KEY TERMS AND DEFINITIONS

Blockchain: A decentralized digital ledger that records executed transactions in the form of blocks with a cryptographic hash and specific timestamp.

Digital Transformation: A transformation referring to the change in business processes and culture due the introduction of digital technology.

Distributed Ledger: A type of a database that records digital transactions whose information and details are documented in multiple places simultaneously.

Public Domain: The services owned and controlled by the government and/or despite being private are funded by governmental authorities.

Public Value: The benefits and rights contributing to the society.

Smart Contract: A self-executing contract whose terms and agreements are written in the form of computer code that ensure the execution of transactions.

Taxonomy: A system of classification according to predefined specific criteria.

Compilation of References

Abdo, J. B., & Zeadally, S. (2020). Multi-utility framework: Blockchain exchange platform for sustainable development. *International Journal of Pervasive Computing and Communications*.

Abeyratne, S., & Monfared, R. (2016). Blockchain Ready Manufacturing Supply Chain Using Distributed Ledger. *International Journal of Research in Engineering and Technology, 5*.

Abeyratne, S. A., & Monfared, R. P. (2016). Blockchain ready manufacturing supply chain using distributed ledger. *International Journal of Research in Engineering and Technology, 5*(9), 1–10. doi:10.15623/ijret.2016.0509001

Abuhantash, A., Grabski, J., Kobeissi, H., White, M., & Sykes, O. (2019). Establishing Blockchain Policy. Academic Press.

ACRAM. (2021, April 28). *ACRAM - Lattoprelevatori di campioni al ricevimento*. Retrieved from, from https://acram.it/it/prodotti/trattamento-acque/lattoprelevatori-di-campioni-al-ricevimento/

Adeodato, R., & Pournouri, S. (2020). Secure Implementation of E-Governance: A Case Study About Estonia. In *Cyber Defence in the Age of AI, Smart Societies and Augmented Humanity* (pp. 397–429). Springer. doi:10.1007/978-3-030-35746-7_18

Adeyemi, A., Yan, M., Shahidehpour, M., Botero, C., Guerra, A. V., Gurung, N., Zhang, L. C., & Paaso, A. (2020). Blockchain technology applications in power distribution systems. *The Electricity Journal, 33*(8), 106817. doi:10.1016/j.tej.2020.106817

Agrawal, P., & Narain, R. (2018). Digital supply chain management: An Overview. *IOP Conf. Ser.*

Ahmed, S., & Broek, N. (2017). Blockchain could boost food security. *Nature, 550*(7674), 43. doi:10.1038/550043e PMID:28980633

Ailawadi, K. L., & Farris, P. W. (2017). Managing Multi- and Omni-Channel Distribution: Metrics and Research Directions. *Journal of Retailing, 93*(1), 120–135. doi:10.1016/j.jretai.2016.12.003

Akbari, M., Khodayari, M., Khaleghi, A., Danesh, M., & Padash, H. (2020). Technological innovation research in the last six decades: A bibliometric analysis. *European Journal of Innovation Management*. Advance online publication. doi:10.1108/EJIM-05-2020-0166

Al Barghuthi, N. B., Ncube, C., & Said, H. (2019, November). State of Art of the Effectiveness in Adopting Blockchain Technology-UAE Survey Study. In 2019 Sixth HCT Information Technology Trends (ITT) (pp. 54-59). IEEE. doi:10.1109/ITT48889.2019.9075108

Albort-Morant, G., & Ribeiro-Soriano, D. (2016). A bibliometric analysis of international impact of business incubators. *Journal of Business Research*, *69*(5), 1775–1779. doi:10.1016/j.jbusres.2015.10.054

Alcarria, R., Bordel, B., Robles, T., Martín, D., & Manso-Callejo, M. Á. (2018). A blockchain-based authorization system for trustworthy resource monitoring and trading in smart communities. *Sensors (Basel)*, *18*(10), 3561. doi:10.339018103561 PMID:30347844

Alharby, M., & Van Moorsel, A. (2017). *Blockchain-based smart contracts: A systematic mapping study.* arXiv preprint arXiv:1710.06372. doi:10.5121/csit.2017.71011

Ali, M. H., Tan, K. H., & Ismail, M. D. (2017a). A supply chain integrity framework for halal food. *British Food Journal*, *119*(1), 20–38. doi:10.1108/BFJ-07-2016-0345

Ali, M. H., Zhan, Y., Alam, S. S., Tse, Y. K., & Tan, K. H. (2017b). Food supply chain integrity: The need to go beyond certification. *Industrial Management & Data Systems*, *117*(8), 1589–1611. doi:10.1108/IMDS-09-2016-0357

Alketbi, A., Nasir, Q., & Talib, M. A. (2020). Novel blockchain reference model for government services: Dubai government case study. *International Journal of System Assurance Engineering and Management*, *11*(6), 1170–1191.

Alkhalifah, A., Ng, A., Kayes, A. S. M., Chowdhury, J., Alazab, M., & Watters, P. A. (2020). A taxonomy of blockchain threats and vulnerabilities. In *Blockchain for Cybersecurity and Privacy* (pp. 3–28). CRC Press. doi:10.1201/9780429324932-2

Alkhudary, R., Brusset, X., & Fenies, P. (2020). Blockchain in general management and economics: A systematic literature review. *European Business Review*, *32*(4), 765–783. doi:10.1108/EBR-11-2019-0297

Al-Megren, S., Alsalamah, S., Altoaimy, L., Alsalamah, H., Soltanisehat, L., & Almutairi, E. (2018, July). Blockchain use cases in digital sectors: A review of the literature. In *2018 IEEE International Conference on Internet of Things (iThings) and IEEE Green Computing and Communications (GreenCom) and IEEE Cyber, Physical and Social Computing (CPSCom) and IEEE Smart Data (SmartData)* (pp. 1417-1424). IEEE. 10.1109/Cybermatics_2018.2018.00242

Alnafrah, I., Bogdanova, E., & Maximova, T. (2019). Text mining as a facilitating tool for deploying blockchain technology in the intellectual property rights system. *International Journal of Intellectual Property Management*, *9*(2), 120–135. doi:10.1504/IJIPM.2019.100207

Angeles, R. (2005). Rfid Technologies: Supply-Chain Applications and Implementation Issues. *Information Systems Management*, *35*(2), 60–64. doi:10.1201/1078/44912.22.1.20051201/85739.7

Antonopoulos, A. M., & Wood, G. (2018). *Mastering Ethereum - Building smart contracts and apps.* O'Reilly Media, Inc.

Antonucci, F., Figorilli, S., Costa, C., Pallottino, F., Raso, L., & Menesatti, P. (2019). A Review on blockchain applications in the agri-food sector. *Journal of the Science of Food and Agriculture*, *99*(14), 6129–6138. doi:10.1002/jsfa.9912 PMID:31273793

Appolloni, A., & Cheng, W. (2021). *Sustainable Procurement: knowledge and practice towards sustainable development*. Giappichelli.

Apte, S., & Petrovsky, N. (2016). Will blockchain technology revolutionize excipient supply chain management? *Journal of Excipients and Food Chemicals*, *7*(3).

Aste, T., Tasca, P., & Di Matteo, T. (2017). Blockchain Technologies: The Foreseeable Impact on Society and Industry. *Computer*, *50*(9), 18–28. doi:10.1109/MC.2017.3571064

Auger, P., Devinney, T. M., Louviere, J. J., & Burke, P. F. (2008). Do social product features have value to consumers? *International Journal of Research in Marketing*, *25*(3), 183–191. doi:10.1016/j.ijresmar.2008.03.005

Aung, M. M., & Chang, Y. S. (2014). Traceability in a food supply chain: Safety and quality perspectives. *Food Control*, *39*, 172–184. doi:10.1016/j.foodcont.2013.11.007

Australian Government. (2020). *The national blockchain roadmap*. Author.

Ayoade, G., Karande, V., Khan, L., & Hamlen, K. (2018). Decentralized IoT data management using blockchain and trusted execution environment. *Proceedings - 2018 IEEE 19th International Conference on Information Reuse and Integration for Data Science, IRI 2018*, 15–22. 10.1109/IRI.2018.00011

Ayoub, H. F., Abdallah, A. B., & Suifan, T. S. (2017). The effect of supply chain integration on technical innovation in Jordan: The mediating role of knowledge management. *Benchmarking*, *24*(3), 594–616. doi:10.1108/BIJ-06-2016-0088

Badia-Melis, R., Mishra, P., & Ruiz-García, L. (2015). Food traceability: New trends and recent advances. A review. *Food Control*, *57*, 393–401. doi:10.1016/j.foodcont.2015.05.005

Badzar, A. (2016). *An explorative study of blockchain technology in logistics*. Master.

Bai, Y. (2018). Researchain: Union Blockchain Based Scientific Research Project Management System. *Chinese Automation Congress (CAC)*, 4206-4209. 10.1109/CAC.2018.8623571

Bakker, P., Holdorf, D. B., & Cairns, A. (2020). *CEO Guide to Food System Transformation*. Available at: https://www.wbcsd.org/Programs/Food-and-Nature/Food-Land-Use/Resources/CEO-Guide-to-Food-System-Transformation

Baltzer, K. (2004). Consumers' willingness to pay for food quality – The case of eggs. *Food Economics - Acta Agriculturae Scandinavica, Section C, 1*(2), 78–90.

Banerjee, M., Lee, J., & Choo, K. K. R. (2018). A blockchain future for internet of things security: A position paper. *Digital Communications and Networks*, *4*(3), 149–160. doi:10.1016/j.dcan.2017.10.006

Beck, R., Avital, M., Rossi, M., & Thatcher, J. B. (2017). *Blockchain technology in business and information systems research*. Academic Press.

Beck, R., Stenum Czepluch, J., Lollike, N., & Malone, S. (2016). *Blockchain–the gateway to trust-free cryptographic transactions*. Academic Press.

Behnke, K., & Janssen, M. F. W. H. A. (2020). Boundary conditions for traceability in food supply chains using blockchain technology. *International Journal of Information Management*, *52*, 101969. doi:10.1016/j.ijinfomgt.2019.05.025

Bellifemine, F. L., Gotta, D., & Trucco, T. (2017). *System and method for managing supply of electric energy through certified measures*. patents.google.com/patent/WO2019081298A1/en

Beloglazov, A., Abawajy, J., & Buyya, R. (2012). Energy-aware resource allocation heuristics for efficient management of data centers for cloud computing. *Future Generation Computer Systems*, *28*(5), 755–768. doi:10.1016/j.future.2011.04.017

Bengtsson, A., Bardhi, F., & Venkatraman, M. (2010). How global brands travel with consumers: An examination of the relationship between brand consistency and meaning across national boundaries. *International Marketing Review*, *27*(5), 519–540. doi:10.1108/02651331011076572

Bentov, I., Gabizon, A., & Mizrahi, A. (2016, February). Cryptocurrencies without proof of work. In *International conference on financial cryptography and data security*, (pp. 142-157). Springer.

Berryhill, J., Bourgery, T., & Hanson, A. (2018). *Blockchains unchained: Blockchain technology and its use in the public sector*. Academic Press.

Bettina Warburg, B. W. (2019). *The Basics of Blockchain*. Animal Ventures LLC.

Bhardwaj, S., & Kaushik, M. (2018). Blockchain—technology to drive the future. In *Smart Computing and Informatics* (pp. 263–271). Springer. doi:10.1007/978-981-10-5547-8_28

Bhatia, S., & Wright de Hernandez, A. D. (2019). Blockchain is already here. What does that mean for records management and archives? *Journal of Archival Organization*, *16*(1), 75–84. doi:10.1080/15332748.2019.1655614

Bhat, M., & Vijayal, S. (2017). A Probabilistic Analysis on Crypto-Currencies Based on Blockchain. *International Conference on Next Generation Computing and Information Systems (ICNGCIS)*, 69-74. 10.1109/ICNGCIS.2017.37

Bhatt, T., Buckley, G., McEntire, J. C., Lothian, P., Sterling, B., & Hickey, C. (2013). Making traceability work across the entire food supply chain. *Journal of Food Science*, *78*(s2), B21–B27. doi:10.1111/1750-3841.12278 PMID:24138197

Bhuiyan, M. Z. A., Zaman, A., Wang, T., Wang, G., Tao, H., & Hassan, M. M. (2018). Blockchain and big data to transform the healthcare. *Proceedings of the International Conference on Data Processing and Applications*, 62-68. 10.1145/3224207.3224220

Biswas, K., Muthukkumarasamy, V., & Tan, W. L. (2017). Blockchain based wine supply chain traceability system. *Future Technologies Conference (FTC) 2017, 56–62*. Retrieved from https://acuresearchbank.acu.edu.au/item/86y07/blockchain-based-wine-supply-chain-traceability-system

Biswas, K., Muthukkumarasamy, V., & Tan, W. L. (2017). Blockchain based wine supply chain traceability system. In *Future Technologies Conference (FTC) 2017* (pp. 56-62). The Science and Information Organization.

Bleve, D., Costa, M., Ghilardi, R., Lanzillo, E., Picinati di Torcello, A., Ripa, P., & Tagliaferri, B. (2018). Il Mercato Dell'arte e Dei Beni Da Collezione Report 2018. Italia.

Bogdan, R. C., & Biklen, S. K. (1998). *Qualitative Research for Education: An Introduction to Theory and Methods*. Allyn and Bacon.

Bonneau, J., Miller, A., Clark, J., Narayanan, A., Kroll, J. A., & Felten, E. W. (2015). *Sok: Research perspectives and challenges for bitcoin and cryptocurrencies. In 2015 IEEE symposium on security and privacy*. IEEE. doi:10.1109/SP.2015.14

Bosona, T., & Gebresenbet, G. (2013). Food traceability as an integral part of logistics management in food and agricultural supply chain. *Food Control, 33*(1), 32–48. doi:10.1016/j.foodcont.2013.02.004

Boukis, A., & Christodoulides, G. (2020). Investigating Key Antecedents and Outcomes of Employee-based Brand Equity. *European Management Review, 17*(1), 41–55. doi:10.1111/emre.12327

Brandon, D. (2016). The blockchain: The future of business information systems. *International Journal of the Academic Business World, 10*(2), 33–40.

BRC Global Standard. (2021). Retrieved from www.brcglobalstandards.com

Brilliantova, V., & Thurner, T. W. (2019). Blockchain and the future of energy. *Technology in Society, 57*, 38–45. doi:10.1016/j.techsoc.2018.11.001

Brophy, R. (2019). Blockchain and insurance: A review for operations and regulation. *Journal of Financial Regulation and Compliance*.

Browne, R. (2021). *Crypto collectibles are selling for thousands — and celebrities like Mark Cuban are cashing in*. CNBC.

Bryła, P. (2015). The role of appeals to tradition in origin food marketing. A survey among Polish consumers. *Appetite, 91*, 302–310. doi:10.1016/j.appet.2015.04.056 PMID:25916623

Budhiraja, S., & Rani, R. (2020). TUDoc Chain-Securing Academic Certificate Digitally on Blockchain. Inventive Computation Technologies. ICICIT. *Lecture Notes in Networks and Systems., 98*, 150–160. doi:10.1007/978-3-030-33846-6_17

Bui, T., Cooper, D., Collomosse, J., Bell, M., Green, A., Sheridan, J., Higgins, J., Das, A., Keller, J. R., & Thereaux, O. (2020). Tamper-proofing video with hierarchical attention autoencoder hashing on blockchain. *IEEE Transactions on Multimedia*, *22*(11), 2858–2872. doi:10.1109/TMM.2020.2967640

Bumblauskas, D., Mann, A., Dugan, B., & Rittmer, J. (2020). A blockchain use case in food distribution: Do you know where your food has been? *International Journal of Information Management*, *52*, 102008. doi:10.1016/j.ijinfomgt.2019.09.004

Buratto, A., Cesaretto, R., & De Giovanni, P. (2019). Consignment contracts with cooperative programs and price discount mechanisms in a dynamic supply chain. *International Journal of Production Economics*, *218*, 72–82. doi:10.1016/j.ijpe.2019.04.027

Bureau of the Fiscal Service. (n. d.). *DEEE blockchain fit update*. FIT: Financial Innovation & Transformation. https://www.fiscal.treasury.gov/fit/updates/deee-blockchain-fit-update.html

Caro, M. P., Ali, M. S., Vecchio, M., & Giaffreda, R. (2018, May). Blockchain-based traceability in Agri-Food supply chain management: A practical implementation. In *2018 IoT Vertical and Topical Summit on Agriculture-Tuscany (IOT Tuscany)* (pp. 1-4). IEEE.

Caro, M.P., Ali, M.S., Vecchio, M., & Giaffreda, R. (2020). Blockchain-based traceability in agri-food supply chain management: a practical implementation. In *IoT Vertical and Topical Summit on Agriculture-Tuscany (IOT Tuscany)*. IEEE.

Carter, L., & Ubacht, J. (2018, May). Blockchain applications in government. In *Proceedings of the 19th Annual International Conference on Digital Government Research: governance in the data age* (pp. 1-2). 10.1145/3209281.3209329

Carter, C., & Rogers, D. (2008). A framework of sustainable supply chain management: Moving toward new theory. *International Journal of Physical Distribution & Logistics Management*, *38*(5), 360–387. doi:10.1108/09600030810882816

Casado-Vara, R., Prieto, J., De la Prieta, F., & Corchado, J. M. (2018). How blockchain improves the supply chain: Case study alimentary supply chain. *Procedia Computer Science*, *134*, 393–398. doi:10.1016/j.procs.2018.07.193

Casino, F., Dasaklis, T. K., & Patsakis, C. (2019). A systematic literature review of blockchain-based applications: Current status, classification and open issues. *Telematics and Informatics*, *36*, 55–81. doi:10.1016/j.tele.2018.11.006

Cauchon, N. S., Oghamian, S., Hassanpour, S., & Abernathy, M. (2019, July 1). Innovation in Chemistry, Manufacturing, and Controls—A Regulatory Perspective From Industry. *Journal of Pharmaceutical Sciences*. doi:10.1016/j.xphs.2019.02.007

Cavallone, M., & Palumbo, R. (2020). Debunking the myth of industry 4.0 in health care: Insights from a systematic literature review. *The TQM Journal*, *32*(4), 849–868. doi:10.1108/TQM-10-2019-0245

Cesaroni, F., & Baglieri, D. (2012). Technology intelligence: New challenges from patent information. In *Information systems: crossroads for organization, management, accounting and engineering* (pp. 267–274). Physica. doi:10.1007/978-3-7908-2789-7_30

Chang, P. L., Wu, C. C., & Leu, H. J. (2010). Using patent analyses to monitor the technological trends in an emerging field of technology: A case of carbon nanotube field emission display. *Scientometrics*, *82*(1), 5–19. doi:10.100711192-009-0033-y

Chellasamy, A., & N, A. (2019). An Outlook in Blockchain Technology- Architecture, Applications and Challenges. *International Journal of Engineering Research & Technology (Ahmedabad)*, *12*(12), 1–5.

Chen, G., Xu, B., Lu, M., & Chen, N. S. (2018). Exploring blockchain technology and its potential applications for education. *Smart Learning Environments*, *5*(1), 1–10. doi:10.118640561-017-0050-x

Cheng, T., & Zhang, G. (2013). Worldwide research productivity in the field of rheumatology from 1996 to 2010: A bibliometric analysis. *Rheumatology*, *52*(9), 1630–1634. doi:10.1093/rheumatology/ket008 PMID:23502075

Chen, M. A., Wu, Q., & Yang, B. (2019). How valuable is FinTech innovation? *Review of Financial Studies*, *32*(5), 2062–2106. doi:10.1093/rfs/hhy130

Chi, J., Lee, J., Kim, N., Choi, J., & Park, S. (2020). Secure and reliable blockchain-based eBook transaction system for self-published eBook trading. *PLoS One, 15*(2). doi:10.1371/journal.pone.0228418

Choe, Y. C., Park, J., Chung, M., & Moon, J. (2009). Effect of the food traceability system for building trust: Price premium and buying behavior. *Information Systems Frontiers*, *11*(2), 167–179. doi:10.100710796-008-9134-z

Chohan U. W. (2017). Blockchain and Securities Exchanges: Australian Case Study. *Available at* SSRN 3085631. doi:10.2139/ssrn.3085631

Christidis, K., & Devetsikiotis, M. (2016). Blockchains and Smart Contracts for the Internet of Things. *IEEE Access: Practical Innovations, Open Solutions*, *4*, 2292–2303. doi:10.1109/ACCESS.2016.2566339

Clarke, N. S., Jürgens, B., & Herrero-Solana, V. (2020). Blockchain patent landscaping: An expert based methodology and search query. *World Patent Information*, *61*, 101964. doi:10.1016/j.wpi.2020.101964

Cledou, G., Estevez, E., & Barbosa, L. S. (2018). A taxonomy for planning and designing smart mobility services. *Government Information Quarterly*, *35*(1), 61–76. doi:10.1016/j.giq.2017.11.008

Coeckelbergh, M., DuPont, Q., & Reijers, W. (2018). Towards a Philosophy of Financial Technologies. *Philosophy & Technology*, *31*(1), 9–14. doi:10.100713347-017-0261-7

Coldiretti. (2020, Sept 2). *Covid: il cibo diventa la prima ricchezza del Paese, vale 538 mln.* Retrieved from Coldiretti: https://www.coldiretti.it/economia/covid-il-cibo-diventa-la-prima-ricchezza-del-paese-vale-538-mln

Comunicazione, C. (2017). *La filiera del vino del vino guarda al Blockchain.* https://www.corrierecomunicazioni.it/digital-economy/la-filiera-del-vinoguarda-al-blockchain-in-nome-del-made-in-italy/

Cong, L. W., & He, Z. (2019). Blockchain disruption and smart contracts. *Review of Financial Studies, 32*(5), 1754–1797. doi:10.1093/rfs/hhz007

Conoscenti, M., Vetro, A., & De Martin, J. C. (2016). Blockchain for the Internet of Things: A systematic literature review. In *2016 IEEE/ACS 13th International Conference of Computer Systems and Applications (AICCSA)* (pp. 1-6). IEEE. 10.1109/AICCSA.2016.7945805

Constantinides, P., Henfridsson, O., & Parker, G. G. (2018). *Introduction—platforms and infrastructures in the digital age.* Academic Press.

Conti, M., Kumar, E. S., Lal, C., & Ruj, S. (2018). A survey on security and privacy issues of bitcoin. *IEEE Communications Surveys and Tutorials, 20*(4), 3416–3452. doi:10.1109/COMST.2018.2842460

Costa, C. (2020, October 7). *La carta d'identità del tonno Rio Mare grazie al Cloud e a IBM Services - Agrifood.Tech.* Agrifood.Tech. Retrieved from, https://www.agrifood.tech/food-industry/la-carta-didentita-del-tonno-rio-mare-grazie-al-cloud-e-a-ibm-services

Creydt, M., & Fischer, M. (2019). Blockchain and more-Algorithm driven food traceability. *Food Control, 105*, 45–51. doi:10.1016/j.foodcont.2019.05.019

Crosby, R. (2015). King of Memorabilia sentenced to 20 months in prison for fraud. *Chicago Tribune*, pp. 1–7.

Crosby, M. (2016). *Blockchain Technology: Beyond Bitcoin.* Giugno.

Dabbagh, M., Sookhak, M., & Safa, N. S. (2019). The evolution of blockchain: A bibliometric study. *IEEE Access: Practical Innovations, Open Solutions, 7*, 19212–19221. doi:10.1109/ACCESS.2019.2895646

Dai, J., & Vasarhelyi, M. A. (2017). Toward blockchain-based accounting and assurance. *Journal of Information Systems, 31*(3), 5–21. doi:10.2308/isys-51804

Daim, T., Lai, K. K., Yalcin, H., Alsoubie, F., & Kumar, V. (2020). Forecasting technological positioning through technology knowledge redundancy: Patent citation analysis of IoT, cybersecurity, and Blockchain. *Technological Forecasting and Social Change, 161*, 120329. doi:10.1016/j.techfore.2020.120329

Davis, F. D. (1989). Perceived usefulness, perceived ease of use, and user acceptance of information technology. *Management Information Systems Quarterly, 13*(3), 319–340. doi:10.2307/249008

De Giovanni, P. (2019a). *Eco-Digital Supply Chains Through Blockchains*. Available at SSRN 3488925.

De Giovanni, P. (2020b). Smart Contracts and Blockchain for Supply Chain Quality Management. In *Dynamic Quality Models and Games in Digital Supply Chains*. Springer Nature.

De Giovanni, P. (2021). *Dynamic Quality Models and Games in Digital Supply Chains: How Digital Transformation Impacts Supply Chain Quality Management*. Springer Nature.

De Giovanni, P. (2021). Smart Contracts and Blockchain for Supply Chain Quality Management, in Dynamic Quality Models and Games in Digital Supply Chains. *Springer Nature*.

De Giovanni, P. (2021a). *Dynamic Quality Models and Games in Digital Supply Chains: How Digital Transformation Impacts Supply Chain Quality Management*. Springer Nature.

De Giovanni, P. (2016). Coordination in a distribution channel with decisions on the nature of incentives and share-dependency on pricing. *The Journal of the Operational Research Society*, *67*(8), 1034–1049. doi:10.1057/jors.2015.118

De Giovanni, P. (2019). Digital supply chain through dynamic inventory and smart contracts. *Mathematics*, *7*(12), 1235. doi:10.3390/math7121235

De GiovanniP. (2019). Eco-Digital Supply Chains Through Blockchains. Available at SSRN 3488925.

De Giovanni, P. (2019b). Eco-Digital Supply Chains Through Blockchains. *International Journal of Business and Management Study*, *6*(2).

De Giovanni, P. (2020). Blockchain and smart contracts in supply chain management: A game theoretic model. *International Journal of Production Economics*, *228*, 107855. doi:10.1016/j.ijpe.2020.107855

De Giovanni, P. (2020c). An optimal control model with defective products and goodwill damages. *Annals of Operations Research*, *289*(2), 419–430. doi:10.100710479-019-03176-4

De Giovanni, P. (2021). Smart Contracts and Blockchain for Supply Chain Quality Management. In *Dynamic Quality Models and Games in Digital Supply Chains* (pp. 91–110). Springer. doi:10.1007/978-3-030-66537-1_5

De Giovanni, P. (2021). Smart Supply Chains with vendor managed inventory, coordination, and environmental performance. *European Journal of Operational Research*, *292*(2), 515–531. doi:10.1016/j.ejor.2020.10.049

De Giovanni, P., & Cariola, A. (2020). Process innovation through industry 4.0 technologies, lean practices and green supply chains. *Research in Transportation Economics*, 100869. doi:10.1016/j.retrec.2020.100869

De Giovanni, P., & Ramani, V. (2017). Product cannibalization and the effect of a service strategy. *The Journal of the Operational Research Society*, 1–17.

De Giovanni, P., & Zaccour, G. (2019). Optimal quality improvements and pricing strategies with active and passive product returns. *Omega, 88*, 248–262. doi:10.1016/j.omega.2018.09.007

de Riedmatten, A., Barr, P., Ringquist, J., & Eng, V. (2013). *The Food Value Chain A Challenge for the next Century Contents*. Deloitte.

Declerck, P. J. (2012). Biologicals and biosimilars: A review of the science and its implications. *GaBi Journal, 1*(1), 13–16. doi:10.5639/gabij.2012.0101.005

Dedeoglu, V., Jurdak, R., Putra, G. D., Dorri, A., & Kanhere, S. S. (2019, November). A trust architecture for blockchain in IoT. *Proceedings of the 16th EAI International Conference on Mobile and Ubiquitous Systems: Computing, Networking and Services*, 190-199. 10.1145/3360774.3360822

Deines, G., & Linhardt, K. (2020). *Nourishing the Food Industry with Profitable Growth*. Available at: https://www.accenture.com/us-en/_acnmedia/pdf-70/accenture-future-of-food-new-realities-for-the-industry.pdf

Delaney, C. (2020, January). *Bonds of trust: Blockchain and disaster relief*. Blockchain Pulse: IBM Blockchain Blog. https://www.ibm.com/blogs/blockchain/2020/01/bonds-of-trust-blockchain-and-disaster-relief/

Deloitte Report. (2018). *When two chains combine Supply chain meets blockchain*. Author.

Deloitte. (2018). *Blockchain in Public Sector Transforming government services through exponential technologies*. Retrieved from https://www2.deloitte.com/content/dam/Deloitte/in/Documents/public-sector/in-ps-blockchain-noexp.pdf

Deloitte. (2018). *Leadership: Driving innovation and delivering impact*. Deloitte.

Deloitte. (2018). *Survey finds biopharma companies lag in digital transformation It is time for a sea change in strategy*. Retrieved from https://www2.deloitte.com/content/dam/Deloitte/de/Documents/life-sciences-health-care/DI_CHS-MIT-survey_Final.pdf

DEMETER Project. (2021, February). *Interview Series: Antonio Caruso from Engineering Ingegneria Informatica S.p.A. (ENG) – Demeter*. Retrieved from https://h2020-demeter.eu/interview-series-antonio-caruso-from-engineering-ingegneria-informatica-s-p-a-eng/

Dey, S., Saha, S., Singh, A. K., & McDonald-Maier, K. (2021). FoodSQRBlock: Digitizing Food Production and the Supply Chain with Blockchain and QR Code in the Cloud. *Sustainability, 13*(6), 3486. doi:10.3390u13063486

Dhillon, G., & Backhouse, J. (2000). Technical opinion: Information system security management in the new millennium. *Communications of the ACM, 43*(7), 125–128. doi:10.1145/341852.341877

Dickinson, D. L., & Bailey, D. (2002). Meat traceability: Are US consumers willing to pay for it? *Journal of Agricultural and Resource Economics*, 348–364.

Dierksmeier, C., & Seele, P. (2020). Blockchain and business ethics. *Business Ethics (Oxford, England), 29*(2), 348–359. doi:10.1111/beer.12259

Dongoski, R., & Ramsey, N. (2020). *Vertical Integration in Food and Agribusiness.* Available at: https://www.google.com/url?sa=t&rct=j&q=&esrc=s&source=web&cd=&ved=2ahUKEwjJjorF66rwAhXdwQIHHUbXAbsQFjAKegQIIhAD&url=https%3A%2F%2Fassets.ey.com%2Fcontent%2Fdam%2Fey-sites%2Fey-com%2Fen_us%2Ftopics%2Fconsumer-products%2Fey-vertical-integration-in-food-and-agribusiness.pdf%3Fdownload&usg=AOvVaw3hMrD8qsc3B94tWYYjm3Vc

Dong, X. (2018). A method of image privacy protection based on blockchain technology. *International Conference on Cloud Computing, Big Data and Blockchain (ICCBB)*, 1-4. 10.1109/ICCBB.2018.8756447

Dos Santos, R. B., Torrisi, N. M., Yamada, E. R. K., & Pantoni, R. P. (2019). IGR Token-Raw Material and Ingredient Certification of Recipe Based Foods Using Smart Contracts. *Informatics (MDPI), 6*(1), 11. doi:10.3390/informatics6010011

Drobyazko, S., Makedon, V., Zhuravlov, D., Buglak, Y., & Stetsenko, V. (2019). Ethical, technological and patent aspects of technology blockchain distribution. *Journal of Legal, Ethical and Regulatory Issues, 22*, 1-6. https://www.proquest.com/openview/f0773b7791a9063857d02fe4659a9329/1?pq-origsite=gscholar&cbl=38868

Duan, B., Zhong, Y., & Liu, D. (2017). Education application of blockchain technology: Learning outcome and meta-diploma. In *2017 IEEE 23rd International Conference on Parallel and Distributed Systems (ICPADS)* (pp. 814-817). IEEE.10.1109/ICPADS.2017.00114

Duhaylongsod, J. B., & De Giovanni, P. (2019). The impact of innovation strategies on the relationship between supplier integration and operational performance. *International Journal of Physical Distribution & Logistics Management, 49*(2), 156–177. doi:10.1108/IJPDLM-09-2017-0269

Duy, P. T., Hien, D. T. T., Hien, D. H., & Pham, V. H. (2018). A survey on opportunities and challenges of Blockchain technology adoption for revolutionary innovation. *Proceedings of the Ninth International Symposium on Information and Communication Technology*, 200-207. 10.1145/3287921.3287978

Economist, T. (2015). The promise of the blockchain: the trust machine. *The Economist, 31*, 27. https://www.economist.com/leaders/2015/10/31/the-trust-machine.

EEA. (2019). Adaptation challenges and opportunities for the European energy system. Luxembourg: Publications Office of the European Union.

Efanov, D., & Roschin, P. (2018). The all-pervasiveness of the blockchain technology. *Procedia Computer Science, 123*, 116–121. doi:10.1016/j.procs.2018.01.019

Eliaz, S., & Jagt, R. (2020a). *The global food system transformation The time to change is now.* Deloitte. Available at: https://www2.deloitte.com/global/en/pages/consumer-business/articles/global-food-system-transformation.html

Eliaz, S., & Jagt, R. (2020b). *Future of Food : Responsible Production Connecting yield increase and sustainability.* Deloitte. Available at: https://www2.deloitte.com/global/en/pages/consumer-business/articles/gx-future-of-food-responsible-production.html

Elkington, J. (1994). Towards the Sustainable Corporation: Win-Win-Win Business Strategies for Sustainable Development. *California Management Review, 36*(2), 90–100. doi:10.2307/41165746

Elliot, H. (2020, September) *An introduction of tokenization.* Cardano Foundation. https://medium.com/cardanorss/an-introduction-to-tokenization-5ce087a7b6c3

EMA. (2016a). *Guidance on good manufacturing practice and good distribution practice: Questions and answers.* European Medicines Agency. Retrieved from https://www.ema.europa.eu/en/human-regulatory/research-development/compliance/good-manufacturing-practice/guidance-good-manufacturing-practice-good-distribution-practice-questions-answers

EMA. (2016b). *Track-change version following public consultation Guideline on good pharmacovigilance practices (GVP) Product-or Population-Specific Considerations II: Biological medicinal products.* Retrieved from https://www.ema.europa.eu/en/documents/scientific-guideline/guideline-good-pharmacovigilance-practices-gvp-product-population-specific-considerations-ii_en-0.pdf

Engelmann, F., Holland, M., Nigischer, C., & Stjepandić, J. (2018). Intellectual property protection and licensing of 3d print with blockchain technology. *Transdisciplinary Engineering Methods for Social Innovation of Industry, 4*, 103–112. doi:10.3233/978-1-61499-898-3-103

Eni. (2021, February 27). *Eni, Abiut us.* Retrieved from Eni corporation website: https://www.eni.com/en

Eni. (2021, March). *Media press.* Retrieved from Eni website: www.eni.com

Enk, A. J. (1967). *U.S. Patent No. 3,340,636.* Washington, DC: U.S. Patent and Trademark Office.

Epstein, J. (2017). *Blockchain and the CMO.* Whitepaper. Available online at: https://s3.us-east-2.amazonaws.com/brightline-website/downloads/reports/Brightline_Epstein_Blockchain-and-the-CMO_Blockchain-Research-Institute.pdf?utm_source=resource-page&utm_medium=skip-link

Ernst & Young Report. (2019). *E&Y Opschain traceability.* Author.

Ertemel, A. V. (2018). Implications of blockchain technology on marketing. *Journal of International Trade, Logistics and Law, 4*(2), 35-44.

Eskildsen, J., & Kristensen, K. (2007). Customer Satisfaction – The Role of Transparency. *Total Quality Management & Business Excellence, 18*(1-2), 39–47. doi:10.1080/14783360601043047

Ethereum Documentation. (2021). *Networks.* Ethereum. Retrieved from, https://ethereum.org/en/developers/docs/networks/

EU Science Hub. (2021). *Food authenticity and quality | EU Science Hub.* Retrieved from, https://ec.europa.eu/jrc/en/research-topic/food-authenticity-and-quality#

EU. (2021). *Falsified medicines*. Retrieved January 4, 2021, from https://ec.europa.eu/health/human-use/falsified_medicines_en

European Commission. (2002). *General Food Law Principles*. Retrieved from, https://ec.europa.eu/food/safety/general_food_law_en

European Commission. (2018). *Case Study Report e-Estonia*. Retrieved from https://jiip.eu/mop/wp/wp-content/uploads/2018/10/EE_e-Estonia_Castanos.pdf

European Commission. (2019). *2019 EBA Italy Fact Sheet*. European Commission.

European Commission. (2019). *Blockchain for digital government*. Retrieved from https://joinup.ec.europa.eu/sites/default/files/document/2019-04/JRC115049%20blockchain%20for%20digital%20government.pdf

European Commission. (2020). *DESI 2020*. Author.

European Commission. (2020). *Horizon 2020 multi-actor projects*. www.eip-agri.eu

European Union Council. (2019). European Parliament, & European Union Council Regulation (EC) No 178/2002 of the European Parliament and of the Council of 28 January 2002 laying down the general principles and requirements of food law, establishing the European Food Safety Authority and laying down procedures in matters of food safety *Official Journal of the European Union*, 02002R0178-EN-26.07.2019-007.001

Eurostat. (2018). *EU energy in figures: statistical pocketbook*. Author.

Everest Group. (2016). *Smart contracts on a distributed ledger – life in the smart lane*. Available at: www2.everestgrp.com/Files/previews/Smart%20Contracts%20on%20Distributed%20Ledger%20-%20Life%20in%20the%20Smart%20Lane.pdf

Eyal, I., & Sirer, E. G. (2014, March). Majority is not enough: Bitcoin mining is vulnerable. In *International conference on financial cryptography and data security* (pp. 436-454). Springer. 10.1007/978-3-662-45472-5_28

Eyassu, S. E. (2019). Overview of blockchain legislation and adoption: Status and challenges. *Issues in Information Systems, 20*(1).

Farid, S. S., Baron, M., Stamatis, C., Nie, W., & Coffman, J. (2020). Benchmarking biopharmaceutical process development and manufacturing cost contributions to R&D. *mAbs, 12*(1), 1754999. doi:10.1080/19420862.2020.1754999 PMID:32449439

FCA. (2019). *Guidance on cryptoassets* (Policy Statement PS19/22). https://www.fca.org.uk/publication/policy/ps19-22.pdf

FDA. (2011). *Food Safety Modernization Act (FSMA) | FDA*. Retrieved from, https://www.fda.gov/food/food-safety-modernization-act-fsma/full-text-food-safety-modernization-act-fsma

FDA. (2014). *Pharmaceutical Quality Control Labs (7/93)*. Retrieved June 11, 2021, from https://www.fda.gov/inspections-compliance-enforcement-and-criminal-investigations/inspection-guides/pharmaceutical-quality-control-labs-793

FDA. (2019). *DSCSA Pilot Project Program*. Retrieved from https://www.fda.gov/drugs/drug-supply-chain-security-act-dscsa/dscsa-pilot-project-program

FDA. (2020a). *Drug Supply Chain Security Act pilot project program and enhanced drug distribution security*. Retrieved from https://www.fda.gov/drugs/news-events-human-drugs/drug-supply-chain-security-act-pilot-project-program-and-enhanced-drug-distribution-security

FDA. (2020b). *New Drug Therapy Approvals*. Retrieved from https://www.fda.gov/media/133911/download

Feng, H., Wang, X., Duan, Y., Zhang, J., & Zhang, X. (2020). Applying blockchain technology to improve agri-food traceability: A review of development methods, benefits and challenges. *Journal of Cleaner Production, 260*, 121031. doi:10.1016/j.jclepro.2020.121031

Feng, L., Zhang, H., Tsai, W. T., & Sun, S. (2019). System architecture for high-performance permissioned blockchains. *Frontiers of Computer Science, 13*(6), 1151–1165. doi:10.100711704-018-6345-4

Ferreira, F. A. (2018). Mapping the field of arts-based management: Bibliographic coupling and co-citation analyses. *Journal of Business Research, 85*, 348–357. doi:10.1016/j.jbusres.2017.03.026

Ferreira, J. J., Fernandes, C. I., & Kraus, S. (2019). Entrepreneurship research: Mapping intellectual structures and research trends. *Review of Managerial Science, 13*(1), 181–205. doi:10.100711846-017-0242-3

Filippova, E. (2019). *Empirical Evidence and Economic Implications of Blockchain as a General Purpose Technology. In IEEE Technology & Engineering Management Conference*. TEMSCON. doi:10.1109/TEMSCON.2019.8813748

Filippova, E., Scharl, A., & Filippov, P. (2019). Blockchain: An Empirical Investigation of Its Scope for Improvement. In J. Joshi, S. Nepal, Q. Zhang, & L. J. Zhang (Eds.), Lecture Notes in Computer Science: Vol. 11521. *Blockchain – ICBC 2019. ICBC 2019*. Springer. doi:10.1007/978-3-030-23404-1_1

FINMA. (2018). *FINMA publishes ICO guidelines*. https://www.finma.ch/en/news/2018/02/20180216-mm-ico-wegleitung

Finzer, D. (2020). *The Non-Fungible Token Bible: Everything You Need to Know about NFTs*. Available at: https://opensea.io/blog/guides/non-fungible-tokens/#:~:text=Non-fungibletokens(NFTs),ownership records for physical assets.

Firdaus, A., Ab Razak, M. F., Feizollah, A., Hashem, I. A. T., Hazim, M., & Anuar, N. B. (2019). The rise of "blockchain": Bibliometric analysis of blockchain study. *Scientometrics, 120*(3), 1289–1331. doi:10.100711192-019-03170-4

Fisch, C. (2019). Initial coin offerings (ICOs) to finance new ventures. *Journal of Business Venturing, 34*(1), 1–22. doi:10.1016/j.jbusvent.2018.09.007

Fisher, C., Poll, J., & Wetklow, M. (2020). The benefits of blockchain to tokenize grants payments. *Journal of Government Financial Management, 69*(2), 24–29.

Folke, C. (2006). Resilience: The emergence of a perspective for social–ecological systems analyses. *Global Environmental Change, 16*(3), 253–267. doi:10.1016/j.gloenvcha.2006.04.002

Folliot Lalliot, L., & Yukins, C. R. (2020). COVID-19: Lessons Learned in Public Procurement. Time for a New Normal? *Time for a New Normal*, 46-58.

Food and Drug Administration. (2016). *Data Integrity and Compliance With CGMP Guidance for Industry*. Retrieved from https://www.fda.gov/files/drugs/published/Data-Integrity-and-Compliance-With-Current-Good-Manufacturing-Practice-Guidance-for-Industry.pdf

Foxley, W. (2021). *Ethereum Transaction Fees Hit Record Highs as Ether, DeFi Coins Soar*. Yahoo Finance.

França, A. S. L., Neto, J. A., Gonçalves, R. F., & Almeida, C. M. V. B. (2020). Proposing the use of blockchain to improve the solid waste management in small municipalities. *Journal of Cleaner Production, 244*, 118529. doi:10.1016/j.jclepro.2019.118529Fulmer, N. (2018). Exploring the legal issues of blockchain applications. *Akron Law Review, 52*, 161.

Francisco, K., & Swanson, D. (2017). *The Supply Chain Has No Clothes: Technology Adoption of Blockchain for Supply Chain Transparency*. Department of Marketing & Logistics, University of North Florida.

Francisco, K., & Swanson, D. (2018). The Supply Chain Has No Clothes: Technology Adoption of Blockchain for Supply Chain Transparency. *Logistics, 2*(1), 2. doi:10.3390/logistics2010002

Galvez, J. F., Mejuto, J. C., & Simal-Gandara, J. (2018). Future challenges on the use of blockchain for food traceability analysis. *Trends in Analytical Chemistry, 107*, 222–232. doi:10.1016/j.trac.2018.08.011

Gartner, W. B., Davidsson, P., & Zahra, S. A. (2006). Are you talking to me? The nature of community in entrepreneurship scholarship. *Entrepreneurship Theory and Practice, 30*(3), 321–331. doi:10.1111/j.1540-6520.2006.00123.x

Gassmann, O., Frankenberger, K., & Csik, M. (2013). *The Business Model Navigator: 55 Models That Will Revolutionise Your Business*. FT Publishing.

Gaviria-Marin, M., Merigó, J. M., & Baier-Fuentes, H. (2019). Knowledge management: A global examination based on bibliometric analysis. *Technological Forecasting and Social Change, 140*, 194–220. doi:10.1016/j.techfore.2018.07.006

Ge, L., Brewster, C., Spek, J., Smeenk, A., & Top, J. (2017). *Blockchain for Agriculture and Food*. Wageningen Economic Research. Available at: www.wur.eu/economic-research

Ge, L., Brewster, C. A., Macdonald, B., Termeer, K., Opdam, P., & Soma, K. (2016). Informational institutions in the agrifood sector: Meta-information and meta-governance of environmental sustainability. *Current Opinion in Environmental Sustainability, 18*, 73–81. doi:10.1016/j. cosust.2015.10.002

Genuino. (2020). *About us.* Available at: https://genuino.world/page.html

Gervais, A., Karame, G. O., Wüst, K., Glykantzis, V., Ritzdorf, H., & Capkun, S. (2016, October). On the security and performance of proof of work blockchains. *Proceedings of the 2016 ACM SIGSAC conference on computer and communications security*, 3-16. 10.1145/2976749.2978341

Gilgamesh Platform. (n.d.). static.gilgameshplatform.com/pdf/whitepaper.pdf

Gipp, Breitinger, Meuschke, & Beel. (2017). CryptSubmit: Introducing Securely Timestamped Manuscript Submission and Peer Review Feedback Using the Blockchain. *ACM/IEEE Joint Conference on Digital Libraries (JCDL)*, 1-4. 10.1109/JCDL.2017.7991588

Glänzel, W., & Czerwon, H. J. (1996). A new methodological approach to bibliographic coupling and its application to the national, regional and institutional level. *Scientometrics, 37*(2), 195–221. doi:10.1007/BF02093621

Glass, R. L., & Vessey, I. (1995). Contemporary application-domain taxonomies. *IEEE Software, 12*(4), 63–76. doi:10.1109/52.391837

Goderdzishvili, N., Gordadze, E., & Gagnidze, N. (2018, April). Georgia's Blockchain-powered Property Registration: Never blocked, Always Secured: Ownership Data Kept Best! In *Proceedings of the 11th International Conference on Theory and Practice of Electronic Governance* (pp. 673-675). 10.1145/3209415.3209437

Goedde, L., Horil, M., & Sanghvi, S. (2015). *Pursuing the Global Opportunity in Food and Agribusiness.* Available at: https://www.mckinsey.com/insights/Food_Agriculture/Pursuing_the_ global_opportunity_in_food_and_agribusiness?cid=other-eml-alt-mip-mck-oth-1507

Gopal, G., Suter-Crazzolara, C., Toldo, L., & Eberhardt, W. (2019). Digital transformation in healthcare - Architectures of present and future information technologies. In *Clinical Chemistry and Laboratory Medicine* (Vol. 57, pp. 328–335). De Gruyter. doi:10.1515/cclm-2018-0658

Grieco, G., Song, W., Cygan, A., Feist, J., & Groce, A. (2020). Echidna: effective, usable, and fast fuzzing for smart contracts. *Proceedings of the 29th ACM SIGSOFT International Symposium on Software Testing and Analysis*, 557-560. 10.1145/3395363.3404366

Grunert, K. G. (2005). Food quality and safety: Consumer perception and demand. *European Review of Agriculture Economics, 32*(3), 369–391. doi:10.1093/eurrag/jbi011

Grunert, K. G. (2011). Sustainability in the Food Sector A Consumer Behaviour Perspective. *International Journal on Food System Dynamics, 2*(3), 207–218.

GS1. (2010a). *Healthcare supply chain traceability.* Available from: https://www.gs1.org/docs/ gdsn/support/20101025_Traceability_White_Paper_final.pdf

GS1. (2012). *GS1 Standards Document*. Business Process and System Requirements for Full Supply Chain Traceability. GS1 Global Traceability Standard.

Guo, J., Li, C., Zhang, G., Sun, Y., & Bie, R. (2019). Blockchain-enabled digital rights management for multimedia resources of online education. *Multimedia Tools and Applications*, 1–21. doi:10.100711042-019-08059-1

Gupta, N., & Bedi, P. (2018). E-waste management using blockchain based smart contracts. In *2018 International Conference on Advances in Computing, Communications and Informatics (ICACCI)* (pp. 915-921). IEEE. 10.1109/ICACCI.2018.8554912

Gürkaynak, G., Yılmaz, İ., Yeşilaltay, B., & Bengi, B. (2018). Intellectual property law and practice in the blockchain realm. *Computer Law & Security Review, 34*(4), 847–862. doi:10.1016/j.clsr.2018.05.027

Gurtu, A., & Johny, J. (2019). Potential of blockchain technology in supply chain management: A literature review. *International Journal of Physical Distribution & Logistics Management, 49*(9), 881–900. doi:10.1108/IJPDLM-11-2018-0371

Guzman, Z. (2021). *This blockchain startup selling collectible NBA highlights just had $50 million in sales in 30 days. Yahoo!* Finance.

Hackius, N., & Petersen, M. (2017). Blockchain in Logistics and Supply Chain: Trick or Treat. *Hamburg International Conference of Logistics*.

Hahn, A., Singh, R., Liu, C. C., & Chen, S. (2017). Smart contract-based campus demonstration of decentralized transactive energy auctions. *IEEE Power & Energy Society Innovative Smart Grid Technologies Conference, 1–5*.

Haig, S. (2021). *Ethereum posts new highs as DeFi gas fees go through the roof*. Cointelegraph.

Hall, B. H., & Khan, B. (2003). *Adoption of new technology* (No. w9730). National Bureau of Economic Research.

Han, Y., Makarova, E., Ringel, M., & Telpis, V. (2019). *Industry 4.0, innovation, and pharmaceutical quality control*. Retrieved May 28, 2021, from https://www.mckinsey.com/industries/pharmaceuticals-and-medical-products/our-insights/digitization-automation-and-online-testing-the-future-of-pharma-quality-control

Handelman, J. M., & Arnold, S. J. (1999). The Role of Marketing Actions with a Social Dimension: Appeals to the Institutional Environment. *Journal of Marketing, 63*(3), 33–48. doi:10.1177/002224299906300303

Hao, D. P. (n.d.). *TrialChain: A Blockchain-Based Platform to Validate Data Integrity in Large*. Biomedical Research Studies.

Hassani, H., Huang, X., & Silva, E. (2018). Banking with blockchain-ed big data. *Journal of Management Analytics, 5*(4), 256–275. doi:10.1080/23270012.2018.1528900

Hawlitschek, F., Notheisen, B., & Teubner, T. (2018). The limits of trust-free systems: A literature review on blockchain technology and trust in the sharing economy. *Electronic Commerce Research and Applications, 29,* 50–63. doi:10.1016/j.elerap.2018.03.005

Hechler-Fayd'herbe, N., & Picinati di Torcello, A. (2020). Collectibles: An Integral Part of Wealth. Academic Press.

Hegnsholt, B. E., Unnikrishnan, S., Pollmann-larsen, M., Askelsdottir, B., & Gerard, M. (2018). *Tackling the 1.6-billion-ton food loss and waste crisis.* BCG Henderson Institute. Available at: https://www.bcg.com/it-it/publications/2018/tackling-1.6-billion-ton-food-loss-and-waste-crisis

Heitner, D. (2016). Playing Ball In The Multi-Billion Dollar Sports Collectible Market. *Forbes,* 2–7.

Helo, P., & Hao, Y. (2019). Blockchains in operations and supply chains: A model and reference implementation. *Computers & Industrial Engineering, 136,* 242–251. doi:10.1016/j.cie.2019.07.023

Hewa, T., Ylianttila, M., & Liyanage, M. (2020). Survey on blockchain-based smart contracts: Applications, opportunities and challenges. *Journal of Network and Computer Applications, 102857.* Advance online publication. doi:10.1016/j.jnca.2020.102857

Hewett, N., Lehmacher, W., & Wang, Y. (2019). *Inclusive Deployment of Blockchain for Supply Chains: Part 1 – Introduction.* World Economic Forum.

Heyman, H. M., Senejoux, F., Seibert, I., Klimkait, T., Maharaj, V. J., & Meyer, J. J. M. (2015). Identification of anti-HIV active dicaffeoylquinic-and tricaffeoylquinic acids in Helichrysum populifolium by NMR-based metabolomic guided fractionation. *Fitoterapia, 103,* 155–164. doi:10.1016/j.fitote.2015.03.024 PMID:25841639

Hoek, R. (2019). Exploring blockchain implementation in the supply chain. *International Journal of Operations & Production Management, 39*(6/7/8), 829–859. doi:10.1108/IJOPM-01-2019-0022

Hoek, R. v. (2020). Unblocking the chain – findings from an executive workshop on blockchain in the supply chain. *Supply Chain Management,* 255–261.

Hölbl, M., Kompara, M., Kamišalić, A., & Nemec Zlatolas, L. (2018). A systematic review of the use of blockchain in healthcare. *Symmetry, 10*(10), 470. doi:10.3390ym10100470

Holland, M., Nigischer, C., & Stjepandic, J. (2017). Copyright protection in additive manufacturing with blockchain approach. *Transdisciplinary Engineering: A Paradigm Shift, 5,* 914-921. doi:10.3233/978-1-61499-779-5-914

Holland, M., Stjepandić, J., & Nigischer, C. (2018). Intellectual property protection of 3D print supply chain with blockchain technology. In *2018 IEEE International conference on engineering, technology and innovation (ICE/ITMC)* (pp. 1-8). IEEE. 10.1109/ICE.2018.8436315

Hollos, D. C. B., Blome, C., & Foerstl, K. (2012). Does sustainable supplier co-operation affect performance? Examining implications for the triple bottom line. *International Journal of Production Research, 50*(11), 2968–2986. doi:10.1080/00207543.2011.582184

Hollyer, J. R., Rosendorff, B. P., & Vreeland, J. R. (2011). Democracy and transparency. *The Journal of Politics*, *73*(4), 1191–1205. doi:10.1017/S0022381611000880

Homburg, C., Koschate, N., & Hoyer, W. D. (2005). Do Satisfied Customers Really Pay More? A Study of the Relationship between Customer Satisfaction and Willingness to Pay. *Journal of Marketing*, *69*(2), 84–96. doi:10.1509/jmkg.69.2.84.60760

Hong, Y., Yoon, S., Kim, Y. S., & Jang, H. (2021). System-level virtual sensing method in building energy systems using autoencoder: Under the limited sensors and operational datasets. *Applied Energy*, *301*, 117458. doi:10.1016/j.apenergy.2021.117458

Hou, H. (2017). The application of blockchain technology in E-government in China. In *2017 26th International Conference on Computer Communication and Networks (ICCCN)* (pp. 1-4). IEEE. 10.1109/ICCCN.2017.8038519

Ho, Y. S. (2014). Classic articles on social work field in Social Science Citation Index: A bibliometric analysis. *Scientometrics*, *98*(1), 137–155. doi:10.100711192-013-1014-8

Huang, Bian, Li, Zhao, & Shi. (2019). Smart Contract Security: A Software Lifecycle Perspective. IEEE Access, 7, 150184-150202. doi:10.1109/ACCESS.2019.2946988

Huang, Z., Su, X., Zhang, Y., Shi, C., Zhang, H., & Xie, L. (2018). A decentralized solution for IoT data trusted exchange based-on blockchain. *2017 3rd IEEE International Conference on Computer and Communications, ICCC 2017*, 1180–1184.

Hu, D., Li, Y., Pan, L., Li, M., & Zheng, S. (2021). A blockchain-based trading system for big data. *Computer Networks*, *191*, 107994. doi:10.1016/j.comnet.2021.107994

Hughes, L., Dwivedi, Y. K., Misra, S. K., Rana, N. P., Raghavan, V., & Akella, V. (2019). Blockchain research, practice and policy: Applications, benefits, limitations, emerging research themes and research agenda. *International Journal of Information Management*, *49*, 114–129. doi:10.1016/j.ijinfomgt.2019.02.005

Hwang, J., Choi, M. I., Lee, T., Jeon, S., Kim, S., Park, S., & Park, S. (2017). Energy Prosumer Business Model Using Blockchain System to Ensure Transparency and Safety. *Energy Procedia*, *141*, 194–198. doi:10.1016/j.egypro.2017.11.037

Hyvärinen, H., Risius, M., & Friis, G. (2017). A blockchain-based approach towards overcoming financial fraud in public sector services. *Business & Information Systems Engineering*, *59*(6), 441–456. doi:10.100712599-017-0502-4

Iansiti, M., & Lakhami, K. (2017). The Truth About Blockchain. *Harvard Business Review*. Retrieved 1 June 2021, from https://hbr.org/2017/01/the-truth-about-blockchain

Iasiniti, M., & Lakhani, K. R. (2017). The Truth About The Blockchain. *Harvard Business Review*.

IBM. (2021). What is a REST API? *IBM Cloud Education.* Retrieved from https://www.ibm.com/cloud/learn/rest-apis

ISO 9001. (2015). *Quality Management Systems: Requirements.* London: BS EN ISO 9001.

ISO. (2007). 22005: Traceability in the feed and food chain—General principles and guidance for system design and development. International Organisation for Standardization.

Ito, R. (2020). The future of collectibles is digital. *Tech Crunch.* Available at: https://techcrunch. com/2020/03/25/the-future-of-collectibles-is-digital/

Ito, K., & O'Dair, M. (2019). A Critical Examination of the Application of Blockchain Technology to Intellectual Property Management. In *Business transformation through blockchain* (pp. 317–335). Palgrave Macmillan. doi:10.1007/978-3-319-99058-3_12

Ivanov, D., Dolgui, A., & Sokolov, B. (2018). Scheduling of recovery actions in the supply chain with resilience analysis considerations. *International Journal of Production Research, 56*(19), 6473–6490. doi:10.1080/00207543.2017.1401747

Jagrat, C. P., & Channegowda, J. (2020, February). A Survey of Blockchain Based Government Infrastructure Information. In *2020 International Conference on Mainstreaming Block Chain Implementation (ICOMBI)* (pp. 1-5). IEEE. 10.23919/ICOMBI48604.2020.9203152

Jansen-Vullers, M. H., van Dorp, C. A., & Beulens, A. J. M. (2003). Managing traceability information in manufacture. *International Journal of Information Management, 23*(5), 395–413. doi:10.1016/S0268-4012(03)00066-5

Jing, N., Liu, Q., & Sugumaran, V. (2021). A blockchain-based code copyright management system. *Information Processing & Management, 58*(3), 102518. doi:10.1016/j.ipm.2021.102518

Jung, C., & Food, U. S. (2014). *Drug Supply Chain Security Act.* Retrieved January 4, 2021, from https://www.fda.gov/Drugs/DrugSafety/DrugIntegrityandSupplyChainSecurity/ DrugSupplyChainSecurityAct/

Kafetzopoulos, D., Gotzamani, K., & Psomas, E. (2013). Quality systems and competitive performance of food companies. *Benchmarking, 20*(4), 463–483. doi:10.1108/BIJ-08-2011-0065

Kalis, R. B. (2018). Validating Data Integrity with Blockchain. In *2018 IEEE International Conference on Cloud Computing Technology and Science* (pp. 272-277). IEEE.

Kamali, A. (2019). Blockchain's Potential to Combat Procurement Frauds. *International Journal of Biometrics and Bioinformatics*, 101 - 107.

Kamath, R. (2018). Food traceability on blockchain: Walmart's pork and mango pilots with IBM. *The Journal of the British Blockchain Association, 1*(1), 3712. doi:10.31585/jbba-1-1-(10)2018

Kamble, S. S., Gunasekaran, A., & Sharma, R. (2020). Modeling the blockchain enabled traceability in agriculture supply chain. *International Journal of Information Management, 52,* 101967. doi:10.1016/j.ijinfomgt.2019.05.023

Kamilaris, A., Fonti, A., & Prenafeta-Boldύ, F. X. (2019). The Rise of Blockchain Technology in Agriculture and Food Supply Chains. *Trends in Food Science & Technology, 91*, 640–652. doi:10.1016/j.tifs.2019.07.034

KaneE. (2017). Is Blockchain a General Purpose Technology? *Available at* SSRN 2932585. doi:10.2139/ssrn.2932585

Kang, J., Yu, R., Huang, X., Maharjan, S., Zhang, Y., & Hossain, E. (2017). Enabling localized peer-to-peer electricity trading among plug-in hybrid electric vehicles using consortium blockchains. *IEEE Transactions on Industrial Informatics, 13*(6), 3154–3164. doi:10.1109/TII.2017.2709784

Karafiloski, E., & Mishev, A. (2017). Blockchain solutions for big data challenges: A literature review. *17th IEEE International Conference on Smart Technologies, EUROCON 2017 - Conference Proceedings*, 763–768. 10.1109/EUROCON.2017.8011213

Kay, G. (2021). *Selling crypto art can come with huge hidden fees, leading some people to lose hundreds of dollars.* Business Insider.

Keeley, B. (2012). *From aid to development: the global fight against poverty.* OECD Publishing. doi:10.1787/9789264123571-4-en

Kehoe, L. (2017). *When two chains combine: Supply chain meets blockchain.* Deloitte.

Kellogg, G., Sporny, M., & Longley, D. (2019). *JSON-LD 1.1.* JSON-LD Documentation. Retrieved from, https://json-ld.org/spec/latest/json-ld/#basic-concepts

Kennedy, Z. C., Stephenson, D. E., Christ, J. F., Pope, T. R., Arey, B. W., Barrett, C. A., & Warner, M. G. (2017). Enhanced anti-counterfeiting measures for additive manufacturing: Coupling lanthanide nanomaterial chemical signatures with blockchain technology. *Journal of Materials Chemistry. C, Materials for Optical and Electronic Devices, 5*(37), 9570–9578. doi:10.1039/C7TC03348F

Kessler, M. M. (1963). Bibliographic coupling extended in time: Ten case histories. *Information Storage and Retrieval, 1*(4), pp. 169-187. doi:10.1016/0020-0271(63)90016-0

Keybase.io. (2019). *Keybase.* Available online at: https://keybase.io/docs/server_security

Khalilov, M. C. K., & Levi, A. (2018). A survey on anonymity and privacy in bitcoin-like digital cash systems. *IEEE Communications Surveys and Tutorials, 20*(3), 2543–2585. doi:10.1109/COMST.2018.2818623

Khan, M. A., & Salah, K. (2018). IoT security: Review, blockchain solutions, and open challenges. *Future Generation Computer Systems, 82*, 395–411. doi:10.1016/j.future.2017.11.022

Kiesnoski, K. (2019). *Are collectibles for collecting or investing? Advisors weigh in.* Available at: https://www.cnbc.com/2019/06/21/are-collectibles-for-collecting-or-investing-advisors-weigh-in.html

Klein, K., & Stolk, P. (2018). Challenges and Opportunities for the Traceability of (Biological) Medicinal Products. *Drug Safety*, *41*(10), 911–918. doi:10.100740264-018-0678-7 PMID:29721822

Klöckner, M., Kurpjuweit, S., Velu, C., & Wagner, S. M. (2020). Does Blockchain for 3D Printing Offer Opportunities for Business Model Innovation? *Research Technology Management*, *63*(4), 18–27. doi:10.1080/08956308.2020.1762444

Knowage. (2021). *The Open Source Business Analytics - Knowage suite*. Retrieved from, https://www.knowage-suite.com/site/

Köhler, S., & Pizzol, M. (2020). Technology assessment of blockchain-based technologies in the food supply chain. *Journal of Cleaner Production*, *269*, 122193. Advance online publication. doi:10.1016/j.jclepro.2020.122193

Konashevych, O. (2017, June). The concept of the blockchain-based governing: Current issues and general vision. In *Proceedings of 17th European Conference on Digital Government ECDG* (p. 79). Academic Press.

Kosba, A., Miller, A., Shi, E., Wen, Z., & Papamanthou, C. (2016, May). Hawk: The blockchain model of cryptography and privacy-preserving smart contracts. In 2016 IEEE symposium on security and privacy (SP), 839-858. IEEE.

Kotula, M. (2020, Mar 11). *Can A Supply Chain Be Really Transparent In A Digital World?* Retrieved from Digitalist Magazine: https://www.digitalistmag.com/digital-supply-networks/2020/03/11/can-supply-chain-be-really-transparent-in-digital-world-06202976/

Kouhizadeh, M., & Sarkis, J. (2018). Blockchain Practices, Potentials, and Perspectives in Greening Supply Chains. *Sustainability*, *10*(10), 3652. doi:10.3390u10103652

Kraft, C. (2020). *Future smart contracts, loosed of oracles*. LinkedIn. https://www.linkedin.com/pulse/future-mart-contracts-loosed-oracles-conrad-kraft/?trackingId=s1Dog16USrCmLRnGVrGqow%3D%3D

Kraft, C., & Carmona, M. (2020, April). *How blockchain spells the end of corruption in public sector procurement*. LinkedIn. https://www.linkedin.com/pulse/how-blockchain-spells-end-corruption-public-sector-mariana-carmona/

Krogsbøll, M., Borre, L. H., Slaats, T., & Debois, S. (2020, February). Smart Contracts for Government Processes: Case Study and Prototype Implementation (Short Paper). In *International Conference on Financial Cryptography and Data Security* (pp. 676-684). Springer. 10.1007/978-3-030-51280-4_36

KruhW. (2019). *Consumer Currents*. Available at: https://www.google.com/url?sa=t&rct=j&q=&esrc=s&source=web&cd=&cad=rja&uact=8&ved=2ahUKEwjc2b7q66rwAhWD7KQKHZhwCrcQFjABegQIAhAD&url=https%3A%2F%2Fassets.kpmg%2Fcontent%2Fdam%2Fkpmg%2Fxx%2Fpdf%2F2019%2F05%2Fconsumer-currents-issues-driving-consumer-organizations.pdf&usg=AOvVaw0MQAkem-_mCZ1OQVwkSKMA

Kshetri, N. (2018). 1 Blockchain's roles in meeting key supply chain management objectives. *International Journal of Information Management, 39*, 80–89. doi:10.1016/j.ijinfomgt.2017.12.005

Kurpjuweit, S., Schmidt, C. G., Klöckner, M., & Wagner, S. M. (2021). Blockchain in additive manufacturing and its impact on supply chains. *Journal of Business Logistics, 42*(1), 46–70. doi:10.1111/jbl.12231

la Torre, B. G., & Albericio, F. (2021). The Pharmaceutical Industry in 2020. An Analysis of FDA Drug Approvals from the Perspective of Molecules. *Molecules (Basel, Switzerland), 26*(3), 627. Advance online publication. doi:10.3390/molecules26030627 PMID:33504104

Labazova, O., Dehling, T., & Sunyaev, A. (2019, January). From hype to reality: A taxonomy of blockchain applications. *Proceedings of the 52nd Hawaii International Conference on System Sciences (HICSS 2019).* 10.24251/HICSS.2019.552

Lacheca, D. (2021). *Case Study: Digital Transformation of a Legacy Paper-Based Process (U.N. Joint Staff Pension Fund).* Gartner. Retrieved from https://www.gartner.com/en/documents/3996055/case-study-digital-transformation-of-a-legacy-paper-base

Lacity, M. C. (2018). Addressing key challenges to making enterprise blockchain applications a reality. *MIS Quarterly Executive, 17*(3), 201-222. https://aisel.aisnet.org/misqe/vol17/iss3/3

Lakhani, K. R., & Iansiti, M. (2017). The truth about blockchain. *Harvard Business Review, 95*(1), 119-127. https://hbr.org/2017/01/the-truth-about-blockchain

Lampe, J., Kraft, P. S., & Bausch, A. (2019). Mapping the field of research on entrepreneurial organizations (1937–2016): A bibliometric analysis and research agenda. *Entrepreneurship Theory and Practice, 44*(4), 784–816. doi:10.1177/1042258719851217

Laouar, M. R., Hamad, Z. T., & Eom, S. (2019). Towards blockchain-based urban planning: Application for waste collection management. In *Proceedings of the 9th International Conference on Information Systems and Technologies* (pp. 1-6). 10.1145/3361570.3361619

Laurent Probst, L. F.-D. (2016). *Blockchain applications and services.* European Union: European Commission.

Lauslahti, K., Mattila, J., & Seppälä, T. (2017). Smart contracts – how will blockchain technology affect contractual practices? *ETLA Reports*, (68). https://pub.etla.fi/ETLA-Raportit-Reports-68.pdf

Le, T. V., & Hsu, C. L. (2021, April). A Systematic Literature Review of Blockchain Technology: Security Properties, Applications and Challenges. *Journal of Internet Technology.*

Lemieux, V. L. (2016). Trusting records: Is Blockchain technology the answer? *Records Management Journal, 26*(2), 110–139. doi:10.1108/RMJ-12-2015-0042

Leong, C., Viskin, T., & Stewart, R. (2018). *Tracing the Supply Chain: How Blockchain Can Enable Traceability in the Food Industry.* Available at: https://www.bcg.com/publications/2020/benefits-of-automation-in-the-agriculture-industry

Lin, J., Long, W., Zhang, A., & Chai, Y. (2019). Using Blockchain and IoT Technologies to Enhance Intellectual Property Protection. In *Proceedings of the 4th International Conference on Crowd Science and Engineering* (pp. 44-49). 10.1145/3371238.3371246

Lin, J., Shen, Z., Zhang, A., & Chai, Y. (2018, July). Blockchain and IoT based food traceability for smart agriculture. In *Proceedings of the 3rd International Conference on Crowd Science and Engineering* (pp. 1-6). 10.1145/3265689.3265692

Lin, Q., Wang, H., Pei, X., & Wang, J. (2019). Food safety traceability system based on blockchain and EPCIS. *IEEE Access: Practical Innovations, Open Solutions, 7,* 20698–20707. doi:10.1109/ACCESS.2019.2897792

Li, P., Xu, H., Ma, T., & Mu, Y. (2018). Research on fault-correcting blockchain technology. *Journal of Cryptologic Research, 5*(5), 501–509.

Li, S., & Lin, B. (2006). Accessing information sharing and information quality in supply chain management. *Decision Support Systems, 42*(3), 1641–1656. doi:10.1016/j.dss.2006.02.011

Liu, B., & De Giovanni, P. (2019). Green process innovation through Industry 4.0 technologies and supply chain coordination. *Annals of Operations Research,* 1–36. doi:10.100710479-019-03498-3

Liu, S. H., Liao, H. L., Pi, S. M., & Hu, J. W. (2011). Development of a Patent Retrieval and Analysis Platform–A hybrid approach. *Expert Systems with Applications, 38*(6), 7864–7868. doi:10.1016/j.eswa.2010.12.114

Li, X., Pak, C., & Bi, K. (2020). Analysis of the development trends and innovation characteristics of Internet of Things technology–based on patentometrics and bibliometrics. *Technology Analysis and Strategic Management, 32*(1), 104–118. doi:10.1080/09537325.2019.1636960

Li, X., Wang, D., & Li, M. (2020). Convenience analysis of sustainable E-agriculture based on blockchain technology. *Journal of Cleaner Production, 271,* 122503. doi:10.1016/j.jclepro.2020.122503

Li, Z., Kang, J., Yu, R., Ye, D., Deng, Q., & Zhang, Y. (2017). Consortium blockchain for secure energy trading in industrial internet of things. *IEEE Transactions on Industrial Informatics, 14*(8), 3690–3700. doi:10.1109/TII.2017.2786307

Loebnitz, N., & Aschemann-Witzel, J. (2016). Communicating organic food quality in China: Consumer perceptions of organic products and the effect of environmental value priming. *Food Quality and Preference, 50,* 102–108. doi:10.1016/j.foodqual.2016.02.003

Low, K., & Mik, E. (2020). Pause the blockchain legal revolution. *The International and Comparative Law Quarterly, 69*(1), 135–175. doi:10.1017/S0020589319000502

Lo, Y. C., & Medda, F. (2020). Assets on the blockchain: An empirical study of tokenomics. *Information Economics and Policy, 53,* 100881. doi:10.1016/j.infoecopol.2020.100881

Lucena, P., Binotto, A. P., Momo, F. D. S., & Kim, H. (2018). *A case study for grain quality assurance tracking based on a Blockchain business network.* arXiv, 1803.07877.

Lundkvist, C., Heck, R., Torstensson, J., Mitton, Z., & Sena, M. (2017). *Uport: A platform for self-sovereign identity.* https://whitepaper.uport.me/uPort_whitepaper_DRAFT20170221.pdf

Lu, Q., & Xu, X. (2017). Adaptable Blockchain-Based Systems: A Case Study for Product Traceability. *IEEE Software, 34*(6), 21–27. doi:10.1109/MS.2017.4121227

Lysons, K., & Farrington, B. (2006). *Purchasing and supply chain management.* Pearson Education.

Macrinici, D., Cartofeanu, C., & Gao, S. (2018). Smart contract applications within blockchain technology: A systematic mapping study. *Telematics and Informatics, 35*(8), 2337–2354. doi:10.1016/j.tele.2018.10.004

Maesa, D. D. F., & Mori, P. (2020). Blockchain 3.0 applications survey. *Journal of Parallel and Distributed Computing, 138*, 99–114. doi:10.1016/j.jpdc.2019.12.019

Magnin, C. (2016). *How Big Data Will Revolutionize the Global Food Chain.* Available at: https://www.mckinsey.com/business-functions/mckinsey-digital/our-insights/how-big-data-will-revolutionize-the-global-food-chain

Majchrzak, A., Markus, M. L., & Wareham, J. (2016). Designing for digital transformation: Lessons for information systems research from the study of ICT and societal challenges. *Management Information Systems Quarterly, 40*(2), 267–277. doi:10.25300/MISQ/2016/40:2.03

Makurvet, F. D. (2021). Biologics vs. small molecules: Drug costs and patient access. *Medicine in Drug Discovery, 9*, 100075. doi:10.1016/j.medidd.2020.100075

Marke, A. (Ed.). (2018). *Transforming Climate Finance and Green Investment with Blockchains.* Academic Press.

Martinez, V., Zhao, M., Blujdea, C., Han, X., Neely, A., & Albores, P. (2019). Blockchain-driven customer. *International Journal of Operations and Production Management, 39*(6-8), 993-1022.

Martyn, J. (1964). Bibliographic coupling. *The Journal of Documentation, 20*(4), 236. doi:10.1108/eb026352

Mascarello, G., Pinto, A., Parise, N., Crovato, S., & Ravarotto, L. (2015). The perception of food quality. Profiling Italian consumers. *Appetite, 89*, 175–182. doi:10.1016/j.appet.2015.02.014 PMID:25681654

Maxham, J. G. III, & Netemeyer, R. G. (2003). Firms Reap what they Sow: The Effects of Shared Values and Perceived Organizational Justice on Customers' Evaluations of Complaint Handling. *Journal of Marketing, 67*(1), 46–62. doi:10.1509/jmkg.67.1.46.18591

Mazzù, M. F., Marozzo, V., Baccelloni, A., & de'Pompeis, F. (2021b). Measuring the Effect of Blockchain Extrinsic Cues on Consumers' Perceived Flavor and Healthiness: A Cross-Country Analysis. *Foods, 10*(6), 1413. doi:10.3390/foods10061413 PMID:34207107

Mazzù, M. F., Romani, S., Baccelloni, A., & Gambicorti, A. (2021a). A cross-country experimental study on consumers' subjective understanding and liking on front-of-pack nutrition labels. *International Journal of Food Sciences and Nutrition*, 1–15. PMID:33657942

McConaghy, M., McMullen, G., Parry, G., McConaghy, T., & Holtzman, D. (2017). Visibility and digital art: Blockchain as an ownership layer on the Internet. *Strategic Change*, 26(5), 461–470. doi:10.1002/jsc.2146

McKenzie, S. (2004). *Social Sustainability: Towards Some Definitions*. Hawke Research Institute.

McLoone, M., & McCanny, J. V. (2003). Generic architecture and semiconductor intellectual property cores for advanced encryption standard cryptography. *IEE Proceedings. Computers and Digital Techniques*, 150(4), 239–244. doi:10.1049/ip-cdt:20030499

McMillan, G. S. (2008). Mapping the invisible colleges of R&D Management. *Research Management*, 38(1), 69–83. doi:10.1111/j.1467-9310.2007.00495.x

Mdakane, R. (2018). *VBS Bank impact on municipalities' finances; Municipal Councillors Pension Fund*. Parliamentary Monitoring Group. https://pmg.org.za/committee-meeting/26233/

Medicines & Healthcare products Regulatory Agency. (2018). *Medicines & Healthcare products Regulatory Agency (MHRA) "GXP" Data Integrity Guidance and Definitions*. Author.

Meehan, J., & Bryde, D. (2011). Sustainable procurement practice. *Business Strategy and the Environment*, 20(2), 94–106. doi:10.1002/bse.678

Mehrabi, Z., McDowell, M. J., Ricciardi, V., Levers, C., Martinez, J. D., Mehrabi, N., Wittman, H., Ramankutty, N., & Jarvis, A. (2021). The global divide in data-driven farming. *Nature Sustainability*, 4(2), 154–160. doi:10.103841893-020-00631-0

Mehrwald, P., Treffers, T., Titze, M., & Welpe, I. (2019). *Blockchain technology application in the sharing economy: A proposed model of effects on trust and intermediation.* doi:10.24251/HICSS.2019.555

Mengelkamp, E., Notheisen, B., Beer, C., Dauer, D., & Weinhardt, C. (2018). A blockchain-based smart grid: Towards sustainable local energy markets. *Computer Science -. Research for Development*, 33(1–2), 207–214.

Meng, W., Tischhauser, E. W., Wang, Q., Wang, Y., & Han, J. (2018). When intrusion detection meets blockchain technology: A review. *IEEE Access: Practical Innovations, Open Solutions*, 6, 10179–10188. doi:10.1109/ACCESS.2018.2799854

Mentzer, J. T., DeWitt, W., Keebler, J. S., Min, S., Nix, N. W., Smith, C. D., & Zacharia, Z. G. (2001). Defining Supply Chain Management. *Journal of Business Logistics*, 22(2), 1–25. doi:10.1002/j.2158-1592.2001.tb00001.x

Meynhardt, T., Brieger, S. A., Strathoff, P., Anderer, S., Bäro, A., Hermann, C., & Gomez, P. (2017). Public value performance: What does it mean to create value in the public sector? In *Public sector management in a globalized world* (pp. 135–160). Springer Gabler. doi:10.1007/978-3-658-16112-5_8

Miau, S., & Yang, J. M. (2018). Bibliometrics-based evaluation of the Blockchain research trend: 2008–March 2017. *Technology Analysis and Strategic Management, 30*(9), 1029–1045. doi:10.1080/09537325.2018.1434138

Milkbox Website. (2021, April 28). *Lattoprelevatore Milk Box - Lattoprelevatore*. Retrieved from, http://www.lattoprelevatore.it/product/lattoprelevatore/

Millington, A. (2008). *Responsible Supply Chain Management - The Oxford Handbook of Corporate Social Responsibility*. Oxford University Press.

Mishra, N., Mistry, S., Choudhary, S., Kudu, S., & Mishra, R. (2020). Food Traceability System Using Blockchain and QR Code. In *IC-BCT 2019. Blockchain Technologies*. Springer. doi:10.1007/978-981-15-4542-9_4

MITRE. (2019, June). *Assessing the potential to improve grants management using blockchain technology*. MITRE Grants Management Blockchain Supply. https://www.mitre.org/sites/default/files/publications/PR-19-1654-MITRE%20Grants%20Mgt%20Blockchain%20Study%20Report.pdf

Modic, D., Hafner, A., Damij, N., & Cehovin Zajc, L. (2019). Innovations in intellectual property rights management: Their potential benefits and limitations. *European Journal of Management and Business Economics, 28*(2), 189–203. doi:10.1108/EJMBE-12-2018-0139

Mohanta, B. K., Jena, D., Ramasubbareddy, S., Daneshmand, M., & Gandomi, A. H. (2020). Addressing security and privacy issues of IoT using blockchain technology. *IEEE Internet of Things Journal, 8*(2), 881–888. doi:10.1109/JIOT.2020.3008906

Moll, O., Heun, J., Eising, R., Gersemsky, U., Norpoth, B., Appel, E., . . . Walloshek, T. (2005). *U.S. Patent Application No. 10/909,660*. US Patent Office.

Mollah, M. B., Zhao, J., Niyato, D., Lam, K. Y., Zhang, X., Ghias, A. M., Koh, L. H., & Yang, L. (2020). Blockchain for future smart grid: A comprehensive survey. *IEEE Internet of Things Journal, 8*(1), 18–43. doi:10.1109/JIOT.2020.2993601

Montecchi, M., Plangger, K., & Etter, M. (2019). It's real, trust me! Establishing supply chain provenance using blockchain. *Business Horizons, 62*(3), 283–293. doi:10.1016/j.bushor.2019.01.008

Moore, M. H. (1995). *Creating public value: Strategic management in government*. Harvard university press.

Morrell, B. (2017). *How to strengthen product life cycle management using blockchain*. Retrieved June 11, 2021, from https://www.ey.com/en_gl/life-sciences/how-to-strengthen-product-life-cycle-management-using-blockchain

Mueller, B. (2020). Why public policies fail: Policymaking under complexity. *Economía, 21*(2), 311–323. doi:10.1016/j.econ.2019.11.002

Mukhopadhyay, U., Skjellum, A., Hambolu, O., Oakley, J., Yu, L., & Brooks, R. (2016). A brief survey of cryptocurrency systems. In *2016 14th annual conference on privacy, security and trust (PST)* (pp. 745-752). IEEE. 10.1109/PST.2016.7906988

Mullard, A. (2014). New drugs cost US$2.6 billion to develop. *Nature Reviews. Drug Discovery, 13*(12), 877–877. doi:10.1038/nrd4507 PMID:25435204

Mun, C., Yoon, S., & Park, H. (2019). Structural decomposition of technological domain using patent co-classification and classification hierarchy. *Scientometrics, 121*(2), 633–652. doi:10.100711192-019-03223-8

Nakamoto, S. (2008). *Bitcoin: a peer-to-peer electronic cash system.* Bitcoin. *Decentralized Business Review, 21260.* https://bitcoin.org/bitcoin.pdf

Nakamoto, S. (2008). Bitcoin: A peer-to-peer electronic cash system. *Decentralized Business Review,* 21260.

Nakamoto, S., & Bitcoin, A. (2008). *A peer-to-peer electronic cash system. Bitcoin.* https:// bitcoin. org/bitcoin. pdf

Nancarrow, C., Tiu Wright, L., & Brace, I. (1998). Gaining competitive advantage from packaging and labelling in marketing communications. *British Food Journal, 100*(2), 110–118. doi:10.1108/00070709810204101

Narayanan, A., Bonneau, J., Felten, E., Miller, A., & Goldfeder, S. (2016). *Bitcoin and cryptocurrency technologies: A comprehensive introduction.* Princeton University Press.

Narayanan, A., Bonneau, J., Felten, E., Miller, A., & Goldfeder, S. (2016). *Bitcoin and cryptocurrency technologies: a comprehensive introduction.* Princeton University Press. https:// scholar.google.com/scholar_lookup?title=Bitcoin+and+cryptocurrency+technologies%3A+A+ comprehensive+introduction&author=Narayanan+A.&author=Bonneau+J.&author=Felten+E .&author=Miller+A.&author=Goldfeder+S&publication+year=2016

Nasdaq. (2017). *Cryptocurrency Agnosticism and a Vision for Privacy.* Nasdaq. Available at: https://www.nasdaq.com/articles/cryptocurrency-agnosticism-and-vision-privacy-2017-09-08

Naspetti, S., & Zanoli, R. (2009). Organic Food Quality and Safety Perception Throughout Europe. *Journal of Food Products Marketing, 15*(3), 249–266. doi:10.1080/10454440902908019

Natoli, C., & Gramoli, V. (2017, June). The balance attack or why forkable blockchains are ill-suited for consortium. In *2017 47th Annual IEEE/IFIP International Conference on Dependable Systems and Networks (DSN),* (pp. 579-590). IEEE. 10.1109/DSN.2017.44

Nickerson, R. C., Varshney, U., & Muntermann, J. (2013). A method for taxonomy development and its application in information systems. *European Journal of Information Systems, 22*(3), 336–359. doi:10.1057/ejis.2012.26

Nicoletti, B. (2017). Agile Procurement. Volume I: Adding Value with Lean Processes. Springer International Publishing.

Nicoletti, B. (2018). *Procurement Finance*. Springer International Publishing. doi:10.1007/978-3-030-02140-5

Nicoletti, B., & Appolloni, A. (2020). Big Data Analytics in Supply Chain Management: Theory and Applications. In *Big Data Analytics in Supply Chain Management: Theory and Applications*. CRC Press.

Niskala, M., Pajunen, T., & Tarna-Mani, K. (2015). *Yritysvastuu: Raportointi-ja laskentaperiaatteet*. ST-Akatemia Oy.

Notheisen, B., Cholewa, J. B., & Shanmugam, A. P. (2017). Trading real-world assets on blockchain. *Business & Information Systems Engineering, 59*(6), 425–440. doi:10.100712599-017-0499-8

O'Connell, A. A., Borg, I., & Groenen, P. (1999). Modern multidimensional scaling: Theory and applications. *Journal of the American Statistical Association, 94*(445), 338–339. doi:10.2307/2669710

O'Dwyer, R. (2020). Limited edition: Producing artificial scarcity for digital art on the blockchain and its implications for the cultural industries. *Convergence., 26*(4), 874–894. doi:10.1177/1354856518795097

O'Leary, K., O'Reilly, P., Feller, J., Gleasure, R., Li, S., & Cristoforo, J. (2017). Exploring the application of blockchain technology to combat the effects of social loafing in cross functional group projects. In *Proceedings of the 13th International Symposium on Open Collaboration* (pp. 1-8). 10.1145/3125433.3125464

OCCRP. (2020). *Crime, corruption and coronavirus*. https://www.occrp.org/en/coronavirus/

OECD. (2021, April). *COVID-19 spending helped to lift foreign aid to an all-time high in 2020. Detailed Note*. https://www.oecd.org/dac/financing-sustainable-development/development-finance-data/ODA-2020-detailed-summary.pdf

Ojo, A., & Adebayo, S. (2017). Blockchain as a next generation government information infrastructure: A review of initiatives in D5 countries. *Government 3.0–Next Generation Government Technology Infrastructure and Services*, 283-298.

Olivares-Rojas, J. C., Reyes-Archundia, E., Gutiérrez-Gnecchi, J. A., Molina-Moreno, I., Cerda-Jacobo, J., & Méndez-Patiño, A. (2021). *A transactive energy model for smart metering systems using blockchain*. CSEE Journal of Power and Energy Systems.

Ølnes, S., Ubacht, J., & Janssen, M. (2017). *Blockchain in government: Benefits and implications of distributed ledger technology for information sharing*. Academic Press.

Ølnes, S. (2016, September). Beyond bitcoin enabling smart government using blockchain technology. In *International conference on electronic government* (pp. 253-264). Springer. 10.1007/978-3-319-44421-5_20

Olsen, P., & Borit, M. (2013). How to define traceability. *Trends in Food Science & Technology*, *29*(2), 142–150. doi:10.1016/j.tifs.2012.10.003

Olsen, P., & Borit, M. (2018). The components of a food traceability system. *Trends in Food Science & Technology*, *77*, 143–149. doi:10.1016/j.tifs.2018.05.004

Oracle. (2019, Feb 28). *Oracle Certified Origins Italia*. Retrieved from Oracle: https://www.oracle.com/it/customers/certified-origins-1-blockchain-story.html

Orr, B. (2002). The case for web-based procurement. *ABA Banking Journal*, *59*.

Oxcert. (2018, April). *Fungible vs non-fungible tokens on the blockchain*. Oxcert. https://medium.com/0xcert/fungible-vs-non-fungible-tokens-on-the-blockchain-ab4b12e0181a

Ozcan, S., & Unalan, S. (2020). Blockchain as a General-Purpose Technology: Patentometric Evidence of Science, Technologies, and Actors. *IEEE Transactions on Engineering Management*, 1–18. Advance online publication. doi:10.1109/TEM.2020.3008859

Papakostas, N., Newell, A., & Hargaden, V. (2019). A novel paradigm for managing the product development process utilising blockchain technology principles. *CIRP Annals*, *68*(1), 137-140. doi:10.1016/j.cirp.2019.04.039

Passarelli, M., Landi, G. C., Cariola, A., & Sciarelli, M. (2020). Open innovation in the new context of proof of concepts: Evidence from Italy. *European Journal of Innovation Management*, *24*(3), 735–755. Advance online publication. doi:10.1108/EJIM-02-2020-0052

Patole, D., Borse, Y., Jain, J., & Maher, S. (2020). Personal Identity on Blockchain. In *Advances in Computing and Intelligent Systems* (pp. 439–446). Springer. doi:10.1007/978-981-15-0222-4_41

Perona, M., & Miragliotta, G. (2002). Complexity management and supply chain performance assessment. A field study and a conceptual framework. *International Journal of Production Economics*, 103–115.

Petrescu, D. C., Vermeir, I., & Petrescu-Mag, R. M. (2019). Consumer Understanding of Food Quality, Healthiness, and Environmental Impact: A Cross-National Perspective. *International Journal of Environmental Research and Public Health*, *17*(1), 169. doi:10.3390/ijerph17010169 PMID:31881711

Pharma R&D Annual Review. (2020). Retrieved from https://pharmaintelligence.informa.com/~/media/informa-shop-window/pharma/2020/files/whitepapers/rd-review-2020-whitepaper.pdf

Piatek, K., Firlit, A., Chmielowiec, K., Dutka, M., Barczentewicz, S., & Hanzelka, Z. (2021). Optimal selection of metering points for power quality measurements in distribution system. *Energies*, *14*(4), 1202. doi:10.3390/en14041202

PICS/S Secretariat. (2018). *Guidance on Data Integrity*. Retrieved from https://picscheme.org/users_uploads/news_news_documents/PI_041_1_Draft_3_Guidance_on_Data_Integrity.pdf

Pilichowski, E., & Turkisch, E. (2008). *Employment in Government in the Perspective of the Production Costs of Goods and Services in the Public Domain.* OECD Working Papers On Public Governance. doi:10.1787/19934351

Pinder, S., Walsh, P., Orndorff, M., Milton, E., & Trescott, J. (2017). *The Future of Food: New Realities for the Industry.* Accenture.

Pizzuti, T., & Mirabelli, G. (2015). The Global Track & Trace System for food: General framework and functioning principles. *Journal of Food Engineering, 159,* 16–35. doi:10.1016/j.jfoodeng.2015.03.001

Pownall, R. (2017). *TEFAF Art Market Report 2017, The European Fine Art Foundation (Tefaf).* Helvoirt. Available at: www.ideebv.com

Pradip, S. M. (2018). *Performance Analysis of Blockchain Platforms* (Thesis). The University of Nevada, Las Vegas, NV.

Prandelli, E., & Verona, G. (2020). *Le cinque regole del business in Rete.* Academic Press.

Prashar, D., Jha, N., Jha, S., Lee, Y., & Joshi, G. P. (2020). Blockchain-based traceability and visibility for agricultural products: A decentralized way of ensuring food safety in india. *Sustainability, 12*(8), 3497. doi:10.3390u12083497

Preeker, T., & De Giovanni, P. (2018). Coordinating innovation projects with high tech suppliers through contracts. *Research Policy, 47*(6), 1161–1172. doi:10.1016/j.respol.2018.04.003

Probst, L., Frideres, L., Cambier, B., & Martinez-Diaz, C. (2016). Blockchain Applications and Services, Directorate-General for Internal Market, Industry, Entrepreneurship and SMEs. European Union.

Publication office of the European Union. (2020). *Annual Report 2019 - The EU Food Fraud Network and the Administrative Assistance & Cooperation System.* . doi:10.2875/326318

Pun, H., Swaminathan, J. M., & Hou, P. (2018). Blockchain Adoption for Combating Deceptive Counterfeits. SSRN *Electronic Journal.*

Pursuing the digital future amid macro-gloom. (2019, Jan 18). Retrieved from Deloitte: https://www2.deloitte.com/us/en/insights/focus/industry-4-0/italy-4-0-digital-future-technology.html

Qi, R., Feng, C., Liu, Z., & Mrad, N. (2017). Blockchain-powered internet of things, e-governance and e-democracy. In *E-Democracy for Smart Cities* (pp. 509–520). Springer. doi:10.1007/978-981-10-4035-1_17

Quillhash. (2020, Jan 28). *Blockchain in Supply of Saffron: A prevention of frauds on the World's most expensive spice.* Retrieved from Quillhash: https://blog.quillhash.com/2020/01/28/blockchain-in-supply-of-saffron-a-prevention-of-frauds-on-the-worlds-most-expensive-spice/

Radanović, I., & Likić, R. (2018). Opportunities for Use of Blockchain Technology in Medicine. *Applied Health Economics and Health Policy, 16*(5), 583–590. doi:10.100740258-018-0412-8 PMID:30022440

Radovilsky, Z. (n.d.). *Enterprise Resource Planning.* California State University.

Rafferty, J. P. (2018). *The Rise of the Machines: Pros and Cons of the Industrial Revolution.* Retrieved January 4, 2021, from https://www.britannica.com/story/the-rise-of-the-machines-pros-and-cons-of-the-industrial-revolution

Rahmanzadeh, S., Pishvaee, M. S., & Rasouli, M. R. (2020). Integrated innovative product design and supply chain tactical planning within a blockchain platform. *International Journal of Production Research, 58*(7), 2242–2262. doi:10.1080/00207543.2019.1651947

Rana, N. P., Dwivedi, Y. K., & Hughes, D. L. (2021). Analysis of challenges for blockchain adoption within the Indian public sector: An interpretive structural modelling approach. *Information Technology & People.* Advance online publication. doi:10.1108/ITP-07-2020-0460

Ranganthan, V. P., Dantu, R., Paul, A., Mears, P., & Morozov, K. (2018). A decentralized marketplace application on the ethereum blockchain. *Proceedings - 4th IEEE International Conference on Collaboration and Internet Computing, CIC 2018*, 90–97. 10.1109/CIC.2018.00023

Raskin. (2017). The law and legality of smart contracts. *Georgetown Law Technol. Rev.,* 305-341.

Rathor, M., & Sengupta, A. (2020). IP Core Steganography Using Switch Based Key-Driven Hash-Chaining and Encoding for Securing DSP Kernels Used in CE Systems. *IEEE Transactions on Consumer Electronics, 66*(3), 251–260. doi:10.1109/TCE.2020.3006050

Rattan, A. K. (2018, March). Data integrity: History, issues, and remediation of issues. *PDA Journal of Pharmaceutical Science and Technology.* doi:10.5731/pdajpst.2017.007765

Red, C. (2020). Sports Memorabilia Is Booming, But Industry Has Its Share Of Past Scandal. *Forbes,* 1–6.

Reddick, C. G. (2021). Analyzing the Case for Adopting Distributed Ledger Technology in the Bank of Canada. In *Blockchain and the Public Sector* (pp. 219–238). Springer. doi:10.1007/978-3-030-55746-1_10

REGULATION (EC) No 178/2002 of the European parliament and of the council, of 28 January 2002

Reid, L. M., O'Donnell, C. P., & Downey, G. (2006). Recent technological advances for the determination of food authenticity. *Trends in Food Science & Technology, 17*(7), 344–353. doi:10.1016/j.tifs.2006.01.006

Rensing, L. (2021). *The future of sports is embracing digitisation.* SportsPro.

Reyburn, S. (2021). Art's NFT Question: Next Frontier in Trading, or a New Form of Tulip? *The New York Times,* pp. 3–7.

Rieger, A., Stohr, A., Wenninger, A., & Fridgen, G. (2021). Reconciling Blockchain with the GDPR: Insights from the German Asylum Procedure. In *Blockchain and the Public Sector* (pp. 73–95). Springer. doi:10.1007/978-3-030-55746-1_4

Roberts, J. J. (2020). *UFC and Dapper Labs offer crypto collectibles of MMA fighters*. Fortune.

Rodriguez. (2018). Agrifood: The $8 Trillion Industry That's Worth Your Salt. *Tech Crunch*. Available at: https://techcrunch.com/2018/11/01/agrifood-the-8trn-industry-thats-worth-your-salt/

Roettgers, J. (2020). Who is buying into IBM's blockchain dreams? *Protocol*. Available at: https://www.protocol.com/ibm-blockchain-supply-produce-coffee

Rogers, S., & Pieters, L. (2020). Small positive signs in the consumers' dual-front crisis The road to recovery may be opening, but. *Deloitte Insight*. Available at: https://www2.deloitte.com/us/en/insights/industry/retail-distribution/consumer-behavior-trends-state-of-the-consumer-tracker/covid-19-recovery.html

Rossi, M., Mueller-Bloch, C., Thatcher, J. B., & Beck, R. (2019). Blockchain research in information systems: Current trends and an inclusive future research agenda. *Journal of the Association for Information Systems*, 20(9), 14. doi:10.17705/1jais.00571

Rot, A., Sobińska, M., Hernes, M., & Franczyk, B. (2020). Digital Transformation of Public Administration Through Blockchain Technology. In *Towards Industry 4.0—Current Challenges in Information Systems* (pp. 111–126). Springer. doi:10.1007/978-3-030-40417-8_7

Saberi, S., Kouhizadeh, M., Sarkis, J., & Shen, L. (2019). Blockchain technology and its relationships to sustainable supply chain management. *International Journal of Production Research*, 57(7), 2117–2135. doi:10.1080/00207543.2018.1533261

Sacco, A., & De Giovanni, P. (2019). Channel coordination with a manufacturer controlling the price and the effect of competition. *Journal of Business Research*, 96, 97–114. doi:10.1016/j.jbusres.2018.09.001

Sadilek, T. (2019). Perception of food quality by consumers: Literature review. *European Research Studies Journal*, 22(1), 57–67. doi:10.35808/ersj/1407

SAHRC. (2019, March). *Who will save us when governance decays?* South African Human Rights Commission. https://www.sahrc.org.za/index.php/sahrc-media/opinion-pieces/item/1855-who-will-save-us-when-governance-decays

Salah, K., Nizamuddin, N., Jayaraman, R., & Omar, M. (2019). Blockchain-based soybean traceability in agricultural supply chain. *IEEE Access : Practical Innovations, Open Solutions*, 7, 73295–73305. doi:10.1109/ACCESS.2019.2918000

SALGA. (2018, April). *VBS: VBS Bank impact on municipalities' finances; Municipal Councillors Pension Fund*. Parliamentary Monitoring Group. https://pmg.org.za/ committee-meeting/26233/

Sanchez, S. N. (2019). The Implementation of Decentralized Ledger Technologies for Public Procurement. *European Procurement and Public Private Partnership Law Review*, 180 - 196.

Santhanam, N., Varanasi, S., Surana, K., Jacobson, Z., & Zegeye, A. (2018). *Food Processing & Handling Ripe for Disruption?* McKinsey & Company.

Santosh, B., & Rane, S. V. (2019). Green procurement process model based on blockchain–IoT. *Management of Environmental Quality*, 741–763.

SAP. (n.d.). *What Is ERP?* Retrieved from Sap Insights: https://insights.sap.com/what-is-erp/

Saraj, S., & Khalaf, C. (2021). Blockchain Applications in the Energy Industry. In *Regulatory Aspects of Artificial Intelligence on Blockchain*. IGI Global.

Sarkintudu, S. M., Ibrahim, H. H., & Abdwahab, A. B. (2018, September). Taxonomy development of blockchain platforms: Information systems perspectives. In. AIP Conference Proceedings: Vol. 2016. *No. 1* (p. 020130). AIP Publishing LLC. doi:10.1063/1.5055532

SaterS. (2018). Blockchain transforming healthcare data flows. *Available at* SSRN 3171005. doi:10.2139/ssrn.3171005

Scannell, J. W., Blanckley, A., Boldon, H., & Warrington, B. (2012, March). Diagnosing the decline in pharmaceutical R&D efficiency. *Nature Reviews. Drug Discovery*, *11*(3), 191–200. Advance online publication. doi:10.1038/nrd3681 PMID:22378269

Schmidt, S. L. (2020). *21st Century Sports: How Technologies Will Change Sports in the Digital Age*. Springer Nature. doi:10.1007/978-3-030-50801-2

Scholl, H. J., Pomeshchikov, R., & Rodríguez Bolívar, M. P. (2020). Early regulations of distributed ledger technology/blockchain providers: A comparative case study. *Proceedings of the 53rd Hawaii International Conference on System Sciences*. 10.24251/HICSS.2020.218

Schönhals, A., Hepp, T., & Gipp, B. (2018). Design thinking using the blockchain: enable traceability of intellectual property in problem-solving processes for open innovation. In *Proceedings of the 1st Workshop on Cryptocurrencies and Blockchains for Distributed Systems* (pp. 105-110). 10.1145/3211933.3211952

Schwägele, F. (2005). Traceability from a European perspective. *Meat Science*, *71*(1), 164–173. doi:10.1016/j.meatsci.2005.03.002 PMID:22064062

Seebacher, S., & Schüritz, R. (2017). Blockchain technology as an enabler of service systems: A structured literature review. In *International Conference on Exploring Services Science* (pp. 12-23). Springer. 10.1007/978-3-319-56925-3_2

Seideman, D. (2018). Tech Entrepreneur Determines First Estimate Of U.S. Sports Memorabilia Market: $5.4 Billion. *Forbes*, 5–10.

Seino, K., Kuwabara, S., Mikami, S., Takahashi, Y., Yoshikawa, M., Narumi, H., Koganezaki, K., Wakabayashi, T., & Nagano, A. (2004). Development of the traceability system which secures the safety of fishery products using the QR code and a digital signature. *Ocean '04 - MTS/IEEE Techno-Ocean '04: Bridges across the Oceans - Conference Proceedings, 1*, 476–481.

Sengar, G. D. M., & Chowdhury, D. R. (2007). Secured Flipped Scan-Chain Model for Crypto-Architecture. *IEEE Transactions on Computer-Aided Design of Integrated Circuits and Systems, 26*(11), 2080–2084. doi:10.1109/TCAD.2007.906483

Shin, D. D. (2019). Blockchain: The emerging technology of digital trust. *Telematics and Informatics, 45,* 101278. doi:10.1016/j.tele.2019.101278

Sivianes, M., & Bordons, C. (2021, October). Application of Blockchain to Peer-to-Peer Energy Trading in Microgrids. In *International Congress on Blockchain and Applications,* (pp. 138-148). Springer.

Skute, I., Zalewska-Kurek, K., Hatak, I., & de Weerd-Nederhof, P. (2019). Mapping the field: A bibliometric analysis of the literature on university–industry collaborations. *The Journal of Technology Transfer, 44*(3), 916–947. doi:10.100710961-017-9637-1

Small, H. (1973). Co-citation in the scientific literature: A new measure of the relationship between two documents. *Journal of the American Society for Information Science, 24*(4), 265–269. doi:10.1002/asi.4630240406

Sobolewski, M., & Allessie, D. (2021). Blockchain Applications in the Public Sector: Investigating Seven Real-Life Blockchain Deployments and Their Benefits. In *Blockchain and the Public Sector* (pp. 97–126). Springer. doi:10.1007/978-3-030-55746-1_5

Somin, S., Altshuler, Y., Gordon, G., & Shmueli, E. (2020). network Dynamics of a financial ecosystem. *Scientific Reports, 10*(1), 1–10. doi:10.103841598-020-61346-y PMID:32165674

Spain, C., Freund, D., Mohan-Gibbons, H., Meadow, R., & Beacham, L. (2018). Are They Buying It? United States Consumers' Changing Attitudes toward More Humanely Raised Meat, Eggs, and Dairy. *Animals (Basel), 8*(8), 128. doi:10.3390/ani8080128 PMID:30044402

Steinwandter, V., & Herwig, C. (2019). Provable data integrity in the pharmaceutical industry based on version control systems and the blockchain. *PDA Journal of Pharmaceutical Science and Technology, 73*(4), 373–390. doi:10.5731/pdajpst.2018.009407 PMID:30770485

Stericycle. (n.d.). *Recall Index.* Retrieved June 11, 2021, from https://pages.stericycleexpertsolutions.co.uk/2020-q3-recall-index-ous

STOA. (2020). Blockchain for supply chain and international trade. Brussels: European Union.

Storøy, J., Thakur, M., & Olsen, P. (2013). The TraceFood Framework–Principles and guidelines for implementing traceability in food value chains. *Journal of Food Engineering, 115*(1), 41–48. doi:10.1016/j.jfoodeng.2012.09.018

Strauss, J., & Frost, R. (2014). *E-Marketing* (S. Wall, Ed.). Pearson.

Sullivan, C. (2021). Blockchain-Based Identity: The Advantages and Disadvantages. In *Blockchain and the Public Sector* (pp. 197–218). Springer. doi:10.1007/978-3-030-55746-1_9

Sun Yin, H. H., Langenheldt, K., Harlev, M., Mukkamala, R. R., & Vatrapu, R. (2019). Regulating cryptocurrencies: A supervised machine learning approach to de-anonymizing the bitcoin blockchain. *Journal of Management Information Systems*, *36*(1), 37–73. doi:10.1080/0742122 2.2018.1550550

Sun, H., Wang, X., & Wang, X. (2018). Application of Blockchain Technology in Online Education. *International Journal of Emerging Technologies in Learning*, *13*(10), 252. doi:10.3991/ijet. v13i10.9455

Suominen, K., Chatzky, A., Reinsch, W., & Robison, J. (2018). *What Should U.S. Blockchain Policy Be?* CSIS.

Swedberg, C. (2015). *Ford Motor Co. Uses Omni-ID 64-kbit Tag to Monitor Engine Production.* RFID Journal.

Sylvester, G. (2019). E-Agriculture in Action: Blockchain for Agriculture Opportunities and Challanges. Academic Press.

Takyar, A. (2019). Retrieved from LeewayHertz: https://www.leewayhertz.com/cost-of-blockchain-implementation/

Tapscott, D., & Tapscott, A. (2016). *Blockchain Revolution: How the Technology Behind Bitcoin Is Changing Money, Business, and the World.* Penguin Random House LLC.

Tasca, P., & Tessone, C. (2019). A Taxonomy of Blockchain Technologies: Principles of Identification and Classification. *Ledger*, *4*. Advance online publication. doi:10.5195/ledger.2019.140

Taş, R., & Tanrıöver, Ö. Ö. (2020). A systematic review of challenges and opportunities of blockchain for E-voting. *Symmetry*, *12*(8), 1328. doi:10.3390ym12081328

Tchankova, L. (2002). Risk identification–basic stage in risk management. *Environmental Management and Health*, *13*(3), 290–297. doi:10.1108/09566160210431088

TDM Website. (2021a, April 28). *Afiact® | TDM | Total Dairy Management*. Retrieved from https://www.tdm.it/en/project/afiact/

TDM Website. (2021b, April 28). *Afilab® | TDM | Total Dairy Management*. Retrieved from https://www.tdm.it/project/afilab/

Thakur, V., Doja, M. N., Dwivedi, Y. K., Ahmad, T., & Khadanga, G. (2020). Land records on blockchain for implementation of land titling in India. *International Journal of Information Management*, *52*, 101940. doi:10.1016/j.ijinfomgt.2019.04.013

The Federal Bureau of Investigation. (2005). *Operation Bullpen*. Available at: https://archives.fbi.gov/archives/news/stories/2005/july/operation-bullpen-overview

Thejaswini, S., & Ranjitha, K. R. (2021). Blockchain for Management of Natural Resources Using Energy Trading as a Platform. In *International Conference on Communication, Computing and Electronics Systems: Proceedings of ICCCES 2020 (Vol. 733*, p. 475). Springer Nature. 10.1007/978-981-33-4909-4_36

Thomas, M. (2020). *Sports Memorabilia Market Estimated at $5.4 Billion, but Beware of the Fakes*. Sports Casting.

Tian, F. (2016, June). An agri-food supply chain traceability system for China based on RFID & blockchain technology. In *2016 13th international conference on service systems and service management* (ICSSSM), (pp. 1-6). IEEE.

Tian, F. (2017, June). A supply chain traceability system for food safety based on HACCP, blockchain & Internet of things. In *2017 International conference on service systems and service management* (pp. 1-6). IEEE.

Tian, F. (2016). *An Agri-food Supply Chain Traceability System for China Based on RFID & Blockchain Technology*. Vienna University of Economics and Business.

Tiscini, R., Testarmata, S., Ciaburri, M., & Ferrari, E. (2020). The blockchain as a sustainable business model innovation. *Management Decision, 58*(8), 1621–1642. Advance online publication. doi:10.1108/MD-09-2019-1281

TokenSoft. (2018). *ERC-1404: Simple restricted token standard*. Medium. https://medium.com/erc1404/erc-1404-simple-restricted-token-standard-f71290a48faa

Tönnissen, S., & Teuteberg, F. (2018). Using blockchain technology for business processes in purchasing— concept and case study-based evidence. In *International Conference on Business Information Systems* (pp. 253-264). Springer. 10.1007/978-3-319-93931-5_18

Tonurist, P., & Cook, J. (2019). *Public Value in Public Service Transformation Working with Change*. OECD. Retrieved from https://www.oecd.org/governance/public-value-in-public-service-transformation-47c17892-en.htm

Torres de Oliveira, R. (2017). *Institutions, middleman, and blockchains. Shuffle and re-start*. Academic Press.

Toufaily, E., Zalan, T., & Ben Dhaou, S. (2021). A framework of blockchain technology adoption: An investigation of challenges and expected value. *Information & Management, 58*(3), 103444. doi:10.1016/j.im.2021.103444

Trees, M., & Storage, D. F. (2014). *A next-generation smart contract and decentralized application platform*. https://ethereum.org/en/whitepaper/

Treiblmaier, H. (2018). The impact of the blockchain on the supply chain: A theory-based research framework and a call for action. *Supply Chain Management, 23*(6), 545–559. doi:10.1108/SCM-01-2018-0029

Trienekens, J. H., Wognum, P. M., Beulens, A. J. M., & Van Der Vorst, J. G. A. J. (2012). Transparency in complex dynamic food supply chains. *Advanced Engineering Informatics, 26*(1), 55–65. doi:10.1016/j.aei.2011.07.007

Trong, T. D. (2018). Issuing and Verifying Digital Certificates with Blockchain. *International Conference on Advanced Technologies for Communications*.

Truong, Um, Zhou, & Lee. (2018). Strengthening the Blockchain-Based Internet of Value with Trust. *IEEE International Conference on Communications (ICC)*, 1-7. 10.1109/ICC.2018.8423014

Tsai, Feng, Zhang, You, Wang, & Zhong. (2017). Intellectual-Property Blockchain-Based Protection Model for Microfilms. *2017 IEEE Symposium on Service-Oriented System Engineering (SOSE)*, 174-178. 10.1109/SOSE.2017.35

Tsang, Y. P., Choy, K. L., Wu, C. H., Ho, G. T., Lam, C. H., & Koo, P. S. (2018). An Internet of Things (IoT)-based risk monitoring system for managing cold supply chain risks. *Industrial Management & Data Systems, 118*(7), 1432–1462. doi:10.1108/IMDS-09-2017-0384

Tse, D., Zhang, B., Yang, Y., Cheng, C., & Mu, H. (2017). Blockchain application in food supply information security. In 2017 IEEE international conference on industrial engineering and engineering management (IEEM) (pp. 1357-1361). IEEE. doi:10.1109/IEEM.2017.8290114

Tsukerman, M. (2015). The block is hot: A survey of the state of Bitcoin regulation and suggestions for the future. *Berkeley Technology Law Journal, 30*(4), 1127–1170. https://www.jstor.org/stable/26377750

Turley, C. (2021). *If you haven't followed NFTs, here's why you should start.* Tech Crunch.

Underwood, S. (2016). Blockchain beyond bitcoin. *Communications of the ACM, 59*(11), 15–17. doi:10.1145/2994581

Unger, B. (2019). *An Analysis Of 2018 FDA Warning Letters Citing Data Integrity Failures.* Retrieved June 1, 2021, from https://www.pharmaceuticalonline.com/doc/an-analysis-of-fda-warning-letters-on-data-integrity-0003

UNI. (2015). Quality management systems - Fundamentals and vocabulary, Milan. *UNI EN ISO, 9000*.

United States Postal Inspection Service. (2019). *Fake Sports Memorabilia.* United States Postal Inspection Service.

Vacca, A., Di Sorbo, A., Visaggio, C. A., & Canfora, G. (2020). A systematic literature review of blockchain and smart contract development: Techniques, tools, and open challenges. *Journal of Systems and Software*, 110891.

Van Doorn, J., & Verhoef, P. C. (2011). Willingness to pay for organic products: Differences between virtue and vice foods. *International Journal of Research in Marketing, 28*(3), 167–180. doi:10.1016/j.ijresmar.2011.02.005

Van Eck, N. J., Waltman, L., Dekker, R., & van den Berg, J. (2010). A comparison of two techniques for bibliometric mapping: Multidimensional scaling and VOS. *Journal of the American Society for Information Science and Technology, 61*(12), 2405-2416. doi:10.1002/asi.21421

Van Norman, G. A. (2016). Drugs, Devices, and the FDA: Part 1: An Overview of Approval Processes for Drugs. *JACC. Basic to Translational Science, 1*(3), 170–179. Advance online publication. doi:10.1016/j.jacbts.2016.03.002 PMID:30167510

Varma, J. R. (2019). Blockchain in finance. *Vikalpa, 44*(1), 1–11. doi:10.1177/0256090919839897

Velčovská, Š., & Del Chiappa, G. (2015). The food quality labels: Awareness and willingness to pay in the context of the Czech Republic. *Acta Universitatis Agriculturae et Silviculturae Mendelianae Brunensis, 63*(2), 647–658. doi:10.11118/actaun201563020647

Venkatesh, V. G., Kang, K., Wang, B., Zhong, R. Y., & Zhang, A. (2020). System architecture for blockchain based transparency of supply chain social sustainability. *Robotics and Computer-integrated Manufacturing, 63*, 101896. doi:10.1016/j.rcim.2019.101896

Verdú Jover, A. J., Lloréns Montes, F. J., & Fuentes Fuentes, M. (2004). Measuring perceptions of quality in food products: The case of red wine. *Food Quality and Preference, 15*(5), 453–469. doi:10.1016/j.foodqual.2003.08.002

Verma, S., & Gustafsson, A. (2020). Investigating the emerging COVID-19 research trends in the field of business and management: A bibliometric analysis approach. *Journal of Business Research, 118*, 253–261. doi:10.1016/j.jbusres.2020.06.057 PMID:32834211

Vial, G. (2019). Understanding digital transformation: A review and a research agenda. *The Journal of Strategic Information Systems, 28*(2), 118–144. doi:10.1016/j.jsis.2019.01.003

Vukolić, M. (2015, October). The quest for scalable blockchain fabric: Proof-of-work vs. BFT replication. In *International workshop on open problems in network security*, (pp. 112-125). Springer.

Walker, D., Van Wyck, J., Nannes, H., & Pérez, D. (2020). *The Future of Food Is Automated.* Boston Consulting Group. Available at: https://www.bcg.com/publications/2020/benefits-of-automation-in-the-agriculture-industry

Waltman, L., Van Eck, N. J., & Noyons, E. C. (2010). A unified approach to mapping and clustering of bibliometric networks. *Journal of Informetrics, 4*(4), 629–635. doi:10.1016/j.joi.2010.07.002

Wang, F., Cao, R., Ding, W., Qian, H., & Gao, Y. (2011, July). Incentives to enable food traceability and its implication on food traceability system design. In *Proceedings of 2011 IEEE International Conference on Service Operations, Logistics and Informatics* (pp. 32-37). IEEE. 10.1109/SOLI.2011.5986524

Wang, J., Wang, S., Guo, J., Du, Y., Cheng, S., & Li, X. (2019). A summary of research on blockchain in the field of intellectual property. *Procedia Computer Science, 147*, 191–197. doi:10.1016/j.procs.2019.01.220

Wang, S., Zhang, Y., & Zhang, Y. (2018). A blockchain-based framework for data sharing with fine-grained access control in decentralized storage systems. *IEEE Access: Practical Innovations, Open Solutions, 6*, 38437–38450. doi:10.1109/ACCESS.2018.2851611

Wang, Y., Singgih, M., Wang, J., & Rit, M. (2019). Making sense of blockchain technology: How will it transform supply chains? *International Journal of Production Economics, 211*, 221–236. doi:10.1016/j.ijpe.2019.02.002

Warkentin, M., & Orgeron, C. (2020). Using the security triad to assess blockchain technology in public sector applications. *International Journal of Information Management, 52*, 102090. doi:10.1016/j.ijinfomgt.2020.102090

Wattana, V. D. (2019). Blockchain characteristics and consensus in modern business processes. *Journal of Industrial Information Integration*, 32 - 39.

Weber, I., Gramoli, V., Staples, M., & Ponomarev, A. (2017). On Availability for Blockchain-Based Systems. *SRDS'17: IEEE International Symposium on Reliable Distributed Systems.*

Weil, D. (2019). The Market for Sports Memorabilia Continues to Score Big. *The Wall Street Journal*, pp. 1–2.

Weiss, E. H. (1973). Grants management: A systems approach. *Socio-Economic Planning Sciences, 7*(5), 457–470. doi:10.1016/0038-0121(73)90042-6

Weking, J., Mandalenakis, M., Hein, A., Hermes, S., Böhm, M., & Krcmar, H. (2019). The impact of blockchain technology on business models–a taxonomy and archetypal patterns. *Electronic Markets*, 1–21.

Wenyan,, S., & Z., X.-C. (2017). Developing sustainable supplier selection criteria for solar air-conditioner manufacturer: An integrated approach. *Renewable & Sustainable Energy Reviews*, 1461–1471.

Westermeier, C. (2020). Money is data–the platformization of financial transactions. *Information Communication and Society, 23*(14), 2047–2063. doi:10.1080/1369118X.2020.1770833

WHO. (2016). *Annex 5 Guidance on good data and record management practices. WHO Technical Report Series.* Retrieved from https://www.who.int/medicines/publications/pharmprep/WHO_TRS_996_annex05.pdf

Wieninger, S., Schuh, G., & Fischer, V. (2019, June). Development of a Blockchain Taxonomy. In *2019 IEEE International Conference on Engineering, Technology and Innovation (ICE/ITMC)* (pp. 1-9). IEEE.

Willrich, S., Melcher, F., Straub, T., & Weinhardt, C. (2019). Towards More Sustainability: A Literature Review Where Bioeconomy Meets Blockchain. In ICETE (vol. 1, pp. 113-120). doi:10.5220/0007786301070114

Wintermeyer, L. (2021). Non-Fungible-Token Market Booms As Big Names Join Crypto's Newest Craze. *Forbes*, 1–7.

Wong, C. W. Y., Wong, C. Y., & Boon-Itt, S. (2013). The combined effects of internal and external supply chain integration on product innovation. *International Journal of Production Economics, 146*(2), 566–574. doi:10.1016/j.ijpe.2013.08.004

World Bank. (2018). *Italy Trade Statistics*. Retrieved from World Bank: https://wits.worldbank.org/CountryProfile/en/ITA

World Economic Forum. (2020). *Inclusive Deployment of Blockchain: Case Studies and Learnings from the United Arab Emirates*. Retrieved from https://www3.weforum.org/docs/WEF_Inclusive_Deployment_of_Blockchain_Case_Studies_and_Learnings_from_the_United_Emirates.pdf

Wright, J. (2019, Aug 1). *Case Study: Decathlon: getting smart with RFID tags*. Retrieved from Internet Retailing: https://internetretailing.net/magazine-articles/magazine-articles/case-study-decathlon-getting-smart-with-rfid-tags

Wuehler, M. (2018, September 6). *Rinkeby consensus post-mortem*. Infura Blog. Retrieved from https://blog.infura.io/rinkeby-consensus-post-mortem-4abbcace0539/

Xiao, L. W., Huang, W., Xie, Y., Xiao, W., & Li, K.-C. (2020). A Blockchain-Based Traceable IP Copyright Protection Algorithm. *IEEE Access: Practical Innovations, Open Solutions, 8*, 49532–49542. doi:10.1109/ACCESS.2020.2969990

Xu, X., Weber, I., Staples, M., Zhu, L., Bosch, J., Bass, L., . . . Rimba, P. (2017, April). A taxonomy of blockchain-based systems for architecture design. In 2017 IEEE international conference on software architecture (ICSA) (pp. 243-252). IEEE. doi:10.1109/ICSA.2017.33

Xu, X., Lu, Q., Liu, Y., Zhu, L., Yao, H., & Vasilakos, A. V. (2019). Designing blockchain-based applications a case study for imported product traceability. *Future Generation Computer Systems, 92*, 399–406. doi:10.1016/j.future.2018.10.010

Yalcin, H., & Daim, T. (2021). Mining research and invention activity for innovation trends: Case of blockchain technology. *Scientometrics, 126*(5), 3775–3806. doi:10.100711192-021-03876-4

Yang & Li. (2016). Research framework and anticipated results of cyberspace digital virtual asset protection. *Advanced Engineering Science, 50*(4), 1–11. doi:10.15961/j.jsuese.20180066

Yang, F. (2019). The Survey on Intellectual Property Based on Blockchain Technology. *2019 IEEE International Conference on Industrial Cyber Physical Systems (ICPS)*, 743-748. 10.1109/ICPHYS.2019.8780125

Yang, F., Zhou, W., Wu, Q., Long, R., Xiong, N. N., & Zhou, M. (2019). Delegated Proof of Stake With Downgrade: A Secure and Efficient Blockchain Consensus Algorithm With Downgrade Mechanism. *IEEE Access: Practical Innovations, Open Solutions, 7*, 118541–118555. doi:10.1109/ACCESS.2019.2935149

Yang, Y. J., & Hwang, J. C. (2020). Recent development trend of blockchain technologies: A patent analysis. *International Journal of Electronic Commerce Studies, 11*(1), 1–12. doi:10.7903/ijecs.1931

Yanik, S., & Kiliç, A. S. (2018). A framework for the performance evaluation of an energy blockchain. In *Energy Management—Collective and Computational Intelligence with Theory and Applications* (pp. 521–543). Springer. doi:10.1007/978-3-319-75690-5_23

Yan, L., Angang, Z., Huaiying, S., Lingda, K., Guang, S., & Shuming, S. (2021, July). Blockchain-Based Reliable Collection Mechanism for Smart Meter Quality Data. In *International Conference on Artificial Intelligence and Security*, (pp. 476-487). Springer. 10.1007/978-3-030-78612-0_38

Yavuz, E., Koç, A. K., Çabuk, U. C., & Dalkılıç, G. (2018). Towards secure e-voting using ethereum blockchain. In *2018 6th International Symposium on Digital Forensic and Security (ISDFS)* (pp. 1-7). IEEE. Available: https://followmyvote.com/online-voting-platform-benefits/open-source-code/

Yin, R. K. (2011). *Applications of case study research*. Sage. doi:10.3138/cjpe.30.1.108

Yli-Huumo, J., Ko, D., Choi, S., Park, S., & Smolander, K. (2016). Where Is Current Research on Blockchain Technology? - A Systematic Review. West Virginia University.

Yli-Huumo, J., Ko, D., Choi, S., Park, S., & Smolander, K. (2016). Where is current research on blockchain technology?—A systematic review. *PLoS One, 11*(10), e0163477. doi:10.1371/journal.pone.0163477 PMID:27695049

Yu, D., & Pan, T. (2021). Tracing the main path of interdisciplinary research considering citation preference: A case from blockchain domain. *Journal of Informetrics, 15*(2), 101136. doi:10.1016/j.joi.2021.101136

Yu, D., & Sheng, L. (2020). Knowledge diffusion paths of blockchain domain: The main path analysis. *Scientometrics, 125*(1), 471–497. doi:10.100711192-020-03650-y

Yukins, C. R. (2006). A Case Study in Comparative Procurement Law: Assessing UNCITRAL's Lessons for US Procurement. *Public Contract Law Journal*, 457-484.

Zeilinger, M. (2018). Digital Art as 'Monetised Graphics': Enforcing Intellectual Property on the Blockchain. *Philosophy & Technology, 31*(1), 15–41. doi:10.100713347-016-0243-1

Zhang, S., & Lee, J. H. (2020). Analysis of the main consensus protocols of blockchain. *ICT Express, 6*(2), 93-97.

Zhang, A., Zhong, R. Y., Farooque, M., Kang, K., & Venkatesh, V. G. (2020). Blockchain-based life cycle assessment: An implementation framework and system architecture. *Resources, Conservation and Recycling, 152*, 104512. doi:10.1016/j.resconrec.2019.104512

Zhang, J., & Bhatt, T. (2014). A guidance document on the best practices in food traceability. *Comprehensive Reviews in Food Science and Food Safety, 13*(5), 1074–1103. doi:10.1111/1541-4337.12103

Zhang, R., Xue, R., & Liu, L. (2019). Security and privacy on blockchain. *ACM Computing Surveys, 52*(3), 1–34. doi:10.1145/3316481

Zhaofeng, M., Xiaochang, W., Jain, D. K., Khan, H., Hongmin, G., & Zhen, W. (2020). A Blockchain-Based Trusted Data Management Scheme in Edge Computing. *IEEE Transactions on Industrial Informatics*, *16*(3), 2013–2021. doi:10.1109/TII.2019.2933482

Zhao, G., Liu, S., Lopez, C., Lu, H., Elgueta, S., Chen, H., & Boshkoska, B. M. (2019). Blockchain technology in agri-food value chain management: A synthesis of applications, challenges and future research directions. *Computers in Industry*, *109*, 83–99. doi:10.1016/j.compind.2019.04.002

Zimmerman, D. V. (2016). *SMEs and digitalisation: The current position, recent developments and challenges*. KfW Research.

Zimmermann, V. (2018). *SME Digitalisation Report 2018*. kWF Research.

Zink, K. (2008). *Corporate Sustainability as a Challenge for Comprehensive Management*. Physica-Verlag. doi:10.1007/978-3-7908-2046-1

Zorloni, L. (2018). Cryptokitties, il Tamagotchi con i gattin che si paga in criptovaluta. *Wired*, *11*, 1–7.

About the Contributors

Andrea Appolloni is an Associate Professor at the University of Rome Tor Vergata, Italy. He is also a permanent visiting fellow at Cranfield University in the UK and Research Associate at the Italian Research Council (CNR). His research areas and teaching activities are concentrated on Operations, Supply Chain, and Procurement Management with a focus on Sustainability. He is the coordinator of the EU Horizon 2020 Marie-Curie project on Sustainable Public Procurement. He was a visiting scholar in the area of Procurement Management at Tianjin University and Shanghai Jia Tong University (China), at the University of Tennessee (USA), and ETH Zurich (CH).

Angelo Baccelloni is a PhD Scholar in Marketing at Sapienza University of Rome and lecturer at Luiss Business School for Master's degree in Marketing Management and Executive Programs. He collaborates with the X.ITE Research Centre as a research fellow for scientific and applied research. He has worked on several projects concerning the Food, Fashion, Pharma and Banking industry. His main research interests focus on the effects of recommendation algorithms on the consumer decision-making process.

Andrea Benetton is the President of Maccarese Spa (Rome, Italy), and of Cirio Agricola, (Caserta, Italy), two of the largest cow breeding farms and zootechnics companies of the country. He owns them together with his family, and he manages them with a keen eye towards sustainability, animal welfare and technical and technological innovation. These two properties, alongside the activities of sustainable energy production and agriculture, have a combined milk output of almost 40 millions litres of milk per year, giving the family a prominent role in the national milk supply chain. Before shifting to management positions in the agricultural sector, his previous professional experience includes working internationally in the U.S.A. for Prince Sports Group and for a cosmetics and sports start-up. He has an MBA, a degree in Sociology of mass communications, and he is a textile expert thanks to his attendance of a technical secondary school. All studies were carried out in Italy.

Gabriele Bernasconi is Co-Founder and CO-CEO at Genuino. A creative, results-driven, brand lover with an extensive experience at Nike, spent inspiring and serving football obsessed generation X and Z consumers across Europe, and the Middle East. Join us to empower fans to Collect Digital and Own Physical at genuino.world.

Giuseppe Bongiorno is a researcher of innovation at the Management Department, University of Calabria.

Alfio Cariola is graduated with honors in Engineering and Ph.D. in Management, is full professor of Economics, Business and Management; at the University of Calabria, where he also teaches Corporate Finance and Operations Management. Since 2018 he has been Director of the Department of Business and Legal Sciences of Unical and member of the Academic Senate.

Mariana Carmona has a MSc in Digital Currencies from the University of Nicosia and is an Economist and public policy expert. Recently working as a cryptocurrency knowledge manager and researcher, Mariana has nineteen years of professional experience in financial inclusion, policy design, evaluation studies and regulation. She is an expert in applied economic research, market and evaluation studies. She has researched for international organizations, including UNPD, NAID-UCLA, IADB, W.K. Kellogg, Rural Finance Latin America and the Caribbean Forum. She has experience training professionals and developing business-oriented courses, workshops, and seminars. For over a decade, she worked as a lobbying strategist.

Pietro De Giovanni is Full Professor of Circular Economy, Operations and Supply Chain at the Department of Business and Management at Luiss University. He holds a PhD from ESSEC Business School, and was visiting PhD candidate at GERAD, HEC Montréal. Before joining Luiss, he has held positions at ESSEC Business School, Vrije Universiteit Amsterdam, and NOVA School of Business and Economics. His research interests are supply chain, operations management, sustainability, and digital transformation. He is Associate Editor of International Transactions of Operations Research. He has published in Journal of Operations Management, European Journal of Operational Research, Transportation Research. Part D Transport and Environment, Annals of Operations Research, International Journal of Production Economics, Journal of Business Research, 4OR, Omega, Research Policy. He has recently published the book entitled "How Digital Transformation impacts Supply Chain Quality Management" edited by Springer.

Tommaso Federici habilitated as associate professor, presently teaches Organization Theory and Human Resource Management at University of Tuscia (Viterbo, Italy), and Digital and Organizational Innovation at LUISS University (Rome, Italy). His most recent research interests are: Online Communities for collective action, Influence of digital technologies on Political Processes, Socio-technical innovation in public organizations. His works are published on journals – Information Systems Journal (ISJ), Journal of Information Technology-Teaching Cases (JITTC), Information & Organization, Government Information Quarterly (GIQ), Journal of Enterprise Information Management (JEIM), Journal of Cases in Information Technology (JCIT), Communications of the AIS (CAIS) and others – chapters of book, and proceedings.

Conrad Kraft is an Accountant and Cryptocurrency Analyst with over a decade's worth of experience in Finance. He has worked in some of the most challenging communities in Africa on finance turnaround projects and also provided oversight, audit, monitoring, and financial support to government organizations in his role as a Provincial Treasury Deputy Director. In addition to his finance experience, he has written articles on the future of Blockchain architecture and its integration within the Finance and Public Sectors. He is multi-disciplinary holding a Postgraduate qualification in Business Management, qualifications in Blockchain Strategy and Fintech from the University of Oxford - Said Business School. He has developed cryptocurrency portfolio methodologies for a hedge fund and provided academic support on the MIT Sloan School of Business Blockchain Technologies: Business Innovation and Application online short course. He is currently completing an MSc in Digital Currencies and Blockchain from the University of Nicosia.

Ludovico Lavini is a Teaching and Research Assistant at Luiss Guido Carli, working for the X.Ite Research Center on New Technologies and Behaviors as a Research Fellow. He obtained his Master's Degree in Management at Luiss University, after a study period at Singapore Management University in Singapore. He holds a BSc in Electronic Engineering. He has worked as a Digital Consultant for different projects in several industries.

Audet Victoire Malonga Bibila is a master's degree student in Business and Management at Luiss Guido Carli. She holds a master's degree in Industrial Engineering and has a strong background in engineering, operations management, and International Management. Her current work focuses on Blockchain applications in supply chain management.

Marco Francesco Mazzù is a Professor of Practice at Luiss, where he teaches in M.Sc. and Executive programs. He is also Director of the Knowledge Transfer Unit of the Luiss X.ITE Research Center, with recent academic publications in the area of Food, Director of the Major in Digital Marketing in the Master in Marketing, and Director of the Executive Program in Marketing (English track). His (25-year) experience as Manager, Consultant and Board Member in top international companies spans multiple industries and more than 15 markets. He holds an MBA from INSEAD.

Mario Miozza is a Ph.D. student in Management at Luiss Guido Carli University, his research focuses on Startups as source of innovation for Manufacturing Companies willing to centralize their efforts in a Digital Ecosystem. Subjects of Interest: Digital Transformation, Blockchain, Artificial Intelligence, Industry 4.0, Startup, Sustainable Development and History of Economics.

Bernardo Nicoletti is a Professor of Management Science at Temple University, Rome, Campus. Bernardo also provides consulting and management coaching internationally. Projects emphasize Lean and Digitizing processes, primarily to financial institutions. He has consulted with several companies worldwide. A frequent speaker at international events, Bernardo is the author of more than 30 business books, published in Italy, the UK, and China. His most recent books are "Procurement 4.0", "Agile Procurement"; "Digital Insurance", and "Banking 5.0". He also teaches Advanced Procurement Management at the University of Rome Tor Vergata, Rome, Italy.

Mariacarmela Passarelli is an adjunct professor of Management and Technology Transfer at the University of Calabria. She got a PhD in Economics and Management at Sant 'Anna School of Advanced Studies (Pisa, Italy) and she was visiting scholar at HAAS Business School (Berkeley). She worked also as an expert for exploitation research activities with international players (AREA Science Park, Ernst &Young and PricewaterhouseCoopers). She is also an expert on European Founds. Her main research streams are technology transfer, innovation, neuroscience, and entrepreneurship. She published several articles and papers on international journals and magazines.

Daniel Ruzza is currently a PhD student at Luiss Guido Carli in the department of Business and Management. He was a research fellow at Ca' Foscari Venice University and he received a M.Sc. in Accounting and Finance at Ca' Foscari University of Venice. His research interests include blockchain, legitimation, institutional technology, business models.

Abhijeet Satwekar is currently working at Merck Group as an Innovation Manager, with 10+ years of scientific experience in the biotech industry spanning USP, DSP, Analytical Development. Driving Innovations by Phase-appropriate approach and steering with a combination of Agile, Design Thinking and Lean approaches to have E2E management of Innovation Projects from scouting, conceptualization, negotiations (external contractor, legal/IP), business case assessments to leading the execution strategy - Process Analytical Technologies, Automation, Advanced Analytical Technologies. Engaged on the topics of Digitalization to enhance digital capabilities across people, processes, and technology. Leading Digital Innovations (AI, Data Science, Automation, Digital Culture) projects in dev. and GxP environments.

Paolo Spagnoletti is Associate Professor at Luiss University, Italy, and at University of Agder (partial appointment), Norway. He is a board member of the Italian Competence Center Cyber 4.0. His research interests include the design and governance of digital platforms, cybersecurity, and data control. His works appears in the Journal of Information Technology, Journal of Strategic Information Systems, Information & Management, Information Systems Frontiers, IEEE Transactions in Engineering Management, Communications of AIS and other journals. He has edited four books and serves as Executive Editor of the Springer series LNISO. He holds a M.Sc. degree in Electronic Engineering from Sapienza University and a Ph.D. degree in Information Systems from Luiss University.

Esli Spahiu is a PhD candidate in Management at LUISS Guido Carli in Rome, Italy. Her doctoral research concerns the application and adoption of blockchain as an alternative to current practices and its effects on the governance and architecture of platforms and infrastructures. Since joining the PhD program, she has also collaborated with Center for Leadership, Innovation and Organizations at LUISS as a researcher on measuring change induced by smart working and various field analysis. Prior to arriving at LUISS she received a MSc. Degree in Strategic Marketing from Imperial College London with a strong focus on technology adoption and data-driven decision making in multinational firms and organizations.

Behzad Maleki Vishkaei is graduated in the field of Industrial Engineering and currently, he is continuing his career as a researcher at Luiss University. His research interests are in the areas of Supply Chain Management, Transportation, Reliability, and Operations Research. He is extending his research in new fields such as Digital Transformation and Smart Cities.

Tiziano Volpentesta is a PhD student in Management at Luiss Guido Carli University, his research focuses on Digital Transformation, Artificial Intelligence and Sustainability.

Index

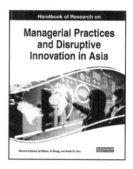
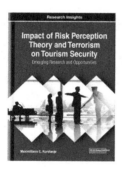

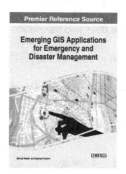

Printed in the United States
by Baker & Taylor Publisher Services